Written according to new syllabus of **BCA/ BBA/BBM** prescribed by
University of Pune from June, 2009.
Also useful for other universities in Maharashtra.

Management Accounting

For
BCA/ BBA/BBM

Prof. Suresh Bhirud
Ex-member, Board of Studies and
Faculty of Commerce, Pune University, Pune

Prof. Bhaskar Naphade
Ex-member, Board of Studies and
Faculty of Commerce, Pune University, Pune

Diamond Publications, Pune

Management Accounting

Prof. Suresh Bhirud
Prof. Bhaskar Naphade

First Edition : August 2009
Reprint : 2016

ISBN : 978-81-8483-173-3

© Diamond Publications

Typesetting :
Aksharwel, Pune

Cover Page :
Shri. Sham Bhalekar

Printed & Published by :
Diamond Publications
264/3 Shaniwar Peth, 302 Anugrah Apartment
Near Omkareshwar Temple, Pune - 411 030
☎ 020-24452387, 24466642
info@diamondbookspune.com

For Online Shopping Visit to
www.diamondbookspune.com

Sole Distributor :
M/s Diamond Book Depot
661, Narayan Peth
Appa Balwant Chowk, Pune 411030

Preface

We have atmost pleasure in placing this standard text book on "Management Accounting" for BCA/ BBA / BBM - semester III students. This text book is prepared according to new syllabus prescribed by University of Pune for BCA/ BBA / BBM - semester III from June 2009. The book contains comprehensive and exhaustive treatment on all topics covered in the new syllabus. The book contains large number of illustrations, involving all types and variations. The book gives equal importance to the theoretical aspects as well as to the practical problems. Hence, this book will be an ideal companion not only to the scholars but also to the normal students. While selecting illustrations as well as the practical exercises, we have used many question papers of various universities and C. A., I. C. W. A., C. S. Examinations. We hope that this book will complete all the requirements of the students and teachers.

The highlight of this book is that, it has been written in a simple language and answers have been given below to the objective questions and the practical exercises wherever possible.

We sincerely thank the senior teachers of the subject for guiding us and constantly encouraging in our enterprise. We are specially thankful Shri. E. S. Zaware, Librarian, Bharatratna Dr. Babasaheb Ambedkar College, Aundh, Pune - 7 for giving co-operation by supplying books on Management Accounting.

We are very much thankful to Mr. Dattatray Pashte and the entire staff of Diamond Publications for their earnest help in bringing out this text book with vigour and accuracy.

We hope that the students would find this text book and very useful for appearing University Examination.

Prof. Suresh Bhirud
Prof. Bhaskar Naphade

INDEX

CHAPTER - 1

Management Accounting

- 1:1 Introduction ● 1:2 Meaning and Definitions ● 1:3 Need of Management Accounting
- 1:4 Essentials of Management Accounting ● 1:5 Importance of Management Accounting
- 1:6 Objectives of Management Accounting ● 1:7 Scope of Management Accounting ● 1:8 Functions of Management Accounting ● 1:9 Methods and Techniques of Management Accounting ● 1:10 Advantages of Management Accounting ● 1:11 Limitations of Management Accounting ● 1:12 Distinction between Management Accounting and Financial Accounting ● 1:13 Distinction between Cost Accounting and Management Accounting ● 1:14 Questions

1:1 Introduction :

Today, an organisation operates in a highly dynamic business enviornment. The main features of such an environment are – presence of large - scale production, research, products improvement and diversification, widening of markets and intense compelition. As a consequence, profit margins get narrowed. To overcome the above factors, a business firm needs greater co-ordination and control to ensure its survival and growth.

Financial accounting is developed over the time to record, summarise and present the financial transactions or events which can be expressed in terms of money, This function was primarily concerned with record keeping leading to preparation of Profit and Loss Account and Balance Sheet. The information obtained through financial accounts is useful to the management in several respects. However, the information generated by financial accounting for several purposes is not sufficient for many areas, such as :

a) acquisition of plant and machinery or other assets;
b) determining product selection, addition or dropping or changing product combination in the case of multi-product company;
c) determining output level;
d) determining or revising prices of products;
e) Whether profit earned is optimum as compared with competitors as well as earlier years.

The need of data for such details lead to development of Cost Accounting.

Cost Accounting is the system of accounting which is concerned with the determination of costs of doing something which can be manufacturing or producing an article or rendering some service or even conducting any activity or function. Cost accounting is the technique and process of ascertainment of costs, which begins with recording of expenses or the bases on which they are calculated and ends with preparation of statistical data. From the above, it is clear that, there are three functions of Cost Accounting.

    a) ascertainment of cost;

    b) control over costs; and

    c) reporting or presentation.

Management Accounting refers to the application of accounting skill to problems of management, thus making the accounting data of the greatest possible value to management of a business or industry. The information received by the management is required to be arranged and this is done by Management Accounting. It refers to the presentation of accounting information in such a way as to assist management in the creation of policy and in the day-to-day operations of an undertaking.

1:2 Meaning and Definitions :

The term "Management Accounting" was first coined by the British Team of Accountants that visited the United States in 1950 under the auspicies of Anglo-American Productivity Council.

1. According to Institute of Chartered Accountants of England the and Wales, " any form of accounting which enables a business to be conducted more efficiently can be regarded as *Management Accounting"*.

2. According to Lamperi & Thurston, "Management cannot obtain full control and co-ordination of operations without a properly designed Accounting System."

3. According to the report of Anglo-American Council of Productivity (1950), "Management Accounting is the presentation of accounting information in such a way as to assist the management in the creation of policy and the day-to-day operations of an undertaking".

4. According to Robert Anthony, "Management Accounting is concerned with accounting information which is useful to management."

5. In the words of Betty, "Management Accountancy is the term used to describe the accounting methods, systems and techniques which, coupled with special knowledge and ability, assist management in its task of maximising profits or minimising losses."

6. Broad and Carmichael observe, "the term Management Accounting covers all those services by which the accounting department can assist the formulation of the policy, control of execution and appreciation of effectiveness."

1:3 Need of Management Accounting

1. Planning and control of business operations: Management Accounting is an advisory service function and is primarily concerned with the efficient management of the business through presenting to the management such information as will facilitate the efficient and appropriate planning and control of business operations.

2. To serve the needs of management : Management Accounting by furnishing relevant information enables the management to manage its business in a more objective and better manner.

3. Future phenomena : Management accounting system seeks to provide information to the management on matters of policy of action to be followed in future. Since, it deals with future phenomena, it is probabilistic in nature.

4. Changing philosophy of management : Managements these days like to collect all relevant information before a decision is made. The owner of the business is more interested about the profits in future. Management need such information which may help them in taking correct decisions so as to increase the profits. In this regard, *"Budget"* helps the management.

1:4 Essentials of Management Accounting

1. A detailed study of the needs of each business.
2. Existence of a sound system of financial accounting.
3. Selection of right accounting and statistical technique for the purpose of measuring and forecasting business activity.
4. The recognition of the human factor in management.
5. The use of targets for incentive.
6. The use of forecasts and budgeting for forward planning.
7. The measurements of individual performance to encourage personal responsibility and initiative.
8. A controlled delegation of duties to individuals.
9. It is most common for a good system of management accounting to utilise, besides pure financial accounting budgetary control, standard costing, and marginal costing.
10. A proper system of recording the relationship between actua performance of the business as compared with present standards.
11. Providing prompt information to management for planning future action.
12. Proper formulation and tabulation of results and diagnosis of weaknesses, if any, of the business is achieved.

1:5 Importance of Management Accounting

Management Accounting has emerged as an important subject of practical value in the modern complex business world. The subject assumes greater significance as it contributes significantly in understanding and solving the problems of business. Management Accounting is very useful to a large scale business organisation. Management Accounting is important due to the following reasons :

1. Efficient planning : Proper planning is necessary for the development of proper strategy to achieve the desired results. The success of any business organisation depends on the effectiveness of plans. Management Accounting is important because it helps to develop realistic plans. Budgetary control technique involves preparation of various financial budgets which are the plans of a business organisation. Through efficient planning, the available resources are put to optimum use.

2. Efficient business operations : Various techniques such as ratio analysis and budgeting are used to appraise the performance of the organisation. It provides scope for further improvement of the operations.

3. Efficient control : Better planning, budgeting, standard costing, performance appraisal etc., bring about an efficient control which is very important for the growth and development of an organisation.

4. Optimum labour efficiency : Labour is an active factor of production which can show miracles if it is properly dealt with. Management accounting aims at improving labour productivity through proper education and training of labour. It develops a greater sense of responsibility among the workers which, in turn, improves their performance.

5. Customer satisfaction : If the tools and techniques of management accounting are applied properly in controlling production volume, cost and quality, the customers can be served better. The customers get better quality of goods at a reasonable price. As a result, good relations are developed with customers.

6. Managerial efficiency : Management accounting contributes a lot to improve managerial efficiency. Evaluation of performance, realistic decision-making by scientific method of analysis and effective control help improve the managerial efficiency of an organisation.

7. Maximising profitability : The use of various techniques help in controlling cost of production and increases the efficiency of each individual in the organisation. This helps to improve the profitability of an organisation.

8. Increase in production : It is possible to increase production by utilising the available resources to the maximum extent possible. Scientific forecast, budgeting and controlling prove to be useful in this respect.

9. Better customer service : The techniques of control used by Management Accounting helps to bring down the cost and reduce the selling price. Goods of good quality are made available to the customers at cheaper rates. As a result, customers are happy.

10. Protection against seasonal fluctuations and trade cycles : Effective planning and budgetary control bring regularity in business operations. It makes the business free from seasonal fluctuations. Analysis of past data enables the management to know in advance the trade cycle. The management can, therefore, prepare a advance safety plan to protect against these trade cycles in future.

1:6 Objectives of Management Accounting

The important objectives of Management Accounting are as follows :

1. Planning and policy formulation : The object of management accounting is to supply the necessary data to the management for formulating plans and policies of the organisation. The information supplied by the management accountant helps the management in policy formulation.

2. **Controlling performance :** The object of management accounting is to control the performance by using the techniques of standard costing and budgetary control.

3. Organising : Management accounting is concerned with the establishment of cost centres, preparation of budgets, fixation of responsibility for different functions. All these aspects help to organise the activities effectively.

4. Interpretation of financial statements : The main object of management accounting is to present the financial information in such a manner as to enable the management to understand the problems properly.

5. Decision–making : Management is concerned with decision-making. The purpose of management accounting is to supply information to the management for decision-making.

6. Co-ordination : Budgetary control is an important technique of co-ordination. Various budgets prepared help to co-ordinate the activities of the organisation.

7. Employee motivation : Management accounting sets the targets by adopting standard costing and budgetary control techniques. The employees are thus motivated to achieve the objectives of the organisation.

1:7 Scope of Management Accounting

At the Seventh International Congress of Accountants held in Amsterdam in 1957, the main facets of Management Accounting emphasised were - Budgetary Control, Cost Accounting and Inventory Control, Interim Reporting, Special Cost and Economic Studies, determination of the most efficient and economic accounting system and assisting the management in the interpretation of financial data.

The principal systems and techniques included in the framework of the Management Accounting are as below :

1. Sources *and* applications of funds : This is also termed as *"Funds flow Analysis"*. It is an attempt to report the flow of funds between various assets and liabilities during the accounting period.

2. Financial analysis : The financial statement analysis is largely a study of relationships among the various financial factors in a business as disclosed by a single set of statements for ascertaining the strengths and weaknesses of a business.

3. Financial planning : The management accounting covers financial policies, such as, Equity-Debts Ratio, the extent of long-term and short-term finance, the management of working capital, etc.

4. Return on investment : The management accounting measures the overall performance of the enterprise in terms of profitability.

5. Historical cost accounting : It concerns with the recording of transactions immediately at the time it takes place or afterwards at the actual costs.

6. Techniques : Control accounting consists of techniques of standard costing, budgetary control, internal check, internal audit and reports.

7. Marginal Cost and break-even analysis : Marginal costing is the technique which measures variable cost per unit of output. In other words, marginal cost is the amount by which total expenditure will increase if one additional unit is produced or will decrease if output is reduced by one unit.

A Break-even point is a stage, where the level of output achieved shows neither profit nor loss. This position invariably procedes the point from where the level of output starts showing profit.

A Break-even point may be determined by means of a graph.

It is a technique of division of total costs into fixed costs and variable costs. It forms a cornerstone of decision-making.

8. Budgetary control : It consists of the determination of the objectives to be achieved, laying an exact and detailed course of action, translation of the course of action into quantitative and monetary terms, constant comparison of the actuals with the budget, noting discrepancies and their reasons and taking steps to remove causes of shortcomings, wastages, losses, etc., and to consolidate reasons leading to good results.

9. Standard costing : Costs of each article or service are determined beforehand on some what idealistic basis, which are called standard costs; then actual costs are constantly compared with the pre-determined costs; and any variances thereof are noted and reasons for them ascertained.

Thus, the exact reason for wastage, loss or gain will be known and the necessary steps can be taken.

A system of standard costing is therefore an essential part of budgetary control.

10. Cost volume profit relationship : Decision is the basic function of management. It is taken after studying the alternative data in terms of costs, prices and profits.

11. Interim reporting : This includes monthly, or quarterly Profit & Loss Account, together with sufficient data as at the end of these periods. For e.g. statement of Current Assets & Liabilities, Orders on Hand, etc.

12. Material control : The management accounting includes material control in connection with inventories, stores, material usage during manufacturing, purchasing, issuing of materials to production units, etc.

13. Statistical methods : Management accounting adopts a technique of statistical methods. For e.g., graphs, index numbers, charts, pictorial representation, etc.

1.8 Functions of Management Accounting

1. Forecasting and planning : Forecasting is a technique of anticipation. Planning is done on the basis of forecasting. For this purpose, use of probability, trend study, co-relation, regression, fund-flow statements, budgeting, standard costing, marginal costing etc., is made. Management accounting makes a valuable contribution by making available forecasts of sales, production, cash and others.

2. Controlling : The control function is an evaluation of performance with a view to ensure that the actual performance coincides with the planned one. For this purpose, use of standard costing, budgetary control, ratios, comparative statements, fund-flow statements are made.

3. Co-ordination : It is a process of inter-linking the functions of different sectors or departments of the organisation. It increases efficiency, resulting in maximisation of profits. Budgeting, financial reporting, financial analysis and interpretation are some of the means of securing co-ordination.

4. Organising : It relates to the organisation of human and non-human resources of the business. The management accounting helps the management in performing this function. In a proper system of accounting, the spheres of activities and responsibilities of each individual or group should be more or less well-defined.

5. Financial analysis and interpretation : Management accountancy is the art or technique of interpretation and presentation in non-technical language (as far as possible) of facts, results and information revealed by cost and financial accounts and other books and records of the business. This is to be done for the benefit of that large body of persons who are in charge of managing the business but are not expected to be experts in accountancy.

6. Communication : The management accountant communicates the data to the management by means of his reports and communicates to the outer world the progress of the business through published accounts and returns etc.

7. Special cost and economic studies : The fundamental object of the management accounting is to assist the management in its main task of maximising profits. In this direction, the management accounting helps the management in its special cost by undertaking economic studies.

In addition to above functions, the management accounting supplies useful information on various matters to different functional authorities, which helps in making strategic decisions like temporary suspension of production etc.

As the management accounting renders invaluable help to management in increasing the managerial efficiency, it is aptly called as 'a tool of management'.

1:9 Methods and Techniques of Management Accounting

The tools used by management accountants are as follows :-
1. Analysis of financial statements and financial planning and control.
2. Ratio analysis.
3. Budgetary control.
4. Profit volume analysis,
5. Costing techniques, such as marginal costing, standard costing and variance analysis.
6. Statistical and graphical techniques.
7. Communication and reporting.

1:10 Advantages of Management Accounting

1. Maximum returns on capital : Management accounting enables the business to get maximum returns on capital by helping it in planning, distribution and controlling activities.

2. Free from adverse effects of trade cycle : Management accounting helps the business in forecasting future events and thus makes it free from the adverse effects of trade cycles.

3. Improving Labour - Management relations : Management accounting helps in improving Labour - Management relations by avoiding unreasonable standards of work.

4. Customer's benefit : Management accounting helps in improving services to its customers.

5. Management's benefit : Management accounting will save the management from being immersed in accounting routine.

1:11 Limitations of Management Accounting

1. Conclusions on accuracy : Management accountant derives the information from financial accounting, cost accounting and other records. Hence, conclusions drawn by him depend to a large extent on the accuracy of financial records and cost records.

2. Sincere efforts at all levels : Execution of the plan drawn by the management accountant will depend upon the sincere efforts at various levels of management.

3. Tool of Management : Management Accounting will not replace the Management and Administration of a Company. It is a decision-making tool of Management and not of the Management Accountant.

4. Useful to big concerns : Installation of a system of management accounting requires a very elaborate organisation with a very large number of rules and regulations, and being a costly affair, can be adopted only by very big concerns.

5. Opposition from some quarters : Adoption of a system of management accounting brings about a radical change in the established pattern of activity of the management personnel. This is bound to encounter opposition from some quarters.

1:12 Distinction Between Management Accounting and Financial Accounting

Financial Accounting and Management Accounting are the two branches of accounting. Financial Accounting is concerned with recording of day-to-day transactions, classification of transactions and ascertainment of profit or loss. On the other hand, Management Accounting is concerned with the analysis of information and its presentation to the management so that it can take a right decision. Management Accounting is an offshoot of Financial Accounting. Both are complementary to each other. The differences between the two branches of accounting are as follows :

Point of distinction	Financial Accounting	Management Accounting
1. Object	The object is to record various transactions in order to find out profit /loss and financial position of the organisation.	The object is to help the management in formulation of policies and strategies.
2. Nature	It is concerned with historical data.	It is concerned with projection of data for the future.
3. Subject Matter	It is concerned with analysis of the results of the organisation as a whole.	It is concerned with analysis of results of different units or departments.
4. Compulsion	It is compulsory.	It is optional.
5. Precision	It records only the actual figures. It gives more emphasis on precision.	It does not lay emphasis on actual figures. It is less precise as compared to financial accounting.
6. Reporting	Reports are useful to outsiders viz bankers, investors, shareholders, Government etc.	Reports are useful to different levels of management.
7. Monetary/ Non-monetary	It records only monetary transactions or events.	It records monetary as well as non-monetary events.
8. Speed of reporting	The speed of reporting is slow but accurate.	The speed of reporting is fast and approximate.
9. Accounting principles	It is governed by GAAP	It is not governed by any set principles.

Point of distinction	Financial Accounting	Management Accounting
10. Period	Financial accounts are prepared for a certain period, i.e., at the end of accounting year.	Reports are prepared as and when required. The frequency of reporting is much higher as compared to financial accounting.
11. Publication	Financial accounts are published for the benefit of public.	Management Accounting statements are not published. They are for internal use.
12. Audit	Financial accounts are audited. It is mandatory.	Statements under management accounting are not audited. It is not mandatory.

1:13 Distinction between Cost Accounting and Management Accounting

Cost Accounting is primarily concerned with the determination of product cost and the techniques of product costing. It deals with cost and price data as well as with procedures of product costing and related information processing. It furnishes valuable information to management which is useful in planning and controlling of production and distribution activities. It is rather very difficult to demarcate between Cost Accounting and Managerial Accounting. Cost Accounting and Management Accounting systems are closely linked. Both these systems use common basic data and report to the managerial personnel. Information provided by cost accounting is also used in Management Accounting. Cost Accounting system uses data pertaining to production, sales, wages and overhead services. This data is also used in Management Accounting. It also uses additional data so as to assist the management in carrying out its primary task of decision-making. The areas covered by management accounting reports are special decision methods, use of highly quantitative methods, behavioural techniques, information system and budgeting system.

Distinction between Cost Accounting and
Management Accounting

Point of distinction	Cost Accounting	Management Accounting
1. Meaning	It is concerned with ascertainment, allocation, apportionment and accounting aspect of costs	It is concerned with the effect and impact of cost on business.
2. Base	It provides a base for Management Accounting.	It is derived from both Cost Accounting and Financial Accounting
3. Role	It helps in collecting costing information for the management.	It helps the management in decision-making.
4. Status	The status of cost accountant comes after the management accountant.	The position of management accountant is senior to cost accountant.

Point of distinction	Cost Accounting	Management Accounting
5. Tools and Techniques	It employs standard costing, marginal costing and budgetary control as techniques of cost accounting.	It employs alongwith these, the techniques of cash flow and fund flow.
6. Scope	It does not include financial accounting, tax planning and tax accounting.	It includes financial and cost accounting, tax planning and tax accounting.
7. Installation	It can be installed without Management Accounting.	It cannot be installed without Financial and Cost Accounting.

1:14 Questions

Objective Type

A) State whether the following statements are True or False :

1) Management Accounting is concerned with historical data.
2) Financial Accounting is concerned with analysis of the results of the organasation as a whole.
3) The object of Management Accounting is to know Profit/Loss and financial position of the organisation.
4) Management accounting records both monetary and non-monetary events.
5) Under management accounting, reports are prepared as and when required.
6) Audit is mandatory under management accounting.
7) Cost accounting provides a base for management accounting.
8) Cost accounting includes, financial accounting also.

Answers : 1) False 2) True 3) False 4) True 5) True 6) False 7) True 8) False

B) Fill in the blanks :-

1) An Organisation today works in a dynamic -------- environment.
2) Cost Accounting is concerned with ------ of cost.
3) Management Accounting helps the management in -------
4) Management Accounting is concerned with projection of data for ---------.
5) Financial Accounting is --------.
6) Management Accounting statements are only for ------ use.
7) Audit is compulsory in --------- accounting.
8) Under Management Accounting, reports are prepared at ----- time.
9) Financial Accounting is concerned with ------ data.
10) The scope of Management Accounting is -------- than Cost Accounting.

Answer : - 1) bunsiness 2) Ascertainment 3) decision-making 4) the future 5) mandatary 6) internal 7) financial 8) any 9) historical 10) wider

Theory Questions

1) Define 'Management Accounting'. What are its objectives ?
2) Explain the term 'Management Accounting'. State its importance.
3) Outline the scope of Management Accounting.
4) What are the functions of Management Accounting?
5) What are the advantages of Management Accounting ? State its limitations?
6) Define 'Management Accounting'. State its objects. How it differs from Financial Accounting?
7) What do you mean by "Management Accounting"? What purposes does it serve ?
8) Explain the term "Management Accounting". Distinguish between the Management Accounting and other forms of Accounting.
9) What are the limitations of Management Accounting ? Discuss the essentials for the success of Management Accounting.
10) Explain the characteristic features of Management Accounting. What are the tools that it makes use of in order to help management?

■ ■ ■

CHAPTER - 2

Analysis and Interpretation of Financial Statement

● **2:1 Methods of Analysis** ● **2:1.1 Comparative Statements** ● **2:1.2 Common-size statements** ● **2:1.3 Trend Percentages** ● **2:1.4 Ratios** ● **2:1.5 Fund Flow Statement** ● **2:2 Ratio Analysis** ● **2:2.1 Meaning of Ratio** ● **2:2.2 Necessity and Advantages of Ratio Analysis** ● **2:2.3 Interpretation of Ratios** ● **2:2.4 Types of Ratios** ● **2:2.4.1 According to the nature of items : a) Balance Sheet Ratios, b) Revenue Statements or Profit and Loss Accounting Ratios c) Inter Statement or Composite Ratios** ● **2.2.4.2 Functional Classification : a) Liquidity Ratios, b) Leverage Ratios, c) Activity Ratios, d) Profitability Ratios**

2:1 Methods of Analysis

Financial Statements - Nature

Financial statements are those which are prepared at the end of a financial year. There are two important financial statements, the balance sheet and the income statement. These two statements summarise all the information contained in the books of accounts of a business. The Balance Sheet is also called 'statement of financial position' and the Profit and Loss Account is called 'statement of income'. The purpose of a balance sheet is to show the financial position of a concern at a particular date. A balance sheet which is prepared at the end of each financial year contains a list of assets and liabilities of the business and also the position of the owner's equity. The Profit and Loss Account discloses the net income or loss resulting from the operations of a business during a specified period. It also discloses the increase or decrease in the owner's equity of an entity arising from profit-seeking operations during a given period.

"Financial statements are prepared for the purpose of presenting a periodical review or report on progress made by the management and deal with the status of the investment in the business and the results achieved during the period under review. They reflect a combination of recorded facts, accounting conventions, personal judgements and the judgements and conventions applied that affect them materially. The soundness of the judgement necessarily depends upon the competence and integrity of those who make them and on their adherence to generally accepted accounting principles and conventions". *(American Institute of Accountants)*. The Balance Sheet has significant uses of its own. The information regarding the assets, liabilities and the owner's equity contained in the Balance Sheet is a very useful complement to the Profit and Loss Account. The Balance Sheet implies two main concepts of financial position – (1) Historical Cost concept, and (2) Current Cost concept. Under the first concept, assets are essentially based on original cost less estimated depreciation or amortisation whereas under the second category assets are based upon their current replacement cost or net realisation values. The first approach alone is generally accepted whereas the second one is rarely used in practice, except by the investment companies.

The figures appearing in the financial statements may be said to have significance in the following aspects :

(i) They are the measures of absolute quantity. Where the financial statement contains an item of current asset, the analyst understands this figure in terms of the current purchasing power and it cannot tell him whether it is sufficient to meet the current obligations. Therefore, some other means of determining its significance is necessary.

(ii) Where figures are compared with those of other years and of similar types of industries, a degree of significance is disclosed by the financial statements.

(iii) The margin of safety can be assessed by comparing the current assets with current liabilities by the analyst.

Uses

Financial statements are very useful for the following reasons :-

They supply the reader relevant information to enable him to make material economic decisions. The most important users of the financial statements are the present and pros- pective shareholders, creditors, employees, financial analysts, customers and some Government agencies. These users have different needs for the kind of financial information derived from the statements. They are concerned with investment decisions, evaluation of management credit decisions, employment terms and other related economic matters. It is generally agreed that the income statement is more important than the balance sheet. "The first possible presentation of the periodic net income, with neither material overstatement nor understatement is important with the increasing importance of income statement. There has been a tendency to regard the balance sheet as the connecting link between successive income statements; however, this concept should not obscure the fact that the balance sheet has significant use of its own."– *(Accounting Research Bulletin – AICPA)*. In this connection, it will be relevant to quote the opinion of Accounting Principles Board of U.S.A., which runs as follows :

"When both financial position and results of operations are presented, disclosure of changes, in the separate account comprising stock-holder equity (in addition to retained earnings) and of the changes in the number of shares of equity securities......is required to make the financial statements ...... sufficiently informative. Disclosure of such changes may take the form of separate statements or may be made in the basic financial statements or notes thereto."

The proper function of the balance sheet is admirably explained in the following passage from the recommendations of accounting principles issued to its members by the Institute of Chartered Accountants of England and Wales –

"The primary purpose of the annual accounts of a business is to present information to the proprietors showing how their funds have been utilised and the profits derived from such use. It has long been accepted in accounting practice that a balance sheet prepared for this purpose is a historical record and not a statement of current worth. Stated briefly, its function is to show in monetary terms the capital, reserves and liabilities of a business at the date at which it is prepared and the manner in which the total monies representing them have been distributed over the several types of assets.

Similarly, a profit and loss account is a historical record. It shows as the profit or loss the difference between the revenue for the period covered by the account and the expenditure chargeable in that period, including charges for the amortisation of capital expenditure. Revenue and expenditure are brought into the account at their respective monetary amounts. The basis of accounting is frequently described as the historical cost basis..." An important feature of the historical cost basis of preparing annual accounts is that, it reduces to a minimum, the extent to which the accounts can be affected by the personal opinions of those responsible for them. For example, the cost of a fixed asset is known so that in calculating depreciation based on that cost, the only respects in which estimates enter into the matter are in relation to the probable useful life of the asset and its realisable value, if any, at the end of its life. Depreciation provisions computed on this basis are intended, by making charges against revenue over the useful life of an asset, to amortise the capital expenditure incurred in acquiring it. For this purpose, estimates of current value or replacement costs do not arise. Again, there are limits within which estimates and operations can properly operate in relation to stock-in-trade, provided the basis of calculation are same in principle and used consistently – *Report on Company Law Committee, London.*

It has already been pointed out that the profit and loss account is generally looked into by the owners of the business with a view to assess the return on their investment. It is significant for the following reasons also as compared to balance sheet :

1. The balance sheet contains several kinds of assets employed in the business for the purpose of earning income. The value of such assets, therefore, depend mainly on their earning power. Fixed assets such as land, building and machinery appearing in the balance sheet may have little value, unless they are effectively utilised by the management in its operations. Intangible assets such as goodwill and trade marks have, strictly speaking, no value unless they have some kind of relationship with the profits of the business.

2. Shareholders are primarily interested to know the return on their investment in the business. As the profits are the source from which, the return on investment will be assessed, the shareholders are more interested in the profit and loss account.

3. The profitability of the business depends upon a number of factors such as efficiency of the utilisation of assets, physical condition of the assets, the ability of the management and not by mere existence of physical assets in the balance sheet. These factors are affected only in the profit and loss statement. For a proper assessment of the return on investments by the shareholders, operating ratios, earnings and trends can be constructed only from the data available in the profit and loss statement.

4. Although the shareholder is interested in a reasonable return on the investment, yet payments of dividends depend upon the liquidity position of a company, which can be ascertained only from the balance sheet. In order to assess the liquidity position of a concern, the working capital position is essential. This can be constructed from the current assets and current liabilities in the balance sheet. The working capital can be compared with some important items contained in the statement of profit and loss to assess the liquidity position, solvency and profitability of a concern.

5. The shareholder has also to consider the balance sheet as important, because only the

comparison of the balance sheet of the past years with the current one will help disclose the policy of the management as regards expansion programme and financing.

But one limitation of the balance sheet is that it contains items recorded in historical value which have no bearing on the changing value of the rupee and thereby make the items difficult of comparison.

Therefore, from the shareholders' point of view, for a proper evaluation of a business, balance sheet is an indispensable factor and the profit and loss account serves as a complementary to the balance sheet.

Sources of Information

As already pointed out, outsiders who want to make analysis do not have access to the internal accounting records. They have to rely upon the published accounts to a considerable extent. These are usually published by the business concerns annually. In the case of large concerns, these statements are usually accompanied by additional reports, containing supplementary information. The following parties are generally interested in the financial statement's analysis.

1. Equity Shareholders : An equity shareholder is the supplier of basic risk capital. This equity capital, which we will discuss in detail later, provides a cushion or shield to the preference or loan capital which are fixed interest bearing securities. Equity interest is usually referred to as 'residual interest'. Their claims for dividend as a Going Concern operations are of residual or deferred interest, i.e. after the interest of the preference and loan capital holders are paid. In view of these circumstances, their investment is of a risky nature. The share value may fluctuate depending upon the amount of profit earned in the business. They are, therefore, interested to know the prospects of the business and to what extent their interest will be affected by the result of the business operations, the profitability and financial condition and as to the future earnings and the return on their capitals.

2. Credit granters : A concern receives short-term and long-term credit on loans from various sources. Short-term credit is usually provided by the owners or banks or other individuals. Long-term credit is provided in the form of long-term loans by financial institutions and other special type of banks and by issue of debentures to the public. The credit granter as opposed to the equity shareholder is primarily concerned with the security provided for his loan. He is concerned with the market value of the assets hypothecated for the repayment of the principal and payment of interest charges regularly. He has, therefore, to rely on the financial statement analysis with a view to satisfy himself as to the ability of the management to maintain sound financial condition for the safeguard of his interests.

3. Management : An analysis of data contained in financial statement is an important tool adopted by the management. This analysis comprises the use of ratios, trends etc. The primary purpose in utilising the tool of analysis by the management is to exercise control over the business operations to know the changes in the financial and operating conditions and to check adverse trends then and there, if any.

Financial Statement Analysis – Techniques

The purpose of financial statement analysis is merely to regard the results "as signals which require further investigation to determine their cause." The purpose is to suggest questions or areas for further investigation, rather than provide answers. According to Mr. W.H. Beaver, "there are two broad purposes of financial statement analysis : (1) Solvency determination, and (2) Profitability evaluation. Solvency determination involves determination of the assessment of the probability that an undertaking will fail. By the use of trend percentages technique, it is possible to predict the failure of a business in advance. The ratios of failed firms implied substantially higher probability of failure than the population as a whole, and this higher probability of failure was evident in the ratio data five years before failure".

The purpose of the profitability evaluation is to assess the probability in the matter of returns on investment in an undertaking.

In analysing the financial statements, the analyst has a number of tools to employ. He can choose the best to suit his need. The following are the principal tools of analysis :

1. Comparative financial statements.
2. Trend percentages.
3. Common-size financial statements.
4. Ratio analysis.
5. Specialised analysis.
6. Statement of changes in working capital or funds flow analysis.

Understanding Financial Statements

Anyone seriously interested in understanding the enterprise must study the financial statements and analyse the data contained in them in order to comprehend their significance and implications.

To understand adequately and to evaluate the financial statement data, an individual must:

(1) Understand the nature and limitations of accounting. Without such an understanding, it is likely that he is unduly impressed by the apparent accuracy and finally of accounting data, as the amounts reported in the income statement and balance sheet are based upon approximation and estimation which are subject to possible error and constant adjustment.

(2) Understand the terminology in accounting and business. Unless a reader is aware of the terms in usage, the financial statements which he studies are not understandable to him.

(3) Have some knowledge of the business, as modern business is complex and variable and the financial statements, even though prepared carefully, cannot make a complex subject simple and clear that anyone can understand it; unless the reader is presumed to have some knowledge of the business, so that he may understand business reports. Unless he is acquainted with the peculiarities of the particular type of business in which he is interested, he will not understand the business reports and statements.

(4) Be acquainted with the nature and tools of financial statement analysis.

Significance of Financial Statement Data

In analysing the data contained in the financial statements, several devices are used. Each device is aimed at disclosure or emphasising the significance of the information contained therein. The usefulness of these devices can be understood only when their significance can be known.

The financial statements have significance in the following aspects :

1. As measures of quantity.
2. In comparing with the similar amounts for other periods and similar companies.
3. When considered alongwith the other figures.

Use of measurements : In interpreting the financial statements, the analyst uses data that show the financial condition of the business. The objective of the measurement by a financial analyst differs from that of an economist. The difference lies in the measurement of fundamental forces governing economic behaviour by the economist and the measurement of fundamental forces, behaviour by the analyst. But in both the cases, precise measurement cannot be made. The analyst cannot formulate valid conclusions unlike the physical scientist as regards the financial statement ratios used. The analyst, therefore, considers his measurements only as indicators. He will concentrate his attention on any given factor which may be abnormal or disproportionate. If the analyst finds there is a variation, he tries to seek an explanation for it. It should, therefore, be remembered that the various ratios are not ends in themselves, but only a means to an end. The analyst is able to form opinions from financial statement by working suitable adjustments depending upon his experience. It is not necessary that he should make mechanical mathematical calculations. If the analyst concentrates only on internal data available from the financial statements to him, his conclusions may not be real. This must be supplemented by external data such as information relating to that particular type of business and the general conditions prevailing in industries. The success of the analyst in interpretation, therefore, depends upon analysing the statements keeping in mind the limitations of the data in the financial statements.

2:1.1 Comparative Financial Statements

The changes in the financial data over a period can be best understood if the statements containing data for a period of two or more years are placed side by side in adjustment columns. Such statements are called *Comparative Financial Statements*. Published annual reports in foreign countries often contain comparative financial statements covering a period of about 10 years. By comparing the change in various items, period by period, the analyst will be able to get some valuable clues as to the growth and other important trends relating to the business.

The analysis of financial statement involves a study of the relationships and trends to determine whether or not the financial position and the results of the operations to measure the relationships among the financial statement's item of single set of statements and the changes that have occurred in these items as shown by the financial statements of subsequent periods. The work of the analyst consists of reducing the data in an understandable manner, by analysing and interpreting the same. A study of the financial position of a company and the results of its operations for a period is more meaningful if the analyst has the statements of financial position and income statements for several periods available, when comparison is made. If two or more financial statements are available, the trends can be better assessed. Statements of three years are usually prepared by large companies for the purpose of comparison. For an effective analysis, the statements to be compared must be based on the consistent application of generally accepted accounting principles over the period. In this connection, the A.I.C.P.A., makes the following recommendations :-

"An adequate understanding and analysis of financial statements data can be achieved only, if the analyst (1) understands the nature and limitation of accounting; (2) understands the terminology of accounting and business; (3) has some knowledge of business; and (4) is acquainted with the nature and tools of financial analysis".

Horizontal and Vertical Analysis

There are two types of analysis, called the horizontal and vertical which form the "backbone" of financial statement analysis.

Horizontal Statement is a statement containing the balance sheet figures of successive periods. The current year's figures are compared with the standard or base year. Usually the statement will contain figures for two years, in one column - the figures for the current year, and the next column will show the rupee changes in percentage. The percentage change is arrived at by dividing the net rupee change by the older of the two figures. The change column indicates the changes in the balance sheet figures that have taken place during the current year. The first of these columns shows the changes in the rupee amounts and the second in terms of percentage. These figures are useful in assessing the change in proper perspective. This will reveal major changes in the nature of current assets to total assets. Similarly, the items in the income statement are prepared in horizontal form. This will disclose the percentage change in sales to other items in the statements; such as selling, general and administrative expenses. Analysis of change in the statements will give the management considerable insight into the levels and areas of strengths and/or weaknesses. This is considered a dynamic type of analysis because it shows the changes that have taken place. The behaviour of each of the entities in the statements can be assessed.

Vertical Statement will contain each item in the balance sheet expressed as a percentage of total assets and in the income statement, the net sales is used as the base. They are useful in analysing and comparing several companies in the same group or divisions within a company. The comparison will be useful because of the analysis of comparing common-size statements. This is a static type of analysis. This deals with the study of the quantitative relationships of the various items in the statements at a particular date.

Comparative Balance Sheets

As against a single balance sheet having the balance of accounts after the accounts are closed, the comparative balance sheet contains the balances of different dates, and also the extent of their increases or decreases in columnar form. The increases and decreases are the results of the changes in the assets and business operations. Usually, the increases and decreases will be represented not only in amounts but also by way of percentages. This facilitates easy comparison of the trends of the business. The comparative balance sheet forms a connecting link between the balance sheet and income statement of different dates. A balance sheet shows the assets, liabilities and the owner's equity of a business at a specified date. On the other hand a comparative balance sheet shows the assets, liabilities and owners' equity of a business for two or more dates with increases and decreases in the absolute data in terms of rupees and percentages. The changes contained in the statements are very important because they indicate the direction in which the financial characteristics are developing. The changes in the balance sheet items consist of the result of profit and loss, acquisition of assets, changes in current assets, conversion of liabilities into another form, payment of liabilities and issue of shares.

Comparative Income Statements

The profit and loss account shows the net income or net loss for a specified period. The comparative income statement will show the operating results for two or more dates. The changes in the data will be shown in terms of rupees and percentages. All items in the income statement are expressed as a percentage of net sales. Such a statement is sometimes called a common-size income statement.

Purposes of Comparison

The comparative financial statements are very useful for analysis because they not only contain certain data but also information necessary for showing the financial and operative trends for a period of years. The nature and trends of these changes indicate the direction to which the financial position and operating results of the business move. Comparison will have no use or will be misleading if the data contained in the statements do not reflect the consistent application of accounting principles. It must be remembered that the data contained in the statements are recorded at the date of the transaction. Naturally, the accounts reflect the data recorded at different price levels. The profit and loss account contains data as regards purchase, sales, and expenses expressed in terms of the rupee value prevailing at the date of purchase or sale or payment. Items such as depreciation, amortisation and opening stock will reflect price levels of the past. As a result of the changes in the price levels of the current period, it is necessary that the analyst must be cautious in interpreting the trends of the items in the comparative balance sheets. As the 'average reader' cannot be expected to understand the relationship of the data, it is necessary to show for each item, the net increase or decrease in the amounts. This will enable him for understand the significance only when each item in the statement is compared with each item of the previous year in the statement. The advantage in showing the increase or decrease in the data is that major changes in the figures will be evident and will pave the way for further study, investigation and interpretation. The extent of net changes in the data from one period to another can be observed only if the relative changes are determined in percentages. Additional column may be provided to show the changes during the year in ratios. The ratios are determined by dividing the amount of the current year by the amount of the previous or base year and comparison can also be made by taking the data of the earliest period as the base year or with the preceding year. No percentage will be shown if the figure is negative in the base period. If it is not possible to compute ratios for certain items, the amounts are shown when there is an amount in the base year and no amount in the following period, the decrease is noted for the item in the following year. When the comparative statements showing the net changes in absolute amounts, and in percentages have been prepared, the analyst should study the changes individually, and jointly to determine and ascertain as to whether the changes so shown in the results are favourable or not.

"The presentation of comparative financial statements in annual and other reports enhances the usefulness of such reports and brings out more clearly, the nature and trends, of current changes, affecting the enterprise; such presentation emphasises the fact that statements for a series of periods are far more significant than those for a single period and that accounts of one period are but an instalment of what is essentially a continuous history. In any one year, it is ordinarily desired, that the balance sheet, the income statement and the surplus statement be given for one or more preceding years as well as the current year." (AICPA - Bulletin No. 1).

2:1.2 Common-size Balance Sheet

In analysing the balance sheet, a statement is prepared to work out the ratio of each asset to total assets and each liability and capital to total liabilities and capital. This statement is known as a *common-size or* 100 *per cent balance sheet.* This is so called because, the total of the assets and also the liabilities and capital is 100 per cent. This statement discloses the relationship of each asset to total assets and each liability and capital item to total liabilities and capital.

The common final balance sheet is converted into common-size balance sheet by dividing each item by total assets and arriving at a percentage figure. The income statement is also converted by dividing each item by sales. The financial statements of different periods are compared on an item-by-item basis so as to detect differences in percentage, for a given item between the financial periods.

In order to find out the proportion of a group or sub-group which a single item in the group represent in financial statement, analysis of common-size statements are made. The assets, liabilities and capital are each expressed as 100 per cent and each item in the group is expressed as a percentage of the respective total. In the income statement, the net sales is taken at 100 per cent and every item in the statement is expressed as a percentage of the net sales. This kind of analysis as already explained, is referred to, as *vertical* analysis and the trend analysis as *horizontal* analysis. This is an analysis of the internal structure of the financial statements. The common-size balance sheet analysis reveals the sources of capital and the distribution of capital sources in the assets of an enterprise.

Comparison of the common-size balance sheet of a single enterprise over the past years is very useful as the changing proportions in the components vary within the group. It must be remembered that the percentages as disclosed in the common-size balance sheet show only the relation of each of the assets to the total assets for each year. When the common-size balance sheet is analysed, and scrutinised horizontally, the trends of the individual items in the balance sheet give information in respect of the same, but they will show their relationship only to the total. As variations in the constituents will affect the total, it is very difficult to interpret the trends. If the trends are to be correctly interpreted, it is necessary to determine the normal percentage of individual assets to the total assets. It is, therefore, advisable to use the common-size balance sheet to study only the proportions therein. Comparison of the comparative balance sheets of two enterprises at a certain date is also done to compare the financial position of the one with the other. This is possible only when the two statements are prepared by the adoption of uniform accounting methods.

Common-size Income Statement

Just as the common-size balance sheet is prepared, so is the common-size income statement prepared with a view to compare the various items in the statement to the total amount of sales. For example, items such as cost of goods sold, selling, administrative expenses and also items of income are reduced to percentage by taking the sales figures as 100%. The changes in the cost of goods sold to sales are very important in financial statement analysis. The difference represents the gross margin which must be sufficient enough to cover the fixed expenses incurred in running the business. The net income is arrived at after. adjustment of expenses against the gross profit. The net income of a business should be reasonable when compared to sales. Similar to common-size balance sheets, a vertical common-size income statement is prepared. We have seen that in the common-size balance sheet, each item of asset is compared to total assets and the item of each liability is compared to the total liabilities. Similarly, the cost of goods sold, and each item of expenses are compared to sales. Each item of expenses is expressed in percentage comparing the total amount of sales which is taken as 100. Common-size income statement can also be prepared in a horizontal form. It is easy to construct the ratios of the various items of expenses to sales for a number of periods and easily interpreted. This will disclose the trends of the expense items to sales. It is also the practice to prepare the common-size income statements of two concerns, so that the results of the operations can be compared with each other. As already pointed out here, the difficulty arises in the matter of the value stated therein. It is necessary for the analyst to satisfy himself whether the same accounting methods are adopted by the two companies. It must be noted that the success of the comparison depends upon the valuation of inventory. The cost of goods sold will be affected by the basis upon which the inventory is valued, since the two companies may be adopting two different methods in the valuation. We have seen that when the income statement is analysed horizontally, the statement will disclose the rate of change in the items affecting the income, and if analysed vertically, shows the distribution of the income, from sales among the items responsible to produce the same. Unlike the common-size balance sheets, there is no difficulty in the case of common-size income statement in the matter of analysis, as each statement serves different purposes. The statements will show the increase or decrease in the expenses to net sales. It is advisable to use both the statements so that the analyst can get supplementary information for the variation noted in the horizontal analysis by reference to the vertical statement.

2:1.3 Trend Percentages

Comparative financial statements for several years may be expressed in terms of trend percentages. Changes in financial statements between periods can be easily studied by establishing a base year and expressing other years in terms of the base year. The trend percentage statement is an 'analytical device for condensing the absolute rupee data' by comparative statements. This device is valuable to the management because by the substitution of percentages for large amounts, the brevity and readability are achieved. They are generally computed for major items in the statements; minor amounts are omitted. The purpose is to highlight significant changes. Trend percentages require careful analysis of the items. Favourable trends are increase in sales, accompanied by a decrease in the cost of goods sold, and selling expenses and increase in current assets with corresponding decrease in current liabilities. Unfavourable trends include an upward trend in debtors and stock with downward trend in sales. Trend percentages indicate the degree of increase or decrease but they cannot indicate the cause for the changes. Changes may have been due to inconsistency in the application of accounting principles, by fluctuating price levels and increase in stock. A series of financial statements are available where each item measured in terms of its growth or decline relative to the base period. Selection of a typical year as base year is very important.

If the accounting principles and practices are not followed consistently throughout the period for which analysis is made, the comparability will be adversely affected. As trend ratios indicate increase or decrease of an item and also the degree of the change, they are useful in finding out the extent to which they give clues that are favourable and/or unfavourable. Trend percentages which are index numbers reveal the relative changes in the financial data. In the statement that will be used as the base, the amount of each item is stated as 100 per cent. In the statement to be compared, if the amount of an item is less than that in the base statement, the trend percentage will be below 100 per cent. If the amount of an item is more than that in the base statement, the trend percentage will be above 100 per cent. Trend percentages are computed by dividing each amount in the statement by the corresponding items in the base statement. The trend percentages represent only percentages of the base statement. They do not indicate the amount of increase unless 100 per cent is deducted from the percentage, or the ratio subtracted from 100. As already stated, trend percentages are computed only for the items that have some relationship and not for all items. If the base year is not typical or representative of the items in the statement, variations in the subsequent period will affect the comparability. In order that the trend percentages may be reliable, it is necessary to study the rupee variations and also the relationship of the items after changes have taken place before arriving at the conclusion whether the trends are favourable or unfavourable. In interpreting the trend, the analyst should consider the 'profitableness of the change', compare the trend data for the particular business with that of business in general and of the industry involved and determine to what extent, changes are the result of price level changes. The most important value of trend analysis is that it can disclose to the analyst a better understanding of management's policies and motives which are the causes for the changes.

It must be remembered that though the trends are important when percentages of various relative items are compared, undue emphasis cannot be laid when there is a smaller number in the base year. To bring out this danger, Mr. J. N. Myer gives a fine example -

"In a college, it was announced one morning that during the nigsht $33 \frac{1}{3}$ per cent of the female students had eloped. However, the college had only three female students". Therefore, it is always desirable that when comparison is made, regard should be had both to absolute and relative changes.

Trend percentage can be represented in the following ways :

(1) Horizontal manner - where the percentage of each year appears one after the other.

(2) Vertical manner - where the percentage appears for each year one below the other.

(3) By a chart containing inventory and sales for some years in rupees.

(4) On semi-logarithmetic scale showing the inventory and sales for some years in rupees.

(5) Showing the trends of average selling prices using as the trend of 'X' as index.

Therefore, the trends may be prepared to show the graphic history of a concern by slotting curves of the trend ratios for several years.

Comparison with prior periods

Comparisons are made on the basis of the past performance of the same company. Changes from year to year will reveal the trends and tendencies as compared to historical relationships. It should be noted that the comparison should be made with comparable data and the accounting methods might have changed, the money value might have been different owing to changing price levels.

Comparison with pre-determined goals

A statement is set up in advance and comparison is made with the same. This will disclose the results as reflected in the financial statements with the results expected or should be. This kind of comparison is very useful when actual income is compared to the budgeted income. If the pre-determined goals are carefully set up, the comparison will reveal why the actual results are different.

Comparison with other companies

Comparisons are often made by investors by employing inter-company data. This is called inter-firm comparison. In this case, there must be caution on the part of the analyst. The only drawback is the difference in the accounting procedure of the companies, and the difficulty in identifying the major companies in a particular industry.

Limitations of trend percentages analysis

(1) In respect of the variation of the least significant factors in the balance sheet, undue emphasis is attached. This will not be of much help in measuring the changes precisely.

(2) If the items in the base year selected are not normal, and much emphasis is made for the same in the matter of measurement of the changes with the item contained in the balance sheets of subsequent years, the result will not be reliable.

(3) If the balance sheet changes are grouped together instead of leaving them as unrelated items, in the preparation of funds statement, the net inflow of funds cannot be considered to be precisely prepared.

(4) If the changes in the assets are shown as net instead of as gross, i.e., depreciation shown separately instead of deduction from the assets, it will be easy to ascertain the increase or decrease in the assets and depreciation, separately.

Financial Statements - Limitations

Financial statements cannot serve the purpose of giving a free and complete picture of the financial position, or the 'financial health' and capabilities of an enterprise because of the following limitations :

1. The data contained in the financial statements cannot be expected to be precise because they are prepared on the basis of the application by precedents, conventions, postulates, assumptions and personal judgment of the accountant preparing them. As the preparation of the statements require the use of judgment and estimates by the accountant, they may not be uniform and reliable owing to differences in the exercise of personal judgment. Principles governing the preparation of financial statements vary from one company to another. There is no agreement as to the principles adopted by the company. Not all companies apply the general principles

governing the preparation of financial statements. If alternative practices are followed, the results will be different.

2. Although the shareholder is interested in a reasonable return on the investment, yet payment of dividends depends upon the liquidity position of the concern which can be ascertained only from the balance sheet. In order to assess the liquidity position of a company, the working capital position is essential. This can be constructed from the current assets, and current liabilities.

3. As the statements are prepared for the use of 'an average reader', it will not be possible to satisfy the requirements of the user for special purpose.

4. The financial statements do not contain full details necessary for the proper assessment of the company's position as regards profitability and solvency. There are many factors which do not form part of financial statements and which have important bearing on the financial position. Unless the data contained in the statements are converted into ratios and percentages, they cannot be said to disclose the real position of an undertaking.

5. The values of the assets contained in a balance sheet do not reflect the current market value at the date of the balance sheet. It is only a historical document, and therefore, does not purport to show the realisable value of the assets appearing therein. It is not a statement of net worth of an undertaking. A balance sheet is prepared on the basis of "going concern" concept and as such the assets are stated at their historical cost. The assets do not reflect what they will fetch if the business is sold. Items of deferred revenue expenditure like preliminary expenses, advertising expenses, and discount on issue of debentures appearing as assets in the balance sheet have no value in liquidation. Even though the rupee values contained in the statements may be accurate, they may be different on the basis of concept of value ascribed by the reader of the statements. The user has to make his own assessment of value. He must be aware of the methods adopted for valuation in the financial statements. Investors rely upon the balance sheets in appraising their holdings in a company. They are interested only in the market value of the assets, *viz* the investment, inventory and fixed assets. The balance sheet contains only the historical costs, and therefore, not useful to them. The value of the rupee is markedly falling with the result that its purchasing power has recorded a downward trend. For example, a machine which was erected 20 years ago cannot be replaced now even for twice its original cost. Therefore, depreciation charged on this machine will only be half of the amount to be charged on replacement basis. If there is an increase in sales value, the increase may not necessarily be due to increase in the number of units sold, but it may be due to increase in the selling price without a similar increase in costs.

6. As financial statements are prepared only for interim periods, they cannot be considered final. To determine the accurate profit or loss of an undertaking, a long period of time is required. For various reasons, it has been found necessary to have the accounting period generally for a period of twelve months and the statements have to be prepared for that period. Transactions affecting income and expenses have to be "cut off" at the date of closing the accounts, and in this regard, numerous differences of opinion are experienced. As the fixed assets are used for a longer period, the uses to which they are put in the business is based only

on estimates. There is, therefore, greater amount of uncertainty in the financial statements and the data contained in it cannot be considered as accurate.

The statements include primarily only information that can be stated in monetary units, and hence, represents only a portion of the total information required for many decisions.

7. Financial statements do not reflect many factors affecting financial conditions because they cannot be recorded in the books in monetary terms. Examples are : Goodwill created by a company, efficiency in the management of business operations, the reputation of the company, and the company's cordial relationship with its employees. They do not contain information as regards the quality of research and development, plant efficiency, marketing organisation, product levels, and future planning. In the absence of uniform unit of measurement, financial statements cannot be reliable.

8. It will be very difficult to correctly understand the position of a company if the financial statements have been prepared under abnormal conditions. During the war period, if production is concentrated by an undertaking in different types of goods for supplies to war and thereby production and sales volume increase and when normal policies of production and sales are not followed, it is natural that the items contained in the financial statements may result either in overstatement or understatement.

9. As the financial statements to be presented involve highly complex and diverse economic activities, it is necessary to portray the same in a simple and summarised form to enable the user of the data to understand the same, without difficulty. In most cases of financial statements, simplicity is not achieved. If the statements are to be kept within a reasonable size, a high degree of summarisation is involved not only at the time of recording the transactions but also in the presentation of statements. In this process, comprehensiveness and clarity are usually lost. Financial statements include only selected quantitative terms, which for further clarity, are condensed. In order to be useful, unbiased, and not misleading, financial statements should disclose all significant financial data essential for making rational economic decisions.

10. There is a time lag between the ocurrence of a gain or loss and the time it appears in the income statements.

11. Occurrence of extraordinary and non-recurring items may distort the net income for a given period.

12. Tax regulations may inappropriately influence the method of reporting. For example : Tendency to treat an item as revenue rather them capitalise the same.

13. Some assets like discovery values of minerals, gas and oil and liabilities like lease contracts are omitted in the financial statements. Gains or losses by holding non-monetary assets occur but are not reported in financial statements.

2:1.4 Ratios :

A ratio is a simple mathematical expression. It is a statistical yardstick that provides a measure of relationship between two figures. Accounting ratio relates to the ratio expressed by analysis of accounting data contained in the published accounts or financial statements. Ratios are an aid to analysis and interpretation. They are a substitute for sound thinking. They are employed to test the solvency, liquidity of the assets and the profitability of the concern.

2.1.5 Fund Flow statement

We know that a Balance sheet is a statement of financial position of a particular concern. But it does not throw hight on the movement of funds. The success or the failure of any business depends upon the availability of funds and their better utilisation. This purpose is served by the fund flow statement. It describes the sources from which additional funds were derived and the use to which these funds were put. It is a statement of sources and application of funds which analyse the changes in the financial condition of a business concern between two dates. Details of ratio analysis and fund flow analysis are discussed in further pages.

2.2 Ratio Analysis

Ratio Analysis is a very important tool of financial analysis. It is the process of establishing a significant relationship between the items of financial statement to provide a meaningful understanding of the performance and financial position of a firm.

2.2.1 Meaning of Ratio

A ratio may be defined as the mathematical expression of the relationship between two accounting figures. But these figures must be related to each other (i.e. these figures must have a mutual cause and effect relationship) to produce a meaningful and useful ratio. Ratio is expressed by dividing one figure by the other related figure. Thus, a ratio is an expression of relating one number to another. It is simply the quotient of two numbers. A ratio may be expressed in the following three ways :

   a) Ratio : Specifically the simple division of one number by another. For eg. 2 : 1, 1 : 2 etc.
   b) Rate : The ratio between two numerical facts usually over a period of time. For e.g. "Stock turnover is three times a year."
   c) Percentage : A special type of rate which expresses the relation in 100. For e.g. "Gross Profit is 20% on sales."

2.2.2 Necessity of Ratio Analysis :

The necessity of computing the relationship between two related items in the form of ratios or percentages arises from the fact that absolute data is often incapable of revealing the soundness or otherwise of a company's financial position or performance. For e. g. a net profit of Rs. 2,00,000 shown by the profit & loss account will be considered quite impressive, when considered without reference to the capital invested in the business. But, when it is compared with the capital invested, say Rs. 25,00,000, it will prove to be inadequate as it works out to just 8 % only. By the application of the percentage and ratio analysis to the various items in the financial statements one can guess accurately the financial health and capabilities of a business.

Thus, ratio analysis is a very valuable tool of management control for diagnosing the financial health of an enterprise.

Advantages

The following are the principal advantages.

1. Ratios simplify the comprehension of financial statements. They tell the whole story in a condensed form.

2. They act as an efficiency index of an enterprise. As such, they serve as an instrument of management control. It is an instrument for diagnosing the financial health of an enterprise. The efficiency of the various individual units similarly situated can be judged through inter-firm comparisons.

3. The ratio analysis can be of invaluable aid to management in the discharge of its basic function of forecasting, planning, co-ordination, communication and control. A study of the trend of strategic ratio may help the management in this respect. Past ratios indicate trends in cost, sales, profit and other relevant facts.

   Ratios besides showing the trends, also indicate changes in the direction and degree of the trend itself. They also indicate the causes leading up to the present position to a large extent.

4. Investment decisions can at times be based on the conditions revealed by certain ratios.

5. They make it possible to estimate the other figures when one figure is known.

   Thus, the ratio analysis points out the financial condition of business - whether it is very strong, good, questionable or poor and thus, enables the management to take necessary steps. According to J. Betty, "Ratio analysis used properly can be a great boon to assessing important characteristics such as solvency, over-trading and profitability."

Limitations

1. The benefits of a ratio analysis depend to a great extent upon the correct interpretation. The interpretation may be based on a single ratio. But a single ratio in itself is meaningless as it does not provide a complete picture of a company's financial position. A single ratio may direct attention to only one aspect of its financial status or operating results. Unless the other aspects of its financial position are analysed and found to be satisfactory, the company cannot be pronounced to be in good health financially. It is to get as complete a picture as possible of the financial health of a company that a number of ratios are to be computed and studied together.

2. Reliability of ratio depends upon the reliability of data.

3. White comparing ratios of the two firms, it must be seen that both of them follow the same accounting plans or bases, otherwise the comparison has no meaning.

4. Changes in prices distort the comparison over a period of years.

5. Ratios sometimes give a misleading picture. It would therefore be proper to study absolute figures along with ratios.

6. Ratios and percentages have little signficance unless they can be compared with or matched against appropriate standards. Unless measuring devices or standards are available , the analyst will not be able to determine whether the ratios indicate favourable or unfavourable conditions.

   Hence, immense benefit is likely to flow out if the ratios are studied :

   i)   for the same firm over a period of years;

   ii) for one firm against another;

   iii) for one firm against the industry as a whole;

iv) for one division or department of a firm against the other division or department; and

v)   actual ratios against standard ratios set.

It may be noted that like any other statistical measurement, ratios are only a convenient means of expressing the relationship between two items. They are not final in any sense of the word and cannot be a substitute for "thinking" on the part of the analyst. They are merely a starting point and focus attention on specific relationships which require further study. Each industry has its own typical ratios and the particular characteristics of the industry should always be kept in mind while a firm is being studied. For instance, if an industry is seasonal, a ratio at a particular point of time will always differ from ratios at the end of the year or throughout the year. Hence, the particular point of time of the study, therefore, becomes important.

Ratios are at best only symptoms and like the symptoms displayed by a human body, may have their origin at a place different from where the symptom appears. One may say that ratios indicate whether there is anything wrong and, if so, probably where; but it becomes the duty of the management to unearth the underlying causes

2.2.3 Interpretation of Ratios

The benefits of ratio analysis depend to a great extent upon their correct interpretation. Interpretation requires considerable ability on the part of the analyst. He has to decide whether the relationship disclosed by the ratio is satisfactory or not. He has to base his decision on experience, or on comparison with normal or average ratios.The ratios may be interpreted in any one of the following ways –

1. Based on single ratio and group of ratio : The interpretation may be based on individual ratio. For e. g. if a current ratio persistently falls and goes below one, it can be interpreted as an indication of short-term solvency. However, one cannot guess correctly by studying individual ratio in isolation. It is, therefore, a common practice to study and interpret a set of several related ratios. For e. g. for short-term solvency, both the ratios viz., Current Ratio and Acid Test Ratio must be studied.The ratios, whose significance is not fully understood, are made more meaningful by the computation and study of additional relevant ratios.

2. Comparison over time : Ratio analysis is primarily useful for studying trends, indicating rise, decline or stability over a period of time. For this purpose, ratios by themselves are of no particular significance. For revealing such trends, the same ratio or a group of ratios is studied over a period of years. Thus, the movements in the ratios, rather than the ratios themselves, are important.

3. Inter-firm Comparison : Ratios of the undertaking are compared with the respective ratios of other firms in the same industry and with the industry average. An immense benefit is likely to flow from such a comparison as the concerns similarly situated are, as a matter of fact, ' to sail in the same boat.'

Procedure of Analysis

First of all the depth, object and extent of analysis must be determined so that necessary information can be collected.

The analyst is required to go through various financial statements of the business and collect other required information from the management.

The analyst is required to re-arrange the data given in the financial statements in a manner which will help him to analyse the statements easily and conveniently.

After analysing the statements, the interpretation is made and the conclusions are drawn.

2.2.4 Types of Ratios

Classification of ratios is done in two ways viz., – i) according to nature of items; and ii) according to purpose or function.

2.2.4.1. According to nature of items

a) Balance Sheet Ratios : The ratios exhibiting the relationship between two items or groups of items in the balance sheet. For e. g. relation between current assets and current liabilities.

b) Revenue Statement or Profit & Loss Account Ratios : The ratios disclosing the relationship between two items or groups of items in the profit & loss account. For e. g. relationship between sales and gross profit or net profit.

c) Inter-statement or Composite Ratios : The ratios indicating the relationship of certain items in the balance sheet with some figures in the revenue statement. For e. g., net profit and capital or sales and fixed assets etc.

2.2.4.2. Functional Classification

a) Liquidity Ratios : These ratios measure the liquidity position of the enterprise i, e. whether the current assets are sufficient to pay off current liabilities as and when they mature. Thus these ratios indicate short-term solvency of the business.

b) Leverage Ratios : They indicate the relative use of debt and equity in financing the assets of the firm. The extent to which the practice of trading on equity can be carried on safely can be known through these ratios.

c) Activity Ratios : These ratios measure the efficiency in the employment of funds in the business operations. They reflect the company's level of activities in relation to its turnover.

d) Profitability Ratios : These ratios measure the overall performance and profit-earning capacity of the business. They reveal the total effect of the business transactions on the profit position of the enterprise.

Some important terms

1. Capital employed, or Long-term funds, or Permanent capital or Proprietors Funds.
   The term means
   (Share Capital + Reserves & Surplus + Premium + Long-term loans) less (Non-business Assets + Fictitious Assets.)
   or it can also be calculated as :-
   Fixed Capital (i.e. Fixed Assets at written down value)
   + Working Capital or Net Current assets (i. e. Current Assets less Current Liabilities.)

2. **Operating Profits**
   = Gross Profit less Operating Expenses (i.e. Trading Expenses) before Interest and Taxation.

3. **Equity or Net Worth**
   = Preference Share Capital + Equity Share Capital + Reserves & Surplus Less Losses and Fictitious Assets.

4. **Common Equity**
   = Equity Share Capital + Reserves & Surplus + Share Premium Less Losses.

5. **Liquid Assets or Quick Assets**
   = Current Assets Excluding Stock and Pre-paid Expenses.

6. **Liquid Liabilities**
   = Current Liabilities excluding Bank Overdraft and Accrued Expenses.

Chart Showing the Important Ratios

Name of Ratio	Formula for calculation of Ratio	Type of Ratio according to	
		Nature	**Function**
1. Current Ratio or 2:1 Ratio	$\dfrac{\text{Current Assets}}{\text{Current Liabilities}}$	Balance Sheet	Liquidity
2. Acid Test Ratio or Quick Ratio or Liquid Ratio	$\dfrac{\text{Quick or Liquid Assets}}{\text{Quick or Liquid Liabilities}}$	Balance Sheet	Liquidity
3. Inventory to Working Capital Ratio	$\dfrac{\text{Closing Stock}}{\text{Working Capital}}$	Balance Sheet	Liquidity
4. Proprietory Ratio, or Tangible Net Worth to Total Assets Ratio or Capital to Total Assets Ratio	$\dfrac{\text{Proprietors' Funds}}{\text{Total Assets}}$	Balance Sheet	Leverage
5. Fixed Assets Ratio or Fixed Assets to Tangible Net Worth Ratio	$\dfrac{\text{(Depreciated value of) Fixed Assets}}{\text{Proprietors' Fund}} \times 100$	Balance Sheet	Leverage
6. Current Assets to Proprietors' Fund	$\dfrac{\text{Current Assets}}{\text{Proprietors' Fund}} \times 100$	Balance Sheet	Leverage
7. Debt to Equity Ratio or Total Liabilities to Proprietors' Funds Ratio	$\dfrac{\text{Total Debt}}{\text{Net Worth}}$	Balance Sheet	Leverage

8. Capital Gearing Ratio	$$\frac{\text{Equity Share Capital Plus Reserves \& Surplus}}{\text{Preference Share Capital \& Loan Capital}}$$	Balance Sheet	Leverage
9. Gross Profit Ratio	$$\frac{\text{Gross Profit}}{\text{Net Sales}} \times 100$$	Revenue	Profitability
10. Net Profit Ratio	$$\frac{\text{Net Profit}}{\text{Net Sales}} \times 100$$	Revenue	Profitability
11. Operating Ratio	$$\frac{\text{Cost of goods sold plus Operating Expenses}}{\text{Net Sales}} \times 100$$	Revenue	Profitability
12. Interest Coverage Ratio or Fixed Charges Cover Ratio	$$\frac{\text{Net profit before deduction of Interest \& Income Tax}}{\text{Fixed Interest Charges}}$$	Revenue	Profitability
13. Inventory Turnover Ratio	$$\frac{\text{Cost of Goods Sold}}{\text{Average Inventory}}$$	Composite	Activity
14. Debtors' Turnover **OR** Receivable Turnover Ratio	$$\frac{\text{Accounts Receivable}}{\text{Average Daily Sales}}$$	Composite	Activity
15. Fixed Assets Turnover Ratio	$$\frac{\text{Sales}}{\text{Net Fixed Assets}}$$	Composite	Activity
16. Total Assets Turnover Ratio	$$\frac{\text{Sales}}{\text{Total Assets}}$$	Composite	Activity
17. Return on Shareholders' Investments or Proprietors' Fund	$$\frac{\text{Net Profit after Taxes}}{\text{Shareholders' Fund}} \times 100$$	Composite	Activity
18. Return on Capital Employed or Net Profit to Total Assets Ratio	$$\frac{\text{Net Profit after Taxes}}{\text{Capital Employed}} \times 100$$	Composite	Activity
19. Return on Equity Capital Ratio	$$\frac{\text{Net Profit (after Taxes and Preference dividend)}}{\text{Equity Capital}} \times 100$$	Composite	Activity
20. Earnings per Equity Share	$$\frac{\text{Net Profit (after Taxes and Preference dividend)}}{\text{Number of Equity shares}}$$	Composite	Activity

According to **Weston and Brigham**, accounting ratios are classified as under :

1) Liquidity :
    a) Current ratios
    b) Quick Ratios

2) Leverage :
    a) Debt to total assets
    b) Times interest earned
    c) Fixed charge coverage

3) Activity :
    a) Inventory turnover
    b) Average collection period
    c) Fixed assets turnover
    d) Total assets turnover

4) Profitability :
    a) Gross profit on sales
    b) Return on total assets
    c) Return on net worth

1. Current Ratio or 'Working Capital Ratio' or 2 :1 Ratio

It is a ratio of current assets to current - liabilities. The ratio is calculated by dividing the current assets by the current liabilities

$$\text{Current Ratio} = \frac{\text{Currents Assets}}{\text{Current Liabilities}}$$

Certain authorities have suggested that in order to ensure solvency of a concern, current assets should be at least twice, the current liabilities, and therefore, this ratio is known as 2 : 1 ratio. This ratio is also named as "Working Capital Ratio" as it represents the working capital being the excess of the current assets over current liabilities.

Significance : This ratio indicates the solvency of the business i. e. ability to meet the liabilities of the business as and when they fall due. The current assets are the sources from which the current liabilities have to be met. It is also a measure of the margin of safety that management maintains in order to allow for the inevitable unevenness in the flow of funds through .the current assets and liability accounts.

Though 2 : 1 ratio is considered desirable, it is not a must as it depends upon the nature of the industry. What is important is not the size of the current ratio but the distribution and characteristics of current assets and current liabilities and their relation to the prospective sales volume.

Precautions : This ratio is sensitive to a number of factors which must be taken into account, if dependable results are to be obtained, some of which are given below :-

i) It must be ascertained whether the current assets and the current liabilities are properly valued. If any of the current assets or current liabilities are not correctly valued, the ratio will be distorted to that extent i. e. the ratio will either be high or low and will not reflect the correct position. It must therefore be seen that proper provisions concerning current assets, such as provision for Doubtful Debts etc. are made.

ii) Window-Dressing :- It means to show off the financial position as better than it actually exists. Accordingly, current assets and current liabilities are shown in the balance sheet in such a way that they result in a more favourable current ratio than the actual one. This is done by resorting to malpractices, such as inflating the value of inventory, omitting certain liabilities, treating a short-term liability as a long-term liability etc.

The analyst must, therefore, get himself assured that such window dressing is not resorted to.

iii) In interpreting the ratio consideration, the proportion of various types of current assets is important. A Company with a high percentage of its current assets in cash is more liquid than the one with a high percentage in inventory. Large stocks may have been accumulated only for a seasonal trade or in anticipation of a rise in the price of goods.

4. For studying the solvency of the concern from the current ratio, still another factor must not be lost sight of i.e. shrinkage in value of current assets on a forced liquidation.

It would thus be clear that in order to get accurate results it is essential that the effect of the aforementioned factors should be eliminated. There is a danger in treating this ratio too rigidly, especially where a business has reached a normal state of progress it should only move within settled limits over an accounting period. Any movement outside these limits should be closely investigated.

(Note : Current Assets include Cash in Hand/Bank, Marketable Securities, other short-term high quality investments, Bills Receivable Pre-paid expenses, Work-in-progress, Sundry Debtors and Inventories. Current Liabilities are composed of Sundry Creditors, Bills Payable, Outstanding and Accrued Expenses, Income Tax payable, Overdraft.)

2. Liquid ratio or acid test ratio or quick ratio

The current ratio fails to serve as a realistic guide to the solvency of the concern as the major portion of the current assets may comprise of such assets which cannot be converted immediately into cash (e.g. stock) to meet the immediate liabilities.

$$\text{Liquid Ratio} = \frac{\text{Quick Assets}}{\text{Quick Liabilities}}$$

The quick ratio indicates the relation of 'quick assets' with 'quick liabilities' Quick or liquid assets include all current assets except stock and pre-paid expenses whereas lquid liabilities include all current liabilities except overdraft and accrued expenses.

If this ratio is 1:1, it is considered that all claims will be met when they arise.

Significance : It is a measure of the extent to which liquid resources are immediately available to meet current obligations. Insofar as it eliminates inventories as part of current assets, this ratio is a more rigorous test of liquidity than the current ratio and, when used in conjunction with, it gives a better picture of the firm's ability to meet its short-term debts out of short-term assets.

This ratio does not take into account two important factors i.e. certain portions of stocks would be sold over to meet current liabilities and all creditors would not be required to be paid at the same time.

Precautions : Same as Current ratio

Care must be exercised before placing too much reliance on 100 per cent acid-test ratio without further investigation. For e.g., a seasonal business which seeks to stabilise production will tend to have a weak acid-test ratio during its period of slack sales, and probably a powerful one in its period of heavy selling. Hence, the earlier weak position would have to be judged in relation to the market prospects for the firm's products in the latter period.

3. Inventory to Working Capital Ratio

This ratio is calculated as under :-

$$\frac{\text{Closing Stock}}{\text{Working Capital}}$$

There is a need to supplement the ratio of net sales to inventory by another ratio to confirm the position shown by the inventory and net working capital. This provides a relatively more stable basis for comparison than is supplied by the inventory turnover ratio.

Significance : The ratio is an index of the position of over-stocking. It shows what part of the working capital is represented by the closing stocks. The size of closing stocks must bear a proper proportion to the quantum of working capital. The higher the cover given by working capital, the lower the risk of loss by the likely fall in the value of inventories in future.

The ratio should be interpreted with great care. It should be treated as a conclusive proof of over-stocking. This ratio should be studied with the stock turnover ratio to arrive at the correct decision.

4. Proprietory Ratio

Ratio of tangible net worth to total assets is also called as proprietory ratio or capital total assets ratio. It is calculated as under :

$$\frac{\text{Proprietors' Funds (i.e. Share Capital, Reserves and surplus)}}{\text{Total Assets}}$$

This ratio establishes the relationship between proprietors' funds and total assets. 100% less percent ago of this ratio = ratio of total liabilites to total assets. If this ratio is 80% it means ratio of total liabilities to total assets is 20%

Significance : The greater the percentage of proprietors' fund, the stronger the financial position of the concern This ratio is normally a test of strength of creditworthiness of the concern. To the extent the percentage of liabilities increase or the percentage of capital dwindles, the credit strength of the concern deteriorates. This ratio, therefore, should be considered alongwith the current ratio while considering the solvency of the concern.

A high proprietory ratio is, however, frequently indicative of over-capitalisation and an excessive investment in fixed assets in relation to actual needs. A ratio nearing 100 per cent often gives low earnings per share, and consequently, a low rate of dividend to shareholders.

A low proprietory ratio on the other hand, is a symptom of under-capitalisation and an excessive use of creditor funds to finance the business.

5. Fixed Assets Ratio or Fixed Assets to Tangible Net Worth Ratio or Capital to Fixed Assets Ratio :

$$\frac{\text{Depreciated value of Fixed Assets}}{\text{Proprietors' Funds}} \times 100$$

Significance : Normally, a proprietor should provide all the funds required to purchase fixed assets. If the ratio exceeds 100%, it indicates that the company has used short-term funds for acquiring fixed assets, which policy, is not desirable. To the extent, the fixed assets exceed the amount of capital and reserves, the working capital is depleted. When the amount of proprietors' funds exceed the value of fixed assets i.e. when the percentage is less than 100, a part of the net working capital is supplied by the shareholders, provided that there are no other non-current assets. Though it is not possible to lay down a rigid standard as regards the percentage of capital which should be invested in fixed assets in each industry, there always is a maximum which should not be exceeded so that the harmony among the fixed assets, debtors and stock is not disturbed. This ratio should generally be 65%.

6. Ratio of Current Assets to Proprietors' Funds :-

It is arrived at as under -,

$$\frac{\text{Current Assets}}{\text{Proprietors' Funds}} \times 100$$

This ratio shows the percentage of proprietors' funds invested in current assets. It must be studied in the relation of fixed assets to proprietory funds ratio.

7. Debt to Equity Ratio or Total Liabilities to Proprietors' Funds Ratio

It is a measure of the relative claims of creditors and owners against the assets of the firm. It is calculated as under :

$$\text{Debt to Equity Ratio} = \frac{\text{Total Debt}}{\text{Net Worth}}$$

The term 'total debt' includes all debts i. e. long-term, short- term, mortgages, bills, debentures etc., whereas the term net worth means equity share capital, preference share capital, reserves and surplus i. e., proprietors' funds or Equity.

(There is difference of opinion regards preference share capital as to whether it is to be included in creditors or in ownership claims)

Significance : It is a measure of the financial strength of a concern. The lower the ratio, the greater is the security available to creditors. A satisfactory current ratio and ample working capital may not always be a guarantee against insolvency if the total liabilities are inordinately large.

The purpose of this ratio is to derive an idea of the amount of capital supplied by the owners and of assets 'cushion' available to creditors on liquidation. Generally, 1:1 ratio is acceptable. The greater the interest of the owners as compared with that of the creditors, the more satisfactory is the financial structure of the business because, in such a situation, the management is less handicapped by interest charges and debt repayment requirements.

A company having a stable profit can afford to operate on a relatively high debt-equity ratio;

whereas in the case of a company having an unstable profit, a high debt-equity ratio reflects a speculative situation.

8. Capital Gearing Ratio

The proportion of the equity share capital to the total capital of the concern is known as gear ratio or capital gearing, According to J. Betty, "the relation of ordinary shares (equity capital) to preference share capital and loan capital is described as "capital gearing". Equity capital means share capital plus undistributed profit items.

$$\text{Capital Gearing Ratio} = \frac{\text{Equity Capital} + \text{Surplus and Reserves}}{\text{Pref. Share and Loan Capital}}$$
$$\text{or Fixed Interest Capital}$$

This ratio is a means of analysis of the capital structure.

If the proportion of preference shares and loan capital is high or where the proportion of ordinary share capital to the total capital is low, then such a capital is said to be highly geared. The reverse is true in the case of low gearing.

Low gearing indicates that the equity share capital is not paid an adequate return because the profits are swallowed up by the high fixed charges in the form of interest and dividends.

Capital gearing signifies the process of maintaining a desired and an appropriate gear ratio in an enterprise. When inflationary conditions are expected, high gearing is to be employed, and in the periods marked by trade depression, low gearing needs to be employed.

9. Gross Profit Ratio

This ratio reflects the efficiency with which the management produces each unit of product. The ratio is calculated as under :-

$$\frac{\text{Gross Profit}}{\text{Sales}} \times 100$$

It is the ratio which is most commonly employed by accountants for comparing the earnings of business for one period with those of other or earnings of one concern with those of another in the same industry.

It indicates 'the degree to which selling prices of goods per unit may decline without resulting in losses on operations for the firm.

A high gross profit ratio as compared with that of other firm in the same industry implies that the firm in question produces its products at lower cost. It is a sign of good management.

A low gross profit ratio may indicate unfavourable purchasing and mark-up policies, the inability of management to develop sales volume, theft, damage, bad maintenance, marked reduction in selling prices not accompanied by proportionate decrease in cost of goods etc.

The reasons for the increase or decrease of gross profit percentage over the preceding period may be any of the following :-

The reasons for increase
  i) Higher sales price, cost price remaining unchanged
  ii) Lower cost of goods, sales price remaining constant

iii) A combination of variations in sales price and costs, with widening margin.

iv) Change in the method of valuation of stock resulting in over-valuation of closing stock.

v) Omission of some of the purchases.

vi) Some sales might have been entered more than once.

vii) The goods which have been sold but not delivered might have been included in closing stock.

The reasons for decrease -

i) Under-valuation of stock.

ii) Higher cost price, sales price remaining the same.

iii) Lower sales price, cost price remaining unchanged.

iv) Pilferage of stock.

v) Some purchases might have been entered more than once.

vi) Goods entered as bought might not have been received and thus not included in the closing stock.

vii) Some sales might not have been recorded to misappropriate cash advertantly or may have been left unrecorded inadvertantly.

10. Net Profit Ratio

Net Profit is that proportion of net sales which remains with the owners or the shareholders after all costs, charges and expenses, including income tax, have been deducted. It is calculated as under :-

$$\frac{\text{Net Profit (After taxes)}}{\text{Net Sales}} \times 100$$

It differs from the ratio of operating profits to net sales inasmuch as it is calculated after adding non-operating income, like interest, dividends on investments etc., to operating profits and deducting non-operating expenses, such as loss on sale of old assets, provision for legal damages etc., from such profits –

This ratio is widely used as a measure of the overall profitability and is very useful to the proprietors. When read alongwith the operating ratio, it gives an idea of the efficiency as well as profitability of the business to a limited extent.

11. Operating Ratio

$$\frac{\text{Cost of goods sold plus Operating Expenses}}{\text{Net Sales}} \times 100$$

Operating expenses consist of –

i) Factory expenses like factory rent, wages, factory insurance etc.

ii) Administrative expenses like rent, insurance, office staff salaries, printing of stationery etc.

iii) Selling and distribution expenses like salesman's salaries , advertising, travelling expenses, delivery van expenses etc.

(Instead of having only one composite ratio for each type of the above expenses, a separate ratio may be computed by dividing each type of expenses by net sales)

The ratio shows the percentage of net sales that is absorbed by the cost of goods sold and operating expenses. Naturally, the higher the ratio, the less favourable it is, because it would leave a smaller margin to meet interest, dividends and other corporate needs.

This ratio is an index of the operating efficiency of the enterprise. It is advisable to study the ratio over a number of years so as to view the direction of the operating efficiency.

12. Fixed Charge Coverage Ratio or Interest Coverage Ratio

This ratio is calculated as under :-

$$= \frac{\text{Net profit before Interest \& Taxes}}{\text{Total Interest Charges}} = \text{No. of times}$$

The answer shows as to how many times (say 10 times, 15 times etc.) the interest charges are covered by the funds that are ordinarily available to pay the interest charges. The standard for coverage fixed is six to seven times. The weakness of the ratio would indicate difficulty in securing additional funds from outside sources. However, too high a ratio may mean that very conservative use of debt is being made by the firm. A lower ratio indicates excessive use of debt and points out that the firm should improve the operating efficiency or repay the debt to improve the coverage. Normally, the standard ratio is taken as 6 or 7 times.

13. Inventory Turnover Ratio

The term "Inventory Turnover" refers to the number of times in a year inventories are sold and replaced. This ratio is computed as under :

$$\frac{\text{Cost of goods sold}}{\text{Average Inventory at Cost}} \quad \text{or} \quad \frac{\text{Net Sales}}{\text{Average Inventory at Selling Price}}$$

(Where cost of goods sold is not available, net sales are taken.)

Significance : It is an indication of the velocity with which merchandise moves through the business. This helps in the test of inventory to discover possible trouble in the form of over-stocking or over-valuation. It assists the financial manager in evaluating inventory policy.

A low inventory turnover may reflect dull business, over-investment in inventory or accumulation of obsolete and unsaleable goods.

A high inventory turnover indicates relatively lower amount of working capital inventories.

An inventory turnover ratio, standing by itself, means absolutely nothing, because there is no fixed form for turnover. To give meaning to a turnover figure, one must compare it with other such figures so that a comparative analysis with industry or over a time is possible.

The relation is between two variables. If both items increase in same proportion, the ratio remains unchanged, and a situation may develop that may inadvertently lead to an unsound financial condition. For e.g.

Net Sales	10,00,000	15,00,000	25,00,000
Inventory	1,00,000	1,50,000	2,50,000
Ratio	10:1	10:1	10:1
Working Capital	1,25,000	1,25,000	1,25,000

Though the ratio is constant for 3 years, inventory may prove excessive for the size of business and could result in bankruptcy.

In order to discern this danger point, this ratio must be supplemented by ratio of inventory to working capital.

(**Note :** Average stock is the total of opening stock and closing stock divided by 2)

14. Debtors Turnover Ratio

Since sundry debtors constitute an important item of current assets, the amount of the accounts receivable at any particular time should not exceed a reasonable proportion of net sales. This proportion is expressed as a ratio, which is computed as under :

$$\frac{\text{Accounts Receivable (i.e. Sundry Debtors and B/R)}}{\text{Average Daily Sales}}$$

$$OR$$

$$\frac{\text{Accounts Receivable}}{\text{Net Sales}} \times 365 \text{ (or 360)}$$

$$= \text{No. of days}$$

Significance : It is an enabling device to find out as to how many days' average sales are tied up in the value of amounts owed by debtors,s according to the balance sheet. It is also an excellent supplementary check to be used for judging the adequacy of current ratio.

A rule of thumb is that the collection period should not **exceed** $1\frac{1}{3}$ times of the regular payment period. For e.g., if regular payment period is 30 days, then average collection period should not exceed 40 days. Changes in the ratio indicate changes in the company's credit policy or changes in its ability to collect its receivables.

The lower this ratio with reference to usual credit terms, the less likely is the receivable accounts to contain old and valueless amounts. Where this ratio is high, the greater must be the allowance for loss of value in the liquidation of receivables and the higher must be the current ratio in order to protect creditors.

The objective of the comparison implied in the debtors turnover ratio is to learn how old the accounts are and partly to learn how fast cash will flow from their collections. If the credit period is 30 days and the ratio shows 60 days, it shows that at least half the accounts are overdue as 60 days sales are locked up in trade debtors. This situation is thought of as over-investment in receivables and may be the result of over-extension of credit, lack of effective collection policies, and is an index of the collection department's ability to make collection in time etc. Thus, this ratio is an index of the number of days for which the period of credit is allowed, or in other words, it indicates the number of day for which the amounts remain uncollected.

15. Fixed Assets Turnover Ratio

The ratio is arrived at as under :

$$\frac{\text{Sales}}{\text{Net Fixed Assets}} = \text{No. of times}$$

Significance : This ratio measures the efficiency in the utilisation of fixed assets and indicates whether the fixed assets are being fully utilised. While high ratio is an index of over-trading; a low ratio suggests idle capacity and excessive investment in fixed assets. Normally, a standard ratio is taken as five times.

16. Total Assets Turnover Ratio

The ratio is arrived at by dividing sales by the total assets i.e.

$$\frac{\text{Sales}}{\text{Total Assets}} = \text{No. of times}$$

This ratio indicates the sales generated per rupee of investment in total assets. An increase in ratio indicates that more revenue is generated per rupee of total investment in assets. Some analysts take only tangible assets, and in that case, the ratio will be arrived at by dividing sales by tangible assets only, i. e., goodwill, patents, trademarks etc., are not taken into account. Normally, a standard ratio is taken as 2 times.

17. Return on Shareholder's Investment or Propreitors' Funds

$$\frac{\text{Net Profit (after taxes)}}{\text{Shareholders' Funds or Equity}}$$

Shareholders' equity will include equity share capital, preference share capital and reserves and surplus (less accumulated losses, if any). It is also termed as 'net worth'.

This ratio shows how well the firm has used the resources of the owners and is a measure of the profitableness of an enterprise. The realisation of a satisfactory net income is the major objective of a business and the ratio shows the extent to which this objective is being achieved. Normal percentage is 15 to 18.

18. Returns on Capital Employed or Net Profit to Total Assets

$$\frac{\text{Net Profit (after tax)}}{\text{Capital Employed}} \times 100$$

The term 'capital employed' means either non-current liabilities plus shareholders' funds or working capital plus non-current assets. (If the term 'capital employed' is taken as gross capital employed, then it means total assets.)

This ratio is a measure of the return on the total resources of the business enterprise. It shows how efficiently management has used the funds provided by the creditors and the owners. This ratio can be used effectively for inter-firm and inter-industry comparisons in order to find out the relative efficiency.

19. Return on Equity Capital or Common Equity

$$= \frac{\text{Net Profit (after Taxes and Preference Dividend)}}{\text{Equity Share Capital}} \times 100$$

= Rate of Returns on Equity Capital

OR

20. Earnings per Equity Share

$$= \frac{\text{Net Profits (after Taxes \& Preference Dividend)}}{\text{Number of Equity Shares}} \times 100$$

= Earnings per Equity Share

This ratio shows the percentage of profits available to equity shareholders or how much return they will get per share. It is used to compare the performance of a company's equity capital with those of other companies. The shares of the oompany with higher rate of returns will have a greater demand in the market; resulting in increase in the market value.

Illustrations

Illustrations 1 : The following are the financial statements of 'S' Ltd., for the year 2007-08

Balance Sheet as on 31-03-2008

1,00,000 Equity Shares		Fixed Assets	12,50,000
of Rs. 10 each.	10,00,000	Stock	3,50,000
General Reserve	9,00,000	Sundry Debtors	1,80,000
Profit & Loss A/c	25,000	Cash	5,15,000
6% Debentures	2,00,000		
Sundry Creditors	1,20,000		
Proposed Dividends	50,000		
	22,95,000		22,95,000

Profit & Loss Account for the year ended 31-03-2008

Sales	24,00,000
Less Cost of goods sold	16,00,000
Gross Profit	8,00,000
Expenses	7,00,000
Net Profit	1,00,000

You are required to compute the following ratios :

1) Current Ratio 2) Acid Test Ratio 3) Gross Profit Ratio 4) Net Income to Capital 5) Debt to Equity Ratio 6) Fixed Assets to Net Tangible Worth Ratio 7) Current Assets to Proprietors' Funds

Ratio 8) Net Profit Ratio 9) Total Assets Turnover Ratio 10) Operating Ratio 11) Return on Capital employed.

Solution : 1

1. Current Ratio $= \dfrac{\text{Current Assets}}{\text{Current Liabilities}} = \dfrac{10,45,000}{1,70,000} = 6.15{:}1$

2. Acid Test Ratio $= \dfrac{\text{Liquid Assets}}{\text{Liquid Liabilities}} = \dfrac{6,95,000}{1,70,000} = 4{:}1$

3. Gross Profit Ratio $= \dfrac{\text{Gross Profit}}{\text{Capital}} \times 100 = \dfrac{8,00,000}{24,00,000} \times 100 = 33.33\%$

4. Net Income to Capital $= \dfrac{\text{Net Profit}}{\text{Capital}} \times 100 = \dfrac{1,00,000}{19,25,000} \times 100 = 5.2\%$

5. Debt to Equity Ratio $= \dfrac{\text{Total Debts}}{\text{Net Worth}} \times 100 = \dfrac{3,70,000}{19,25,000} \times 100 = 19.22\%$

6. Fixed Assets to Net Tangible Worth Ratio

$= \dfrac{\text{Fixed Assets (WDV)}}{\text{Proprietors Funds}} \times 100 = \dfrac{12,50,000}{19,25,000} \times 100 = 64.9\%$

7. Current Assets to Proprietors Funds

$= \dfrac{\text{Current Assets}}{\text{Proprietors Funds}} \times 100 = \dfrac{10,45,000}{19,25,000} \times 100 = 54.3\%$

8. Net Profit Ratio $= \dfrac{\text{Net Profit}}{\text{Net Sales}} \times 100 = \dfrac{1,00,000}{24,00,000} \times 100 = 4.16\%$

9. Total Assets Turnover Ratio

$= \dfrac{\text{Sales}}{\text{Total Assets}} = \dfrac{24,00,000}{22,95,000} = 1.04 \text{ times}$

10. Operating Ratio $= \dfrac{\text{Cost of Goods sold plus Operating Expenses}}{\text{Net Sales}} \times 100 = \dfrac{23,00,000}{24,00,000} \times 100 = 95.8\%$

11. Return of Capital Employed

$= \dfrac{\text{Net Profit}}{\text{Capital Employed}} \times 100 = \dfrac{1,00,000}{21,25,000} \times 100 = 4.7\%$

Illustration : 2 From the following statement of financial position of Amar Corporation as at 31-03-2009, compute Four Ratios to acess the financial health :

Balance Sheet

Liabilities	Rs.	Assets	Rs.
Preference Share Capital	20,000	Fixed Assets	70,000
Equity Share Capital	50,000	Cash	5,000
Reserve	10,000	Bills Receivable	10,000
Long-term Fixed Loan	20,000	Debtors	15,000
Bank Overdraft	20,000	Stock-in-Trade	60,000
Bills Payable	10,000		
Trade Creditors	30,000		
Total Rs.	1,60,000	Total Rs.	1,60,000

Solution : 2

1. Current Ratio :

$$\frac{\text{Current Assets}}{\text{Current Liabilities}}$$

$$= \frac{\text{Cash + B. R. + Drs. + Stock}}{\text{B. O. D. + B. P. + Crs.}}$$

$$= \frac{90,000}{60,000} = 1.5 : 1$$

Significance : The acceped Current Ratio is 2 : 1. In the above case, it is less than an ideal Current Ratio, As such, the financial position is not satisfactory.

2. Liquid Ratio / Acid Test Ratio :

$$= \frac{\text{Liquid Current Assets (excluding stock)}}{\text{Liquid Current Liabilities (excluding B. O. D.)}}$$

$$= \frac{\text{Cash + B. R. + Drs.}}{\text{B. P. + Crs.}}$$

$$= \frac{30,000}{40,000} = 0.75 : 1$$

Significance : The accepted Liquid Ratio is 1 : 1. Hence, the company will be put into financial difficulty at the time of maturity of quick liabilites.

3. Equity Debt Ratio :

$$= \frac{\text{Owner's Equity}}{\text{Debt Equity}}$$

$$= \frac{\text{Pref. Cap. + Eq. Cap. + Reserve}}{\text{Long-term Loan + B. O. D. + B. P. + Crs.}}$$

$$= \frac{80,000}{80,000} = 1:1$$

Significance : The acceptable Equity Debt Ratio is 1 : 1. Here, we can say the financial structure of the organisation is sound.

4. Ratio of Fixed Assets to Fixed Liabilities :

$$= \frac{\text{Fixed Assets}}{\text{Fixed Liabilities}}$$

$$= \frac{70,000}{20,000} = 3.5:1$$

Significance : Usually, the minimum allowable Ratio is 2:1. The above ratio is more than satisfactory and the company can obtain further long-term lons on the Fixed Assets.

Illustration : 3 From the following summarised Profit & Loss Account and Balance Sheet, calculate -
a) Current Ratio,   b) Operating Ratio,
c) Stock Turnover, and   d) Return on Total Resources

Dr.   **Profit Assets A/c**   Cr.

		Rs.			Rs.
To Opening Stock		9,950	By Sales		85,000
To Purchases		54,525	By Closing Stock		14,900
To Sundry Expenses		1,425			
To Gross Profit c/d.		34,000			
		99,900			99,900
To Operating Expenses			By Gross Profit B/d		34,000
Selling & Distribution	3,000		By Non-operating Income		
Administrative	15,000		Interest (Bank)	300	
Financial	1,500		Profit on Sale of Shares	600	
		19,500			900
To Non-operating					
Expenses					
Loss on Sale of					
Plant & Machinery		400			
To Net Profit c/d		15,000			
		34,900			34,900

Balance Sheet

Liabilities	Rs.	Assets	Rs.
2,000 Shares of Rs. 10	20,000	Land & Building	15,000
Reserves	9,000	Plant & Machinery	8,000
Current Liabilities	13,000	Stock-in-Trade	14,900
Profit & Loss A/c.	6,000	Sundry Debtors	7,100
		Cash at Bank	3,000
	48,000		48,000

Solution 3

a) Current Ratio :

$$\text{Formula} = \frac{\text{Current Assets}}{\text{Current Liabilities}}$$

$$= \frac{\text{Stock} + \text{Drs} + \text{Cash at Bank}}{\text{Current Liabilities}}$$

$$= \frac{14,900 + 7,100 + 3,000}{13,000}$$

$$= \frac{25,000}{13,000} = 1.92 : 1$$

b) Operating Ratio

$$\text{Formula} = \frac{\text{Cost of Goods Sold} + \text{Operating Expenses}}{\text{Net Sales}} \times 100$$

Note :

$$
\begin{aligned}
\text{Cost of Goods Sold} &= \text{Sales - G. P.} \\
&= 85,000 - 34,000 \\
&= 51,000
\end{aligned}
$$

$$\text{Operating Ratio} = \frac{51,000 + 19,500}{85,000} \times 100$$

$$= 82.9\%$$

c) Stock - Turnover Ratio

$$\text{Formula} = \frac{\text{Cost of Goods Sold}}{\text{Average Stock}} \times 100$$

Notes :

i) Cost of Goods Sold Rs. 51,000
   (Sales - G. P.)

ii) Average Stock

$$= \frac{\text{Opening Stock} + \text{Closing Stock}}{2}$$

$$= \frac{9,950 + 14,900}{2}$$

$$= \frac{24,850}{2} = \text{Rs. } 12,425$$

Stock Turnover Ratio

$$= \frac{51,000}{12,425} = 4.09 \text{ Times}$$

d) Return on Total Resources :

$$\text{Formula} = \frac{\text{Operating Profit}}{\text{Capital Employed}} \times 100$$

Notes :

i) Operating Profit
= Net Profit - Non-operating Income + Non-operating Expenses,
= Rs. 15,000 - 900 + 400 = 14,500.

ii) Capital Employed = Share Capital + Reserve + P & L A/c
= Rs. 20,000 + 9,000 + 6,000 = 35,000

$$\text{Return on Total Resources} = \frac{14,500}{35,000} \times 100 = 41.43\%$$

Illustration : 4 The following are the summarised Trading & Profit & Loss Accounts for the year 2008-09 and the Balance Sheets as on 31-03-2009 of Wise Ltd., & Clever Ltd.

Dr.   Trading & Profit & Loss A/c   Cr.

	Wise Ltd Rs.	Clever Ltd Rs.		Wise Ltd. Rs.	Clever Ltd Rs.
To Opening Stock	48,000	8,000	By Sales	3,60,000	3,60,000
To Purchases	3,19,000	3,34,000	By Closing Stock	52,000	12,000
To Gross Profit	45,000	30,000			
	4,12,000	3,72,000		4,12,000	3,72,000
To Expenses	16,200	7,600	By Gross Profit	45,000	30,000
To Net Profit	28,800	22,400			
	45,000	30,000		45,000	30,000

Balance Sheets

Liabilities	Wise Ltd. Rs.	Clever Ltd. Rs.	Assets	Wise Ltd. Rs.	Clever Ltd Rs.
Share Capital	1,00,000	1,00,000	Fixed Assets	1,27,800	1,07,500
Reserves	80,000	16,000	Stock	52,000	12,000
Profit & Loss	60,000	24,000	Debtors	40,000	24,000
Creditors	43,800	40,500	Bank	84,000	37,000
Bank Overhead	20,000	-			
	3,03,800	1,80,500		3,03,800	1,80,500

Your are required to compute the following ratios of the above companies and ofter at least one remark on each of them after comparing the same -

i) Current Ratio,

ii) Liquid Ratio,

iii) Gross Profit as a percentage of sales,

iv) Stock Turnover Ratio.

Solution : 4

i) Current Ratio :

$$= \frac{\text{Current Assets}}{\text{Current Liabilities}}$$

Wise Ltd's Current Ratio =

$$= \frac{52,000 + 40,000 + 84,000}{43,800 + 20,00} = \frac{1,76,000}{63,800} = 2.75{:}1$$

Clever Ltd's Current Ratio :

$$= \frac{12,000 + 24,000 + 37,000}{40,500} = \frac{73,000}{40,500} = 1.8{:}1$$

Remarks :

1. An ideal Current Ratio is 2.1 as accepted.

2. The Current Ratio of Wise Ltd., is 2.75:1. It means it is most satisfactory. The excessive Current Ratio is also treated as a sign of managerial ineffciency.

3. The Current Ratio of Clever Ltd., is below the accepted Ratio. It is not a satisfactory Ratio. This is also treated as a sign of managerial inefficiency.

ii) Liquid Ratio :

$$= \frac{\text{Liquid Assets/Quick Assets (excluding Stock)}}{\text{Liquid Liabilities/Quick Liabilities (excluding B.O.D.)}}$$

Wise Ltd's Liquid Ratio :

Liquid Assets of Wise Ltd., are Debtors and Bank (Stock is excluded)

Liquid Liabilities of Wise Ltd., include Creditors (Bank Overdraft is excluded)

$$= \frac{40,000 + 84,000}{43,800} = \frac{1,24,000}{43,800} = 2.83 :$$

Clever Ltd,'s Liquid Ratio

Liquid Assets of Wise Ltd., Consist of Debtors and Bank (excluding Stock).

Liquid Liabilities include creditors

$$= \frac{24,000 + 37,000}{40,500} = \frac{61,000}{40,500} = 1.5:1$$

Remarks :

1) Normally, the liquid Ratio should be 1:1
2. Liquid Ratio of Wise Ltd., is most satisfatory. The company may not be put into difficulty. But excessive Liquidity Ratio is also treated as a sign of idle funds with the Co.
3. Liquid Ratio of Clever Ltd., is satisfactory. It is a good sign of managerial efficiency.
iii) Gross Profit as Percentage of Sales

$$= \frac{\text{Gross Profit}}{\text{Net Sales}} \times 100$$

G. P. Ratio of Wise Ltd.

$$= \frac{45,000}{3,60,000} \times 100 - 12.5\%$$

G. P. Ratio of Clever Ltd.

$$= \frac{30,000}{3,60,000} \times 100 = 8.33\%$$

Remarks :

1. Gross profit should be adequate to cover the operating expenses and to provide for fixed charges. dividends and reserves.
2. Comparatively, the Gross Profit Ratio of Wise Ltd., is most satisfactory.
3. The turnover of the both companies are similar even though the G. P. Ratio of Clever Ltd., is very low which may indicate unfavourable purchasing policies, inability of management to develop sales volume etc.
iv) Stock Turnover Ratio :

$$= \frac{\text{Cost of Goods Sold}}{\text{Average Inventory}}$$

a) Cost of Goods Sold of Wise Ltd :
Sales - Gross profit = Cost of Sales.
3,60,000 - 45,000 = 3,15,000

Average Inventory (Stock) of Wise Ltd.

$$= \frac{\text{Opening Stock} + \text{Closing Stock}}{2}$$

$$= \frac{48,000 + 52,000}{2} = 50,000$$

Stock Turnover of Wise Ltd.

$$= \frac{3,15,000}{50,000} = 6.3 \text{ times}$$

b) Cost of Goods Sold of Clever Ltd.
   = Sales - Gross profit
   = 3,60,000 - 30,000 = 3,30,000
   Average Stock of Clever Ltd.

$$= \frac{\text{Opening Stock} + \text{Closing Stock}}{2}$$

$$= \frac{8,000 + 12,000}{2} = 10,000$$

Stock Turnover of Clever Ltd.

$$= \frac{3,30,000}{10,000} \ 33 \text{ times}$$

Remarks :

1) A higher ratio suggests efficient business activity, while a lower ratio suggest that some steps should be taken to push up the sales.

2) Comparing the above Inventory Turnover Ratios of Wise Ltd., and clever Ltd., it is clear that the Ratio of Wise Ltd., is too low which may reflect dull business, over-investment in inventory etc.

Illustration : 5 Following is the Trading Account of Mr. 'X' for the year ending 31st March, 2008.

Dr.   **Trading A/c**   Cr.

	Rs.		Rs.
To Opening Stock	13,300	By Sales	74,800
To Purchases	58,400	By Closing Stock	12,100
To Gross Profit	15,200		
	86,900		86,900

And following is the Balance Sheet of Mr. 'X' as at 31st March, 2008

Balance Sheet
as on 31-03 2008

Liabilities		Rs.	Assets	Rs.
Capital :			Premises	7,400
Balance	24,000		Plant and Machinery	14,000
Add : Net profit	4,500		Motor Vechicles	3,800
	28,500		Stock	12,100
Less : Drawings	6,000	22,500	Debtors	502
Bank Loan		10,000	Bank Current A/c	650
Creditors		6,000	Cash in Hand	48
		38,500		38,500

Calculate :
  i) Gross Profit Ratios,
 ii) Working Capital Ratio,
iii) Acid Test Ratio, and
 iv) Return on Proprietors Equity.

And Answer the following :
 1) Is Mr. 'X' Solvent?
 2) Is he over-trading?
 3) Is return on capital invested satisfactory?
 4) What can cause a rise or fall in the Gross Profit Ratio?

Solution : 5
  i) Gross Profit Ratio :

$$= \frac{\text{Gross Profit}}{\text{Net Sales}} \times 100$$

$$= \frac{15,200}{74,800} \times 100$$

$$= 20.33 \%$$

 ii) Working Capital Ratio :
OR
Current Ratio

$$= \frac{\text{Current Assets}}{\text{Current Liabilities}}$$

Current Assets include, Stock, Debtors, Bank Current A/c, and Cash in Hand.
Current Liabilities include, Bank Loan and Creditors. (Here, it is presumed that Bank Loan is a short-term one payable within one year)

$$\text{Current Ratio} = \frac{21,000 + 502 + 650 + 48}{10,000 + 6,000}$$

$$= \frac{13,300}{16,000} = 0.83{:}1$$

iii) Acid Test Ratio / Liquidity Ratio :

$$= \frac{\text{Liquid Asstets (Current Assets - Stock)}}{\text{Liquid Liabilities (Current Liabilities - Bank Loan)}}$$

$$= \frac{502 + 650 + 48}{6,000} = \frac{1,200}{6,000} = 0.5{:}1$$

iv) Return on Proprietors Equity :

$$= \frac{\text{Net Profit after Taxes and Interest}}{\text{Capital (excluding Drawings)}} \times 100$$

$$= \frac{4,500}{24,000 - 6,000} \times 100 = \frac{4,500}{18,000} \times 100 = 25\%$$

Answers to the above Queries :

1) Is Mr. 'X' Solvent?

Answer : Mr. 'X' is not a solvent business man. The Solvency Ratios, i.e., Working Capital Ratio and Acid Test Ratio, are not satisfactory. The accepted Working Capital Ratio is 2:1, but in this case, the working Capital Ratio is 0.83:1. It is too low. Hence, Mr. 'X' may be put into difficulties at the maturity of current liabilities.

The Acid Test Ratio should be 1:1.

But, in this case, it is 0.5:1. Mr. 'X' is unable to meet his Current Liabilities out of his liquid funds immediately.

2) Is he over-trading?

Answer : Over-trading is the result of excessive sales. Over-trading is a curse to the business. Increasing tendency of credit sales, Piling of Stock, Price spiral, reduction in turnover, poor cash position are the signs of over-trading. In over-trading, credit period taken is more than normally allowed.

The overall liquidity declines and the net working capital position becomes precarious.

There is an increase in Current Liabilities to a great extent.

These are the signs of over-trading The above signs are applicable in the case of business man Mr. 'X'.

Hence, Mr. 'X's business is in a state of over-trading.

3) Is the return on capital invested satisfactory?

Answer : Return on his capital shows a ratio of 25%. It can be said to be satisfactory. But, his financial position is very weak.

4) What can cause a rise or fall in the G.P. Ratio?

Answer : A low Gross Profit Ratio may include unfavourable purchasing policies, inability of management to develop Sales volume, over the investment in plant facilities etc.

Illustration : 6 State the significance of the following Ratios and calculate the same from the following statements :

1) Current Ratio
2) Stock Turnover
3) Debtor's Turnover
4) Turnover to Fixed Assets
5) Selling Expenses to Sales.

Bharat Traders Ltd.
Balance Sheet as on 31-03-08

Liabilities	Rs.	Assets	Rs.
50,000 Shares of Rs. 10 each	5,00,000	Land & Buildings	5,00,000
General Reserve	4,00,000	Plant & Machinery	2,00,000
Sundry Creditors	2,00,000	Stock	1,50,000
Profit & Loss A/c	1,50,000	Sundry Debtors	2,50,000
		Bank	1,50,000
	12,50,000		12,50,000

Profit & Loss A/c
for the year ending 31-03-08

Dr.   Cr.

	Rs.		Rs.
To Opening Stock	2,50,000	By Sales	18,00,000
To Purchases	10,50,000	By Closing Stock	1,50,000
To Selling Expenses	1,00,000	By Profit on sale	
To Administration Exp.	2,30,000	of Fixed Assets	50,000
To Finance Exp.	20,000		
To Net Profit	3,50,000		
	20,00,000		20,00,000

Solution 6

1) Current Ratio :

$$\text{Formula} = \frac{\text{Current Assets}}{\text{Current Liabilities}}$$

$$= \frac{\text{Stock + Drs + Bank}}{\text{Sundry Creditors}}$$

$$= \frac{1,50,000 + 2,50,000 + 1,50,000}{2,00,000}$$

$$= \frac{5,50,000}{2,00,000} = 2.75{:}1$$

Significance : The accepted Current Ratio is 2:1. The above Ratio indicates that for every Re 1 of Current Liabilities, there are Rs. 2.75 of the Current Assets. The Current Assets are 2.75 times the Current Liabilities at maturity. It also signifies that the excess funds are available with the Company which may be idle.

2) Stock Turnover Ratio :

$$\text{Formula} = \frac{\text{Cost of Goods Sold}}{\text{Average Inventory}}$$

Cost of Goods Sold

= Opening Stock + Purchases - Closing Stock

= 2,50,000 + 10,50,000 = 13,00,000 - 1,50,000

= 11,50,000

OR

Sales - Gross Profit

= 18,00,000 - 6,50,000 (Prepare Trading A/c)

= 11,50,000 Cost of Good Sold

$$\text{Average Stock} = \frac{\text{Opening Stock + Closing Stock}}{2}$$

$$= \frac{2,50,000 + 1,50,000}{2} = \frac{4,00,000}{2}$$

$$= 2,00,000$$

$$\text{Stock Turnover Ratio} = \frac{11,50,000}{2,00,000} = 5.75 \text{ times}$$

Significance : This ratio is an indication of the velocity of the movement of goods during the year. In case of decrease in sales, this ratio will decrease. This serves as a check on the control of stocks in a business.

If stocks are accumulated and if the profits fall, there is bound to be a loss to the business. If the business has too much stocks and heavy liabilities, it is a sign of bankruptcy.

A higher ratio suggests efficient business activity while a lower rate suggest that some steps should be taken to push up the sales.

In the above case, Goods sold are 5.75 times of the average inventory which indicate efficient business.

3) Debtors Turnover Ratio :

$$\text{Formula} = \frac{\text{Total Receivables (Drs.+B.R.)}}{\text{Sales per day}}$$

OR

$$\frac{\text{Total B.R. +Total Debtors}}{\text{Net Sales}} \times 360 \text{ (Working days)}$$

Debtors Turnover Ratio :

$$= \frac{2,50,000}{1,80,000} \times 360 \text{ days} = 50 \text{ days}$$

Significance : Thus, debtors represent uncollected accounts in respect of 50 days of sales.

There should always be a relationship between the period of credit allowed by a business and the Debtors Turnover Ratio.

If the period of credit allowed is 30 days, the outstanding Debtors figure represents 50 days, then, in the above case, we can conclude that the credit collection system is faulty.

If the average date is high, immediate steps should be taken to collect the outstanding.

Some leading accountants are of the opinion that the average collection period should be "no more than one-third higher than the net selling terms."

4) Turnover To Fixed Assets :

$$\text{Formula} = \frac{\text{Sales}}{\text{Fixed Assets}} \times 100$$

If the Sales are more than the amount of Fixed Assets, then it is not necessary to multiply by 100. In the above problem, the Sales are more than the Fixed Assets.

Turnover to Fixed Assets Ratio

$$= \frac{\text{Sales}}{\text{Land, Building + Plant Machinery}}$$

$$= \frac{81,00,000}{5,00,000 + 2,00,000} = 2.57$$

Significance : This ratio measures the efficiency in the utilisation of Fixed Assets. Investment in Fixed Assets is made for the ultimate purpose of increasing sales. Therefore, Ratio of Sales to Fixed Assets is an important measure of the efficient and profit-earning capacity of the concern.

The higher the Ratio, the greater is the intensive utilisation of Fixed Assets. Low Ratio means under-utilisation of Fixed Assets. But, too much sales may also be an indication of over-trading.

In the above case, there is too much sales, and hence, its a case of over-trading.

5) Selling Expenses to Sales :

$$\text{Formula} = \frac{\text{Selling Expenses}}{\text{Sales}} \times 100$$

$$= \frac{1,00,000}{18,00,000} \times 100 = 5.56\%$$

Significance : This percentage should be compared with the percentage of previous year. The decrease in expense ratio will be an indication of increased efficiency and will contribute to more profitability.

Illustration : 7 The balance Sheet of Gauri & Co., as at 31-03-08 was as follows :

Balance Sheet

Liabilities	Rs.	Assets	Rs.
2,000 Equity Shares of Rs.10 each.	20,000	Goodwill	12,000
		Fixed Assets	28,000
Capital Reserve	4,000	Stocks	6,000
Loan on Mortgage	16,000	Debtors	6,000
Bank Overdraft	2,000	Investments	2,000
Creditors on Open A/c	8,000	Cash in hand	6,000
Taxation Reserve	4,000		
Profit & Loss A/c	6,000		
	60,000		60,000

The profit for the year 2007-08 after taxation and interest on fixed deposits amounted to Rs. 12,000, out of which, Rs. 4,000 were transferred to Reserves and Rs. 2,000 paid as dividend. Sales amounted to Rs. 1,20,000.

Calculate the Ratios for :

a) Testing Liquidity,
b) Testing Solvency,
c) Testing Profitability, and
d) Testing Capital Gearing.

Solution : 8

a) **Testing Liquidity Ratios :**

1) **Current Ratio –**

$$\text{Formula} \quad = \frac{\text{Current Assets}}{\text{Current Liabilities}}$$

$$= \frac{\text{Stock} + \text{Drs.} + \text{Investments} + \text{Cash}}{\text{B.O.D.} + \text{Crs.} + \text{Taxation Re serve}}$$

$$= \frac{6,000 + 6,000 + 2,000 + 6,000}{2,000 + 8,000 + 4,000}$$

$$= \frac{20,000}{14,000} = 1.43:1$$

2) Liquid Ratio :

Formula $= \dfrac{\text{Liquid Assets (exculding Stock)}}{\text{Liquid Liabilities (excluding B.O.D.)}}$

$$= \frac{\text{Drs.} + \text{Investments} + \text{Cash}}{\text{Crs.} + \text{Taxation Re serve}}$$

$$= \frac{6,000 + 2,000 + 6,000}{8,000 + 4,000}$$

$$= \frac{14,000}{12,000} = 1.16:1$$

b) Testing Solvency Ratios :

1) Solvency Ratios $= \dfrac{\text{Total Assets}}{\text{Total Liabilities}}$

= Goodwill + Fixed Assets + Stock + Drs. + Investments + Cash

Loan on Mortgage + B.O.D. + Creditors + Taxation Reserve

(**Note :** Capital, Capital Reserve and P & L is not third party Liability).

= 12,000 + 28,000 + 6,000 + 6,000 + 2,000 + 6,000

16,000 + 2,000 + 8,000 + 4,000

$$= \frac{60,000}{30,000} = 2:1$$

Note : Goodwill is a fictitious asset / intangible asset and may not be included in total assets. But, it has been included here assuming that it is purchased by the company.

2) Proprietory Ratio $= \dfrac{\text{Total Assets}}{\text{Proprietors' Funds}}$

$$= \frac{\text{All Assets}}{\text{Capital} + \text{C. Reserve} + \text{P \& L}}$$

$$= \frac{60,000}{20,000 + 4,000 + 6,000}$$

$$= \frac{60,000}{30,000} = 2:1$$

3) Equity Debt Ratio
OR
Proprietors' Funds to External Liability

$$\text{Formula} = \frac{\text{Owners' Equity}}{\text{Debt Equity}}$$

$$= \frac{\text{Capital} + \text{C. Reserve} + \text{P \& L}}{\text{Loan on Mortgage} + \text{B.O.D.} + \text{Crs.} + \text{Taxation Reserve}}$$

$$= \frac{20,000 + 4,000 + 6,000}{16,000 + 2,000 + 8,000 + 4,000} = \frac{30,000}{30,000} = 1:1$$

C) Testing Profitability :

1. Net Profit Ratio $= \dfrac{\text{Net Profit}}{\text{Sales}} \times 100$

$$= \frac{12,000}{1,20,000} \times 100 = 10\%$$

2. Return on Capital Employed :

$$\text{Formula} = \frac{\text{Profit before Tax and Interest}}{\text{Capital employed}} \times 100$$

Notes :

i) Profit before Tax
   = N.P. Given Rs. 12,000 + Taxation Reserve Rs. 4,000
   = Rs. 16,000. Profit before Tax.

ii) Capital Employed = Owners' Capital + Borrowed Capital
   = (Capital + Capital Reserve + P & L) + (Mortgage Loan)
   = (20,000 + 4,000 + 6,000) + (16,000)
   = 30,000 + 16,000
   = 46,000

$$\text{Return on Capital Employed} = \frac{16,000}{46,000} \times 100 = 34.7\%$$

3) Return on Shareholder's Funds :

$$\text{Formula} = \frac{\text{Profit after Tax and Interest}}{\text{Shareholders Funds}} \times 100$$

$$= \frac{12,000}{20,000 + 4,000 + 6,000} \times 100$$

$$= 40\%$$

d) Testing Capital Gearing :

Formula $= \dfrac{\text{Equity Capital} + \text{Free Reserves} + \text{Retained Earnings}}{\text{Preference Capital} + \text{Long-term Debts bearing}}$

$= \dfrac{20,000 + 4,000 + 6,000}{16,000}$

$= \dfrac{30,000}{16,000} = 1.87:1$

Illustration : 8 From the following information, for the accounting year 2008-09, you are required :
a) to arrange them in a form suitable for analysis; and
b) to find out the following ratios :
1) Gross Profit Ratio, 2) Operating Ratio, and 3) Stock Turnover Ratio.

	Rs.		Rs.
Sales	5,20,000	Depreciation	9,300
Purchases	3,22,250	Other charges	16,500
Opening Stock	76,250	Provision for Taxation	40,000
Closing Stock	98,500	Non-operating Incomes :	
Sales Returns	20,000	Dividend on Shares	9,000
Selling & Distribution Expenses :		**Non-trading Expenses**	
Salaries	15,300	Loss on Sale of Asset	4,000
Advertising	4,700	**Administration Expenses**	
Travelling	2,000	Salaries 27,000	
Profit on Sale of Shares	3,000	Rent 2,700	
		Stationery and Postage 2,500	32,200

(B.U.)

Solution 8

Trading & Profit & Loss A/c
for the year ending 31-03-09

Dr.   Cr.

	Rs.			Rs.
To Opening Stock	76,250	By Sales	5,20,000	
To Purchases	3,22,250	Less : Sales Returns	20,000	5,00,000
To Gross Profit c/d	2,00,000	By Closing Stock		98,500
	5,98,500			5,98,500

		Rs.			Rs.
To Operating Expenses :			By Gross Profit b/d		2,00,000
Administrative Expenses :			**Non-operating Income:**		
Salaries	27,000		Dividend	9,000	
Rent	2,700		Profit on sale of shares	3000	12,000
Stationery	2,500				
Depreciation	9,300				
Other Charges	16,500	58,000			
Selling Expenses :					
Salaries	15,300				
Advertising	4,700				
Travelling	2,000	22,000			
Non-Operating Exp. :					
Loss on sale of Assets		4,000			
Proision for Taxation		40,000			
Net Profit		88,000			
		2,12,000			2,12,000

Ratios :

1) Gross Profit Ratio :

$$= \frac{G.P.}{Sales} \times 100$$

$$= \frac{2,00,000}{5,00,000} \times 100 = 40\%$$

2) Operating Ratio :

$$\text{Operating Ratio} = \frac{\text{Cost of Goods Sold} + \text{Operating Expenses}}{\text{Net Sales}}$$

$$= \frac{3,00,000 + 80,000}{5,00,000} \times 100 = 76\%$$

Workings :

i)   Cost of Goods Sold = Sales - G. P.

               = 5,00,000 - 2,00,000

               = 3,00,000

ii) Operating Expenses :

	Rs.
Administrative Exp.	58,000
Selling Exp.	22,000
Total Operating Exp.	Rs. 80,000

3) Stock Turnover Ratio :

$$\text{Stock Turnover ratio} = \frac{\text{Loss of Goods Sold}}{\text{Average Stock}}$$

$$= \frac{3,00,000}{87,375}$$

$$= 3.5 \text{ times}$$

Workings :

$$\text{Average Stock} = \frac{\text{Opening Stock} + \text{Closing Stock}}{2}$$

$$= \frac{76,250 + 98,500}{2}$$

$$= \frac{1,74,750}{2}$$

$$= 87,375$$

Illustration : 9 The following is the Trading and Profit & Loss A/c of a limited company for the year ended on 31st March, 2009

Profit & Loss A/c

	Rs.			Rs.
To Stock	76,250	By Sales		5,00,000
To Purchases	3,15,250	By Stock		98,500
To Carriage & Freight	2,000			
To Wages	5,000			
To Gross Profit	2,00,000			
	5,98,500			5,98,500
To Administrative Expenses	1,01,000	By Gross profit		2,00,000
To Finance Expenses		By Non-operating Incomes		
Interest 1,200		Interest on Security	1,500	
Discount 2,400		Dividend on Shares	3,750	
Bad debts 3,400		Profit on Sale of Shares	750	
	7,000			6,000
To Selling & Distribution Expenses	12,000			
To Non-operating expenses				
Loss on Sale of Securities 350				
Provision for legal Suit 1,650	2,000			
To Net Profit	84,000			
	2,06,000			2,06,000

Calculate : i) Expense Ratio ii) Gross Profit Ratio iii) Net Profit Ratio iv) Operating net profit Ratio v) Operating Ratio & vi) Stock Turnover Ratio.

Solution : 9

i) **Expense Ratio**

   a)   Administrative Expenses Ratio

$$\frac{\text{Administrative Expenses}}{\text{Sales}} \times 100$$

$$= \frac{1,01,000}{5,00,000} \times 100 = 20.2\%$$

   b)   Selling & Distribution Expenses Ratio

$$\frac{\text{Selling and Distribution Expenses}}{\text{Sales}} \times 100 = 2.4\%$$

   c)   Finance Expenses Ratio

$$\frac{\text{Finance Expenses}}{\text{Sales}} \times 100$$

$$= \frac{7,000}{5,00,000} \times 100 = 1.40\%$$

   d)   Non-operating Expenses Ratio

$$\frac{\text{Non-operating Expenses}}{\text{Sales}} \times 100$$

$$= \frac{2,000}{5,00,000} \times 100 = 0.4\%$$

ii) **Gross Profit Ratio**

$$\frac{\text{Gross Profit}}{\text{Sales}} \times 100 = \frac{2,00,000}{5,00,000} \times 100 = 40\%$$

iii) **Net Profit Ratio**

$$\frac{\text{Net Profit}}{\text{Sales}} \times 100 = \frac{84,000}{5,00,000} \times 100 = 16.80\%$$

iv) **Operating Net Profit**

$$\frac{\text{N.P.} + \text{Non-operating Expenses} - \text{Non-operating Incomes}}{\text{Sales}} \times 100$$

$$= \frac{(84,000 + 2,000) - 6,000}{5,00,000} \times 100 = 16\%$$

v) Operating Ratio

$$\frac{*\text{Cost of Goods Sold} + \text{Operating Expenses}}{\text{Sales}} \times 100$$

$$= \frac{*3,00,000 + 1,01,000 + 7,000 + 12,000}{5,00,000} \times 100 = 84\%$$

(* Cost of Goods Sold = Sales Rs. 5,00,000 Less G.P. 2,00,000)

vi) Stock Turnover Ratio

$$\frac{\text{Cost of Goods Sold}}{\text{Average Stock}}$$

$$= \frac{3,00,000}{87,375} = 3.43 \text{ times}$$

$$\left(\text{Average Stock} = \frac{\text{Opening Stock} + \text{Closing Stock}}{2} \right)$$

Illustration : 10 From the following financial statements of Rimzim Ltd.; calculate any three of the Accounting Ratios and comment on the significance thereof –

Zenith Ltd.;

Manufacturing, Trading and Profit and Loss Account for the year ended 31st March 2009

	Rs.			Rs.
To Opening Stock	5,00,000	By Sales		
To Purchases	11,00,000	Cash	3,00,000	
To Wages	3,00,000	Credit	17,00,000	
To Factory Overheads	2,00,000			20,00,000
To Gross Profit c/d	5,00,000	By Closing Stock		6,00,000
	26,00,000			26,00,000
To Adminstrative expenses	75,000	By Gross Profit B/d		5,00,000
To Selling and Distribution expenses	50,000	By Dividend on Investments		10,000
To Debentures Interest	20,000	By Profit on Sale of Furniture		20,000
To Depreciation	60,000			
To Loss on Sale of Motor Car	5,000			
To Net Profit c/d	3,20,000			
	5,30,000			5,30,000
To Preference Dividend		By Balance b/d		2,71,000
(net) Interim	15,000	By Net Profit		3,20,000
To Provision for Taxation	1,76,000			
To Balance c/f	4,00,000			
	5,91,000			5,91,000

Balance Sheet as on 31st March, 2009

Liabilities	Rs.	Assets	Rs.
Equity Share Capital	10,00,000	Goodwill (at Cost)	5,00,000
6% Preference Share Capital	5,00,000	Plant & Machinery	6,00,000
General Reserve	1,00,000	Land & Building	7,00,000
Profit & Loss Account	4,00,000	Furniture & Fixtures	1,00,000
Provision for Taxation	1,76,000	Stock-in-trade	6,00,000
bills Payable	1,24,000	Bills Receivable	30,000
Bank Overdraft	1,20,000	Debtors	1,50,000
Creditors	4,80,000	Bank	2,20,000
	29,00,000		29,00,000

Solution : 10

a) Liquid Ratio

= Quick Assets ÷ Current Liabilities excluding Bank o/d.

$$= \frac{\text{B/R} + \text{Debtors} + \text{Bank}}{\text{B/P} + \text{Creditors} + \text{Prov. for Tax}} = \frac{4,00,000}{7,80,000} = 0.51 : 1$$

If the ratio is 1:1, it shows that all claims will be met when they mature, Here the ratio is less than 1 and therefore it can be concluded that quick assets are not sufficient to pay off the current or quick liabilities, and thus, the short-term solvency of the company is questionable.

b) Operating Ratio

$$= \frac{\text{Cost of Goods Sold} + \text{All Other Operating Expenses}}{\text{Sales}} \times 100$$

Cost of Goods Sold = Sales Less G.P.

$$\text{Hence, Operating Ratio} = \frac{15,00,000 + 75,000 + 50,000 + 60,000}{20,00,000}$$

$$\frac{16,85,000}{20,00,000} \times 100 = 84.25\%$$

A rise in this ratio indicates a decline in effciency. In the present example, the ratio is normal indicating a reasonable margin of profit.

c) Proprietory Ratio

$$= \frac{\text{Proprietors' Funds}}{\text{Total Assets}} = \frac{\text{Eq. \& Pref. Share Capital} + \text{Reserve} + \text{P \& L A/c}}{\text{Total Assets}}$$

$$= \frac{20,00,000}{29,00,000} = 0.69 : 1$$

This ratio shows that the greater the percentage of proprietor's funds the stronger is the financial position of the concern. This ratio is normally a test of strength of credit-worthiness of the conncern.

Illustration : 11 From the following financial statement of Manish Ltd.; you are required -

a) to find out any three accounting ratios for both the years.

b) to state in which year each of the three accounting Ratios is favourable; and

c) to suggest measures for improvement of unfavourable accounting ratios.

Particulars	2006-07 Rs			2007-08 Rs.
Sales				
Cash	60,000		64,000	
Credit	5,40,000	6,00,000	6,84,000	7,48,000
Less : Cost of Sales		4,72,000		5,96,000
Gross Profit		1,28,000		1,52,000
Less : Expenses				
Warehousing and Transport	9,000		12,000	
Administration	48,000		52,000	
Selling	23,000		35,000	
Debenture Interest	10,000		10,000	
Depreciation	8,000		9,000	
		98,000		1,18,000
		30,000		34,000

	31st March 2007 Rs.			31st March 2008 Rs.
Fixed Assets Less Depreciation :	1,60,000			1,80,000
Curent Assets :				
Stock	1,20,000		1,28,000	
Debtors	1,00,000		1,64,000	
Cash	20,000		14,000	
		2,40,000		3,06,000
		4,00,000		4,86,000

	31st March 2007 Rs.	31st March 2008 Rs.
Share Capital	1,50,000	1,50,000
Reserves	30,000	60,000
Profits & Loss Account	20,000	24,000
10 Per cent Debentures	1,00,000	1,00,000
Current Liabilities	1,00,000	1,52,000
	4,00,000	4,86,000

Solution : 11

1. **Net Profit Ratio**

$$\frac{\text{Net Operating Profit}}{\text{Sales}} \times 100$$

$$2006 - 2007 = \frac{40,000}{6,00,000} \times 100 = 6.67\%$$

$$2007 - 2008 = \frac{44,000}{7,48,000} \times 100 = 5.88\%$$

The percentage of N.P. has gone down. On comparing Gross Profit percentage, selling expenses etc., it shows that the efficiency of purchase department and control over expenses have gone down. These items must be controlled properly to improve the position.

(Instead of Net Operating Profit, some take Net Profit)

2. **Gross Profit Ratio**

$$= \frac{\text{Gross Profit}}{\text{Sales}} \times 100$$

$$2006-07 = \frac{1,28,000}{6,00,000} \times 100 = 21.33\%$$

$$2007-08 = \frac{1,52,000}{7,48,000} \times 100 = 20.32\%$$

The Gross Profit percentage has declined by 1% in 2007-08. To imporve the results, efficiency of purchases department must be improved.

3. **Current Ratio**

$$= \frac{\text{Current Assets}}{\text{Current Liabilities}}$$

$$2006-07 = \frac{2,40,000}{1,00,000} = 2.4:1$$

$$2007\text{-}08 \quad = \frac{3,06,000}{1,52,000} = 2\!:\!1$$

Though the ratio has declined in 2007-08, the difference is slight and further, it has not come down below the accepted limit of 2:1. Current assets are therefore sufficient to meet current liabilities. Thus, the short-term solvency of the business is quite good.

Illustration : 12 The following is the balance sheet of Ratio Company Ltd.

	Rs.			Rs.
Authorised Share Capital		Gross Block	2,48,300	
500 9.5% cum. Pref.		Less : Depreciation	39,000	2,09,300
Shares of Rs. 100 each	50,000			
20,000 Equity Shares of		Stock in Trade		98,500
Rs. 10 each	2,00,000	Trade Debtors	95,000	
		Less : Provision for		
Issued Capital :		Doubtful Debts	3,000	92,000
500 9.5% Cum. Pref. Shares	50,000	Bills Receivable		17,000
20,000 Equity Shares of		Pre-paid expenses		5,000
Rs. 10 each, Rs. 5 per		Cash and Bank		1,800
Share, paid-up	1,00,000			
Shares Premium Account	10,000			
General Reserve	52,000			
Profit & Loss Account	40,000			
Trade Creditors	1,00,000			
Bank Overdrafts	20,100			
9% Debentures of Rs. 100				
each (Secured by				
Hypothecation of stock)	50,000			
Outstanding Expenses	1,500			
	4,23,600			4,23,600

From the above Balance Sheet calculate the following :

1.Current Ratio 2. Proprietory Ratio 3. Capital Gearing Ratio 4.Liquid Ratio 5. Stock Working Capital Ratio.

Solution : 12

1. Current Ratio

$$= \frac{\text{Current Assets}}{\text{Current Liabilities}}$$

$$= \frac{98,500 + 92,000 + 17,000 + 5,000 + 1,800}{1,00,000 + 1,500 + 20,100} = \frac{2,14,300}{1,21,600} = 1.76:1,$$

2. Proprietory Ratio

$$= \frac{\text{Proprietor's Fund}}{\text{Total Assets}} = \frac{2,52,000}{4,23,600} = 0.59:1$$

$$\left(\frac{50,000 + 1,00,000 + 10,000 + 52,000 + 40,000}{4,23,600} \right)$$

3. Capital Gearing Ratio

$$= \frac{\text{Equity Capital} + \text{G.R.} + \text{P \& L}}{\text{Pref. Share Capital} + \text{Debentures}}$$

$$= \frac{1,92,000}{1,00,000} = 1.9:1$$

4. Liquid Ratio

$$= \frac{\text{Quick Assets i.e. Current Assets Excluding Stock \& Pre-paid Expenses}}{\text{Current Liabilities}}$$

$$= \frac{1,10,800}{1,01,500} = 1.09:1$$

5. Stock Working Capital Ratio

$$= \frac{\text{Stock}}{\text{Working Capital}}$$

(Working Capital = Current Assets Less Current Liabilities)

$$= \frac{98,500}{1,12,800} = 0.87$$

Illustration 13 : From the following particulars calculate : (a) Current Ratio (b) Liquid Ratio (c) Capital Gearing Ratio & (d) Debtors Turnover Ratio, for both the years.

Blance Sheet

Liabilities	31st Mar. 2008	31st Mar. 2009	Assets	31st Mar. 2008	31st Mar. 2009
	Rs.	Rs.		Rs.	Rs.
Equity Capital	10,00,000	12,00,000	Goodwill	5,00,000	5,00,000
Preference Cap.	5,00,000	5,00,000	Buildings	7,00,000	6,50,000
Debentures	2,00,000	–	Furniture	1,00,000	90,000
General Reserve	5,00,000	6,00,000	Plant	6,00,000	7,70,000
Profit & Loss Account	3,00,000	4,00,000	Stock	5,00,000	6,50,000
Provision for Taxation	1,75,000	2,00,000	Bills Receivable	1,30,000	1,00,000
Bills Payable	1,25,000	50,000	Debtors	2,70,000	4,00,000
Bank Overdraft	–	1,50,000	Bank	1,00,000	–
Creditors	1,00,000	60,000			
	29,00,000	31,60,000		29,00,000	31,60,000

Other Particulars

	31st March, 2008 Rs.	31st March, 2009 Rs.
Sales		
Cash	3,00,000	5,00,000
Credit	18,25,000	20,07,500

Solution : 13

1. Current Ratio

$$= \frac{\text{Current Assets}}{\text{Current Liabilities}}$$

2007-08   2008-09

$$\frac{10,00,000}{4,00,000} = 2.5{:}1 \qquad \frac{11,50,000}{4,60,000} = 2.5{:}1$$

2. Liquid Ratio

$$= \frac{\text{Quick Assets}}{\text{Quick Liabilities}}$$

2007-08   2008-09

$$\frac{5,00,000}{4,00,000} = 1.25{:}1 \qquad \frac{5,00,000}{3,10,000} = 1.6{:}1$$

3. Capital Gearing Ratio

$$= \frac{\text{Equity Capital} + \text{G.R.} + \text{P \& L}}{\text{Pref. Share Capital} + \text{Debentures}}$$

$$= \frac{18,00,000}{7,00,000} = 18:7 = 2.6 \qquad\qquad \frac{22,00,000}{5,00,000} = 22:5 = 4.40$$

4. Debtors Turnover Ratio

$$= \frac{\text{Sundry Debtors} + \text{B/R}}{\text{Net Credit Sales}} \times 365$$

$$= \frac{4,00,000}{18,25,000} \times 365 = 80 \text{ days} \qquad \frac{5,00,000}{20,07,500} \times 365 = 91 \text{ days}$$

Illustration 14 : The following items appear in the accounts as at 31st March, 2009 of Overseas Ltd.,

	Rs.
Cash	48,600
Land & Buildings at Cost	8,00,000
Deposits & Payments in Advance	62,000
Stock	2,72,800
Trade Creditors	4,05,750
General Reserve	1,00,000
Debtors	5,23,000
Bills Receivable	22,600
Plant and Machinery at cost less depreciation	5,44,000
Debentures repayable 2007 (Secured)	2,50,000
Bank Overdraft	52,000
Ordinary Share Capital of Rs. 10 each	10,00,000
Profit & Loss A/c Balance	2,17,000
Proposed dividend for 2008-09 net	86,250
Trade Investments	20,000
Advance payment of Tax	1,00,000
Provision for Taxation	2,64,000
Bills Payable	18,000
Net Sales for the year 2008-09	21,82,400

You are required to arrange the above items in the form of Financial Statement to indicate (a) Working Capital (b) Total funds Employed (c) Shareholders Equity & calculate the following ratios.

a) Current ratio b) Turnover of Debtors

Solution 14 :

Financial Statement

		Rs.
Issued & paid up equity capital		10,00,000
General Reserve		1,00,000
Profit & Loss A/c		2,17,000
Shareholders Equity -		13,17,000
Liabilities -		
Debentures	2,50,000	
Bank Overdraft	52,000	
Bills Payable	18,000	
Trade Creditors	4,05,750	
Proposed Dividend	86,250	
Provision for Taxation(Less advance payment)	1,64,000	9,76,000
Total Funds Employed -		22,93,000
Current Assets		
Stock	2,72,800	
Debtors	5,23,000	
B/R	22,600	
Cash	48,600	
Deposits & Payments in advance	62,000	
Trade Investments	20,000	9,49,000
Less : Current Liabilities		
Creditors	4,05,750	
Bank Overdraft	52,000	
Proposed Dividend	86,250	
Bills Payable	18,000	
Provision for Taxation		
(Less Advance tax paid)	1,64,000	7,26,000
Working Capital		2,23,000

(Bank overdraft is considered to be Current Liability & Trade investments are presumed to be readily saleable)

1) Current Ratio :

$$\text{Current Ratio} = \frac{\text{Current Assets}}{\text{Current Liabilities}}$$

$$= \frac{9,49,000}{7,26,000}$$

$$= 1.30:1$$

2) Turnover of Debtors :

$$\text{Turnover of Debtors Ratio} = \frac{\text{Assets Receivable}}{\text{Net Sales}} \times 365$$

$$= \frac{22,600 + 5,23,000}{21,82,400} \times 365$$

$$= \frac{5,45,600}{21,82,400} \times 365$$

$$= 91 \text{ days}$$

Illustration 15 : You are given the following information pertaining to the financial statements of CD Ltd. as as 31-03-2009. On the the basis of the information supplied, you are required to prepare the Trading and Profit & Loss A/c for the year ended and a Balance Sheet as on that date.

	Rs.
Net Current Assets	Rs. 2,00,000
Issued Share Capital	Rs. 6,00,000
Current Assets Ratio	1.8:1
Quick Assets Ratio	
(Ratio of Debtors & Bank Balance to Current Liabilities)	1.35:1
Fixed Assets to Shareholders Equity	80%
Rate of Gross Profit on Turnover	25%
Net Profit to Issued Share Capital	20%
Average Rate of Stock Turnover (on Cost of goods Sold)	5 Times
Average age of outstanding for the year	36½ days

On 31-03-2009 the Current Assets consisted only of Stock, Debtors and Bank Balance; Liabilities consisted of Share Capital and Current Liabilities; and assets Consisted of Fixed Assets and Current Assets.

Solution 15

1. Current Assets Ratio 1.8:1

i.e. Current Assets 1.8 - Current liabilities 1

= 0.8 Net Current Assets (i.e. Working Capital)

But Net Current Assets given Rs. 2,00,000 = 0.8

$$\text{So, Current Assets } 1.8 = \frac{2,00,000}{1} \times \frac{1.8}{0.8} = \text{Rs. } 4,50,000$$

$$\text{Current Liabilities } 1 = 2,00,000 \times \frac{1}{0.8} = \text{Rs. } 2,50,000$$

2. Quick Assets Ratio 1.35:1

$$\text{So, Quick Assets } = 2,00,000 \times \frac{1.35}{0.8} = \text{Rs. } 3,37,500$$

$$\text{Stock } = \text{Current Assets - Quick Assets}$$
$$= 4,50,000 - 3,37,500 = \text{Rs. } 1,12,500$$

3. Fixed Assets to Shareholders Equity 80%

i.e. Fixed Assets 80 : Shareholders Equity 100.

So, Shareholders Equity 100% = Fixed Assets 80% + Net Current Assets 20%

But Net Current Assets 20% = Rs. 2,00,000 (given)

$$\text{So, Fixed Assets } 80\% = 2,00,000 \times \frac{80\%}{20\%} = 8,00,000$$

Shareholders Equity 100% = Fixed Assets 80% + Net Current Assets 20%
$$= 8,00,000 + 2,00,000 = \text{Rs. } 10,00,000$$

Reserves & Surplus = Shareholders Equity - Issued Share Cap.
$$= 10,00,000 - 6,00,000 - \text{Rs. } 4,00,000$$

4. Average Rate of Stock Turnover 5 Times :

(i.e. on cost of goods sold)

$$\text{Cost of Sales } = \text{Stock} \times 5 \text{ Times (i.e. Purchases)}$$
$$= 1,12,500 \times 5 = \text{Rs. } 5,62,500$$

5. G. P. Ratio 25% on Turnover

i.e. $33\frac{1}{3}\%$ on cost.

$$\text{G. P.} = \text{Purchases (i.e. Cost of Sales)} \times 33\tfrac{1}{3}\%$$

$$= 5,62,500 \times 33\tfrac{1}{3}\% = \text{Rs. } 1,87,500$$

$$\text{Sales} = \text{Cost of Sales (Purchases)} + \text{G.P.}$$
$$= 5,62,500 + 1,87,500 = \text{Rs. } 7,50,000$$

6. Debtors Average Age $36\frac{1}{2}$ days $= \dfrac{73}{2}$

(i.e. Average Age of Outstanding)

i.e. Debtors Turnover Ratio

$$\frac{\text{Total Receivables}}{\text{Sales per day}} \quad \text{OR} \quad \frac{\text{Total Debtors}}{\text{Net Sales}} \times 365$$

So, Debtors

$$= \frac{\text{Debtors Averge Age}}{365} \times \text{Sales}$$

$$= \frac{73}{2} \times \frac{1}{365} \times \frac{7,50,000}{1}$$

$$= \text{Rs. 75,000 Debtors.}$$

7. N.P. Ratio to Issued Share Capital 20%

N.P.   = Share Capital Issued × 20 %
     = 6,00,000 × 20%
     = Rs. 1,20,000 Net Profit

8. Overheads / Expenses   = G. P. - N. P.
     = 1,87,500 - 1,20,000
     = Rs. 67,500 Overheads.

Trading & Profit & Loss A/c
for the year ending 31-03-2009

Dr.   Cr.

	Rs.		Rs.
To Cost of Sales (i. e. Purchases)	5,62,500	By Sales	7,50,000
To G. P. c/d	1,87,500		
	7,50,000		7,50,000
To Expenses (i. e. Overheads)	67,500	By G. P. b/d	1,87,500
To N. P. c/d	1,20,000		
	1,87,500		1,87,5000

Balance Sheet
as on 31-03-2009

Liabilities	Rs.	Assets		Rs.
Share Capital	6,00,000	Fixed Assets		8,00,000
Reserves & Surplus	4,00,000	**Current Assets:**		
(including N.P. Rs. 1,20,000)		Stock	1,12,500	
Current Liabilities	2,50,000	Debtors	75,000	
		Cash / Bank	2,62,500	4,50,000
		(Balancing)		
	12,50,000			12,50,000

Preparation of Financial Statements From Accounting Ratios

Tips

In order to prepare Profit and Loss A/c and Balance Sheet from the given ratios, it is necessary to have an idea of relationship which exists between different terms to compute ratios. The following equations may be used to prepare final accounts,

Trading & Profit & Loss A/c

Gross Profit	= Sales - Cost of goods sold
∴ Cost of Goods sold	= Sales - Gross Profit
Sales	= Cost of goods sold + Gross Profit
Cost of Goods Sold	= Opening Stock + Materials Consumed + Manufacturing expenses - Closing Stock
Operating Profit	= Sales - Operating Costs
Operating Expenses	= Administrative Exp. + Selling & Distribution Exp. + Finance Exp.
Operating Profit	= Sales - Operating Profit
Operating Cost	= Sales – Operating Profit
Sales	= Operating Cost + Operating Profit
Operating Cost	= Cost of Goods sold + Operating Exp.
Net Profit or Earnings before Interest and Tax	= Operating Profit + Non-Operating Income – Non-Operating Expenses
Net Profit after Interest but before Tax	= Net Profit before Interest & Tax - Interest
Net Profit after Interest & Tax	= Net Profit before Tax - Tax

Balance Sheet

Capital Employed	= Fixed Assets + Working Capital
Fixed Assets	= Capital Employed - Working Capital
Working Capital	= Capital Employed - Fixed Assets
	OR
Working Capital	= Current Assets - Current Liabilities
Current Assets	= Working Capital - Current Liabilities
	OR
Current Liabilities	= Current Assets - Working Capital
Current Assets	= Liquid Assets + Stock
Liquid Assets	= Current Assets - Stock
Stock	= Current Assets - Liquid Assets

Liquid Assets	= Debtors + Cash & Bank Balance
Debtors	= Liquid Assets - Cash & Bank Balance
Cash at Bank	= Liquid Assets - Debtors

Capital Employed (Liabilities Side) :

Capital Employed	= Net Worth + Long-term Loans
Net worth / Proprietor's Fund	= Capital Employed - Long-term Loans
Long-term Loans	= Capital Employed - Net worth
Net Worth	= Share Capital + Reserve & Surplus
Equity Share Capital	= Equity Net worth - Reserve & Surplus
Reserves & Surplus	= Equity Net Worth - Equity Share Capital

Stock Turnover Ratio Connects

Sales, Cost of Sales, Operating Profits and Stock

Debtor's Turnover Ratio Connects

Sales, Cost of Sales, Operation Profits Debtors

Stock to Working Capital Ratio helps to ascertain

Composition of Working Capital or between Current & Quick Assets

llustration 16 - You are given the following figures worked out from the Profit and Loss Account and Balance Sheet of 'Z' Ltd., relating to the year 2008. Prepare the Balance Sheet.

	Rs.
Fixed Assets (Net after writing off 30%)	Rs. 10,50,000
Fixed Assets Turnover Ratio	2
Finished Goods Turnover Ratio	6
Rate of Gross Profit on Sales	25%
Net Profit (before Interest) to Sales	8%
Fixed charges Cover (Debentures Interest 7%)	8%
Debt Collection Period	1½ Months
Materials Consumed in Sales	30%
Stock of Raw Materials (in terms of number of month's consumption)	8
Current Ratio	2.4
Quick Ratio	1.0
Reserves to Capital	0.20

Solution 16 -

Balance Sheet

	Rs.		Rs.
Share Capital	13,00,000	Fixed Assets	10,50,000
Reserves & Surplus	2,60,000	Stock	9,10,000
Debentures	4,00,000	Debtors	3,50,000
Current Liabilities	6,50,000	Cash	3,00,000
	26,10,000		26,10,000

Workings

1) Fixed Assets Turnover Ratio = 2

Fixed Assets Rs. 10,50,000

$\therefore$ Cost of Goods Sold 10,50,000 $\times$ 2 = Rs. 21,00,000

2) Gross Profit 25% on Sales

$\therefore 33\frac{1}{3}$% on Cost of Goods Sold.

$= 21,00,000 \times \dfrac{33\frac{1}{3}}{100} =$ Rs. 7,00,000

Sales = Rs. 21,00,000 + Rs. 7,00,000 = Rs. 28,00,000

3) Net Profit (before Interest) to sales 8%

Net Profit = 28,00,000 $\times \dfrac{8}{100} =$ Rs. 2,24,000

4) Finished Goods Stock to Turnover = 6

$\dfrac{21,00,000}{6} =$ Rs. 3,50,000

5) Debenture Interest :

Fixed Charges Cover (deb. interest) 8

$\dfrac{\text{Net Profit}}{\text{Interest}} = \dfrac{2,24,000}{8} =$ Rs. 28,000

6) Debentures - 7% interest = 28,000 $\times \dfrac{100}{7} =$ Rs. 4,00,000

7) Materials Consumed in Sales 30%

$= 28,00,000 \times \dfrac{30}{100} =$ Rs. 8,40,000

8) **Stock of raw materials (in terms of number of material consumption) = 8**

$$\therefore \text{Consumption of materials} \times \frac{8}{12} = \frac{8,40,000 \times 8}{12} = \text{Rs. } 5,60,000$$

9) **Closing Stock** = Raw materials + finished goods
   = 5,60,000 + 3,50,000 = Rs. 9,10,000

10) **Current Assets** = $9,10,000 \times \dfrac{2.4}{1.4} = \text{Rs. } 15,60,000$

Stock =	Current Assets ratio	2.4
	Quick Assets ratio	1.0
	Stock	1.4

11) **Current Liabilities** = $\dfrac{15,60,000}{2.4} = \text{Rs. } 6,50,000$

12) **Shareholder's Equity -**
    (Fixed Assets + Current Assets) – (Debentures + Current Liabilities)
    = (10,50,000 + 15,60,000) – (4,00,000 + 6,50,000)
    = 26,10,000 – 10,50,000 = Rs. 15,60,000

13) **Share Capital -**

Reserve to Capital	0.20
Shareholder's Equity	1.20
(Capital + Reserve)	

$$\frac{15,60,000}{1.20} = \text{Rs. } 13,00,000$$

14) **Reserves and Surplus -**

$$\frac{13,00,000}{5} = \text{Rs. } 26,00,000$$

15) **Cash -**
    Cash = Current Assets - (Debtors + Stock)
    = 15,60,000 - (3,50,000 + 9,10,000)
    = 15,60,000 - 12,60,000
    = Rs. 3,00,000

Illustration : 17 – From the given information, prepare a Balance Sheet.

	Rs.
1) Working Capital	75,000
2) Reserves & Surplus	100,000
3) Bank Overdraft	60,000
4) Current Ratio	1.75
5) Liquid Ratio	1.15

6) Fixed assets to Proprietor's Fund   0.75
7) Long-term Liabilities   Nil

Solution : 17

Balance Sheet

	Rs.		Rs.
Share Capital	2,00,000	Fixed Assets	2,25,000
Reserves & Surplus	1,00,000	Stock	60,000
Bank Overdraft	60,000	Debtors and Cash	1,15,000
Creditors	40,000		
	4,00,000		4,00,000

Working -

1) **Current Assets –**

   Current ratio - 1.75

   Working Capital should be - 0.75

   $$\text{Working Capital} \times \frac{175}{75}$$

   $$= \text{Rs. } 75,000 \times \frac{175}{75} = \text{Rs. } 1,75,000$$

2) **Liquid Assets (Debtors & Cash) –**

   Liquid ratio 1.15

   If current assets are 175 liquid assets should be 115

   $$\text{Current assets} \times \frac{115}{175}$$

   $$= \text{Rs. } 1,75,000 \times \frac{115}{175} = \text{Rs. } 1,15,000$$

3) **Stock –**

   Current Assets - Liquid Assets

   Rs. 1,75,000 - 1,15,000 = Rs. 60,000

4) **Fixed Assets –**

   Shareholder's Equity should be equal to Total Net Assets. Proprietory Ratio - 0.75

   If fixed assets are 75 to Proprietor's funds, net current assets should be 25 of the total assets.

   Proprietory funds, net current assets should be 25 of the total net assets.

   $$\text{Net current assets} \times \frac{75}{25}$$

$$= \text{Rs. } 75000 \times \frac{75}{25} = \text{Rs. } 2,25,000$$

5) Shareholder's Funds

If fixed assets are 75, shareholder's fund should be 100

$$\text{Fixed Assets} \times \frac{100}{75}$$

$$= \text{Rs. } 2,25,000 \times \frac{100}{75} = \text{Rs. } 3,00,000$$

Share Capital = Shareholder's Funds - Reserves and Surplus
= Rs. 3,00,000 - Rs. 1,00,000
= Rs. 2,00,000

6) Creditors –

Current Assets - Working Capital – Bank Overdraft
Rs. 1,75,000 - 75,000 - 60,000   = Rs. 40,000

Questions

Objective Type

A) State whether the following statements are True or False -

1) Financial statements are prepare at the end of a financial year.
2) The Profit & Loss Account discloses the financial position of a Company.
3) All items in the Income Statement are expressed as a percentage of Net Sales.
4) Horizontal Statement is a statement containing the revenue figures of successive periods.
5) A trend percentage indicate the degree of increase or decrease, but they cannot indicate the cause for the changes.
6) Ratio is a statistical yardstick that provides a measure of relationship between two figures.
7) Interpretation does not require ability on the part of the analyst.
8) Liquidity ratio measure the liquid position of the enterprise.
9) Activity ratio measure the efficiency in the employment of funds in the business operations'
10) Profit ability ratio measures only particular performance of the business.

Answers - 1) True 2) False 3) True 4) False 5) True 6) True 7) False 8) True 9) True (10) False.

B) Fill in the blanks.

1) The ..... income statement will show the operating results for two or more dates.
2) Regular balance sheet is converted into ...... balance sheet by dividing each item by total assets and arriving at a percentage figure.
3) Ratio is a simple ...... expression.
4) Ratio analysis is an important ..... of financial analysis.

5) Ratio analysis is an intrument for diagnosis of the ..... health of an enterprise.

6) The benefits of ratio analysis depends to a great extent upon their .....

7) ..... Ratio indicate the relative use of debts and equity in financing the assets of the firm.

8) Profitablity Ratio measure ..... performance of the business.

9) Current Ratio = $\dfrac{?}{\text{Current Liabilities}}$

10) Operating Ratio = $\dfrac{\text{Cost of Goods Sold Plus Operating Exp.}}{?} \times 100$

Answers - 1) Comparative, 2) common-size, 3) mathematical, 4) tool, 5) financial, 6) interpretation, 7) Leverage, 8) overall, 9) Current Assets, 10) Net Sales.

Essay Type

1) Who are interersted in the financial statements?

2) What is 'Ratio?' What are the limitations of Ratio Analysis?

3) State the different modes of expressing ratios.

4) What are the different types of ratios, according to conventional and functional classification?

5) Distinguish between balance sheet ratios and revenue statement ratios.

6) What is ratio analysis? State its objectives.

7) What is the purpose of a Liquid Ratio.

8) What is Current Ratio? What are the components of current ratio. State its significance.

9) Explain how following ratios help the management in interpretation of financial data :

(a) Acid Test Ratio.

(b) Stock-working Capital Ratio.

(c) Proprietory ratio.

10) Write short notes, on :

(a) Return on Capital Employed.

(b) Importance of Balance Sheet Ratios.

(c) Limitations of Ratio Analysis.

(d) Trading on Equity

(e) Capital Gearing Ratio.

(f) Earnings per share.

Practical Problems

1) You have the following information on the performance of Prosper Co. as also the industry averages.

a)   Determine the indicated ratios for Prosper Company.

b)   Indicate the Company's strengths and weaknesses as shown by your analysis.

Balance Sheet as on 31st March, 2009

	Rs.		Rs.
Equity Share Capital	24,00,000	Net Fixed Assets	12,10,000
10% Debentures	4,60,000	Cash	4,40,000
Sundry Creditors	3,30,000	Sundry Debtors	5,50,000
Bills Payable	4,40,000	Stocks	16,50,000
Other Current Liabilities	2,20,000		
	38,50,000		38,50,000

Statement of Profit
for the year ending 31st March, 2009

		Rs.
Sales		55,00,000
Less : Cost of goods sold :		
Materials	20,90,000	
Wages	13,20,000	
Factory Overheads	6,49,000	40,59,000
Gross Profit		14,41,000
Less : Selling and Distribution Costs	5,50,000	
Administration and General Expenses	6,14,000	11,64,000
Earnings before Interest and Tax		2,77,000
Less : Interest Charges		46,000
Earnings before Tax		2,31,000
Less : Tax (50%)		1,15,500
Net Profit		1,15,500

Ratios to be computed

i)   Current Ratio   ii) Liquid Ratio
iii) Earning Per share   iv) Net Profit Ratio
v)   Operating Ratio   vi) Proprietary Ratio
vii) Stock Turnover Ratio   viii) Debt collection Period
ix) Capital Gearing Ratio, and   x) Return on Capital Employed

Ans. i) 2:67   ii) 1   iii) 48   iv) 2.1%   v) 94.96%   vi) 62.34   vii) 2.46   viii) 37 days
ix) 19   x) 9.69%

2) The XYZ Company's financial statements contain the following information.

	Previous Year (Rs.)	Current Year (Rs.)
Cash	2,00,000	1,60,000
Sundry Debtors	3,20,000	4,00,000
Temporary Investments	2,00,000	4,00,000
Stock	18,40,000	21,60,000
Prepaid Expenses	28,000	12,000
Total Current Assets	25,88,000	31,32,000
Total Assets	56,00,000	64,00,000
Current Liabilities	6,40,000	8,00,000
10% Debentures	16,00,000	16,00,000
Equity Share Capital	20,00,000	20,00,000
Retained Earnings	4,68,000	8,12,000

Statement of Profit
for the year ended June 30

	Rs.
Sales	40,00,000
Less : Cost of goods sold	28,00,000
Less : Interest	1,60,000
Net Profit	10,40,000
Less : Taxes @ 50%	5,20,000
Profit after Taxes	5,20,000
Dividends declared on Equity Shares	2,20,000

From the above, appraise the financial position of the company from the points of view of : (a) Liquidity, (b) Solvency, (c) Profitability and (d) Activity.

Ans. Current Ratio 4.04; 3.91, Acid Test 1.12; 1.2 Debt Equity 0.65; 57 $\dfrac{\text{Outsiders Debt}}{\text{Equity}}$ Gross Profit 30%; Net Profit 13%; Return on Capital 27.19% Debtors to 32 days stock to 1.4 times.)

3) From the following Balance Sheet of B Ltd. as on 31st December, 2001 and the Trading, Profit and Loss Account for the year ending 31st December, 2001, calculate the following ratios.

i) Current Ratio   ii) Liquid Ratio.

iii) Inventory Turnover Ratio.   iv) Debtors Turnover Ratio.

v) Operating Ratio.   vi) Capital Gearing Ratio,

vii) Net Profit Ratio,
ix) Earnings per Equity Share
xi) Creditors Turnover

viii) Stock Working Capital Ratio.
x) Interest Coverage Ratio
xii) Dividend Payout Ratio.

Balance Sheet

Liabilities	Rs.	Assets	Rs.
10% Preference Capital	2,00,000	Fixed Assets	26,00,000
Equity Capital (Rs. 10)	10,00,000	Bank Balance	1,00,000
General Reserve	8,00,000	Short Term Investments	3,00,000
12% Debentures	14,00,000	Debtors	
Creditors	1,20,000	(last year Rs. 2,00,000)	4,00,000
Outstanding Expenses	2,20,000	Stock	6,00,000
Income tax Provision	2,60,000		
	40,00,000		40,00,000

Trading Profit & Loss A/c

	Rs.		Rs.
To Opening Stock	6,00,000	By Sales	60,00,000
To Purchases	51,60,000	By Closing Stock	6,00,000
To Gross Profit	8,40,000		
	66,00,000		66,00,000
To Administrative Expenses	80,000	By Gross Profit	8,40,000
To Rent	56,000	By Profit on Sale of	
To Interest	90,000	Fixed Assets	1,10,000
To Selling Expenses	44,000		
To Depreciation	2,00,000		
To Income Tax Provision	2,40,000		
To Net Profit	2,40,000		
	9,50,000		9,50,000

The Company declared dividend on Equity Share @ 20%.

Ans. (i) 2.33, (ii) 1.33 (iii) 8.6 times. (iv) 20 times, (v) 93.83%, (vi) 0.88, (vii) 4%, (viii) 75%, (ix) 2.2 (x) 5.11 times (xi) 43 times, (xii) 0.91.

4) The following are the final accounts of Excel Ltd., for the year ended 31st March, 2008 and 2009.

Balance Sheet

Liabilities	2008 Rs.	2009 Rs.	Assets	2008 Rs.	2009 Rs.
Equity Shares of Rs. 10/- each, fully paid-up	2,32,570	2,39,150	Fixed Assets net block	2,68,210	4,11520
8% Pref. Shares of Rs. 100 each fully paid-up	—	32,650	Stock at Cost	68,690	2,32,820
			Book debts	1,92,500	2,90,530
			Prepald Expenses	4,150	6,640
			Bank	1,04,360	1,18,430
General Reserve	1,61,560	2,13,430			
Profit and Loss A/c	62,280	82,050			
8% Debentures of Rs. 100 each	92,500	3,20,000			
Sundry Creditors	53,370	1,03,680			
Other Current Liab.	35,630	68,980			
	6,37,910	10,59,940		6,37,910	10,59,940

Revenue Statement

Liabilities	2008 Rs.	2009 Rs.	Assets	2008 Rs.	2009 Rs.
Cost of Sales	6,07,760	12,84,340	Sales	9,19,540	19,32,130
Gross Profit	3,11,780	6,47,790			
	9,19,540	19,32,130		9,19,540	19,32,130
Administration Exp.	90,110	1,83,000	Gross Profit	3,11,780	6,47790
Selling Expenses	90,000	1,79,000	Discount	2,730	9, 560
Interest	7,400	25,600			
Provision for Tax	69,340	1,47,120			
Transfer to Reserve	40,000	50,000			
Net Income	17,660	72,630			
	3,14,510	6,57,350		3,14,510	6,57,350

Assume that stock at cost on 1-4-2007 was Rs. 68,690.

Market Price of Equity Shares of the Company was - Rs. 25 on 31st March, 2006 and Rs. 50 on 31st March. 2009.

You are required to calculate the following ratios.

a) Return on Capital Employed.

b) Return on Proprietors Fund.

c) Return on Equity Capital.

d) Earning per Share.

e) Net Profit Ratio.

f) Stock Turnover Ratio.

g) Debtors Turnover Ratio.

Comment on Operating efficiency and profitability of the company.

5. The following information is given :

Current Ratio	2.5
Liquidity Ratio	1.5
Net Working Capital	Rs. 3,00,000
Fixed Assets Turnover Ratio	2 times
Average Debt Collection Period	2 months
Stock Turnover Ratio	6 times
Fixed Assets to Shareholder's Networth	1 : 1
Gross Profit Ratio	20%
Reserves to Share Capital	0.5 : 1

Draw up a Balance Sheet from the above. (Pune, May, 1996)

6) From the following figures and ratios of M/s. 'ABC' Ltd., draw out Balance Sheet and Trading and Profit & Loss Account as on 31st March, 2009.

	Rs.
Share Capital	1,80,000
Working Capital	63,000
Bank Overdraft	10,000

There is no fictitious asset. In Current Assets, there is no asset other than Stock, Debtors and Cash. Closing Stock is 20% higher than the Opening Stock.

Current Ratio	2.5
Quick Ratio	1.5
Proprietory Ratio (Fixed Assets : Proprietory Fund)	0.7
Gross Profit Ratio	20% (to Sales)
Stock Velocity	4
Debtor's Velocity	36.5 days
Net Profit Ratio (to Average Capital Employed)	10%

Ans. Current Assets - Rs. 1,05,000; Current Liabilities - Rs. 42,000; Closing Stock - Rs. 57,000, Opening Stock - Rs. 47,500; Cost of goods sold - Rs. 2,09,000, Sales - Rs. 2,61,250; Debtors - Rs. 26,125, Fixed Assets Rs. 1,47,000; Proprietors Fund - Rs. 2,10,000; Net Profit - Rs. 20,000)

7) From the Balance Sheet of RAN Ltd. given ahead, compute.

a) Debt Equity Ratio.   b) Funded Debt to Total Capitalisation Ratio.

c) Fixed Assets to Networth Ratio.   d) Current Assets to Proprietor's Fund Ratio.

e) Fixed Assets Ratio.

Balance Sheet

Liabilities	Rs.	Assets		Rs.
Equity Share Capital	3,00,000	Goodwill		90,000
9% Preference Share Capital	1,50,000	Land and Building		1,00,000
Reserve Fund	50,000	Plant and Machinery		2,50,000
Profit & Loss A/c	20,000	Equipment		60,000
Securities Premium	10,000	Furniture and Fittings		80,000
8% Debentures	2,00,000	Sundry Debtors	92,000	
6% Mortgage Loan	60,000	Less : Provision	2,000	90, 000
Sundry Creditors	80,000	Bills Receivables		1,00,000
Income Tax Provision	20,000	Stock-in-Hand		1,20,000
Depreciation Fund	50,000	Cash Balance		45,500
		Prepaid Insurance		1,500
		Preliminary Expenses		2,000
		Discount on issue of Debentures		1,000
	9,40,000			9,40,000

Ans. : (a) 0.49, (b) 0.33, (c) 1.1; (d) 0.67 and (e) 0.73

8. Big Ltd. and Giant Ltd. are competing companies. Following information is obtained from published accounts for the year 1-4-2007 to 31st March. 2008

	Big Ltd. Rs.	Giant Ltd. Rs.
Sales	32,00,000	30,00,000
Net Profit (after Tax @ 50%)	1,28,000	1,50,000
Equity Capital (inshares of Rs. 10 each)	10,00,000	8,00,000
General Reserve	3,32,000	6,42,000
Long-term Debts	8,00,000	5,60,000
Creditors	3,82,000	5,49,000
Bank Credit (Short-term)	60,000	2,00,000
Fixed Assets	15,99,000	15,90,000
Inventories	3,31,000	8,09,000
Other Current Assets	5,44,000	4,52,000

Gross Profit is 5 times the Net Profit for both companies.

You are required to compute appropriate ratios of both companies and comment upon.

a) Liquidity   c) Utilisation (Turnover) of Assets.

b) Profitability   d) Financial Position.

Ans.

	Big Ltd.	Giant Ltd.
Current Ratio	1.98	1.68
Quick Ratio	1.23	0.60
Gross Profit Ratio	20%	25%
Refund on PF	10.39%	10.40%
Stock Turnover	7.73	2.78
Fixed Assets Turnover	2	1.89
Debt Equity	0.65	0.39
Proprietory Ratio	0.50	0.50

9. From the following financial statements of 'X' Ltd., calculate :

a) Current Ratio.

b) Liquid Ratio.

c) Gross Profit Ratio.

d) Fixed Assets Turnover.

e) Sales to Capital Employed.

f) Debtors Turnover.

g) Net Profit to Capital Employed.

Income Statement
for the year ending 31st December, 2002

	Rs.	Rs.
Sales		
Cash	64,000	
Credit	6,84,000	7,48,000
Less : Cost of Sales		5,96,000
Gross Profit		1,52,000
Less : Expenses		
Warehousing and Transport	48,000	
Administration	38,000	
Selling	28,000	
Debenture Interest	4,000	1,18,000
Net Profit		34,000

Balance Sheet
as at 31st December, 2002

Liabilities	Rs.	Assets		Rs.
Share Capital	1,50,000	Fixed Assets (Net)		80,000
Reserves	60,000	**Current Assets :**		
Profit & Loss	24,000	Stock	1,88,000	
Debentures	60,000	Debtors	1,64,000	
Current Liabilities	1,52,000	Cash	14,000	3,66,000
	4,46,000			4,46,000

(Pune, November, 1987)

Ans. (a) 2.41, (b) 1.17, (c) 20.32%, (d) 9.35, (e) 2.54, (f) 88 days, (g) 11.56%.

10. The financial Statements and operating results of Gradpro Ltd. revealed the following position as on 31st March, 2009.

    a) Equity Share Capital (Rs. 10/- fully paid)   Rs. 10,00,000
    b) Working Capital   Rs. 7,80,000
    c) Bank Overdraft   Rs. 1,20,000
    d) Current Ratio   2.5
    e) Quick Ratio   1.5
    f) Proprietory Ratio (Fixed Assets to Proprietory Fund)   0.6
    g) Gross Profit Ratio   25%
    h) Stock Velocity   5 times
    i) Debtor Credit Period   1½ month.
    j) Net Profit to Sales   15%

    Expenses included depreciation Rs. 1,30,000/-, Closing Stock was 25% higher than the Opening Stock. There was also free reserve brought forward from earlier years. Current Assets including Stock. Debtors and Cash only. There were no fictitious assets.

Ans. Current Assets - Rs. 13,00,000; Current Liabilities - Rs. 5,20,000, Quick Liabilities Rs. 4,00,000; Quick Assets - Rs. 6,00,000; Stock - Rs. 7,00,000; Opening Stock - Rs. 5,60,000; Cost of goods sold - Rs. 31,50,000; Gross Profit - Rs. 10,50,000, Sales - Rs. 42,00,000; Debtors - Rs. 5,25,000

■ ■ ■

CHAPTER 3

Fund Flow Statement and Cash Flow Statement

● 3:1 Meaning of Fund ● 3:2 Fund Flow Statement ● 3:3 Flow of Funds ● 3:4 Working Capital ● 3:5 Causes of changes in Working Capital ● 3:6 Proforma of Sources and Application of Funds ● 3:7 Proforma of Adjusted Profit and Loss Account ● 3:8 Cash Flow Statement ● 3:9 Illustrations ● 3:10 Questions

3.1 Meaning of Fund

Fund – The term 'fund' is used in three different meanings in the 'fund flow analysis'. Some take it as 'cash' only, and in that case, the statement prepared is termed as 'Cash Flow Statement', which shows inflow and outflow of cash only. Some take it as cash and marketable securities, whereas others take it as 'net Working Capital.' The first two definitions are inadequate as the fund flow analysis is something more than a mere cash analysis.The assets of a firm represent the net uses of funds and its liabilities, and net worth represents net resource. Therefore, the term 'fund', in its broad sense, stands for net working capital and the term 'fund flow' refers to changes in the working capital.

3:2 Meaning of Fund Flow Statement :

The fund flow statement consists of two terms - 'fund' and 'flow'. While a 'fund' may be interpreted as cash or working capital or all financial resources; 'flow' represents change. Therefore, when the term 'fund' is interpreted as 'working capital', the fund flow statement means a statement of changes in working capital. This statement contains the sources of funds, uses of funds and the changes in net working capital indicating the difference between the total sources and uses.

This statement is also known as ' Statement of Sources and Application of Funds,' and 'Statement of Sources and Uses of Working Capital'.

The working capital flow arises when the net effect of a transaction is either to increase or decrease the amount of working capital. The transaction which affects both the current accounts (e.g. accounts of current assets and current liabilities) and non-current accounts (e.g. accounts of non-current assets and non-current liabilities) causes a change in working capital. Any transaction which increases the amount of working capital is a source of working capital. The major sources of working capital are summarised as under :

a) Issue of Shares (whether Equity or Preference)
b) Raising of Long-term Debt (e.g. issue of Debentures)
c) Sale of Non-current Assets
d) Non-operating Incomes (e.g. Dividend and Interest on Investment)
e) Funds from Operations

Any transaction which decreases the amount of working capital is an application of working capital. The major uses of working capital are summarised as under :

a) Redemption of Redeemable Preference Shares for Cash
b) Repayment of Long-term Debt
c) Purchase of Non-current Assets
d) Payment of Cash Dividend (whether final or interim)
e) Fund (Loss) from Operations.
f) Non-operating Expenses (e.g. payment of Preliminary Expenses, payment of Underwriting Commission)

Though, it it not legally compulsory for the companies in India to prepare and publish this statement, yet it is recommended that this statement should be prepared and published alongwith the annual accounts.

To provide a comparative view of the movements of funds, this statement should be prepared and published for the period covered by the Profit and Loss Account and for the corresponding previous period.

Though, there is no fixed form of presentation, yet each enterprise should adopt the form of presentation which is most informative in the circumstances.

Objective of Fund Flow Statement

The basic objective of a fund flow statement is to indicate the sources from which the funds (i.e. working capital) were obtained and the specific uses to which such funds (i.e. working capital) were applied between the dates of two Balance Sheets.

Distinction between Fund Flow Statement and Balance Sheet

Funds Flow Statement and Position Statement can be distinguished as under:

Basis of Distinction	Balance Sheet	Fund Flow Statement
1. Meaning	It is a statement of assets and liabilities of an enterprise.	It is a statement of changes in assets and liabilities of an enterprise.
2. Objective	It is prepared to ascertain the financial position at a particular date.	It is prepared to indicate how the financial position has changed during a specific period.
3. Legal obligation to prepare	Schedule VI to the Companies Act requires every Company to prepare a Balance Sheet.	There exists no legal obligation to prepare fund flow Statement.
4. Prescribed Format	Company's balance sheet is required to be prepared in a prescribed form.	Fund flow statement is not required to be prepared in a prescribed form.

Basis of Distinction	Balance Sheet	Fund Flow Statement
5. Headings	The headings used in horizontal balance sheet are 'assets' and 'liabilities'	The headings used in fund flow Statement are 'sources of funds' and 'application of funds.'
6. Treatment of retained earnings	Retained earnings are treated as sources of funds.	All earnings (whether retained or distributed) are treated as sources of funds.
7. Basic data required for preparation	It is prepared with the help of ledger balances and additional information.	It is prepared with the help of two consecutive balance sheets and additional information.

Distinction between Fund Flow Statement and Income Statement

Fund flow Statement and an Income Statement can be distinguished as under :

Basis of Distinction	Income Statement	Fund Flow Statement
1. Meaning	It summarises the results of operating activities during a particular period.	It is a statement of changes in assets and liabilities of an enterprise.
2. Objective	It is prepared to ascertain how the profit was earned.	It is prepared to ascertain how the profit has been utilised.
3. Legal obligation to prepare	Schedule Vl to the Companies Act, requires every Company to prepare an Income Statement.	There exists no legal obligation to prepare Fund Flow Statement.
4. Basic data required for preparation	It is prepared with the help of nominal accounts and additional information.	It is prepared with the help of two consecutive balance sheets and additional information.
5. Treatment of difference	An excess of incomes over expenses is known as 'net profit' and vice versa is known as 'net loss'.	An excess of sources over applications is known as increase in working capital and vice versa is known as decrease in working capital.
6. Basis for one source or all sources of funds	It provides a basis for the calculation of funds from operations which is one of the sources of funds.	It shows the funds from various sources (including funds from operations.)

Advantages or Uses of Fund Flow Statement :

1. Fund flow study is a useful tool for financial management. The balance sheet is only a list of assets and liabilities, indicating the financial position at a certain point of time. Its nature is of historical character and it does not meet the dynamic requirements of the financial management. A financial executive must know the flow of funds indicated by the changes in the figures of the balance sheets. This purpose is served by the Fund Flow Statement. These statements bring into light the underlying financial movements and reflect the changes in the financial position or working capital position in two different dates – a complete record of incoming and outgoing funds are maintained.

2. With the help of fund statements, a finance officer can ensure that the business will have funds when they are wanted and will utilise effectively when available.

3. It is an essential tool of financial analysis. In fact, it is the major instrument used for analysing the financial problems and determining the long range financial policies of the business enterprise. It seeks to answer certain financial questions which are of intensive use to the financial management.

4. It gives an insight into the financial operations of the concern and thus helps in analysing the past and future expansion plans.

5. An analysis of the major sources of funds reveals the internal and external sources. It also shows whether the sources are utilised according to plans or not.

6. It helps the financial manager in planning the intermediate and long-term financing of the business. It discloses to him the total need for funds, the expected timings of requirement and their nature.

Limitations of Fund Flow Statement

The major limitations of Fund Flow Statement are summarised below:

a) It ignores the non-fund transactions. In other words, it does not take into consideration those transactions which do not affect the working capital e.g., issue of shares against the purchase of fixed assets, conversion of debentures into equity shares etc.

b) It is a secondary data-based statement. It merely rearranges the primary data already appearing in other statements viz., Income Statement and Balance Sheet.

c) It is basically historical in nature unless projected fund flow statements are prepared to plan for the future.

Working Capital

It is the capital with which the business is worked over. According to Shubin, "Working capital is that amount of funds necessary to cover the cost of operating the enterprise. Thus, the funds required by the business for conducting the day-to-day operations, for e.g., purchase of raw materials, payment of expenses. such as wages, salaries, rent, insurance etc., besides those for carrying out production, investment in stocks and stores, receivables and to be maintained in cash etc., are known as working capital. This capital is also known as circulating capital because cash is converted into stock of goods, and later, the same are sold, which in turn, creates debtors and bills receivables and, is finally turned again into cash. Thus, it completes a cycle. The assets coming under this short operating cycle, viz., stock, debtors, bills receivables, pre-paid expenses, cash/bank balance are termed as circulating assets or current assets. Hence, in the words of Gerstenberg, "Circulating capital means current assets of a company that are changed in the ordinary course of business from one form to another, as for example, cash to inventories, inventories to receivables and receivables to cash."

As there are current assets, there are current liabilities also. Current liabilities are those liabilities which are to be repaid within a year's period and which are paid out of current assets or by creating current liabilities i.e., short-term liabilities. Thus, the term 'current liabilities' include creditors, bills payable, bank overdraft, outstanding expenses etc. (some are of the opinion that 'bank overdraft' being a permanent arrangement, it should not be included in the term 'current liabilities' whereas others rightly plead that as this facility can be withdrawn by bank at any time, it should be treated as a current liability. It is therefore, generally treated as a current liability).

Thus, the balance sheet can be divided into two sections viz. − 1) current accounts i.e. the assets which are constantly changing form and the short-term liabilities, and 2) 'non-current accounts' i.e. fixed assets which are not meant for re-sale, and fixed or long-term liabilities and the net worth.

Now, we can define working capital as 'the excess of current assets over current liabilities i.e. net current assets.' However, in the broad sense, the term 'working capital' is used to denote the total current assets.

Causes of changes in Working Capital

In general terms, it can be said that the transactions which affect the current assets and current liabilities are the cause for changes in working capital. But, if the accounts involved are both of the 'current' category, it will not change the working capital e.g. payment to a creditor. It will reduce cash and creditors by the same amount, and as such, will be not affect the amount of the working capital. Hence, out of the two accounts affected by the transactions, one must be of 'current' category and the other of 'non-current' category.

If as a result of a transaction, current asset or current liability account is debited and 'non-current' account is credited, the working capital is increased. For e.g.

i) Sale of fixed assets
ii) Issue of shares, debentures or bonds
iii) Sales of merchandise
vi) Earnings from non-trading items.

Similarly, when current assets or liabilities are credited and non-current items are debited, working capital is decreased. For e.g.

i) Purchase and improvement or expansion of fixed assets.
ii) Redemption of Preference Share Capital, debentures or bonds.
iii) Payment of non-trading expenses, such as dividend.

Preparation of Fund Flow Statement

The various steps involved in the preparation of Fund Flow Statement are given below :−

Steps involved in the preparation of Fund Flow Statement

Step 1   Prepare Schedule of changes in components of working capital.

Step 2   Analyse the changes in non-current assets and non-current liabilities to find out whether there is inflow or outflow of funds on account of these non-current items.

Step 3   Compute the Funds from Operations.

Step 4   Prepare Fund Flow Statement.

Step 1. Preparation of Schedule of changes in components of working capital

The various steps involved in the preparation of schedule of changes in working capital are given below

Steps involved in the preparation of Schedule of the changes in working capital

Step 1   Enter the names of current assets in 'particular column.'

Step 2   Enter the amounts of current assets for previous year in 'previous year column.'

Step 3   Enter the amounts of current assets for current year in 'current year column.'

Step 4   Enter the increase in current asset as 'Increase in Working Capital and the decrease as 'decrease in working capital column.

Step 5   Total 'previous year column' and 'current year column' for current assets separately.

Step 6   Enter the names of current liabilities in 'particulars' column.

Step 7   Enter the amounts of current liabilities for previous year in 'previous year column.'

Step 8   Enter the amounts of current liabilities for current year in 'current year column.'

Step 9   Enter the increase in current liability in 'decrease in working capital column' and decrease in as current liability 'increase in working capital column.'

Step 10   Total 'previous year column' and 'current year column' for Current Liabilities separately.

Step 11   Calculate the working capital for previous year and current year by taking out the difference between current asscts and current liabilities and enter in 'previous year column' and 'current year column' respectively.

Step 12   Calculate the difference between the working capital for current year and working capital of previous year and enter the Increase in working capital in 'previous year column' and decrease in working capital in 'current year column'.

Step 13   Total 'previous year column', 'current year' column, 'increase in working capital column' and 'decrease in working capital column.'

The purpose of preparing this statement is to arrive at a single figure of net increase or decrease in working capital at the end of the period as compared with that of the beginning.

An increase in working capital means applying long-term funds towards short-term needs and a decrease in working capital means applying short-term funds for long-term needs. A format of schedule of changes in components of working capital is shown below :

Format of Schedule of Changes in Working Capital

Schedule of changes in Working Capital

(1) Particulars	Absolute Amounts		Changes in Working Capital	
	(2) Previous year Rs.	(3) Current year Rs.	(4) Increase (Debit) Rs.	(5) Decrease (Credit) Rs.
A. Current Assets				
(a) Stock-in-trade	.....	.....		
(b) Debtors Gross	.....	.....		
(c) Cash Balance	.....	.....		
(d) Bank Balance	.....	.....		
(e) Bills Receivable	.....	.....		
(f) Pre-paid Expenses	.....	.....		
(g) Accrued Incomes	.....	.....		
(h) Short-term Loans and Advances	.....	.....		
(i) Marketable Investments (Short-term)	.....	.....		
	.....	.....		
B. Current Liabilities				
(a) Creditors for goods	.....	.....		
(b) Bills Payable	.....	.....		
(c) Outstanding Expenses	.....	.....		
(d) Bank Overdraft	.....	.....		
(e) Unclaimed Dividend	.....	.....		
(f) Unaccrued Incomes	.....	.....		
(g) Short-term Loans and Advances	.....	.....		
(h) Provision for Doubtful Debts	.....	.....		
(i) Provision for Discount on Debtors	.....	.....		
	.....	.....		
C. Working Capital (A - B)	.....	.....		
D. Increase in Working Capital or **Decrease in Working Capital**	.....	.....	.....	.....
	.....	.....	.....	.....

Notes :

(i) If all the debtors are considered as good, the Debtors will be shown in the schedule at gross figure and the provision for Doubtful Debts will not appear in the Schedule. However, provision for Discount on Debtors, (if any), will appear in the Schedule.

(ii) The figures of Marketable Investments given in the Balance Sheets should not again be adjusted for purchase, sale or profit / loss on sale of such investments made during the accounting period.

(iii) Increase in value of assets to be shown under the column 'Increase' and 'decrease' in value of assets under the column 'Decrease'. Whereas in the case of liabilities, increase in liabilities is to be shown under the column 'Decrease' and decrease in liabilities to be shown under column 'Increase.'

How to determine whether an asset is a Current Asset or Non-current Asset

An asset is classified either as a current asset or as a non-current asset on the basis of the purpose for which an asset is held in the hands of the user. If all the answers to the following questions are in the negative, the asset will be treated as a non-current asset.

Q. a) Whether it is Cash or Bank Balance.

Q. b) Whether it is expected to be converted into Cash.

Q. c) Whether it is expected to be consumed in the production of goods or rendering services in the normal course of business.

For example :

Items → Questions ↓	Stock of Finished Goods	Stock of Raw Material & Work-in-Progress	Debtors & B/R	Land & Building
Q. (a)	No	No	No	No
Q. (b)	Yes	No	Yes	No
Q. (c)	No	Yes	No	No
Result	Current Asset	Current Asset	Current Asset	Non-current Asset

Examples of Non-current assets include Goodwill, Land & Building, Plant and Machinery, Furniture and Fixtures, Long-term Investments.

Examples of Non-current Liabilities include Share Capital, Long-term loans, Debentures, Public deposits payable after 12 months from the date of Balance Sheet.

Distinction between Fund Flow Statement And Schedule of changes in Working Capital

Fund Flow Statement and Schedule of changes in components of Working Capital can be distinguished as under :

Basis of Distinction	Fund Flow Statement	Schedule of Changes in components of Working Capital
1. Meaning	It contains the sources of funds, uses of funds and the changes in net working capital.	It contains the various items of current assets, current liabilities and changes therein, working capital for the previous year and current year and the net increase/decrease in working capital as compared to previous year.
2. Objective	It is prepared to ascertain how the financial position has changed during a particular period.	It is prepared to ascertain how the various components of working capital have changed during a particular period.
3. Disclosure of changes in non-current items	Changes in non-current items are shown in Fund Flow Statement.	Changes in non-current items are not shown in this schedule.
4. Disclosure of	Funds from operations are shown in fund flow statement.	Funds from operations are not shown in this schedule

Illustration : How will you deal with the following, while preparing the Schedule of Changes in Working Capital?

a) Increase in Patents, b) Decrease in Stock, c) Decrease in Goodwill, d) Increase in Debtors, e) Decrease in Land & Building, f) Decrease in Marketable Securities, g) Increase in Long-term Investments, h) Decrease in Creditors, i) Increase in Share Capital, j) Increase in Bank overdraft, k) Decrease in Debentures, l) Decrease in Dividend Payable, m) Increase in Share Premium, n) Increase in Bills Payable, o) Decrease in Public Deposits (due after 2 years), p) Decrease in Unclaimed Dividend, q) Decrease in Preliminary Expenses, r) Increase in Discount on Issue of Debentures.

Solution :

Items to be shown as increase in working capital - (d), (h), (l), (p)

Items to be shown as decrease in working capital - (b), (f), (j), (n)

Items not to be shown in Schedule - (a), (c), (e), (g), (k), (m), (o), (q), (r)

Illustration : From the following Balance Sheets of Tulsi Ltd., prepare Schedule of Changes in Working Capital.

Liabilities	2007 Rs.	2008 Rs.	Assets	2007 Rs.	2008 Rs.
Equity Share Capital	3,00,000	4,00,000	Goodwill	1,15,000	90,000
Pref. Share Capital	1,50,000	1,00,000	Patents	90,000	1,15,000
General Reserve	40,000	70,000	Land	1,00,000	90,000
Share Premium	5,000	15,000	Plant & Machinery		
Profit & Loss A/c	23,000	54,000	(Net)	1,80,000	1,70,000
Debentures	3,20,000	4,20,000	Furniture	10,000	2,25,000
Creditors for Goods	30,000	50,000	Investments	2,00,000	1,80,000
Bills Payables	20,000	30,000	Stock	77,000	1,09,000
Outstanding Expenses	5,000	3,000	Debtors	1,60,000	2,00,000
Bank Overdraft	20,000	16,000	Bills Receivable	20,000	30,000
(Canara Bank)			Marketable Securities	3,000	2,000
Provision for Taxation	38,000	50,000	Accrued Interest	1,000	3,000
Proposed Dividend	42,000	50,000	Cash in hand	5,000	4,000
Provision for			Cash at Dena Bank	10,000	6,000
Doubtful Debts	4,000	5,000	Prepaid Expenses	10,000	8,000
Provision for			Preliminary Expenses	5,000	3,000
Legal Damages	2,000	-	Underwriting		
			Commission	3,000	8,000
			Discount on Issue of		
			Debentures	10,000	20,000
	9,99,000	12,63,000		9,99,000	12,63,000

Solution : **Schedule of Changes in Working Capital**

	31st Dec.		Changes in Working Capital	
Particulars	2007 Rs.	2008 Rs.	Increase Rs.	Decrease Rs.
A. Current Assets				
Stock	77,000	1,09,000	32,000	
Debtors	1,60,000	2,00,000	40,000	
Bills Receivables	20,000	30,000	10,000	
Marketable Securities	3,000	2,000		1,000
Accrued Interest	1,000	3,000	2,000	
Cash in hand	5,000	4,000		1,000
Cash at Dena Bank	10,000	6,000		4,000
Pre-paid Expenses	10,000	8,000		2,000
	2,86,000	3,62,000		

Particulars	2007 Rs.	2008 Rs.	Increase Rs.	Decrease Rs.
B. Current Liabilities				
Creditors for Goods	30,000	50,000		20,000
Bills Payables	20,000	30,000		10,000
Outstanding Expenses	5,000	3,000	2,000	
Bank O/D (Can Bank)	20,000	16,000	4,000	
Provision for Doubtful Debts	4,000	5,000		1,000
Provision for Legal Damages	2,000		2,000	
	81,000	1,04,000		
C. Working Capital (A-B)	2,05,000	2,58,000		
D. Increase in Working Capital	53,000			53,000
	2,58,000	2,58,000	92,000	92,000

Step 2 : Analysis of the changes in Non-current items

To identify whether there is an inflow or outflow of funds on account of non-current items, the accounts of all non-current items (like Fixed Assets, Investments (Long-term), Goodwill, Patents, Trademarks, Preliminary Expenses, Underwriting Commission, Discount on issue of Shares/ Debentures, Equity Share Capital, Preference Share Capital, Debentures, Long-term Loans) should be prepared after taking into consideration the following.

    a) Opening Balance (given in Opening Balance Sheet)

    b) Closing Balance (given in Closing Balance Sheet)

    c) Relevant additional information, (if any, given).

The following table summarises the meaning, accounting treatment and reasoning for treatment of changes in various non-current items in the absence of any additional information :

Non-current Items	Meaning	Treatment	Reasoning for Treatment
I. Intangible Non-Current Assets (e.g. Goodwill, Patents, Trademarks, Copyrights) a) Increase	It represents the amount of purchase.	Show as an application of fund in Fund Flow Statement.	It involves an outflow of fund.

Non-current Items	Meaning	Treatment	Reasoning for Treatment
b) Decrease	It represents the amount amortised/written off.	Add back to the current years' profits to find out funds from operations.	It merely represents a book entry and does not involve any outflow of fund.
II. Tangible Non-depreciable Non-current Assets (e.g. Investments) a) Increase	It represents the amount of purchase.	Show as an application of Funds in Fund Flow Statement	It involves an outflow of fund.
b) Decrease	It represents the amount of sale proceeds.	Show as a Source of Funds in Fund Flow Statement.	It involves an inflow of fund.
III. Tangible depreciable Non-current Assets (e.g. Land and Building, Plant & Machinery) a) Increase	It represents the amount of purchase.	Show as an Application of Fund in Funds Flow Statement.	It involves an outflow of fund.
b) Decrease	It represents the amount of depreciation provided during the year.	Add back to the current years' profits to find out funds from operations.	It merely represents a book entry and does not involve any outflow of fund.
IV. Fictitious Assets other than Discount (e.g. Preliminary Expenses, Underwriting Commission)			

Non-current Items	Meaning	Treatment	Reasoning for Treatment
a) Increase	It represents the payment.	Show as an Application of Funds in Fund Flow Statement.	It involves an outflow of fund.
b) Decrease	It represents the amount written off.	Add back to the current years' profits to find out funds from operations.	It merely represents a book entry and does not involve any outflow of fund.
V. Discount allowed on Issue of Shares/ Debentures			
a) Increase	It represents the amount of discount allowed on issue of shares/debentures.	Deduct from the increase in Share Capital/Debenture to ascertain the net amount of issue (which is shown as a source of funds in Fund Flow Statement)	It represents less inflow of funds on issue of shares/debentures to the extent of discount allowed.
b) Decrease	It represents the amount written off.	Add back to the current years' profits to find out funds from operations.	It merely represents a book entry and does not involve any outflow of funds.
VI. Share Capital, Debentures, Long-term Loans	It represents an issue of new shares/debentures or raising a fresh loan.	Show as a source of funds in Fund Flow Statement **Note :** While calculating the amount of source, premium (if any received) should be added to or discount (if any allowed) should be deducted from the amount of increase.	It involves an inflow of funds.
a) Increase			
b) Decrease	It represents the repayment of Redeemable Pref. Shares/Debentures / Long-term	Show as an application of funds in Fund Flow Statement.	It involves an outflow of fund.

Non-current Items	Meaning	Treatment	Reasoning for Treatment
	Loan.	**Note :** While calculating the amount of application, premium on redemption (if any paid) should be added to the amount of decrease.	
VII. General Reserve Account a) Increase	It represents transfer of profits from P & L A/c.	Add back to the current years' profits to find out funds from operations.	It merely represents a book entry and does not invoive any inflow of funds.
b) Decrease	It represents transfer of profit from General Reserve to P & L A/c.	Deduct from the current years' profits to find out funds from operations.	It merely represents a book entry and does not involve any outflow of funds.
VIII. Share Premium Account a) Increase	It represents the amount of premium received on issue of shares.	Add to the increase in Share Capital to ascertain the total amount of issue (which is shown as a source of funds in Fund Flow Statement).	It represents more inflow of funds on issue of shares to the extent of premium received.
b) Decrease	It represents the amount of premium utilised for- i) Writing off preliminary expenses, underwriting commission, discount on issue of shares/debentures or ii) Providing for premium on redemption of redeemable preference shares/debentures	No treatment is required, but it may be noted that an amount of decrease in preliminary exp./ underwriting comm.,/ discount allowed, to the extent of decrease in share premium, shall not be added back to current years' profits.	

Non-current Items	Meaning	Treatment	Reasoning for Treatment
		No treatment is required, but it may be noted that premium paid on redemption to the extent of decrease in share premium, shall not be added back to current years' profits.	
IX. Proposed Dividend a) Previous year's	It represents the amount of final dividend declared for the previous year, but paid during the current year.	Show as an Application of funds in Funds Flow Statement.	It involves an outflow of funds.
b) Current year's	It represents the amount of dividend proposed by the Board of Directors for the current year.	Add back to the current year's profits to find out funds from operations.	It is merely a book entry and does not involve an outflow of funds
X. Provision for Doubtful Debts, if all debtors have been considered as good.			Treatment is similar to that of General Reserve (as discussed earlier is item VII).

Step 3 : Computations of the funds from operations (Operational flow) :

Instead of showing sales, closing stock as sources of fund, and opening stock, purchases, and expenses as applications of fund, net profit may be taken as net source or net loss as net application.

If no profit is given after charging the items (such as depreciation on fixed assets, loss on sale of fixed assets, preliminary expenses etc.) which do not result in application of funds, they must be added back to the profit while calculating 'funds from operations'. Similarly, the items which are credited to Profit and Loss A/c but are not the sources of income, such as profit on sale of fixed assets, Re-transfer of excess provision, etc. must be deducted from the profit. The net amount arrived at after making such adjustments, is the amount of fund from operation. In short, it means the expenses and the incomes which result from operation only. (i.e. trade) are to be considered.

Funds from operations :

Net profit as per Profit & Loss A/c

Add : i) Depreciation of fixed assets charged —

ii) Amounts written off in respect of Preliminary expenses, 'Discount on —
issue of Shares/Debentures, Goodwill, Patents, Premium on
redemption of preference shares or Debentures, Deferred revenue
charges, etc.

iii) Provision for taxation charged —

iv) Dividend paid out of Current year's profits. —

v) Appropriations of Retained Earnings —

vi) Loss on sale of fixed assets charged —

vii)Any other expenditure not affecting cash —

Less :

1. Savings from provisions credited back to Profit & Loss A/c —

2. Profit on sale or revaluation of fixed assets credited to P & L A/c.

3. Dividends Received from outside. —

4. Any other income not affecting the fund. —

Funds from Operations —

Or, if opening and closing balances of Profit & Loss A/c are given an Adjusted Profit and Loss A/c should be prepared as under to find out funds from operations.

Adjusted Profit & Loss A/c

	Rs.		Rs.
To Depreciation or loss on sale of fixed assets		By Opening Balance of P & L A/c	
To Amounts written off on account of		By Rents received and receivable	
i) Discount on Shares/Debentures		By Dividends received & receivable	
ii) Preliminary expenses		By Profit on Sale / Appreciation of Fixed Assets	
iii) Goodwill/Trade Marks/Patents		By Income Tax refund	
iv) Other deferred expenses		By Savings in excess provision made	
To Amounts transferred out of profits		OR	
of current year to :			
General Reserve		Decrease in Revenue Reserve caused by	
Capital Reserve		transfer to Profit & Loss A/c	
Dividend Equalisation Reserve		By Funds from Operations (Balancing figure)	
Debenture Sinking Fund			
Provision for Taxation			
Proposed Dividend			
Contingency Reserve			
Any other Revenue Reserve			
To Closing balance of P & L A/c			

(Students to bear in mind that the above non-operating items to be added to or deducted from balance of Net Profit of current year, or to be debited/credited to Adjusted Profit & Loss A/c, only if they were transferred to Profit & Loss A/c or Profit & Loss Appropriation A/c before arriving at the balance of profit.)

From the above it will be clear that 'non-funds and/or non-operating' debits i.e. expenses or losses are added back to the balance of current year's profit, and 'non-funds and/or non-operating' credits, i.e., incomes and gains are deducted.

Illustration :

From the records of a Company, the following information has been extracted :

	Rs.
Net Profit after providing for the following items	80,000
Loss on sale of Equipments	15,000
Premium on Redemption of Debentures Equipments	1,000
Discount on issue of Debentures	2,000
Depreciation on Buildings	15,000
Depletion of Wasting Asset	5,000
Goodwill written off	20,000
Interim Dividend	20,000
Profit on sale of Fixed Assets	35,000
Excess Taxation provided	20,000
Income from Investments	5,000
Transfer to General Reserve	6,000
Preliminary Expenses written off	1,500
Profit on Revaluation of Investments	2,000
Calculate Funds from Operations	

Solution :

	Rs.	Rs.
Net Profit		80,000
Add : Non-cash and Non-operating Charges :		
Loss on Sale of Equipments	15,000	
Discount on Issue of Debentures	2,000	
Depreciation on Buildings	15,000	
Depletion on of Wasting Assets	5,000	
Goodwill written off	20,000	
Excess Provision for Taxation	20,000	
Transfer to General Reserve	6,000	

	Rs.	Rs.
Preliminary Expenses written off	15,00	
Premium on Redemption of Debentures	1,000	
Interim Dividend	20,000	1,05,500
		1,85,500
Less : Profit on Revaluation of Investments	2,000	
Profit on sale of Current Assets (Final Assets)	35,000	
Income from Investments	5,000	42,000
Fund from Operations		1,43,500

Alternatively, funds from operations can be ascertained as below :

Adjusted Profit & Loss A/c

	Rs.		Rs.
To Loss on sale of equipment	15,000	By Profit on reduction	
To Discount on debentures	2,000	of Investments	2,000
To Depreciation on Bldgs.	15,000	By Profit on sale of Non-current	
To Depletion of Working Assets	5,000	Assets	35,000
To Goodswill written off	20,000	By Income from Investment	5,000
To Provision for Taxation	20,000	By Funds from operation	
To Transfer to General Reserve	6,000	(Building figure)	1,43,500
To Preliminary Exp. written off	1,500		
To Premium on Redemption			
of Debentures	1,000		
To Interim Dividend	20,000		
To Bal c/d	80,000		
	1,85,500		1,85,500

Calculation of Funds from Operations when net profit is not given :

Sometimes net profit earned by the business may not be given, instead opening and closing credit balances of profit and loss A/c may be provided. In that case, an adjusted P & L A/c is prepared as usual alongwith the opening balance on the credit side and closing balance on the debit side. The balancing figure is considered as funds from operations. If the debit side exceeds the credit of the Adjusted P & L A/c, it is treated as source of funds. If the balancing figure falls on the debit side, it is considered as an application of funds as it is a loss from operations.

Illustration :

From the following data, calculate funds from operations :

	Rs.		Rs.
Sales	4,00,000	Excess provision for Tax	
Cost of goods sold	2,80,000	written back	31,000
Salaries	30,000	Loss on sale of Fixed Assets	60,000
Rent	20,000	Interest on Investments	10,000
Selling Exp.	7,000	Profit on sale of Investments	20,000
Office Expenses	2,000		
Preliminary Exp. written off	9,000	**Profit and Loss A/c :**	
Transfer to General Reserve	21,000	Opening balance	29,000
Postage & telegram	1,000	Closing stock	60,000

Solution :

Adjusted Profit & Loss A/c

	Rs.		Rs.
To Preliminary Exp. written off	9,000	By Bal b/d(opening)	29,000
To Loss on sale of Fixed assets	60,000	By Interest on Investment	10,000
To General Reserve (Transfer)	21,000	By Excess provision for tax	
To Bal c/d (closing)	60,000	written back	31,000
		By Profit on sale of Investments	20,000
		By Funds from operations	
		(Balancing figure)	60,000
	1,50,000		1,50,000

Alternatively,

	Rs.	Rs.
Sales		4,00,000
Less : Cost of goods sold	2,80,000	
Salaries	30,000	
Rent	20,000	
Selling Expenses	7,000	
Office Expenses	2,000	
Postage & telegram	1,000	3,40,000
Funds from Operations		60,000

Step 4 : Preparation of Fund Flow Statement

Fund Flow Statement : While preparing a Fund Flow Statement, funds from operations, increase in non-current liabilities, non-operating (i.e. non-trading) incomes, such as sale of fixed assets, dividends, rent etc. and decrease in working capital are shown as 'sources' of funds.

Loss from operations, redemption or repayment of non-current liabilities, non-trading payments such as purchase of shares, payment of dividends etc. and increase in working capital are shown as 'Application' of funds.

The statement may be prepared either in Report Form or in the Account Form as shown below :–

(Account Form)
Fund Flow Statement

Sources of Funds	Rs.	Application of Funds	Rs.
i) Funds from Operations		i) Loss from Operations	
ii) Issue of Share Capital		ii) Redemption of Shares	
iii) Issue of Debentures		iii) Redemption of Debentures	
iv) Long-term Loans taken		iv) Repayment of long-term Loans	
v) Sale of Investments and other fixed assets		v) Purchase of Investments or other Fixed Assets	
vi) Non-trading Receipts e.g. dividend received		vi) Non-trading Payments e.g. payment of dividend	
vii) Decrease in Working Capital		vii) Increase in Working Capital	

Report Form
Fund Flow Statement

Sources of Funds :
- i) Funds from Operations ....
- ii) Issue of Share Capital (New) ....
- iii) Issue of Debentures (New) ....
- iv) Long-term Loans ....
- v) Sale of Investments / Fixed Assets ....
- vi) Non-trading Receipts ....
- vii) Decrease in Working Capital ....

Total ....

Application of Funds :
- i) Loss from Operations ....
- ii) Redemption of Pref. Shares ....
- iii) Redemption of Debentures ....
- iv) Repayment of Long-term Loans ....

v) Purchase of Investments / Fixed Assets	....
vi) Non-trading Payments	....
vii) Increase in Working Capital	....
Total	....

Important :-

1) The revenue items which are charged or credited to P & L A/c are <u>not taken</u> in the Fund Flow Statement because their net effect i.e. funds from operations is taken in the Fund Flow Statement.

2) Changes in current assets / liabilities are also not shown item-wise in the Fund Flow Statement because their net effect i.e. increase or decrease in working capital is shown in the Fund Flow Statement.

Items which need particular care :

i) Dividend/Rent Received or Receivable : It results in increasing current asset (cash or debtor), but is not operating income.

It will be taken as separate item of source in the fund flow statement.

ii) Transfer back of excess Provision for Taxation :

a) If it is treated as Current liability, it will be taken as a source in the fund flow statement, as it effects change in working capital-current liability i.e. provision, is reduced and credit is given to non-current account i.e. Profit and Loss Account or Profit and Loss Appropriation Account.

b) If it is treated as an internal reserve i.e. non-current account, both the accounts involved being 'non-current' i.e. of same category, the item will not appear in fund flow statement.

iii) Refund of Tax : Though it increases current assets i.e. cash, it is non-operating income, and hence, it will be shown separately as a source in the fund statement.

iv) Profit or Loss on Sale of Fixed Asset :

a) If it is transferred to some reserve, or it is shown on the liabilities/assets side in the balance sheet, it will neither be added back to or deducted from profit nor it will be considered in fund statement.

b) If it is transferred to Profit and Loss Account, only then it is added to/deducted from profit to find out funds from Operations.

(Unless otherwise stated, it may always be presumed that such profit/loss is transferred to Profit & Loss A/c)

v) Proposed Dividend -
A) If it is treated as current liability :

i) It will appear in the Schedule of Working Capital

ii) Payment of dividend against proposed dividend for previous/earlier year will not appear in fund statement as the accounts involved i.e. Cash A/c and Proposed Dividend A/c, are of the same category i.e. 'Current' accounts.

iii) Proposed dividend for current year results in creation of current liability out of Non-current

A/c (i.e. Profit & Loss Appropriation A/c), and hence, it will be shown as application of funds in the fund statement.

B) If it is treated as Internal Reserve :

i) It will not be taken in Schedule of Working Capital.

ii) Payment of dividend against proposed dividend for previous or earlier year will be shown as an application of the funds in the fund flow statement.

vi) Interim Dividend : It will appear as an application of funds in the funds-flow statement.

vii) Repayment of Capital/Debentures at a Premium : In the fund statement, amount of premium is to be treated as outflow of fund i.e. application of fund. If the premium had charged to Profit & Loss A/c, it should be adjusted back to Profit & Loss A/c to find out 'funds from operation' or 'operational flow.' If it was not charged to Profit & Loss A/c, no adjustment to Profit & Loss A/c is to be made.

viii) If there is transfer from 'loans and advances' to fixed assets account, the item concerned is not to be treated as current asset.

ix) Increase in share capital due to issue of bonus shares is not to be treated as 'source.'

x) Increase in case of certain 'Miscellaneous Expenses' is to be treated as 'Application of Funds' or the source of fund is to be reduced by that amount. For e.g. issue of debentures of Rs.10,000 at discount during the year will result in increasing 'Discount on debentures' by Rs.1,000. In this case, instead of showing Rs.1,000 as application, sources of funds from debentures will be shown as Rs.9,000 (and not Rs.10,000).

xi) Important Rules for Fund Flow Statement

Following are the important rules for fund flow statement :

1. Increase in working capital is to be taken as 'Application of funds',
2. Decrease in working capital is to be taken as 'Sources of funds',
3. Increase in fixed assets is to be taken as 'Application of funds',
4. Decrease in fixed assets is to be taken as 'Source of funds',
5. Increase in fixed liability is to be taken as 'Source of funds',
6. Decrease in fixed liability is to be taken as 'Application of funds',
7. Income from operations to be taken as 'Source of funds',
8. Loss from operations is to be taken as 'Application of funds.'

xii) Provision for Taxation : This item is treated in two different ways.

According to first method, it is treated as internal appropriation and hence as 'non-current liability.' It is taken into consideration for calculating the profit made during the year. i.e. added back to net profit arrived at after charging the provision, and tax paid during the year is treated as an application of fund.

According to second method, the provision for taxation made during the year is treated as 'current liability.' Hence, it is not considered, for adjusting the profits made during the year and the payment of tax is not treated as application of fund.

xiii) Flow of Fund : In simple words, it can be explained as movement of funds i.e. incoming of funds from different sources and their disbursement on various items. Thus, a flow of funds effects change in the amount of fund.

Source of Fund : If the change results in the increase of the amount of fund, the transaction effecting such a change is a 'source' of fund.

Application or use of Fund : If a transaction decreases the amount of fund, it is said to be an 'Application' or a 'use' of fund.

Important : If a transaction does not increase or decrease the fund, there is **no flow of fund.**

If all the accounts involved in a transaction belong to the same category i.e. either 'current' or 'non-current' category, there is no flow of fund. For e.g. payment to creditor (both the accounts being of a 'current' category), or conversion of debentures into shares (both the accounts being of a 'non-current' category) does not result into flow of fund. Hence, such transactions, find no place in the fund flow statement.

From the above, it follows that for flow of fund, the accounts involved in a transaction must be of both the categories i.e. 'current' and 'non-current'. For e.g. purchase of a machinery for cash (machinery is a non-current asset, whereas cash is a 'current asset').

Illustrations

Illustration : 1 : From the figures given below prepare a Statement showing application and sources of funds during the year 2008

Balance Sheet as on 31-12....

Liabilities	2007 Rs.	2008 Rs.	Assets	2007 Rs.	2008 Rs.
Equity Share Capital	3,00,000	3,50,000	Fixed Assets (Net)	5,10,000	6,20,000
9% Preference			Investments	30,000	80,000
Share Capital	2,00,000	1,00,000	Current Assets	2,40,000	3,75,000
8% Debentures	1,00,000	2,00,000	Discount on		
Reserves	1,10,000	2,70,000	Debentures	10,000	5,000
Provision for					
Doubtful Debts	10,000	15,000			
Current Liabilities	70,000	1,45,000			
	7,90,000	10,80,000		7,90,000	10,80,000

The provision for Depreciation stood at Rs.1,50,000 on 31st December, 2007, and at Rs.1,90,000 on 31st December, 2008 during the year.

a) Machine costing Rs.70,000 (book value Rs. 40,000) was disposed off for Rs.25,000.

b) Preference share redemption was carried out at a premium of 5%, on 1-1-2008.

e) Dividend at 15% was paid on Equity Shares for the year 2007.

Solution 1   **Statement of changes In Working Capital**

Particulars	2007 Rs.	2008 Rs.	Increase Rs.	Decrease Rs.
Current Assets :	2,40,000	3,75,000	1,35,000	–
Current Liabilities	70,000	1,45,000	–	75,000
Provision for Doubtful Debts	10,000	15,000	–	5,000
Total Current Liabilities	80,000	1,60,000		
Net Working Capital	1,60,000	2,15,000		
(Current Assets - Current Liabilities)				
(A) Increase in Working Capital	*55,000	–	–	55,000
	2,15,000	2,15,000	1,35,000	1,35,000

Working Notes & Accounts

    (S = Sources, A = Application)

1. Increase of Equity Share Capital Rs.50,000 (Source)
2. Decrease in Preference share Capital Rs.1,00,000. The preference Shares of Rs.1,00,000 are redeemed at 5% Premium i.e. Rs.1,00,000 + 5,000 premium. Total Cash paid Rs.1,05,000 (Application)

   Premium on Preference Shares Rs.5,000 is a Loss and taken on debit of P & L A/c.
3. Increase in Debentures Rs.1,00,000 (Source)
4. Increase in Reserves Rs.1,60,000 (P & L Debit)
5. Discount on Debentures is Reduced by Rs.5,000 (10,000-5,000) i.e. written off against P & L A/c.

6)   **Fixed Assets A/c**

	Rs.		Rs.
To Balance B/d (07)	6,60,000	By Transfer to Sale of Machine	70,000
(5,10,000 + Dep. Res. 1,50,000)		By Balance c/d (08)	8,10,000
To Bank (Purchases) (A)	2,20,000	(6,20,000 + Dep. Res. 1,90,000)	
(Balancing)			
	8,80,000		8,80,000

7)   **Machine Sold A/c**

	Rs.		Rs.
To Fixed Assets A/c (Transfer)	70,000	By Depreciation (Accumulated)	30,000
		By Bank (Sold) (S)	25,000
		By Loss on Sale (P & L)	15,000
	70,000		70,000

8) **Provision for Depreciation A/c**

	Rs.		Rs.
To Machine Sold A/c	30,000	By Balance b/d (07)	1,50,000
(Accumulated Transfer)		By Profit & Loss A/c	
To Balance c/d (08)	1,90,000	(Provision made)	70,000
	2,20,000		2,20,000

9) **Profit & Loss A/c**

	Rs.		Rs.
To Transfer to Reserves	1,60,000	By Net Income	
To Premium on Redemption		from Operation (S)	3,00,000
of Preference Shares	5,000		
To Dividend Paid (A)			
(15% on Rs.3,00,000)	45,000		
To Provision for Depreciation	70,000		
To Loss on Sale of Machine	15,000		
To Discount on Debentures			
written off	5,000		
	3,00,000		3,00,000

10) Increase in Investments Rs.50,000, i.e.
Purchase of Investment (A)

Fund Flow Statement
for the year ending 31-12-2008

Source	Rs.	Application	Rs.
Issue of Equity Share Capital (1)	50,000	Redemption of Preference	
Issue of Debenatures (3)	1,00,000	Share Capital	1,05,000
Sale of Machine (7)	25,000	Purchase of fixed Assets (6)	2,20,000
Income from Operations (9)	3,00,000	Increase in Working Capital *	55,000
		Purchase of Investments (10)	50,000
		Dividend on Equity Shares Paid (9)	45,000
	4,75,000		4,75,000

Illustration : 2

From the following Balance Sheet of 'N' Co. Ltd., as on 31st March, 2007 and 2008, you are required to prepare a statement of sources and applications of funds for the year ended 31st March, 2009.

Balance Sheets

Liabilities	2007 Rs.	2008 Rs.	Assets	2007 Rs.	2008 Rs.
Share Capital	1,00,000	1,25,000	Land & Buildings	1,00,000	95,000
General Reserve	25,000	30,000	Plant	75,000	84,500
Profit & Loss A/c	15,250	15,300	Stock	50,000	37,000
Bank Loan	35,000	67,600	Debtors	40,000	32,100
Creditors	75,000	-	Cash	250	300
Provision for			Bank	-	4,000
Taxation	15,000	17,500	Goodwill	-	2,500
	2,65,250	2,55,400		2,65,250	2,55,400

Additional information :

a) Dividend of Rs.11,500 was paid. b) Depreciation written off on plant Rs.7,000. c) Income Tax provision was made during the year Rs.16,500.

Solution 2

Statement of Changes In Working Capital

	2007 Rs.	2008 Rs.	Increase Rs.	Decrease Rs.
Current Assets :				
Stock	50,000	37,000	-	13,000
Debtors	40,000	32,100	-	7,900
Cash	250	300	50	-
Bank	-	4,000	4,000	-
	90,250	73,400		
Current Liabilities :				
Creditors	75,000	-	75,000	-
	75,000	-		
Net Working Capital (CA - CL)	15,250	73,400		
Inerease in Working Capital (A)	58,150	-	-	58,150
	73,400	73,400	79,050	79,050

Working Notes & Accounts

1. Increase in Share Capital Rs.25,000 by issue of Shares. (i.e. Source of Funds)

2. Increase in General Reserve Rs. 5,000 by Transfer From P & L A/c.

3. Increase in Bank Loan Rs. 32,600 (i.e. Source of Funds). [67,600-35,000]

4. Goodwill appears in 2007 only. So, it is an excess amount paid for purchase of Assets. It is Application of Funds Rs. 2,500.

5) Dr.   **Provision for Taxation A/c**   Cr.

	Rs.		Rs.
To Bank (Application) (Balancing)	14,000	By Balance b/d (07)	15,000
		By Profit & Loss A/c	16,500
To Balance c/d (08)	17,500	(Provision made)	
	31,500		31,500

6) Dr.   **Land & Buildings A/c**   Cr.

	Rs.		Rs.
To Balance b/d (07)	1,00,000	By Depreciation (Balancing)	5,000
		By Balance c/d (08)	95,000
	1,00,000		1,00,000

7) Dr.   **Plant A/c**   Cr.

	Rs.		Rs.
To Balance b/d (07)	75,000	By Depreciation	7,000
To Bank (Application) (Purchase) (Balancing)	16,500	By Balance c/d (08)	84,500
	91,500		91,500

8) Dr.   **Profit & Loss A/c**   Cr.

		Rs.		Rs.
To Depreciation :			By Balance b/d (07)	15,250
Plant	7,000		By Income from Operations	45,050
Building	5,000	12,000	(Balancing) (Sources)	
To Dividend paid (Applications)		11,500		
To Provision for Taxation		16,500		
To Transfer to General Reserve		5,000		
To Balance c/d (08)		15,300		
		60,300		60,300

Fund Flow Statement
For the year ending 31-03-2008

Source	Rs.	Application	Rs.
Issue of Shares (1)	25,000	Payment for Goodwill (4)	2,500
Bank Loan Raised (3)	32,600	Payment of Tax (5)	14,000
Income from Operations (8)	45,050	Purchase of Plant (7)	16,500
		Increase in Working Capital	58,150
		Dividend Paid	11,500
	1,02,650		1,02,650

Illustration : 3

You have given the following financial statements of Taj Mahal Estates Ltd. as on 31st March.

Liabilities	2008 Rs.	2007 Rs.	Assets	2008 Rs.	2007 Rs.
Ordinary Shares			Cash at Bank	45,000	1,30,000
of Rs. 100 each	2,30,000	1,97,000	Debtors	1,40,000	90,700
Reserves & Surplus	3,12,000	1,48,000	Stock in trade	1,96,000	1,42,500
Secured loan from Bank	-	87,000	**Fixed Assets**		
Provision for Taxation	1,72,000	65,000	Less Depreciation	6,00,000	3,60,000
Sundry Creditors	2,98,000	2,51,450	Investments	10,000	11,250
			Pre-paid Expenses	21,000	14,000
	10,12,000	7,48,450		10,12,000	7,48,450

The following further information is available from the records :

i) The position in respect of reserves & surplus is as under :

	Rs.
Balance on 1-4-2007	1,48,000
Net Profit for the year	1,98,500
	3,46,500
Less : Dividend	34,500
	3,12,000

ii) On 31-03-2008, the accumulated depreciation on fixed assets was Rs. 1,80,000 and on 31-03-2007 Rs. 1,60,000. Machinery costing Rs. 20,000 which was one half depreciated was discarded and written off in 2008. Depreciation for the year Rs. 30,000.

iii) Investment costing Rs. 5,000 were sold during the year 2008 for Rs. 4,800 and the Government securities of the face value of Rs. 4,000 were purchased during the year for Rs. 3,750. You are required to prepare the following :

1) Statement of source and application of funds.
2) Statement showing in detail the item-wise increase and decrease in the net Working Capital.

(S.U.)

Solution 3

Statement of changes in Working Capital

Particulars	2007 Rs.	2008 Rs.	Increase Rs.	Decrease Rs.
Current Assets :				
Cash at Bank	1,30,000	45,000	-	85,000
Debtors	90,700	1,40,000	49,300	–
Stock-in-trade	1,42,500	1,96,000	53,500	–
Pre-paid Expenses	14,000	21,000	7,000	–
	3,77,200	4,02,000		
Current Liabilities :				
Sundry Creditors	2,51,450	2,98,000	-	46,550
Net Working Capital	1,25,750	1,04,000		
(S) Decrease in Working Capital (S)	-	* 21,750	21,750	
	1,25,750	1,25,750	1,31,550	1,31,550

Working Notes & Accounts

(S = Source; A = Application)

1) Increase in ordinary Share Capital Rs. 33,000 (S)
2) Secured Bank Loan repaid Rs. 87,000 (A)
3) Dividend paid Rs. 34,500 (A)

(4) **Provision for Taxation A/c**

	Rs.		Rs.
To Cash (Tax Paid for year) (A)	65,000	By Balance b/d (07)	65,000
To Balance c/d (08)	1,72,000	By P & L A/c (Provision)	1,72,000
	2,37,000		2,37,000

(5) **Investment A/c**

	Rs.		Rs.
To Balance b/d (07)	11,250	By Bank (Sold) (S)	4,800
To Bank (Purchase of Rs.4,000 (A)	3,750	By Loss on Sale (P & L)	200
		By Balance c/d (08)	10,000
	15,000		15,000

(6)　　　　　　　　　　　**Fixed Assets A/c**

	Rs.		Rs.
To Balance b/d (07)		By Machinery Discarded A/c	20,000
(3,60,000 + Dep. Reserve	5,20,000	By Balance c/d (08)	
Rs. 1,60,000)		(6,00,000 + Dep. Reserve	7,80,000
To Bank (Balancing)		Rs. 1,80,000)	
(Purchase) (A)	2,80,000		
	8,00,000		8,00,000

(7)　　　　　　　　　　　**Machinery Discarded A/c**

	Rs.		Rs.
To Fixed Assets A/c (Transfer)	20,000	By Depreciation (Accumulated)	10,000
		By P & L A/c (written off)	10,000
	20,000		20,000

(8)　　　　　　　　**Depreciation Provision on fixed Assets A/c**

	Rs.		Rs.
To Machinery Discarded A/c		By Balance b/d (07)	1,60,000
(Accumulated)	10,000	By P & L A/c (Provision)	
To Balance c/d (08)	1,80,000	(Balancing)	30,000
	1,90,000		1,90,000

(9)　　　　　　　　　　　**Profit & Loss A/c**

	Rs.		Rs.
To Dividend paid	34,500	By Balance b/d (07)	1,48,000
To Provision for Taxation	1,72,000	By Income from Operations (S)	4,10,700
To Loss on Sale of Investment	200		
To Machinery written off	10,000		
To Provision for Depreciation	30,000		
To Balance c/d (08)	3,12,000		
	5,58,700		5,58,700

Fund Flow Statement
for the year ending 31-03-2008

	Rs.		Rs.
Issue of Ordinary Shares (1)	33,000	Secured Loan Repaid (2)	87,000
Sale of Investment (5)	4,800	Dividend Paid (3)	34,500
Income from Operation (9)	4,10,700	Payment of Tax (4)	65,000
Decrease in Working Capital	* 21,750	Purchase of Investment (5)	3,750
		Purchase of fixed Assets (6)	2,80,000
	4,70,250		4,70,250

Illustration : 4

Flash Light Industries Ltd., presents you with the following Balance Sheets as on 31-03.....

Liabilities	2007 Rs.	2008 Rs.	Assets	2007 Rs.	2008 Rs.
Equity Share Capital	50,000	60,000	Fixed Assets	85,000	1,04,000
6% Redeemable			Investments	10,000	8,000
Preference Share Capital	20,000	–	Preliminary Exp.	4,000	3,000
Capital Redemption			Current Assets	44,000	56,000
Reserve Fund	–	10,000			
General Reserve	10,000	13,000			
Taxation Reserve	7,000	9,000			
P & L A/c	14,000	27,000			
Proposed Equity					
Dividend	5,000	6,000			
Provision for					
Depreciation	18,000	23,000			
Share Premium	5,000	5,000			
Sundry Creditors	14,000	18,000			
	1,43,000	1,71,000		1,43,000	1,71,000

i) During the year 2008, a fixed asset costing Rs. 3,000 (accumulated depreciation Rs. 1,600) was sold for Rs. 1,000.

ii) Tax liability in respect of 2007 came to Rs. 5,500.

iii) Investments costing Rs. 2,000 were realised Rs. 1,800 in 2008.

iv) During the year 2008, proposed dividend was paid in addition to preference dividend upto 30th Sept., 2007, on which date, preference shares were redeemed at a premium of 5%. Prepare a Fund Flow Statement for the year, 2008.   (B.U.)

Solution 4

Statement of changes in Working Capital

Particulars	2007 Rs.	2008 Rs.	Increase Rs.	Decrease Rs.
Current Assets	44,000	56,000	12,000	–
Current Liabilities :				
Sundry Creditors	14,000	18,000	–	4,000
Net Working Capital	30,000	38,000		
Increase in Working Capital (A)	* 8,000	–	–	8,000
	38,000	38,000	12,000	12,000

Working Notes and Accounts

1) Issue of Equity Shares Rs. 10,000 (S)
2) Share premium is unchanged, so do not consider.
3) Capital Redemption Reserve created from P & L A/c Rs. 10,000 (Take to P & L Debit Side)
4) Transfer to General Reserve Rs. 3,000 (P & L Debit)
5) Preliminary expenses written off Rs.1,000 (P & L Debit)

(6)   **Taxation Reserve A/c**

	Rs.		Rs.
To Cash (Paid for 07) (A)	5,500	By Balance b/d (07)	7,000
To Balance c/d (08)	9,000	By P & L A/c (Difference)	
		(Provision made)	7,500
	14,500		14,500

(7)   **Proposed Equity Dividend A/c**

	Rs.		Rs.
To Cash (paid for 07) (A)	5,000	By Balance b/d (07)	5,000
To Balance c/d (08)	6,000	By P & L A/c (Difference)	
		(Provision made)	6,000
	11,000		11,000

(8)   **Provision for Depreciation A/c**

	Rs.		Rs.
To Fixed Assets	1,600	By Balance b/d (07)	18,000
(Dep. on sale of Asset)		By P & L A/c (Difference)	6,600
To Balance c/d (08)	23,000	(Provision made)	
	24,600		24,600

(9)   **Fixed Assets A/c**

	Rs.		Rs.
To Balance b/d (07)	85,000	By Bank (Sale) (S)	1,000
To Bank (Purchase) (A)		By Provision for	
(Difference)	22,000	Depreciation A/c (on Sale)	1,600
		By Loss on Sale	400
		(3,000-1,600-1,000)	
		By Balance c/d (08)	1,04,000
	1,07,000		1,07,000

(10)   **Investment A/c**

	Rs.		Rs.
To Balance b/d (07)	10,000	By Bank (Sale) (S)	1,800
		By Loss on Sale	200
		By Balance c/d (08)	8,000
	10,000		10,000

(11)   **6% Preference Shareholders A/c**

	Rs.		Rs.
To Bank (Redemption) (A)	21,600	By Preference Share Capital	20,000
		By Preference Dividend	
		(for 6 months @ 6%)	600
		(P & L)	
		By Premium on Redemption	
		(P & L)	1,000
	21,600		21,600

(12)   **Profit and Loss A/c**

	Rs.		Rs.
To Capital Redemption Reserve	10,000	By Balance b/d (07)	14,000
To General Reserve	3,000	By Income from Operations (S)	
To Preliminary Expenses	1,000	(Difference)	49,300
To Taxation Reserve	7,500		
To Proposed Equity Dividend	6,000		
To Provision for Depreciation	6,600		
To Loss on Sale of Fixed Assets	400		
To Loss on Sale of Investment	200		
To Preference Dividend	600		
To Premium on Redemption of			
Preference Shares	1,000		
To Balance c/d (08)	27,000		
	63,300		63,300

Fund Flow Statement
for the year ending 31-03-2008

Source	Rs.	Application	Rs.
Issue of Equity Shares (1)	10,000	Payment of Tax (6)	5,500
Sale of Fixed Assets (9)	1,000	Equity Dividend paid (7)	5,000
Sale of Investment (10)	1,800	Purchase of fixed Assets(9)	22,000
Income from Operations (12)	49,300	Redemption of Preference	
		Shares (11)	21,600
		Increase in Working Capital	* 8,000
	62,100		62,100

Illustration : 5

From the following Balance Sheets, prepare a Statement showing Sources and Application of Funds :

Liabilities	2007 Rs.	2008 Rs.	Assets	2007 Rs.	2008 Rs.
Bank Overdraft	1,860	-	Petty Cash	100	160
R.D.D.	800	900	Bank	–	2,080
Provision for Depreciation			Debtors	38,160	42,480
Machinery	17,400	20,700	Stock	49,920	46,470
Furniture	1,360	1,580	Investments (Short-term)	16,000	–
Delivery Vans	7,900	7,600	Machinery	73,600	1,04,800
Sundry Creditors	12,800	11,200	Furniture	4,400	4,800
Provision for Taxation	7,600	9,000	Delivery Vans	14,800	14,400
Debentures	20,000	40,000	Property	–	18,000
Issued Capital	1,10,000	1,19,400	Provision for Discounts		
Calls in Advance	500	-	Receivable	320	280
General Reserve	10,000	14,000			
Appropriation A/c	7,080	9,090			
	1,97,300	2,33,470		1,97,300	2,33,470

During 2007-2008, dividend of Rs. 10,000 had been paid. A delivery van, which had cost Rs. 2,300 and had been depreciated to Rs. 660 had been sold for Rs. 600. Taxes during the year had been paid Rs. 7,000.

Solution 5

Statement of changes in Working Capital

Particulars	2007 Rs.	2008 Rs.	Increase Rs.	Decrease Rs.
Current Assets :				
Petty Cash	100	160	60	–
Bank	-	2,080	2,080	–
Debtors	38,160	42,480	4,320	–
Stock	49,920	46,470	-	3,450
Investments	16,000	-	-	16,000
Provision for Discounts Receivable	320	280	-	40
	1,04,500	91,470		
Current Liabilities :				
Creditors	12,800	11,200	1,600	–
Bank Overdraft	1,860	-	1,860	–
R.D.D.	800	900	-	100
	15,460	12,100		

Particulars	2007 Rs.	2008 Rs.	Increase Rs.	Decrease Rs.
Net Working Capital	89,040	79,370		
Decrease in Working Capital (S)	-	* 9,670	9,670	–
	89,040	89,040	19,590	19,590

Working Notes & Accounts

	Rs.
1) Increase in Share Capital	9,400
Less : Calls in Advance included being cash received last year	500
Source	8,900

2) Issue of Debentures Rs. 20,000 (S)

3) General Reserve increased by Rs. 4,000 (P & L Dr.)

(4) **Delivery Vans A/c**

	Rs.		Rs.
To Balance b/d (07)	14,800	By Provision for Depreciation of Van (Transfer 2,300-660)	1,640
To Bank (Purchase) (A)		By Bank (Sale) (S)	600
(Difference)	1,900	By Loss on Sale (2,300-1,640-600)	60
		By Balance c/d (08)	14,400
	16,700		16,700

(5) **Provision for Depreciation of Vans A/c**

	Rs.		Rs.
To Vans A/c (Transfer on Sale)	1,640	By Balance b/d (07)	7,900
		By P & L A/c (Provision)	
To Balance c/d (08)	7,600	(Difference)	1,340
	9,240		9,240

6) Depreciation of Machinery provided in this year Rs. 3,300. (20,700 - 17,400)

7) Depreciation of Furniture provided in this year Rs. 220 (1,580 - 1,360)

(8) **Provision for Taxation A/c**

	Rs.		Rs.
To Bank (paid) (A)	7,000	By Balance b/d (07)	7,600
To Balance c/d (08)	9,000	By P & L A/c (Difference)	8,400
	16,000		16,000

(9) P & L (Appropriation) A/c

		Rs.		Rs.
To General Reserve		4,000	By Balance b/d (07)	7,080
To Depreciation :			By Income from Operations (S)	
Vans	1,340		(Difference)	29,330
Machinery	3,300			
Furniture	220	4,860		
To Dividend (A)		10,000		
To Provision for Taxation		8,400		
To Loss on Sale of Vans		60		
To Balance c/d (08)		9,090		
		36,410		36,410

Fund Flow Statement
(for the year ending 31-03-2008)

Source	Rs.	Application	Rs.
Issue of Share Capital (1)	8,900	Purchase of Vans (4)	1,900
Issue of Debentures (2)	20,000	Payment of Tax (8)	7,000
Sale of Vans (4)	600	Payment of Dividend (9)	10,000
Income from Operations (9)	29,330	Purchase of Machinery	
Decrease in Working Capital	9,670	(1,04,800 - 73,600)	31,200
		Purchase of Property	18,000
		Purchase of Furniture	
		(4,800 - 4,400)	400
	68,500		68,500

Illustration : 6 - Following are the summarised Balance Sheets of 'T & T' Ltd., as at 31st Dec, 2008 and 31st March, 2009.

	2007-08 Rs.	2008-09 Rs.
Sundry Creditors	39,500	41,135
Bills Payable	33,780	11,525
Bank Overdraft	59,510	—
Provision for Taxation	40,000	50,000
Reserves	50,000	50,000
Profit & Loss Account	39,690	41,220
Share Capital	2,00,000	2,60,000
Total	4,62,480	4,53,880

	2007-08 Rs.	2008-09 Rs.
Cash at Bank	2,500	2,700
Sundry Debtors	85,175	72,625
Sundry Advances	2,315	735
Stock	1,11,040	97,370
Land and Building	1,48,500	1,44,250
Plant and Machinery	1,12,950	1,16,200
Goodwill	–	20,000
Total	4,62,480	4,53,880

Following additional information is obtained from General Ledger.

1) During the year ended 31st Dec., 2008, an interim dividend of Rs. 26,000 was paid.
2) The assets of another Company were purchased for Rs. 60,000, payable in fully paid shares of the Company. These assets consisted of Stock Rs. 21,640 Machinery Rs. 18,360, and Goodwill Rs. 20,000. In addition, sundry purchases of Plant were made totalling Rs. 5,650.
3) Income Tax paid during the year amounted to Rs. 25,000.
4) The net profit for the year before tax was Rs. 62,530.

You are required to prepare a statement showing the Sources and Application of Funds for the year 2008-09, and a Schedule setting out the changes in Working Capital.   (S.U.)

Solution : 6

T & T Ltd.
Changes in Working Capital Statement

Particulars	2007-08 Rs.	2008-09 Rs.	Increase Rs.	Decrease Rs.
Current Assets :				
Cash at Bank	2,500	2,700	200	–
Sundry Debtors	85,175	72,625	-	12,550
Sundry Advances	2,315	735	-	1,580
Stock	1,11,040	97,370	-	13,670
Current Assets Total	2,01,030	1,73,430		
Current Liabilities :				
Sundry Creditors	39,500	41,135	-	1,635
Bills Payable	33,780	11,525	22,255	–
Bank Overdraft	59,510	-	59,510	
Current Liabilities Total	1,32,790	52,660		

Particulars	2007-08 Rs.	2008-09 Rs.	Increase Rs.	Decrease Rs.
Working Capital Increase in Working Capital (A)	68,240 52,530	1,20,770 -	-	52,530
	1,20,770	1,20,770	81,965	81,965

Working Notes & Accounts :

		Rs.
1)	Increase in Share Capital	60,000
	Less : Shares issued for fixed Assets purchased	
	i.e. Machinery Rs. 18,360	
	Goodwill Rs. 20,000	38,360
	Increase in Share Capital (S)	21,640

(For Current Asset/Closing Stock)

2) **Reserves :** There is neither increase nor decrease. in the Reserves, hence, it is not affecting Profit & Loss A/c.

3) **Goodwill :** There is increase in G.W. this year by Rs. 20,000. It would have been an item of Application, if shares would not have been issued. But here, for purchase of Goodwill, shares are issued and the increase in G.W. is cancelled against the increase in Share Capital (both fixed items).

(4)   **Land & Building A/c**

	Rs.		Rs.
To Balance b/d	1,48,500	By Depreciation (presumed) By Balance c/d	4,250 1,44,250
	1,48,500		1,48,500

(5) Dr.   **Plant & Machinery A/c**   **Cr.**

	Rs.		Rs.
To Balance b/d To Bank (A) To Share Capital A/c	1,12,950 5,650 18,360	By Depreciation (presumed) By Balance c/d	20,760 1,16,200
	1,36,960		1,36,960

(6) Dr.   **Provision for Taxation A/c**   **Cr.**

	Rs.		Rs.
To Cash (Tax Paid) (A)	25,000	By Bal. b/d	40,000
To Balance c/d	50,000	By p & L A/c (Provision)	35,000
	75,000		75,000

(7) Dr.   **Goodwill A/c**   **Cr.**

	Rs.		Rs.
To Share Capital	20,000	By Balance c/d	20,000
	20,000		20,000

(8) Dr.   **Share Capital A/c**   **Cr.**

	Rs.		Rs.
		By Bal. b/d	2,00,000
To Balance c/d	2,60,000	By Current Assets	
		(Stock purchased) (S)	21,640
		By Machinery (fixed)	18,360
		By Goodwill (fixed)	20,000
	2,60,000		2,60,000

(9) Dr.   **Profit & Loss A/c**   **Cr.**

		Rs.		Rs.
To Depreciation :			By Bal. b/d	39,690
Plant & Machinery	20,760		By Income from	
Land & Building	4,250	25,010	Operations (S)	87,540
To Provision for Tax		35,000		
To Interim Dividend		26,000		
To Bal. c/d		41,220		
		1,27,230		1,27,230

Fund Flow Statement

Source	Rs.	Application	Rs.
Income from Operations (9)	87,540	Income tax paid (6)	25,000
Issue of Share Capital		Interim Dividend paid	26,000
For Current Assets only (1)	21,640	Purchase of Plant (5)	5,650
		Increase in Working Capital	52,530
	1,09,180		1,09,180

Illustration : 7

The comparative Balance Sheets of 'Z' Ltd., as at 31st Dec., for the years 2007 and 2008 were as follows :–

Liabilities	2008 Rs.	2007 Rs.	Assets	2008 Rs.	2007 Rs.
Share Capital	50,000	45,000	Cash	11,200	8,500
Retained Earnings	13,950	16,275	Accounts Receivable	21,300	23,500
Provision for			Stock	35,000	30,600
Doubtful Debts	1,350	1,425	Sinking Fund		
Sinking Fund	16,000	12,000	Investments	16,000	12,000
Accounts Payable	15,000	18,000	Land	10,000	10,000
Loan on Mortgage	40,000	40,000	Building	60,000	60,000
Notes Payable	10,000	7,500	Furniture & Fixtures	8,000	7,000
Accumulated Depreciation:					
Building	12,000	9,000			
Furniture & Fixtures	3,200	2,400			
	1,61,500	1,51,600		1,61,500	1,51,600

You are given the following further information :–
i) The net profit for 2008 amounted to Rs. 6,675.
ii) A dividend amounting to Rs. 5,000 was paid during the year.

Prepare a schedule of changes in Working Capital and a statement of Sources and Application of Funds.

Solution 7

Schedule of changes in Working Capital

Particulars	2007 Rs.	2008 Rs.	Changes in Working Capital Increase Rs.	Changes in Working Capital Decrease Rs.
Current Assets				
Cash	8,500	11,200	2,700	–
Accounts Receivable	23,500	21,300	–	2,200
Stock	30,600	35,000	4,400	–
Total (A)	62,600	67,500		

Particulars	2007 Rs.	2008 Rs.	Increase Rs.	Decrease Rs.
Current Liabilities				
* Provision for Doubtful Debts	1,425	1,350	75	–
Accounts Payable	18,000	15,000	3,000	–
Notes Payable	7,500	10,000	–	2,500
Total (B)	26,925	26,350		
Working Capital (A-B)	35,675	41,150		
Increase in Working				
Capital (i.e. 41,150-35,675)	5,475			5,475
	41,150	41,150	10,175	10,175

(* Provisions against current assets, such as provision for doubtful debts or for discount on debtors, provision for loss of stock etc. may be treated as current liabilities, as they reduce the amount of current assets)

Fund Flow Statement

	Rs.
Sources	
Funds from operations	10,475
Issue of Share capital	5,000
	15,475
Application	
Payment of Dividend	5,000
Sinking Fund Investments	4,000
Furniture and Fixture	1,000
	10,000
Increase in Working Capital	5,475
	15,475

Note -   Funds from Operations –

	Rs.
Net Profit for the year	6,675
Add :- Depreciation charged during the year	
Building (12000 - 9000)	3,000
Furniture (3200 - 2400)	800
	= 10,475

Illustration : 8

The comparative Balance Sheets of Bharat Trading Corporation Ltd., as on 31st March, 2008 and 31st March, 2009, were as under :

Balance Sheets as on

Liabilities	31-3-08 Rs.	31-3-09 Rs.	Assets	31-3-08 Rs.	31-3-09 Rs.
Share Capital	3,60,000	4,00,000	Fixed Assets	4,80,000	5,20,000
General Reserve	1,10,000	60,000	Less : Depreciation	1,08,000	1,40,000
Surplus in P & L A/c	20,450	33,450	todate	3,72,000	3,80,000
Current Liabilities			Investments at		
Sundry Creditors	1,33,650	1,95,350	Cost	1,00,000	50,000
Provision for Taxation	50,000	32,000	Stocks	55,600	90,500
Proposed Dividend	28,800	15,000	Sundry Debtors	1,18,300	1,67,800
			Cash and Bank		
			Balance	49,800	47,500
			Preliminary Expenses	7,200	–
	7,02,900	7,35,800		7,02,900	7,35,800

Additional Information

a) The net profits for the year' 08-09 (after making provision for taxation Rs. 32,000, writing off preliminary expenses Rs. 7,200 and providing depreciation Rs. 40,000) amounted to Rs. 38,000.

b) The Company sold during the year, old machinery costing Rs. 9000 for Rs. 3000. The accumulated depreciation on the sold machinery was Rs. 8,000.

c) A portion of Company's investment has become worthless and was written off to general reserve. The cost of these investments was Rs. 50,000.

d) During the year, the Company paid an interim dividend of Rs. 10,000 and Directors have recommended a final dividend of Rs. 15,000 for the year 2008-09.

Prepare a 'Statement of 'Sources and Application of Funds' for the year ended 31st March, 2009 and a 'Schedule of Working Capital Changes.'

Solution 8

Schedule of Working Capital changes

Particulars	31-3-08 Rs.	31-3-09 Rs.	Changes in Working Capital Increase Rs.	Changes in Working Capital Decrease Rs.
Current Assets				
Stock	55,600	90,500	34,900	
Debtors	1,18,300	1,67,800	49,500	
Cash and Bank Balance	49,800	47,500	--	2,300
Total	2,23,700	3,05,800		
Current Liabilities				
Sundry Creditors	1,33,650	1,95,350	-	61,700
Provision for Taxation	50,000	32,000	18,000	
Proposed Dividend	28,800	15,000	13,800	
Total	2,12,450	2,42,350		
Working Capital	11,250	63,450		
Increase in W.C.	52,200			52,200
	63,450	63,450	1,16,200	1,16,200

Statement of Sources and Application of Funds

Sources	Rs.	Application	Rs.
Funds from Operations	83,200	Purchase of Fixed Assets	49,000
Issue of Capital	40,000	Payment of Interim Dividend	10,000
Sale of Machinery	3,000	Proposed Dividend	15,000
		Increase in W.C.	52,200
	1,26,200		1,26,200

Working Notes

1) Funds from Operations -

		Rs.
Net Profit for the year as given		38,000
Add : Preliminary expenses charged	7,200	
Depreciation charged	40,000	47,200
		85,200
Less : Profit on sale of Machinery		2,000
(Cost 9,000 Less Depreciation 8,000 = 1,000 Book		
Value Sale price 3,000-1,000 Book Value)		
Fund from Operations		83,200

(Since, provision for taxation and proposed dividend are treated as current liabilities as stated in the problem, they are not added back to profit)

Similarly, proposed dividend for last year and payment of dividend for last year do not affect funds as both the accounts are 'current' accounts.

2) Purchase of Fixed Asset :

Opening Balance as given at cost	4,80,000
Less : Machinery sold cost	9,000
	4,71,000
Less : Cost price at the end	5,20,000
Purchases of Machinery	49,000

OR

Machinery A/c

	Rs.		Rs.
To Balance b/d	3,72,000	By Cash (Sale)	3,000
To Profit & Loss	2,000	By Depreciation	40,000
To Cash (Balancing figure)	49,000	By Balance c/d	3,80,000
	4,23,000		4,23,000

Illustration : 9

From the following balance sheets of 'A' Ltd., make out –

i) Statement of change in the Working Capital, and

ii) Fund Flow Statement

Balance Sheets

Liabilities	2007 Rs.	2008 Rs.	Assets	2007 Rs.	2008 Rs.
Equity Share Capital	3,00,000	4,00,000	Goodwill	1,15,000	90,000
8% Redeemable			Land & Buildings	2,00,000	1,70,000
Preference Share Captial	1,50,000	1,00,000	Plant	80,000	2,00,000
General Reserve	40,000	70,000	Debtors	1,60,000	2,00,000
Profit & Loss A/c	30,000	48,000	Stock	77,000	1,09,000
Proposed Dividend	42,000	50,000	Bills Receivable	20,000	30,000
Creditors	55,000	83,000	Cash in Hand	15,000	10,000
Bills Payable	20,000	16,000	Cash at Bank	10,000	8,000
Provision for Taxation	40,000	50,000			
	6,77,000	8,17,000		6,77,000	8,17,000

Additional information :

i) Depreciations of Rs. 10,000 and Rs. 20,000 have been charged on plant and buildings respectively, in 1970.

ii) An interim dividend of Rs. 20,000 has been paid in 2008.

iii) Income Tax Rs. 35,000 has been paid during the year 2008.

Solution 9

Working Notes

1. Funds from Operations

Adjusted Profit & Loss A/c

		Rs.		Rs.
To Goodwill (written off)		25,000	By Balance (Opening)	30,000
(1,15,000-90,000)			By Funds from Operations	2,18,000
To Depreciation			(Balancing figure)	
Buildings	20,000			
Plant	10,000	30,000		
To Provision for Taxation		45,000		
To General Reserve		30,000		
To Interim Dividend		20,000		
To Proposed Dividend		50,000		
To Balance (Closing)		48,000		
		2,48,000		2,48,000

2. Provision for Taxation charged during the year

	Rs.
Last year's provision	40,000
Less tax paid during the year	35,000
Excess provision	5,000
Provision required for Current year	50,000
Less Last year's balance as above	5,000
Amount charged to P & L during the year	45,000

3. Land & Building Account

	Rs.		Rs.
To Opening Balance	2,00,000	By Depreciation	20,000
		By Bank (Sale balancing figure)	10,000
		By Closing Balance	1,70,000
	2,00,000		2,00,000

4. Plant A/c

	Rs.		Rs.
To Opening Balance	80,000	By Depreciation	10,000
To Bank		By Closing balance	2,00,000
(purchase balancing figure)	1,30,000		
	2,10,000		2,10,000

Statement of changes in Working Capital

Particulars	2007 Rs.	2008 Rs.	Changes in Working Capital Increase Rs.	Changes in Working Capital Decreace Rs.
Current Assets				
Debtors	1,60,000	2,00,000	40,000	-
Stock	77,000	1,09,000	32,000	-
Bills Receivable	20,000	30,000	10,000	-
Cash in Hand	15,000	10,000	-	5,000
Cash at Bank	10,000	8,000	-	2,000
Total	2,82,000	3,57,000		

Particulars	2007 Rs.	2008 Rs.	Changes in Working Capital Increase Rs.	Changes in Working Capital Decreace Rs.
Current Liabilities				
Creditors	55,000	83,000	-	28,000
Bills Payable	20,000	16,000	4,000	
Total	75,000	99,000		
Working Capital	2,07,000	2,58,000		
Increase in Working Capital	51,000			51,000
	2,58,000	2,58,000	86,000	86,000

Funds Flow Statement

		Rs.
Sources		
Funds from Operations		2,18,000
Issue of Equity Share Capital		1,00,000
Sale of building		10,000
	Total	3,28,000
Application		
Redemption of Pref. Share Capital		50,000
Purchase of Plant		1,30,000
Payment of Dividend		
i) For last year	42,000	
ii) Interim	20,000	62,000
Payment of Tax		35,000
Increase in Working Capital		51,000
		3,28,000

(**Note :** The difference in treatment of provision for taxation, proposed dividend, payment of tax and dividend from Illustrations No. 2 and 3. In illustration No. 2, provisions are treated as No. 2. Current liabilities, in the present Illustration are treated as 'non-current' liabilities)

Illustration : 10

Following are the summerised balance sheets of Anmol Ltd., as on 31st Dec., 2007 and 2008.

Liabilities	2007 Rs.	2008 Rs.	Assets	2007 Rs.	2008 Rs.
Share Capital	2,00,000	2,50,000	Land and Building	2,00,000	1,90,000
General Reserve	50,000	60,000	Machinery	1,50,000	1,68,000
Profit & Loss	30,500	30,600	Stock	1,00,000	74,000
Bank Loan	70,000	–	Sundry Debtors	78,200	64,000
(Long term)			Pre-paid Insurance	1,800	1,200
Sundry Creditors	1,40,000	1,30,000	Cash Balance	500	600
Outstanding Expenses	10,000	5,200	Bills Receivable	–	8,000
			Goodwill	–	5,000
Provision for Taxation	30,000	35,000			
	5,30,500	5,10,800		5,30,500	5,10,800

Additional information

During the year 2008 –

i) Dividend of Rs. 20,000 was paid

ii) Following assets were purchased from other company. Stock of Rs. 10,000 and Machinery of Rs. 35,000. Purchase price paid by issue of shares of Rs. 50,000.

iii) Depreciation written off machinery Rs. 15,000

iv) Loss on sale of machinery Rs. 600 was charged to General Reserve.

v) Income Tax provided during the year was Rs. 32,000.

Solution 10
Working Notes

Machinery A/c

	Rs.		Rs.
To Balance	1,50,000	By Depreciation	15,000
To Share Capital (Purchase)	35,000	By General Reserve (Loss on Sale)	600
		By Cash (Sale-Balancing figure)	1,400
		By Balance c/d	1,68,000
	1,85,000		1,85,000

2. Depreciation of Building
   Opening Balance 2,00,000 Less closing 1,90,000 = Depr. 10,000
3. Payment of Income tax during the year

Closing Provision	Rs. 35,000
Less : Provision made during the year	32,000
Balance brought forward from Previous year's Provision	3,000

Hence, last year's provision 30,000 Less savings 3,000
= Tax paid Rs. 27,000.

4. Goodwill = Price paid for assets taken 50,000 less value of assets taken 45,000 = Goodwill 5,000

5. Addition to General Reserve = Closing Balance 50,000 + Rs. 600 loss of machinery written off = 50,600 - 40,000 Opening Balance = 10,600

Adjusted Profit & Loss A/c

		Rs.		Rs.
To General Reserve		10,600	By Opening Balance	30,500
To Proposed Dividend		20,000	By Funds from Operations	87,700
To Provision for			(Balancing figure)	
Income Tax		32,000		
To Depreciation				
Building	10,000			
Machinery	15,000	25,000		
To Closing Balance		30,600		
		1,18,200		1,18,200

Statement of changes in Working Capital

			Changes in W.C.	
Particulars	2007 Rs.	2008 Rs.	Increase Rs.	Decrease Rs.
Current Assets				
i) Stock	1,00,000	74,000	-	26,000
ii) Debtors	78,200	64,000	-	14,200
iii) Pre-paid Insurance	1,800	1,200	-	600
iv) Cash	500	600	100	-
v) Bills Receivable	–	8,000	8,000	-
	1,80,500	1,47,800		
Current Liabilities				
i) Creditors	1,40,000	1,30,000	10,000	
ii) Outstanding Expenses	10,000	5,200	4,800	
	1,50,000	1,35,200		
Working Capital	30,500	12,600		
Decrease in Working Capital		17,900	17,900	
	30,500	30,500	40,800	40,800

Statement of Sources & Application of Funds

Sources	Rs.	Applications	Rs.
Funds from Operations	87,700	Payment of Bank	70,000
Shares	10,000	Payment of Tax	27,000
Sale of machine	1,400	Payment of Dividend	20,000
Decrease in W.C.	17,900		
	1,17,000		1,17,000

Notes :

The total amount of shares issued during the year is Rs. 50,000, whereas in the fund flow statement, the source from shares is shown Rs. 10,000 only. As the remaining amount of Rs. 40,000 is used for purchase of machinery and goodwill, all the items i.e. shares, machinery and goodwill relate to the same category i.e. 'non-current' and hence they do not appear in fund flow statement. In the case of purchase of stock, the item stock is of 'current' category, and the shares is the item of 'non-current' type. Hence this amount is shown in the fund-flow statement.

Some authors are of the opinion that full amount of shares be shown as source and purchase of machinery and goodwill as application of funds. They plead that the reader of the fund flow statement wants to know both the aspects i.e. acquisition of assets and creation of liabilities. But, this treatment is not proper when we consider funds flow statement from the view point of 'Working Capital' concept.

Illustration : 11

The summarised Balance Sheets of 'AB' Ltd., are set out below :

Balance Sheets

Liabilities	31-12-07 Rs.	31-12-08 Rs.	Assets	31-12-07 Rs.	31-12-08 Rs.
Equity Share Capital (Shares of Rs. 10 each, fully paid)	1,00,000	2,00,000	**Fixed Assets** Building at Cost Plant & Machinery at	60,000	70,000
General Reserve	-	10,000	Cost	50,000	55,000
Share Premium	2,000	12,000	Investments	5,000	45,000
Profit & Loss	10,000	14,000	**Current Assets**		
5% Debentures	1,00,000	50,000	Stock	80,000	1,00,000
Current Liabilities			Bills Receivable	5,000	13,000
Loan	20,000	-	Debtors	58,000	75,000
Bills Payable	15,000	7,000	Cash in Hand	7,000	2,000
Creditors	20,000	40,000	Cash at Bank	40,000	30,000
Accrued Expenses	5,000	7,000	Pre-paid Expenses	2,000	3,000
			Miscellaneous		

Liabilities	31-12-07 Rs.	31-12-08 Rs.	Assets	31-12-07 Rs.	31-12-08 Rs.
Provisions			**Expenditure**		
Provision for Depreciation on Building	25,000	35,000	Preliminary Expenses Loss on sale of Plant	5,000 -	- 2,000
Depreciation on Plant & Machinery	15,000	20,000			
	3,12,000	3,95,000		3,12,000	3,95,000

Profit & Loss Account for the year 2008 is also given

Profit & Loss Account

	Rs.		Rs.
To Depreciation	19,000	By Trading Profit	46,500
To Debenture Interest	2,500	By Balance b/f from	10,000
To Preliminary Expenses	5,000	last year	
To General Reserve	10,000		
To Interim Dividend paid	6,000		
To Balance	14,000		
	56,500		56,500

Further information

1. Debentures were redeemed on 1-7-2008 and the debentureholders were paid as follows :

   a) Rs. 22,500 plus amount of accrued interest in cash.

   b) 2,500 equity shares of Rs. 10 each, issued as fully paid at a premium of Re. 1 per share.

2. The balance of the equity shares were issued for cash at a premium of Re. 1 per share.

3. Certain machinery was sold during 2008 for which the following entry was made.

Cash Account A/c	Dr. Rs. 6,000
Provision for Depreciation A/c	Dr. Rs. 4,000
Loss on sale of Plant A/c	Dr. Rs. 2,000
To Plants & Machinery A/c	Rs.12,000

   Prepare a statement showing the sources and applications of funds during the year, 2008. Also, prepare the statement showing changes in Working Capital.

Solution 11

Working Notes :

1. Funds from Operations

Adjusted Profit & Loss A/c

	Rs.		Rs.
To Depreciation	19,000	By Opening Balance	10,000
To Preliminary Expenses	5,000	By Funds From Operations	44,000
To Interim Dividend	6,000		
To General Reserve	10,000		
To Balance c/d	14,000		
	54,000		54,000

2) Purchase of Builiding = Closing Balance 70,000 - Op. Bal. 60,000   = 10,000

3) Purchase of Machinery = Closing Balance   55,000

     Less =   Opening Bal.   50,000

              Less Sales   12,000   38,000

                     =   17,000   **Rs.**

4) Increase in Capital i.e. fresh issue =   1,00,000

    Out of this, issued for redemption of Debentures.   25,000

    Issued for cash =   75,000

Statement showing changes in Working Capital

			Changes in W.C.	
Particulars	**2007 Rs.**	**2008 Rs.**	**Increase Rs.**	**Decrease Rs.**
Current Assets				
Stock	80,000	1,00,000	20,000	–
Bills Receivable	5,000	13,000	8,000	–
Debtors	58,000	75,000	17,000	–
Cash in Hand	7,000	2,000	–	5,000
Cash at Bank	40,000	30,000	–	10,000
Pre-paid Expenses	2,000	3,000	1,000	–
	1,92,000	2,23,000		

	2007 Rs.	2008 Rs.	Changes in W.C. Increase Rs.	Decrease Rs.
Current Liabilities				
Loan	20,000	–	20,000	–
Bills Payable	15,000	7,000	8,000	
Creditors	20,000	40,000	–	20,000
Accrued Expenses	5,000	7,000	–	2,000
	60,000	54,000		
Working Capital	1,32,000	1,69,000	–	–
Increase in Working Capital	37,000	–	–	37,000
	1,69,000	1,69,000	74,000	74,000

Statement of Sources & Application of Funds

	Rs.
Sources	
Funds from Operations	44,000
Issue of Shares	75,000
Share Premium	7,500
Sale of Machinery	6,000
	1,32,500
Application	
Repayment of Debentures	22,500
Purchase of Machinery	17,000
Purchase of Building	10,000
Purchase of Investments	40,000
Payment of Interim Dividend	6,000
Increase in Working Capital	37,000
	1,32,500

Illustration : 12

From the following balances as on 31st December, 2007 and 2008, prepare a Fund Statement:

Liabilities	2007 Rs.	2008 Rs.
Share Capital	2,00,000	3,00,000
Share Premium	–	10,000
Capital Reserve - Profit on redemption of Debentures	–	1,000
Profit and Loss Account Balance b/f	40,000	40,000
Profit for the year	–	45,000
5% Debentures	1,00,000	75,000
Sundry Creditors	60,000	1,04,000
Taxation Account	20,000	5,000
Proposed Dividends	10,000	10,000
	4,30,000	5,90,000

Assets	2007 Rs.		2008 Rs.
Buildings at Cost		1,50,000	2,30,000
Plant and Machinery at Cost	2,60,000		3,20,000
Less Depreciation	85,000	1,75,000	95,000	2,25,000
Shares in Subsidiary Company		20,000	20,000
Stock		45,000	49,000
Sundry Debtors		15,000	18,000
Bank		25,000	48,000
		4,30,000	5,90,000

During the year 2008, Plant costing Rs. 15,000 (accumulated depreciation thereon Rs. 8,000) was sold for Rs. 5,000, the loss on sale being charged to Profit and Loss Account.

Solution 12

Working Notes :

1) Statement showing changes in Working Capital		
	2007 Rs.	2008 Rs.
Stock	45,000	49,000
Debtors	15,000	18,000
Bank	25,000	48,000
	85,000	1,15,000
Creditors	60,000	1,04,000
Provision for Taxation	20,000	5,000
	80,000	1,09,000
Working Capital	5,000	6,000
Increase	1,000	–
	6,000	6,000

2) **Profit for the year**

	Rs.
Net Profit as per Balance Sheet	45,000
Add : Loss on sale of Plant	2,000
	47,000
Add : Proposed Dividend	10,000
	57,000

3) **Buildings Account**

	Rs.		Rs.
To Balance b/f	1,50,000	By Balance c/d	2,30,000
To Purchases	80,000		
	2,30,000		2,30,000

4) **Plant Account**

	Rs.		Rs.
To Balance b/f	2,60,000	By Sale	5,000
To Purchases	75,000	By Dep. provision	8,000
		By Loss on Sale	2,000
		By Balance c/d	3,20,000
	3,35,000		3,35,000

5) **Provision for Depreciation on Plant Account**

	Rs.		Rs.
To Plant A/c	8,000	By Balance b/f	85,000
To Balance c/d	95,000	By Depreciation	18,000
	1,03,000		1,03,000

Taxation account balances are treated as current liabilities as there is no indication in the problem as to the amount of taxation paid and hence included in the statement of working capital.

The provision of proposed dividend appearing in the opening balance sheet has been shown in the aplication as payment. The closing balance being provision for the year has been charged to the adjusted profit and loss account to arrive at the profit from operations. Alternatively, the two balances may be included in the working capital statement.

Statement showing Source and Application of Funds during the year ended 31st December, 2008

	Rs.	Rs.
Funds provided by		
Profit for the year (2)	57,000	–
Add : Non-cash item - Depreciation (5)	18,000	75,000
Share issue proceeds	1,00,000	
Share premium	10,000	1,10,000
Sale of Plant	–	5,000
		1,90,000
Funds applied by		
Purchase of Buildings (3)	80,000	–
Purchase of Plant (4)	75,000	–
Debentures repaid (1,00,000 - 76,000)	24,000	1,79,000
Dividends paid		10,000
Increase in Working Capital (1)		1,000
		1,90,000

Illustration : 13

From the following Balance Sheets as at 1st January and 31st December, 2008, prepare a Movement of Funds Statement showing the increase or decrease in Working Capital.

Liabilities	1st Jan. 2008 Rs.	31st Dec. 2008 Rs.	Assets	1st Jan. 2008 Rs.	31st Dec 2008 Rs.
Equity Share capital	1,00,000	1,20,000	Land & Building	55,400	1,13,200
Share Premium	–	10,000	Machinery	35,600	51,300
General Reserve	6,000	11,000	Furniture & Fittings	2,400	2,500
Profit & Loss Account	7,500	20,700	Stock	36,500	38, 000
5% Debentures	–	26,000	Sundry Debtors	32,100	38,000
Sundry Creditors	33,500	36,400	Bank	4,800	4,000
Provision for Taxation	9,800	10,900			
Proposed Dividend	10,000	12,000			
	1,66,800	2,47,000		1,66,800	2,47,000

Depreciation written off during the year :	Rs.
Machinery	12,000
Furniture & Fittings	400

Solution 13

Movement of Fund Statement for the year ending 31st December, 2008

	Rs.	Rs.
Sources		
Share Capital issued	20,000	
Share premium received	10,000	
Debentures issued	26,000	
Profit from Operations	30,600	
	86,600	
Application		
Increase in Working Capital	600	
Additions to Land & Building	57,800	
Additions to Machinery	27,700	
Additions to Furniture	500	
	86,600	

Statement showing changes in Working Capital

	1-1-08	31-12-08
Stock	36,500	38,000
Sundry Debtors	32,100	38,000
Bank	4,800	4,000
	73,400	80,000
Sundry Creditors	33,500	36,400
Provision for Taxation	9,800	10,900
Proposed Dividend	10,000	12,000
	53,300	59,300
Working Capital	20,100	20,700
Increase	600	–
	20,700	20,700

Machinery Account

	Rs.		Rs.
To Balance b/d	35,600	By Depreciation	12,000
To Additions	27,700	By Balance c/d	51,300
	63,300		63,300

Furniture and Fittings Account

	Rs.		Rs.
To Balance b/d	2,400	By Depreciation	400
To Additions	500	By Balance c/d	2,500
	2,900		2,900

Profit and Loss Account

	Rs.		Rs.
To Depreciation	12,400	By Balance	7,500
To Reserve	5,000	By Profit	30,600
To Balance	20,700		
	38,100		38,100

Illustration : 14

The following are the summarised Balance Sheets of 'X' Ltd., as at 31st March, 2007 and 2008.

2007

Liabilities	Rs.	Assets	Rs.
Share Capital	4,50,000	Fixed Assets	4,00,000
General Reserve	3,00,000	Investments	50,000
Profit and Loss Account	56,000	Stock	2,40,000
Sundry Creditors	1,68,000	Sundry Debtors	2,10,000
Provision for Taxation	75,000	Bank	1,49,000
	10,49,000		10,49,000

2008

Liabilities	Rs.	Assets	Rs.
Share Capital	4,50,000	Fixed Assets	3,20,000
General Reserve	3,10,000	Investments	60,000
Profit and Loss Account	68,000	Stock	2,10,000
Mortgage Loan	2,70,000	Sundry Debtors	4,55,000
Sundry Creditors	1,34,000	Bank	1,97,000
Provision for Taxation	10,000		
	12,42,000		12,42,000

Additional information available

1. Investments costing Rs. 8,000 were sold during the year for Rs. 8,500 and further investments were purchased during the year for Rs. 18,000.
2. The net profit for the year was Rs. 62,000 after charging depreciation on fixed assets Rs. 70,000 for the year and provision for taxation Rs. 10,000.
3. During the year, part of fixed assets costing Rs. 10,000 was disposed off for Rs. 12,000 and the profit is included in the profit and loss account.
4. Dividend paid during the year amounted to Rs. 40,000.

Prepare a statement of the Source and Application of Funds for the year ended 31st March, 2008.

Solution 14

Statement showing Source and Application of Funds
during the year ended 31st March, 2008

	Rs.
Sources	
Profit for the year	1,39,500
Sale of Investments	8,500
Sale of Fixed Asset	12,000
Proceeds of Loan	2,70,000
	4,30,000
Application	
Increase in Working Capital	2,97,000
Purchase of Investments	18,000
Dividends paid	40,000
Taxation paid	75,000
	4,30,000

Workings :

1)   **Statement showing changes in Working Capital**

	2008 Rs.	2007 Rs.
Stock	2,10,000	2,40,000
Debtors	4,55,000	2,10,000
Bank	1,97,000	1,49,000
	8,62,000	5,99,000
Less : Creditors	1,34,000	1,68,000
Working Capital	7,28,000	4,31,000
Increase	–	2,97,000
	7,28,000	7,28,000

2)

Profit and Loss Account

	Rs.		Rs.
To Depreciation	70,000	By Balance b/d	56,000
To Provision for Taxation	10,000	By Profit on sale of Fixed Assets	2,000
To Dividend	40,000	By Profit on sale of Investments	500
To General Reserve	10,000	By Profits	1,39,500
To Balance c/d	68,000		
	1,98,000		1,98,000

3)

Investments Account

	Rs.		Rs.
To Balance b/d	50,000	By Sale	8,500
To Profit on Sale	500	By Balance c/d	60,000
To Cash	18,000	-	-
	68,500	-	68,500

4)

Fixed Assets Account

	Rs.		Rs.
To Balance b/d	4,00,000	By Depreciation	70,000
To Profit on Sale	2,000	By Sale	12,000
		By Balance c/d	3,20,000
	4,02,000	-	4,02,000

Illustrations : 15

The following are the summarised Balance Sheets of M.N. Ltd., as at 31st December, 2007 and 2008 :–

Liabilities	2007 Rs.	2008 Rs.	Assets	2007 Rs.	2008 Rs.
Share Capital	5,00,000	5,00,000	Land & Buildings at		
Profit & Loss Account	1,50,000	2,52,000	Cost	2,00,000	2,50,000
Debentures	2,00,000	2,00,000	Plant & Machinery at		
Sundry Creditors	1,20,000	1,05,000	Cost	3,50,000	3,60,000
Provision for Doubtful			Sundry Debtors	1,47,000	1,38,000
Debts	5,000	4,000	Stock	2,50,000	2,74,000
Provision for Depreciation			Bank	83,000	1,01,000
Land & Buildings	30,000	34,000	Preliminary Expenses	5,000	4,000
Plant & Machinery	30,000	32,000			
	10,35,000	11,27,000		10,35,000	11,27,000

Additional information :

1. The net profit for the year ending 31st December, 2008 was Rs. 1,52,000 and is arrived at after charging loss on sale of machinery and writing off preliminary expenses and adjusting provision for doubtful debts.
2. During the year, a part of the machinery costing Rs. 7,000, accumulated depreciation thereon being Rs. 1,000 was sold for Rs. 5,000
3. Dividend for Rs. 50,000 was paid during the year ended 31st December, 2008

Prepare statements to show the changes in working capital for the year 2008 and the Source and Application of Funds for 2008.

Solution

Statement showing Source and Application of Funds during the year ending 31st December, 2008

	Rs.
Sources	
Profit for the year	1,60,000
Sale of Machinery	5,000
	1,65,000
Application	
Purchase of Land	50,000
Purchase of Machinery	17,000
Dividend paid	50,000
Increase in Working Capital	48,000
	1,65,000

Workings :

1)   **Statement showing changes in the Working Capital**

	2008 Rs.	2007 Rs.
Sundry Debtors	1,38,000	1,47,000
Stock	2,74,000	2,50,000
Bank	1,01,000	83,000
	5,13,000	4,80,000
Less : Sundry Creditors	1,05,000	1,20,000
Working Capital	4,08,000	3,60,000
Increase	–	48,000
	4,08,000	4,08,000

2)   **Profit for the year ....**

	Rs.
As per question	1,52,000
Add : Loss on Sale of Machinery	1,000
Add : Depreciation on Buildings	4,000
Add : Depreciation on Machinery	3,000
	1,60,000
Less : Over-provision of doubtful debts	1,000
	1,59,000
Add : Preliminary Expenses w/o	1,000
	1,60,000

3)   **Plant and Machinery Account**

	Rs.		Rs.
To Balance b/f	3,50,000	By Loss on Sale	1,000
To Additions (Balancing figure)	17,000	By Sale	5,000
		By Provision for Depreciation	1,000
		By Balance c/f	3,60,000
	3,67,000		3,67,000

4) **Provision for Depreciation on Plant and Machinery Account**

	Rs.		Rs.
To Plant A/c	1,000	By Balance b/f	30,000
To Balance c/d	32,000	By Depreciation	3,000
	33,000		33,000

5) **Land and Buildings Account**

	Rs.		Rs.
To Balance b/f	2,00,000	By Balance b/d	2,50,000
To Purchases (Balancing Figure)	50,000		
	2,50,000		2,50,000

6) **Provision for Depreciation on Buildings Account**

	Rs.		Rs.
To Balance c/d	34,000	By Balance b/f	30,000
		By Depreciation	4,000
	34,000		34,000

Alternatively, the profit from operations can by arrived at by preparing adjusted Profit and Loss Account as under :

Profit and Loss Account

	Rs.		Rs.
To Depreciation on Building	4,000	By Balance	1,50,000
To Depreciation on Machinery	3,000	By Over-provision	
To Loss on sale of Machinery	1,000	of Doubtful Debts	1,000
To Dividend	50,000	By Profit	1,60,000
To Preliminary Expenses w/o	1,000		
To Balance	2,52,000		
	3,11,000		3,11,000

3:2 Cash Flow Statement

3:2.1 Introduction

In earlier pages, we discussed various concepts of Funds. In the preparation of Fund Flow Statement, the term funds was used to mean 'working capital' i.e. current assets less current liabilities. However, over the period there was a shift to 'cash concept' of funds at the international level. In

India, ICAI issued a revised Accounting Standard AS-3 titled 'Cash Flow Statement' in March 1997. This new standard supercedes the earlier AS-3 'Changes in Financial Position' which was issued in June 1981. The earlier standard used the working capital concept of Fund, whereas the new standard used the 'cash concept' of Fund.

3:2.2 Cash Concept of Funds

A balance sheet of any concern shows the financial position stating assets and liabilities on a particular date. As against, a flow statement explains the changes that took place in various items in the balance sheet during the period between the dates of two balance sheets.

Income statement can also be termed as a flow statement since it explains changes that occurred in the profit and loss account (balance) during the given period. However, this income statement does not provide information about cash flow associated with, the operations of the company. Hence, a separate statement is prepared called the 'Cash flow Statement', for the benefit of the readers / users of the financial statements.

A Cash Flow Statement is a statement depicting changes in cash position from one period to another. The cash flow statement explains the reasons for such inflows and outflows of cash, as the case might be. It also helps the management in making plans for the immediate future. A projected cash flow statement or a cash budget will help the management in ascertaining how much cash will be available to meet obligations of trade creditors, to pay bank loans and to pay dividend to the shareholders. A proper planning of the cash resources will enable the management to have cash available whenever needed and put it to same profitable or productive use in case there is surplus cash available.

The term 'cash' here stands for cash and bank balances.

3:2.3 Terms used in Cash Flow Statement :

1) Definition of Cash : As per AS-3, this would include cash in hand and savings. current account balances with banks (also referred to as demand deposits) with banks and cash equivalents.

2) Cash Equivalents : Cash equivalents are defined as short-term and highly liquid investments that are readily convertible into cash and which are subject to insignificant risk of changes in values. (Note : Students would readily recall the term marketable investments, which is described in a similar manner). An investment would normally be called a cash equivalent only when it has a short-term maturity of say 3 months or less from the date of acquisition. Generally, investment in shares would not be considered as cash equivalent.

Since cash and cash equivalent is taken together as a starting point of a cash flow statement, it excludes movements between the items that constitute cash and cash equivalents. (Note : Traditionally, the starting point of cash flow statement was only cash and bank balance. Cash equivalent was not considered as a part of cash balance.)

3. Cash Flow : Cash flows are inflow or outflow of cash and cash equivalents. Major cash flows are listed below:

Cash Inflows

1. Issue of new shares for cash.

2. Receipt of long-term loans from banks, financial institutions etc.
3. Receipt of short-term loans from banks, financial institutions and other entities.
4. Sale of assets and investments.
5. Dividend and interest received.
6. Cash generated from operations.

Cash Outflows

1. Redemption of preference shares.
2. Purchase of fixed assets or investments.
3. Repayment of long-term and short-term borrowings.
4. Decrease in deferred payment-of liabilities.
5. Loss from operations.
6. Payment of tax, dividend etc.

It will be observed that these inflows are similar to sources whereas outflows are similar to applications as discussed in the earlier pages, except the items cash from operations and loss from operations.

3:2.4 Classification of Activities

As per AS-3, the Cash Flow Statement should report cash flows during the period classified by operating, investing and financing activities.

Cash flow from operating activities : The cash flows generated from major revenue producing activities of the entities are covered under this head. Cash flow from operating activities is the indicator of the extent to which the operations of the enterprise have generated suffcient cash to maintain the operating capability to pay dividend, repay loans and make new investments. Examples of cash flows from operating activities are as follows:

1. Cash receipts from sale of goods and services.
2. Cash receipts from royalties, fees, commission etc.
3. Cash payments to employees.
4. Cash payments or refunds of income tax (except when such payments or refunds relate to investing or financing activities)
5. Cash receipts and payments relating to future contracts, forward contract, etc.
6. Cash receipts and payment' arising from purchase and sale of trading securities.

Cash flow from investing activities : These are the acquisition and disposal of long-term assets and other investments not included in cash equivalents. This represents the extent to which the expenditures have been made for resources intended to generate future incomes and cash flows.

Examples of cash flows from investing activities are as follows :
1. Cash payments for purchase of fixed assets.
2. Cash receipts from sale of fixed assets.
3. Cash payments for purchase of shares / debentures etc., in other entities.
4. Loans and advances given to third parties.
5. Repayments of loans given.

Cash flow from financing activities : Financing activities are the activities that result in changes in the size and composition of an owner's capital and borrowings of the enterprise. Separate disclosure is important because it is useful in predicting claims on future cash flows by providers of funds.

Examples of cash flows from financing activities are as follows :
1. Cash receipts from issue of share capital
2. Cash receipts from issue of debentures, loans (short or long-term)
3. Cash repayments of amounts borrowed
4. Cash payment to redeem preference shares.

Note : Investing and financing activities that do not require the use of cash or cash equivalents should be excluded from a cash flow statement. Examples of non-cash transactions are:
1. Acquisition of assets by assuming directly related liabilities.
2. Acquisition of business by means of issue of shares.
3. Conversion of debt into equity

3.2.5 Other items

1) Interest and Dividends : In the case of non-financial enterprises, interest and dividends are not related to operating activities of the enterprise. Hence, they are not shown as a part of cash flow from operating activities. Cash outflows arising from interest and dividend paid are excluded from cash flow operations and are classified as cash outflows from financing activities. Interest and dividends received are classified as non-operating and reported as cash inflow from investing activities. Net profit is adjusted for non-operating expenses and incomes to calculate operating profits as given below :–

	Rs.
Net profit	××
Add : Non-operating expenses	××
Less : Non-operating incomes	××
Net Operating Profit	××

2) Income Tax : Cash flows arising from taxes on income generated and distributed should be disclosed separately as cash flows from operating activities unless they can be specially identified with financing and investment activities.

Corporate dividend tax paid should be disclosed as part of financing activities and capital gain tax on sale of property should be regarded as investing activities.

3) Extraordinary items : Cash flow associated with extraordinary items should be classified as arising from operating, investing or financing as appropriate. Legal expenses incurred in case of disputed land and building is classified as investing activity. Loss of stock by fire should be classified as operating activites.

4) Non-cash transactions : Investing and financing transactions that do not require cash are excluded from a cash flow statement. These transactions do not have a direct impact on current cash flow though they affect the capital and assets of the enterprise. Non-cash transactions include the purchase of assets by issue of shares and debentures, conversion of debentures into shares and so on. These transactions are shown as a footnote in the Cash Flow Statement.

5) Foreign currency cash flows : These flows should be recorded in the organisation's reporting currency by applying the exchange rate at the date of cash flows. The effect of changes in the exchange rate on cash and cash equivalents held in a foreign currency should be reported as a separate item as a part of reconciliation of the changes in the 'cash funds' during the period under consideration.

6) Investment in Subsidiaries, Associates and Joint Ventures : It is reported as cash flow relating to dividends and advances.

7) Acquisitions / disposal of Subsidiaries and other business units : Cash flow arising out of these should be classified as investing activities.

A separate presentation of the cash flow effects of acquisitions and disposals is required.

8) Other disclosures : The organisation should disclose the amount of significant cash and cash equivalent balances held by the enterprise that are not available for use by it. For example, bank balance of a foreign branch is not available due to foreign exchange controls.

3:2.6 Methods of calculation of cash flows from operating activities

The most important piece of information disclosed in a cash flow statement is cash from operating activities. Cash flow from operations include cash receipt from the sale of goods and rendering of services, cash receipt from royalties, fees, commissions, other revenue, cash payment to suppliers of goods, refund of tax, cash payment to employees and so on. Net profit disclosed by the income statement does not indicate the net cash provided for operating activities. In order to calculate net cash provided by operating activities, revenues and expenses are replaced by actual receipts and payments in cash. There are two methods of calculation of cash flow from operating activities as given below :

1) Direct Method :

Under this method, major classes of gross cash receipts and gross cash payments are obtained from the records for determination of cash flow from operating activities.

Following are the examples of usual cash receipts and cash payments resulting from operating activities :

  i) Cash sale of goods and services.
 ii) Collection from customers
iii) Receipt of royalties, fees, commissions and other revenues.
 iv) Cash payment for purchase of inventories.
  v) Cash payment for various operating expenses.
 vi) Cash payment of salaries and wages of employees.
vii) Cash payment of income tax.

The procedure of computation of cash from operating activities is also known as income statement method.

Profit and Loss Account records all the items on accrual basis. Various items in the Profit and Loss Account are adjusted for changes in related items in current assets and current liabilities in order to decide Profit and Loss Account on cash basis. The balancing figure in Profit and Loss Account reveals cash from operating activities.

Some Adjustments :

1. Cash inflow from Sales : Sales in the income statement show cash sales and credit sales. For deciding cash flow from credit sales, it is adjusted in the light of Debtors and Bills Receivable.

	Credit Sales	××
Add :	Debtors and Bills Receivable at the beginning	××
		××
Less :	Debtors and Bills Receivable at the end	××
	Cash flow from Sales	××

2. Cost of Sales on cash basis : Cost of sales as per income statement is adjusted for stock of goods to get purchases and then purchases are adjusted in the light of creditors at the beginning and at the end of the year to decide cash outflow of cost of sales.

Purchases = Cost of Sales - Opening Stock + Closing Stock

Purchases		××
Add :	Opening Creditors	××
		××
Less :	Closing Creditors	××
	Cash Outflow on Purchases	××

3. Expenses on cash basis : Expenses debited to Profit and Loss Account are analysed to decide cash outflow on account of payment of expenses is as follows :

Expenses (in Profit and Loss A/c)		××
Add :	Outstanding in the beginning	××
Less :	Outstanding at the end	××
	Cash Outflow on account of Expenses	××

4. Cash outflow on account of insurance :

Insurance premium (in Profit and Loss A/c)		××
Less :	Pre-paid in the beginning	××
		××
Add :	Pre-paid at the end	××
	Cash Outflow on account of Insurance	××

Note : Non-cash expenses such as depreciation, loss on sale of fixed assets, goodwill written off etc., are deleted.

2) Indirect Method

Under this method, cash from operating activities is calculated by adjusting net profit and loss instead of individual items disclosed in the Profit and Loss Account. Net profit and loss is adjusted in the light of changes during the period. The following formula should be kept in mind for the determination of cash from operating activities :–

A) When Net Profit is given :

		Rs.
Net Profit before Tax and Extraordinary items	××	
Add : Non-cash and Non-operating items :		
Depreciation on Fixed Assets	××	
Goodwill written off	××	
Preliminary Expenses, Discount on Shares / Debentures, Underwriting Commission on cost of issue of Shares and Debentures written off	××	
Loss on Sale of Investments	××	
Loss on Sale of Fixed Assets	××	××
Less : Gains on Sale of Fixed Assets and Investments :		
Gain on Sale of Fixed Assets	××	
Gain on Sale of Investments	××	××
Add : Increase in Current Liabilities (except Bank Overdraft)		××
Add : Decrease in Current Assets (Except Cash and Cash Equivalent)		××
Less : Increase in Current Assets		××
Less : Decrease in Current Liabilities		××
Less : Income Tax Paid		××
Cash provided by Operating Activities		××

B) When Profit and Loss Account balances are given :

Cash Flow from Operating Activities

		Rs.
Profit and Loss A/c balance as per Balance Sheet at the end of the year		××
Less : Profit and Loss A/c balance as per Balance Sheet at the beginning of the year		××
Net Profit after Appropriations		××
Add : **Appropriations**		
Proposed Dividend	××	
Transfer to General Reserve	××	
Transfer to Debenture Redemption Fund	××	
Transfer to Dividend Equalisation Fund	××	××
Net Profit for the year		××

		Rs.
Add : **Non-operating Expenses :**		
(including Extraordinary Expenses)		
Interest paid	××	
Loss by fire	××	××
Less : **Non-operating Incomes :**		
(including Extraordinary Incomes)		××
Interest received	××	
Dividend received	××	××
Net Operating Profit		××
Add : **Non-cash Expenses**		
Depreciation on Fixed Assets	××	
Loss on Sale of Fixed Assets	××	
Provision for Taxation	××	
Goodwill w/off	××	
Preliminary Expenses, Discount on issue of Shares		
and Debentures, Underwriting Commission written off	××	
Loss on Sale of Investments	××	××
		××
Less : **Non-cash Incomes/Gains**		
Profit on Sale of Fixed Assets	××	
Profit on Sale of Investments	××	××
Net Operating Profit before Working Capital changes.		
Add : Increase in Current Liabilities	××	
Decrease in Current Assets	××	××
Less : Increase in Current Assets	××	
Decrease in Current Liabilities	××	××
Cash generated from Operations		××
Less : Payment of Income Tax		××
Add : Refund of Income Tax		××
Cash from Operation after Income Tax		
but before Extraordinary items		××
Add : Cash inflow from Extraordinary Items not related to		
financing and investment activities		××
Less : Cash outflow on Extraordinary Items not related to		
financing and investment activities		××
Cash flow from operating activities.		××

3.2.7 Procedure of preparation of Cash Flow Statement

The procedure of prepration of Cash Flow Statment is similar to that of Fund Flow Statement except the treatment of current assets and current liabilities.

Format of Cash Flow Statement

(Traditional Method)

Cash Flow Statement

(For the year ending on .....)

Balance as on	Rs.	Rs.
Balance as on 1 - 1 -		
Cash Balance	.....	
Bank Balance	.....	....
Add : Sources of Cash :		
Issue of Shares	.....	
Raising of short-term Loans	.....	
Sale of Fixed Assets	.....	
Short-term borrowing	.....	
Cash from Operations	.....	
Add / Less : Adjustment for non-cash items :		
Add : Increase in current Liabilities	.....	
Add : Decrease in current Assets	.....	
Less : Increase in current Assets	.....	
Less : Decrease in current Liability	.....	.....
Total cash available (1)		.....
Less : Application of Cash :		
Redemption of Debentures	.....	
Redemption of Preference Shares	.....	
Redemption of long-term Loans	.....	
Purchase of Fixed Assets	.....	
Decrease in deferred payment of Liability	.....	
Cash outflow on account of Operations	.....	
Tax paid	.....	
Dividend paid	.....	
Decrease in Unsecured Loans, Deposits etc.	.....	.....
Total Applications (2)		.....

Closing Balance as on 31-12-.....

Cash Balance	.....
Bank Balance	.....

Note : It should tally with the balance as shown by (1) - (2)

Following steps are involved in the procedure :

Step   1.   Calculate cash flows from operating activities

        2.   Analyse non-current assets : Non-operating current assets, non-current liabilities, non-operating current liabilities and capital to ascertain the cash inflows and cash outflows which is not related to operating activities of the organisation.

        3.   Find out cash inflows from investing activities and financing activities.

        4.   Prepare a cash flow statement

3:2.8   Proforma of Cash Flow Statement as Per AS-3 issued by ICAI

Cash Flow Statement based on indirect method of calculating cash flows from operating activities :–

	Rs.	Rs.
Cash flows from operating activities :		
Net Profit before taxation and extraordinary items		
Adjustments for :		
Depreciation	××	
Foreign Exchange Loss	××	
Interest Income	(××)	
Dividend Income	(××)	
Interest Expense	××	
Operating profit before working capital changes	××	
Increase in Working Capital	(××)	
Decrease in Working Capital	××	
Cash generated from Operations	××	
Income Tax paid	(××)	
Cash flow before extraordinary item :	××	
Proceeds from earthquake disaster settlement	××	
Net Cash from operating activities :		××
Cash Flows from investing activities		
Purchase of Fixed Assets and Investment	××	
Sale of Fixed Assets and Investment	××	
Interest received	××	
Dividend received	××	
Net cash from investing activities		××
Cash flows from financing activities		
Proceeds from issuance of Share Capital	××	
Proceeds from long-term borrowings	××	
Repayment of long-term borrowings	(××)	
Issue of Debentures	××	

	Rs.	Rs.
Redemption of Debentures	(××)	
Redemption of Preference Shares	(××)	
Interest Paid	(××)	
Dividend paid	(××)	
Net cash used in financing activities		××
		××
Net Increase in cash and cash equivalents :		
Cash and cash equivalents at the beginning of period		××
Cash and cash equivalents at the end of period		××

Illustration on cash flow from operating activities :

Illustration : 1

From the following information, calculate cash flows from operating activities by direct method :

Profit & Loss A/c
for the year ended 31st December, 2008

	Rs.		Rs.
To Cost of goods sold	2,10,000	By Sales	3,60,000
To Gross Profit c/d	1,50,000		
	3,60,000		3,60,000
To Salaries	30,000	By Gross Profit b/d	1,50,000
To Depreciation	45,000		
To Insurance	15,000		
To Net Profit	60,000		
	1,50,000		1,50,000

Additional information :

	1-1-2008 Rs.	31-12-2008 Rs.
Customers	30,000	42,000
Suppliers	21,000	15,000
Stock	36,000	51,000
Outstanding Salaries	3,000	4,500
Pre-paid Insurance	3,000	3,000

Solution 1

Cash flows from operating activities

		Rs.
Cash inflow from Sales		3,48,000
Less : Cash outflow on cost of Sales		2,31,000
Less : Cash outflow on Expenses :		
Salaries	28,500	
Insurance	15,000	43,500
Net cash used in operating activities		73,500

1.   **Customer's A/c**

	Rs.		Rs.
To Balance b/d	30,000	By Bank	3,48,000
To Sales	3,60,000	By Balance c/d	42,000
	3,90,000		3,90,000

2. Purchases = Cost of Sales - Operating Stock + Closing Stock
              = 2,10,000 - 36,000 + 51,000
              = 2,25,000

3. Payment to Creditors :

Supplier's A/c

	Rs.		Rs.
To Bank	2,31,000	By Balance b/d	21,000
To Balance c/d	15,000	By Purchases	2,25,000
	2,46,000		2,46,000

	Rs.
4. Salaries	30,000
Add : Outstanding at the beginning	3,000
	33,000
Less : Outstanding at the end	4,500
Paid	28,500
5. Insurance	15,000
Less : Pre-paid at the beginning	3,000
	12,000
Add : Pre-paid at the end	3,000
	15,000

6. Depreciation has no impact on cash flow.

Illustration : 2

Calculate cash flow from operating activities from the following Profit and Loss Account. (Indirect Method)

	Rs.		Rs.
Salaries	20,000	Gross Profit	50,000
Rent	10,000	Profit on Sale of Land and Building	5,000
Depreciation	5,000	Income Tax Refund	5,000
Loss on Sale of Plant	2,000		
Goodwill written off	5,000		
Proposed Dividend	6,000		
Provision for Taxation	5,000		
Net Profit	7,000		
	60,000		60,000

Solution 2

Cash flows from operating activities

	Rs.	Rs.
Net Profit		7,000
Add : Proposed Dividend	6,000	
Depreciation	5,000	
Loss on Sale of Plant	2,000	
Goodwill written off	5,000	
Provision for Taxation	5,000	23,000
		30,000
Less : Profit on Sale of Land & Building		5,000
		25,000
Less : Income Tax Refund (to be shown separately)		5,000
Cash flow from operating activities		20,000

Illustration : 3

Calculate cash flow from operating activities from the following :

	As on 1-4-2008 Rs.	As on 31-3-2009 Rs.
Profit and Loss A/c	60,000	70,000
General Reserve	20,000	30,000
Provision for Depreciation on Plant	60,000	70,000
Expenses payable	10,000	6,000
Goodwill	40,000	20,000
Debtors	80,000	70,000

An item of Plant costing Rs. 40,000 having a book value of Rs. 28,000 was sold for Rs. 36,000 during the year.

Solution 3

Cash flows form operating activities

	Rs.	Rs.
Profit and Loss A/c balance as on 31-3-2009	70,000	
Less : Profit and Loss A/c balance as on 1-4-2008	60,000	
Net Profit for the year		10,000
Add : Transfer to General Reserve		10,000
Net Profit		20,000
Add : Non-cash Expenses		
Depreciation on Plant	22,000	
Goodwill written off	20,000	42,000
		62,000
Less : Non-cash Incomes		
Profit on Sale of Plant		8,000
Operating Profit		54,000
Add : Decrease in Debtors		10,000
		64,000
Less : Decrease in payable Expenses		4,000
Cash flows from operating activities		60,000

Provision for Depreciation on Plant

	Rs.		Rs.
To Plant A/c	12,000	By Balance b/d	60,000
To Balance c/d	70,000	By Depreciation provided	22,000
	82,000		82,000

Illustration : 4

From the following balances, you are required to calculate cash from operations :–

	31st December	
	2008 Rs.	2009 Rs.
Debtors	50,000	47,000
Bills Receivable	10,000	12,500
Creditors	20,000	25,000
Bills Payable	8,000	6,000
Outstanding Expenses	1,000	1,200
Pre-paid Expenses	800	700
Accrued income	600	750
Income received in advance	300	250
Profit made during the year	–	1,30,000

Solution 4

Cash from Operations

	Rs.	Rs.
Profit made during the year	–	1,30,000
Add : Decrease in Debtors	3,000	
Increase in Creditors	5,000	
Increase in Outstanding Expenses	200	
Decrease in pre-paid Expenses	100	8,300
		1,38,300
Less : Increase in Bills Receivable	2,500	
Decrease in Bills Payable	2,000	
Increase in Accrued Income	150	
Decrease in Income received in advance	50	4,700
Cash from operations		1,33,600

3:2.9 Benefits of Cash Flow Statement

The following are the benefits of cash flow statement :

1. It increases the comparability of reported performance by different organisations.

2. It is useful in checking the accuracy of past assessments of future cash flows.

3. It is helpful in preparation of a cash budget for the subsequent period.

4. It helps to understand the ability of the organisation to meet its financial commitments in time and pay dividends.

5. It provides information of all the investing and financing activities taken place during the year.

6. It shows relationship between profitability and net cash flow.

3:2.10 Limitations of Cash Flow Statement

1. Concept of cash and cash equivalents as a fund is considered as narrower concept as agsinst 'working capital' concept of funds used in the preparation of fund flow statement.

2. Though in case of certain items, netting out is not recommended, the enterprise may show a net portion. For e.g. : In the case of loans given to sister concerns, the repayments during the year would be adjusted and only the net amount would be shown as loans given to conceal the magnitude of loan given. Thus, the meaningful information may not be available to the reader from cash flow statement.

3. Elaborate and detailed preparation of cash flow statement requires access to accounts of the enterprise which may not be possible. As such the analyst preparing the cash flow statement on the basis of available balance sheets and profitability statement will not be able to ascertain the correct picture of cash flows.

4. Cash flow statement is not a substitute for profitability statement.

5. Cash flow statement can be easily manipulated by postponing major payments. For e.g. : Purchases.

3:2.11 Distinction Between Cash Flow Statement and Fund Flow Statement

Point of Distinction	Cash Flow Statement	Fund Flow Statement
1) Scope	Cash flow statement is concerned only with the change in cash position	Fund flow statement is concerned with change in working capital position.
2) Concept	Cash flow statement is based on narrower concept of fund i.e. cash and cash equivalents.	Fund flow statement is based on broader concept of funds i.e. working capital.
3) Legal Position	Cash flow statement is now mandatory for all the listed companies and is more widely used in India and broad.	Fund flow statement is not mandatory and it is not being used by the companies
4) Presentation	Cash flow statement classifies and highlights the cash flows into three categories i.e. operating activities, investing activities and financing activities.	Fund flow statement does not show such meaningful classification of activities.
5) Statement of changes in working capital	Statement of changes in working capital is not prepared in cash flow statement because changes in working capital are adjusted for ascertaining cash generated from operations.	Statement of Changes in working capital is prepared in fund flow statement.
6) Technique used in preparation	In cash flow statement technique, decrease in current liability or increase in current assets results in decrease in cash and vice-versa.	In fund flow statement technique decrease in current liability or increase in current assets brings increase in working capital and vice-versa.
7) Cash position	As cash is a part of working capital, improvement in 'cash position' may indicate improved 'working capital position.'	Sound working capital or fund position may not necessarily mean sound 'cash position.'
8) Time utility	Cash flow analysis is more useful to the management in short period.	Fund flow analysis is not much useful to the management for short period.

AS-3 (Revised) : Cash Flow Statements

The following are the salient features of the Revised Accounting Standard (AS-3), Cash Flow Statements, issued by the Council of the Institute of Chartered Accountants of India in March, 1997. This Standard supersedes AS-3, changes in financial position, issued in June, 1981.

This Accounting Standard (AS) has become mandatory w.e.f. accounting periods beginning from 1.4.2001 for the following enterprises :–

    a) Enterprises whose debt ar equity securities are listed or going to be listed on a recognised stock exchange.

    b) All other commercial, industrial and business reporting enterprises whose turnover for the accounting period exceeds Rs. 50 crores.

Objectives

Information about the cash flows of an enterprise is useful in providing users of financial statements with a basis to assess the ability of the enterprise to generate cash and cash equivalents and the needs of the enterprise to utilise those cash flows. The economic decisions that are taken by users require an evaluation of the ability of an enterprise to generate cash and cash equivalents and the timing and certainty of their generation.

The statement deals with the provisions of information about the historical changes in cash and cash equivalents of an enterprise by means of a cash flow statement which classifies cash flows during the period from operating, investing and financing activities.

Scope

    1. An enterprise should prepare a cash flow statement and should present it for each period for which financial statements are presented.

    2. Users of an enterprise's financial statements are interested in how the enterprise generates and use cash and cash equivalents. This is the case regardless of the nature of the enterprise's activities and irrespective of whether cash can be viewed as the product of the enterprise, as may be the case with a financial enterprise. Enterprises need cash for essentially the same reasons, however, different their principal revenue-producing activities might be. They need cash to conduct their operations, to pay their obligations, and to provide returns to their investors.

Benefits of Cash flow Information

    1. A cash flow statement, when used in conjunction with the other financial statements. provides information that enables users to evaluate the changes in the net assets of an enterprise, its financial structure (including its liquidity and solvency), and its ability to affect the amounts and timing of cash flows in order to adapt to changing circumstances and opportunities. Cash flow information is useful in assessing the ability of the enterprise to generate cash and cash equivalents and enables users to develop models to assess and compare the present value of the future cash flows of different enterprises.

    2. It also enhances the comparability of the reporting of operating performance by different enterprises because it eliminates the effects of using different accounting treatments for the

same transactions and events.

3. Historical cash flow information is often used as an indicator of the amount, timing and certainty of future cash flows. It is also useful in checking the accuracy of past assessments of future cash flows and in examining the relationship between profitability and net cash flow and the impact of changing prices.

Definitions

The following terms are used in this statement with the meanings specified :–

1) Cash comprises cash on hand and demand deposits with banks.
2) Cash equivalents are short-term, highly liquid investments that are readily convertible into known amounts of cash and which are subject to an insignificant risk of changes in value.
3) Cash flows are inflows and outflows of cash and cash equivalents.
4) Operating activities are the principal revenue-producing activities of the enterprise and other activities that are not investing or financing activities.
5) Investing activities are the acquisition and disposal of long-term assets and other investments not included in cash equivalents.
6) Financing activities are activities that result in changes in the size and composition of the owner's capital (including preference share capital in the case of a company) and borrowings of the enterprise.

Presentation of a Cash Flow Statement

The cash flow statement should report cash flows during the period classified as operating, investing and financing activities.

Operating activities : Cash flows from operating activities are primarily derived from the principal revenue-producing activities of the enterprise. Therefore, the general result from the transactions and other events that enter into the determination of net profit or loss. Examples of cash flows from operating activites are –

a) cash receipts from the sale of goods and the rendering of services;
b) cash receipts from royalties, fees, commissions, and other revenue;
c) cash payments to suppliers for goods and services;
d) cash payments to and on behalf of employees;
e) cash receipts and cash payments of an insurance enterprise for premiums and claims, annuities and other policy benefits;
f) cash payments or refunds of income taxes unless they can be specifically identified with financing and investing activities; and
g) cash receipts and payments relating to futures contracts, forward contracts, option contracts, and swap contracts when the contracts are held for dealing or trading purposes.

Investing activities : Examples of cash flows arising from investing activities are –

a) cash payments to acquire fixed assets (including intangibles). These payments include those relating to capitalised research and development cost and self-constructed fixed assets;
b) cash receipts from disposal of fixed assets (including intangibles);
c) cash payments to acquire shares, warrants, or debt instruments of other enterprises and interests

in joint ventures (other than payments for those instruments considered to be cash equivalents and those held for dealing or trading purposes);

d) cash receipts from disposal of shares, warrants, or debt instruments of other enterprises and interests in joint ventures (other than receipts from those instruments considered to be cash equivalents and those held for dealing or trading purposes);

e) cash advances and loans made to third parties (other than advances and loans made by a financial enterprise);

f) cash receipts from the repayment of advances and loans made to third parties (other than advances and loans of a financial enterprise);

g) cash payments for futures contracts, forward contracts, option contracts, and swap contracts except when the contracts are held for dealing or trading purposes or the payments are classified as financing activities; and

h) cash receipts from futures contracts, forward contracts, option contracts and swap contracts except when the contracts are held for dealing or trading purposes, or the receipts are classified as financing activities.

Financing activities : Examples of cash flowing from financing activities are –

a) cash proceeds from issuing shares or other similar instruments;

b) cash proceeds from issuing debentures, loans, notes, bonds and other short or long-term borrowings; and

c) cash repayments of amounts borrowed.

Reporting cash flows from operating activities

1) An enterprise should report cash flows from operating activities using either:

  a) the direct method, whereby major classes of gross cash receipts and gross cash payments are disclosed; or

  b) the indirect method, whereby net profit or loss is adjusted for the effects of transactions of a non-cash nature, any deferrals or accruals of past or future operating cash receipts, payments and items of income or expense associated with investing or financing cash flows.

2) The direct method provides information which may be useful in estimating future cash flows and which is not available under the indirect method, and is therefore, considered more appropriate than the indirect method. Under the direct method, information about major classes of gross cash receipts and gross cash payments may be obtained either –

  a) from the accounting records of the enterprise; or

  b) by adjusting sales, cost of sales (interest and similar income and interest expense and similar charges for a financial enterprise) and other items in the statement of profit and loss for –

    i) changes during the period in inventories and operating receivables and payables;

    ii) other non-cash items; and

    iii) other items for which the cash effects are investing or financing cash flows.

3) Under the indirect method, the net cash flow from operating activities is determined by adjusting

net profit or loss for the effects of:

a) changes during the period in inventories and operating receivables and payables;

b) non-cash items such as depreciation, provisions, deferred taxes and unrealised foreign exchange gains and losses; and

c) all other items for which the cash effects are investing or financing cash flows.

4) Alternatively, the net cash flow from operating activities may be presented under the indirect method by showing the operating revenues and expenses, excluding non-cash items disclosed in the statement of profit and loss and the changes during the period in inventories and operating receivables and payables.

Reporting Cash Flows from Investing and Financing Activities

An enterprise should report separately major classes of gross cash receipts and gross cash payments arising from investing and financing activities, except to the extent that cash flows described in paragraphs VI are reported on a net basis.

Reporting Cash Flows on a Net Basis

1) Cash flows arising from the following operating investing or financing activities may be reported on a net basis :

a) cash receipts and payments on behalf of customers when the cash flows reflect the activities of the customer rather than those of the enterprise.

Examples of cash receipts and payments referred above are as follows:

i) the acceptance and repayment of demand deposits by a bank;

ii) funds held for customers by an investment enterprise; and

iii) rents collected on behalf of and paid over to the owners of properties;

b) cash receipts and payments for items in which the trurnover is quick, the amounts are large and the maturities are short.

Examples of cash receipts and payments referred above are advances made for and the repayments of;

i) principal amounts relating to credit card customers;

ii) the purchase and sale of investments; and

iii) other short-term borrowings, for example, those which have a maturity period of three months or less.

2) Cash flows arising from each of the following activities of a financial enterprise may be reported on a net basis;

a) cash receipts and payments for the acceptance and repayment of deposits within a fixed maturity date;

b) the placement of deposits with and withdrawal of deposits from other financial enterprises; and

c) cash advances and loans made to customers and the repayment of those advances and loans.

Foreign Currency Cash Flows : Cash flows arising from transactions in a foreign currency should be recorded in an enterprise's reporting currency by applying to the foreign currency amount the exchange rate berween the reporting currency and the foreign currency at the date of the cash flow. A rate that approximates the actual rate may be used if the result is substantially the same as would arise if the rates at the dates of the cash flows were used. The effect of changes in exchange rates on cash and cash equivalents held in a foreign currency should be reported as a separate part of the reconciliation of the changes in cash and cash equivalents during the period.

Extraordinary Items : The cash flows associated with extraordinary items should be classified as arising from operating, investing or financing activities as appropriately and separately disclosed.

Interest and Dividends : Cash flows from interest and dividends received and paid should each be disclosed separately. Cash flows arising from interest paid and interest and dividends received in the case of a financial enterprise should be classified as cash flows arising from operating activities. In the case of other enterprises, cash flows arising from interest paid should be classified as cash flows from financing activities while interest and dividend received should be classified as cash flows from investing activities. Dividends paid should be classified as cash flows from financing activities.

Taxes on income : Cash flows arising from taxes on income should be separately disclosed and be classified as cash flows from operating activities unless they can be specifically identified with financing and investing activities.

Investments in Subsidiaries, Associates and Joint Ventures : When accounting for an investment in an associate or a subsidiary in an or a joint venture; an investor restricts its reporting in the cash flow statement to the cash flows between itself and the investee/joint venture. For example, cash flows relating to dividends and advances.

Acquisitions and Disposals of Subsidiaries and other Business Units

1) The aggregate cash flows arising from acquisitions and from disposals of subsidiaries or other business units should be presented separately and classified as investing activities.

2) An enterprise should disclose, in aggregate, in respect of both acquisition and disposal of subsidiaries or other business units during the period of each of the following :–
   a) the total purchase or disposal consideration; and
   b) the portion of the purchase or disposal consideration discharged by means of cash and cash equivalents.

Non-cash Transactions : Investing and financing transactions that do not require the use of cash or cash equivalents should be excluded from a cash flow statement. Such transactions should be disclosed elsewhere in the financial statement in a way that provides all the relevant information about these investing and financing activities.

Disclosure

Components of cash and cash equivalents : An enterprise should disclose the components of cash and cash equivalents and present a reconciliation of the amounts in its cash flow staement with the equivalent items reported in the balance sheet.

Other disclosures : An enterprise should disclose together with a commentary by management, the amount of significant cash and cash equivalent balances held by the enterprise that are not available for use by it.

Illustration on Cash Flow Statement

Illustration : 1 - Statement of financial position of Mr. Arun is given below :

Liabilities	1st Jan., 2008 Rs.	31st Dec., 2008 Rs.	Assets	1st Jan., 2008 Rs.	31st Dec., 2008 Rs.
Accounts Payable	29,000	25,000	Cash	40,000	30,000
Capital	7,39,000	6,15,000	Debtors	20,000	17,000
			Stock	8,000	13,000
			Building	1,00,000	80,000
			Other Fixed Assets	6,00,000	5,00,000
	7,68,000	6,40,000		7,68,000	6,40,000

Additional information :

a) There were no drawings.

b) There were no purchases or sales of either building or other fixed assets.
   Prepare a statement of cash flow.

Solution 1

Cash Flow Statement
(Traditional Method)

			Rs.
Cash Balance as on 1st January, 2008			40,000
Net loss as per Profit and Loss A/c			
Capital at the end of 2008		6,15,000	
Less : Capital at the beginning of 2008		7,39,000	
		(1,24,000)	
Add : Non-cash Charges			
Depreciation on Buildings	20,000		
Depreciation on other Fixed Assets	1,00,000	1,20,000	
Funds from Operations		(4,000)	
Add : Decrease in Current Assets			
Debtors		3,000	
		(1,000)	
Less : Increase in Current Assets or decrease in Current Liabilities			
Increase in Stocks	5,000		
Decrease in Accounts Payable	4,000	9,000	
Cash outflow on account of Operations			(10,000)
Cash Balance as on 31st December, 2008			30,000

Illustration : 2

Balance Sheet of 'A' and 'B' on 1st January, 2008 and 31st December, 2008 were as follows :

Balance Sheet

Liabilities	1st Jan., 2008 Rs.	31st Dec., 2008 Rs.	Assets	1st Jan., 2008 Rs.	31st Dec., 2008 Rs.
Creditors	40,000	44,000	Cash	10,000	7,000
Mrs. A's Loan	25,000	–	Debtors	30,000	50,000
Loans from Bank	40,000	50,000	Stock	35,000	25,000
Capital	1,25,000	1,53,000	Machinery	80,000	55,000
			Land	40,000	50,000
			Building	35,000	60,000
	2,30,000	2,47,000		2,30,000	2,47,000

During the year, a machine costing Rs. 10,000 (accumulated depreciation Rs. 3,000) sold for Rs. 5,000. The provisions for depreciation against machinery as on 1st January, 2008 was Rs. 25,000 and on 31st December, 2008, Rs. 40,000. Net profit for the year 2008, amounted to Rs.45,000. You are required to prepare a cash flow statement.

Solution 2

i) Traditional Approach

Cash Flow Statement

	Rs.	Rs.
Cash Balance as on January, 2008		10,000
Add : Sources		
Cash from Operations	59,000	
Loan from Bank	10,000	
Sale of Machinery	5,000	74,000
		84,000
Less : Application		
Purchase of Land	10,000	
Purchase of Building	25,000	
Mrs. A's Loan repaid	25,000	
Drawings	17,000	77,000
Cash Balance as on 31st December, 2008		7,000

Working Notes :

	Rs.
Cash from Operations	
Profit made during the year	45,000
Add: Depreciation on Machinery 18,000	
Loss on Sales of Machinery 2,000	
Decrease in Stock 10,000	4,000
Increase in Creditors 4,000	79,000
Less : Increase in Debtors	20,000
Cash from Operations	59,000

Machinery Account (At Cost)

Particulars	Rs.	Particulars	Rs.
To Balance b/d	1,05,000	By Bank	5,000
		By Loss on Sale of Machinery	2,000
		By provision for Depreciation	3,000
		By Balance c/d	95,000
	1,05,000		1,05,000

Provision for Depreciation

Particulars	Rs.	Particulars	Rs.
To Machinery A/c	3,000	By Balance b/d	25,000
To Balance c/d	40,000	By P & L A/c	
		(Dep. charged - balancing figure)	18,000
	43,000		43,000

ii) Modern Approach

Cash Flow Statement

	Rs.	Rs.
Net cash flows from operating activities		59,000
Cash flows from investing activities		
Sale of Machinery	5,000	
Purchase of Land	(10,000)	
Purchase of Building	(25,000)	
Net Cash flows from investing activities		30,000
Cash flows from financing activities		
Loan from Bank	10,000	
Mrs. A's Loan repaid	(25,000)	
Drawings	(17,000)	
Net cash flow from financial activities		(32,000)
Net increase (decrease) in cash and cash equivalents		(3,000)
Cash and cash equivalents on Jan., 1, 2008		10,000
Cash and cash equivalents on Dec., 31, 2008		7,000

Illustration : 3

The following are the summarised balance sheet of a Company as on December, 2008 and 2009 :–

Liabilities	2008 Rs.	2009 Rs.	Assets	2008 Rs.	2009 Rs.
Share Capital	2,00,000	2,50,000	Land and buildings	2,00,000	1,90,000
General Reserve	50,000	60,000	Machinery	1,50,000	1,69,000
Profit and Loss	30,500	30,600	Stock	1,00,000	74,000
Bank Loan (Long-term)	70,000	–	Sundry Debtors	80,000	64,200
Sundry Creditors	1,50,000	1,35,200	Cash	500	600
Provision for Taxation	30,000	35,000	Bank	–	8,000
			Goodwill	–	5,000
	5,30,500	5,10,800		5,30,500	5,10,800

Additional information :

During the year ended 31st December, 2009 –
1. Dividend of Rs.23,000 was paid.
2. Assets of another Company were purchased for a consideration of Rs.50,000, payable in shares. The following assets were purchased : Stock Rs.20,000, Machinery Rs.25000.
3. Machinery was further purchased for Rs.8,000.

4. Depreciation written off on Machinery Rs.12,000.
5. Income Tax provided during the year Rs. 33,000.
6. Loss on sale of machinery Rs.200 was written off to General Reserve.
   You are required to prepare a cash flow statement.

Solution 3

i) Traditional Approach

Cash Flow Statement
for the year ending 31st December, 2009

	Rs.	Rs.
Cash Balance as on 1st Jan., 2009		500
Add : Sources of cash		
Sale of Machinery		1,800
Cash from Operations	88,300	
Funds from Operations	46,000	
Add : Decrease in Stock	15,800	
Decrease in Debtors	1,50,100	
Less : Decrease in Creditors	14,800	1,35,300
		1,37,600
Less : Application of Cash		
Payment of Dividend	23,000	
Purchase of Machinery	8,000	
Tax paid (See Note 4)	28,000	
Mortgage Loan repaid	70,000	1,29,000
Closing Cash and Bank Balances		8,600
(Cash in Hand Rs.600 + Cash at Bank Rs.8,000)		

Working Notes :

1. Adjusted Profit And Loss Account

Particulars	Rs.	Particulars	Rs.
To Dividend	23,000	By Balance b/d	30,500
To Depreciation on Building	10,000	By Funds from Operations	
To Provision for Tax	33,000	(balancing figure)	88,300
To Transfer to General Reserve	10,200		
To Dep. on Machinery	12,000		
To Balance c/d	30,600		
	1,18,800		1,18,800

2.   **Machinery Account**

Particulars	Rs.	Particulars	Rs.
To Balance b/d	1,50,000	By Depreciation	12,000
To Share Capital	25,000	By General Reserve	200
To Bank	8,000	By Bank	1,800
		By Balance c/d	1,69,000
	1,83,000		1,83,000

3.   **General Reserve**

Particulars	Rs.	Particulars	Rs.
To Machinery A/c	200	By Balance b/d	50,000
To Balance c/d	60,000	By P & L A/c	10,200
	60,200		60,200

4.   **Provision for Taxation**

Particulars	Rs.	Particulars	Rs.
To Bank	28,000	By Balance b/d	30,000
To Balance c/d	35,000	By P & L A/c	33,000
	63,000		63,000

5.   **Decrease In Stock**

	Rs.
Stock as on 31st December, 2008	1,00,000
Less : Stock as on 31st December, 2009	54,000
(after deducting Stock purchased by issuing Shares)	
Increase in Cash	46,000

ii) Modern Approach as per AS - 3

Cash Flow Statement
for the year ending 31st December, 2009

Particulars	Rs.
Cash flows from operating activities :	
Funds from Operations 88,300	
Adjustments for :	
Decrease in Stock 46,000	
Decrease in Debtors 15,800	
Decrease in Creditors (14,800)	
Tax paid (28,000)	
Net cash from operating activities	1,07,300
Cash flows from investing activities :	
Sale of Machinery 1,800	
Purchase of Machinery (8,000)	
Net cash used for investing activities	(6,200)
Cash flows from financing activities :	
Payment of Dividend (23,000)	
Mortgage Loan repaid (70,000)	
Net cash used in financing activities	(93,000)
Net increase in Cash and Cash equivalents	8,100
Cash and Cash equivalents as on 1st Jan., 2009	500
Cash and cash equivalents as on 31st Dec., 2009	8,600
(Cash 600 + Bank 8,000)	

Illustration : 4

From the following Balance Sheets of Exe. Ltd., make out the statement of sources and uses of cash

Liabilities	2006 Rs.	2007 Rs.	Assets	2006 Rs.	2007 Rs.
Equity Share Capital	3,00,000	4,00,000	Goodwill	1,15,000	90,000
8%, Redeemable	1,50,000	1,00,000	Land & Bldgs.	2,00,000	1,70,000
Preference Share capital					
General Reserve	40,000	70,000	Plant	80,000	2,00,000
Profit and Loss A/c	30,000	48,000	Debtors	1,60,000	2,00,000
Proposed Dividend	42,000	50,000	Stock	77,000	1,09,000
Creditors	55,000	83,000	Bills Receivable	20,000	30,000
Bills Payable	20,000	16,000	Cash in Hand	15,000	10,000
Provision for Taxation	40,000	50,000	Cash at Bank	10,000	8,000
	6,77,000	8,17,000		6,77,000	8,17,000

Additional information :

a) Depreciation of Rs.10,000 and Rs.20,000 have been charged on Plant and Land and Buildings, respectively, in 2007.

b) An interim dividend of Rs.20,000 has been paid in 2007.

c) Rs. 35,000 Income Tax was paid during the year 2007.

Solution 4

Traditional Approach
Cash Flow Statement
for the year ending 31st December, 2007

Particulars		Rs.
Cash Balance as on 1st January, 2007		
Cash in Hand	15,000	
Cash at Bank	10,000	25,000
Add : Sources		
Issue of Share Capital	1,00,000	
Sale of Land and Buildings	10,000	
Cash from Operations (Note V)	1,60,000	2,70,000
Total Sources		2,95,000
Less : Applications		
Redemption of Redeemable Preference Shares	50,000	
Interim Dividend paid	20,000	
Dividend paid	42,000	
Income Tax paid	35,000	
Plant purchased	1,30,000	2,77,000
Cash Balance on 31st December, 2007		
Cash in Hand	10,000	
Cash at Bank	8,000	18,000

Alternatively, the Cash Flow Statement can also be prepared as follows :

Cash Flow Statement
for the year ending 31st December, 2007

Particulars	Rs.	Particulars	Rs.
Cash Balance as on 1st January, 2007		Outflows of Cash :	
Cash in Hand	15,000	Redemption of Redeemable	
Cash at Bank	10,000	Preference Shares	50,000
Add : Inflows of Cash : Issue of Shares	1,00,000	Payment of interim Dividend	20,000
Sale of Land and Building	10,000	Payment of Dividend	42,000

Particulars	Rs.	Particulars	Rs.
Funds from Operations	2,18,000	Payment of Tax	35,000
Increase in Creditors	28,000	Purchase of Plant	1,30,000
		Decrease in Bills Payable	4,000
		Increase in Debtors	40,000
		Increase in Stock	32,000
		Increase in Bills Receivable	10,000
		Cash Balance on 31st Dec., 2007	
		Cash in Hand	10,000
		Cash at Bank	8,000
	3,81,000		3,81,000

Working Notes :

i)   **Adjusted Profit And Loss Account**

Particulars	Rs.	Particulars	Rs.
To Depreciation on Plant	10,000	By Balanced b/d	30,000
To Depreciation on Building	20,000	By Funds from Operations	2,18,000
To Goodwill written off	25,000	(Balancing figure)	
To Provision for Taxation	45,000		
To Interim Dividend	20,000		
To Dividend proposed	50,000		
To Transfer to General Reserve	30,000		
To Balance c/d	48,000		
	2,48,000		2,48,000

ii)   **Provision For Taxation Account**

Particulars	Rs.	Particulars	Rs.
To Bank	35,000	By Balance b/d	40,000
To Balance c/d	50,000	By P & L A/c	45,000
	85,000		85,000

iii)   **Land And Building Account**

Particulars	Rs.	Particulars	Rs.
To Balance b/d	2,00,000	By Depreciation	20,000
		By Bank (Sale)	10,000
		By Balance c/d	1,70,000
	2,00,000		2,00,000

iv)   **Plant Account**

Particulars	Rs.	Particulars	Rs.
To Balance b/d	80,000	By Depreciation	10,000
To Balance (Purchase)	1,30,000	By Balance c/d	2,00,000
	2,10,000		2,10,000

v)   **Cash from Operations**

Particulars		Rs.
Funds from Operations		2,18,000
Add : Increase in Creditors		28,000
		2,46,000
Less : Decrease in Bills Payable	4,000	
Increase in Debtors	40,000	
Increase in Stock	32,000	
Increase in Bills Receivable	10,000	86,000
Cash from Operations		1,60,000

vi) In the absence of information, it has been presumed that there is no profit (loss) and no accumulated depreciation on that part of land and buildings which has been sold.

vii) Modern Approach as per AS - 3 (Revised)

Cash Flow Statement

for the year ending 31st December, 2007

Particulars		Rs.
Net Cash flows from operating activities :		
(1,60,000 - 35,000)		1,25,000
Cash flows from investing activities		
Sale of Land & Buildings	10,000	
Plant purchased	(1,30,000)	(1,20,000)
Net cash used in investing activities		
Cash flows from financing activities :		
Issuance of Share Capital	1,00,000	
Redemption of Redeemable Pref. shares	(50,000)	
Interim Dividend paid	(20,000)	
Dividend paid	(42,000)	(12,000)
Net cash used in financing activities		
Net increase (decrease) in Cash and Cash equivalents		(7,000)
Cash and Cash equivalents as on 1st Jan., 2007		
(Cash 15,000 + Bank 10,000)		25,000
Cash and Cash equivalents as on 31st Dec., 2007		18,000

Illustration : 5

Swastik Oils Ltd., has furnished the following information for the year ended 31st March, 2009 :

	(Rs. in lakhs)
Net profit	37,500.00
Dividend (including interim dividend paid)	12,000.00
Provision for Income Tax	7,500.00
Income Tax paid during the year	6,372.00
Loss on sale of Assets (net)	60.00
Book value of Assets sold	277.00
Depreciation charged to P & L Account	30,000.00
Profit on sale of Investments	150.00
Interest income on Investments	41,647.50
Value of Investments sold	3,759.00
Interest expenses	15,000.00
Interest paid during the year	15,780.00
Increase in Working Capital (excluding cash and bank balance)	84,112.50
Purchase of Fixed Assets	21,840.00
Investments on Joint Venture	5,775.00
Expenditure on construction (Work-in-progress)	69,480.00
Proceeds from long-term borrowings	38,970.00
Proceeds from short-term borrowings	30,862.50
Opening Cash and Bank balances	11,032.50
Closing Cash and Bank balances	2,569.00

You are required to prepare the cash flow statement in accordance with AS-3 for the year ended 31st March, 2009 (Make assumptions wherever necessary).

Solution 5

Swastik Oils Limited
Cash Flow Statement for the year ended 31st March, 2009

	(Rs. in lakhs)
Cash flows from operating activities	
Net Profit before Taxation (37,500 + 7,500)	45,000.00
Adjustment for :	
Depreciation charged to P & L A/c	30,000.00
Loss on sale of Assets (net)	60.00

	(Rs. in lakhs)
Profit on sale of Investments	(150.00)
Interest income on Investments	(3,759.00)
Interest expenses	15,000.00
Operating Profit before working capital changes	86,151.00
Increase (change) in Working Capital (excluding Cash and Bank balance	(84,112.50)
Cash generated from Operations	2,038.50
Income Tax paid	(6,372.00)
Net Cash used in operating activities (A)	(4,333.50)
b) Cash flow from investing activities	
Sale of Assets (277.50-60.00)	217.50
Sale of Investments (41,647.50 + 150)	41,797.50
Interest Income on Investments (assumed)	3,759.00
Purchase of Fixed Assets	(21,840.00)
Investments in Joint Venture	(5,775.00)
Expenditure on Construction (Work-in-progress)	(69,480.00)
Net Cash used in investing activities (B)	(51,321.00)
c) Cash flow from financing activities	
Proceeds from long-term borrowings	38,970.00
Proceeds from short-term borrowings	30,862.50
Interest paid	(15,780.00)
Dividends (including interim dividend paid)	(12,000.00)
Net Cash from financing activities (C)	42,052.50
Net increase in Cash and Cash equivalents (A) + (B) + (C)	(13,602.00)
Cash and Cash Equivalents at the beginning of the year	11,032.50
Cash and Cash Equivalents at the end of the year	2,569.50

Illustration : 6

From the following financial statement, you are required to prepare cash flow statement of Dolphin Ltd., for the year ended 31st March, 2009 :

Liabilities	2008 Rs.	2009 Rs.	Assets	2008 Rs.	2009 Rs.
Share Capital	1,40,000	1,40,000	Plant & Machinery	1,00,000	1,82,000
Secured Loan	–	80,000			
Profit & Loss A/c	14,000	20,000	Inventory	30,000	80,000
Creditors	28,000	78,000	Debtors	10,000	40,000
Tax Payable	2,000	6,000	Cash	40,000	18,000
			Preliminary Expenses	4,000	4,000
	1,84,000	3,24,000		1,84,000	3,24,000

Revenue Statement
for the year ended 31st March. 2009

	Rs.		Rs.
To Opening Inventory	30,000	By Sales	2,00,000
To Purchases	1,96,000	By Closing Inventory	80,000
To Gross Profit c/d	54,000		
	2,80,000		2,80,000
To General Expenses	22,000	By Gross Profit b/d	54,000
To Deprectation	16,000		
To Provision for Tax	8,000		
To Net Profit c/d	8,000		
	54,000		54,000
To Dividend paid	2,000	By Balance b/d	14,000
To Balance c/d	20,000	By Net Profit b/d	8,000
	22,000		22,000

Solution 6

Calculation of Net Profit before Tax

	Rs.
Net Profit Before Appropriation	8,000
Add : Provision for Tax	8,000
Net Profit before Tax	16,000

Dr.		Tax Payable A/c		Cr.
	Rs.			**Rs.**
To Bank A/c	4,000	By Balance b/d		2,000
To Balance c/d	6,000	By Profit & Loss A/c		8,000
	10,000			10,000

Dr.		Plant & Machinery A/c		Cr.
	Rs.			**Rs.**
To Balance b/d	1,00,000	By Profit & Loss A/c (Dep.)		16,000
To Bank A/c	98,000	By Balance c/d		1,82,000
	1,98,000			1,98,000

Dolphin Ltd.
Cash Flow Statement for the year ended 31st March, 2009

	Rs.	Rs.
Cash flows from operating activities		
Net Profit before Tax	16,000	
Adjustment for		
Depreciation written off	16,000	
Operating Profit before Working Capital changes	32,000	
Working Capital changes		
Increase in Inventory	(50,000)	
Increase in Debtors	(30,000)	
Increase in Creditors	50,000	
Cash generated from Operations	2,000	
Less : Tax paid	(4,000)	
Net Cash from operating activities		(2,000)
Cash flows from investing activities		
Plant & Machinery purchased		(98,000)
Cash flows from financing activities		
Secured Loan raised	80,000	
Dividend paid	(2,000)	
Net Cash flow from financing activities		78,000
Net decrease in Cash & Cash equivalent		(22,000)
Cash & Cash equivalent at the beginning of the year		
Cash		40,000
Cash & Cash equivalent at the end of the year		
Cash		18,000

Illustration : 7

The Balance Sheets of PVC Ltd., Pune as on 31.3.2001 and 31.3.2002 are given below :

Balance Sheet

Liabilities	31.3.2008 Rs.	31.3.2009 Rs.	Assets	31.3.2008 Rs.	31.3.2009 Rs.
Equity Share Capital	1,00,000	1,80,000	Freehold Land	1,00,000	1,00,000
10% Redeemable			Plant	1,04,000	1,00,000
Pref. Share Capital	2,00,000	1,00,000	Furniture	56,000	10,000
General Reserve	30,000	17,000	Investments	61,000	79,000
Capital Redemption			Debtors	80,000	70,000
Reserve	–	20,000	Stock	56,000	60,000
Profit & Loss A/c	10,000	20,000	Cash	34,000	50,000
Provision for Taxation	20,000	30,000			
Sundry Creditors	80,000	75,000			
Bills Payable	40,000	20,000			
Bank Overdraft	11,000	7,000			
	4,91,000	4,69,000		4,91,000	4,69,000

Prepare a cash flow statement after considering the following points :

a) Plant having book value Rs.30,000 was sold at a loss of Rs. 2,000.

b) Charge depreciation on Plant at 15% and Furniture at 10% of the opening balance.

c) Taxes paid during the year Rs. 40,000.

d) Interest on investments received Rs.4,000, of which Rs.1,200 is pre-acquisition interest.

Solution 7

Dr.   **Plant A/c**   Cr.

	Rs.		Rs.
To Balance b/d	1,04,000	By Bank	28,000
To Bank A/c	41,600	By Profit & Loss A/c	2,000
		By Depreciation	15,600
		By Balance c/d	1,00,000
	1,45,600		1,45,600

Dr.   **Furniture A/c**   Cr.

	Rs.		Rs.
To Balance b/d	56,000	By Depreciation	5,600
		By Bank	40,400
		By Balance c/d	10,000
	56,000		56,000

Dr.   **Investments A/c**   Cr.

	Rs.		Rs.
To Balance b/d	61,000	By Interest (Pre-acquisition)	1,200
To Bank A/c	19,200	By Balance c/d	79,000
	80,200		80,200

Dr.   **Provision for Taxation A/c**   Cr.

	Rs.		Rs.
To Bank A/c	40,000	By Balance c/d	20,000
To Balance b/d	30,000	By Profit & Loss A/c	50,000
	70,000		70,000

Cash Flow Statement
for the year ended 31st March, 2009

	Rs.	Rs.
Cash flows from operating activities		
P & L A/c Balance at the end of the year	20,000	
Less : P & L A/c Balance at the beginning of the year	10,000	
Net Profit before Adjustment	10,000	
Depreciation :		
Plant	15,600	
Furniture	5,600	
Transfer to Capital Redemption Reserve	20,000	
Transfer from General Reserve	(13,000)	

	Rs.	Rs.
Loss on Sale of Plant	2,000	
Interest on Investment (4,000 - 1,200)	(2,800)	
Provision for Tax	50,000	
Operating Profit before Working Capital changes	87,400	
Working Capital changes :		
Decrease in Debtors	10,000	
Increase in Stock	(4,000)	
Decrease in Creditors	(5,000)	
Decrease in Bills Payable	(20,000)	
Cash generated from Operations	68,400	
Less : Tax paid	(40,000)	
Net Cash from operating activities		28,400
Cash Flow from investing activities :		
Purchase of Plant	(41,600)	
Purchase of Investments	(19,200)	
Sale of Plant	28,000	
Sale of Furniture	40,400	
Interest on Investments	4,000	11,600
Cash Flow from financing activities :		
Issue of Equity Share Capital	80,000	
Redemption of Preference Share Capital	(1,00,000)	(20,000)
Net increase in Cash and Cash equivalent		20,000
Cash & Cash equivalent at the beginning of the year :		
Cash	34,000	
Bank Overdraft	(11,000)	23,000
		43,000
Cash and Cash equivalent at the end of the year :		
Cash	50,000	
Bank Overdraft	7,000	43,000

Illustration : 8

From the following Balance Sheets of Web-Sight Ltd., prepare a statement of sources and applications of cash.

Balance Sheet

Liabilities	2008 Rs.	2009 Rs.	Assets	2008 Rs.	2009 Rs.
Equity Share Capital	3,00,000	4,00,000	Goodwill	1,00,000	80,000
12% Redeemable			Land & Buildings	2,50,000	1,90,000
Preference Shares	1,80,000	1,00,000	Plant and		
Capital Reserve	–	30,000	Machinery	80,000	2,20,000
General Reserve	50,000	60,000	Investments	30,000	40,000
Profit & Loss A/c	40,000	48,000	Debtors	1,00,000	90,000
Proposed Dividend	25,000	27,000	Stocks	50,000	40,000
Sundry Creditors	30,000	50,000	Cash in hand	15,000	21,000
Bills Payable	20,000	16,000	Bank Balance	70,000	80,000
Provision for Taxation	50,000	30,000			
	6,95,000	7,61,000		6,95,000	7,61,000

Notes :

i) A machine costing Rs. 50,000 purchased on 1st January, 2008 was sold at 10% loss at the end of the year. Depreciation is written off by reducing balance method at 10% p.a.

ii) A piece of land has been sold and the profit on sale is credited to Capital Reserve Account.

iii) Interim Dividend of Rs. 20,000 has been paid in the year.

iv) Taxes paid during the year are Rs. 60,000.

v) Compensation of Rs. 10,000 has been paid to a worker who was injured in an accident.

Solution 8

Machinery A/c

	Rs.		Rs.
To Balance b/d	80,000	By Bank	40,500
To Bank A/c	2,07,500	By Loss on Sale	4,500
		By Depreciation (5,000 + 17,500)	22,500
		By Balance c/d	2,20,000
	2,87,500		2,87,500

Land & Buildings A/c

	Rs.		Rs.
To Balance b/d	2,50,000	By Bank A/c	90,000
To Capital Reserve (Profit on Sale)	30,000	By Balance c/d	1,90,000
	2,80,000		2,80,000

Provision for Taxation A/c

	Rs.		Rs.
To Bank A/c	60,000	By Balance c/d	50,000
To Balance c/d	30,000	By Profit & Loss A/c	40,000
	90,000		90,000

Capital Reserve A/c

	Rs.		Rs.
To Balance c/d	30,000	By Land & Buildings A/c	30,000
	30,000		30,000

Loss on Sale of Machinery

		Rs.			Rs.
1.1.2001	Cost of Machinery	50,000	31.12.2001	WDV of	
31.12.2001	Less : Depreciation	5,000		Machinery	2,20,000
	WDV	45,000		Less : WDV of	
	Loss			Machinery Sold	45,000
	(10% of 45,000)	4,500		WDV with the	
	Sale	40,500		Company	1,75,000
				Depreciation @ 10%	17,500

Cash Flow Statement
for the year ended 31st December, 2009

	Rs.	Rs.
Cash Flow from operating activities		
P & L A/c Balance at the end of the year	48,000	
Less : P & L A/c Balance at the beginning of the year	40,000	
Net Profit after Appropriation	8,000	
Transfer from General Reserve	10,000	
Provision for Dividend	27,000	
Provision for Taxation	40,000	
Goodwill Written Off	20,000	
Loss on Sale of Machinery	4,500	
Depreciation	22,500	
Interim Dividend	20,000	
Compensation to Workers provided	10,000	

	Rs.	Rs.
Operating Profit before Working Capital changes	1,62,000	
Changes in Working Capital :		
Decrease in Debtors	10,000	
Decrease in Stock	10,000	
Increase in Creditors	20,000	
Decrease in Bills Payable	(4,000)	
Cash generated from Operations	1,98,000	
Payment of Income Tax	(60,000)	
Cash Flow before extraordinary items	1,38,000	
Payment of compensation to a Worker	(10,000)	
Net Cash from operating activities		1,28,000
Cash Flow from investing activities :		
Sale of Machinery	40,500	
Sale of Land and Building	90,000	
Purchase of Machinery	(2,07,500)	
Purchase of Investments	(10,000)	(87,000)
Cash Flow from financing activities :		
Issue of Equity Share Capital	1,00,000	
Redemption of Preference Share Capital	(80,000)	
Payment of Dividend	(25,000)	
Payment of Interim Dividend	(20,000)	(25,000)
Net increase in Cash and Cash equivalent		16,000
Add : Cash & Cash equivalent		
at the beginning of the year :		
Cash	15,000	
Bank	70,000	85,000
Cash & Cash equivalent at the end of the year :		1,01,000
Cash	21,000	
Bank	80,000	1,01,000

Illustration : 9

From the Balance Sheets as on 31st March, 2009 and 31st March, 2008 of 'Man AC' Ltd., Pune, prepare a cash flow statement.

Balance Sheet

Liabilities	31.3.2008 Rs.	31.3.2009 Rs.	Assets	31.3.2008 Rs.	31.3.2009 Rs.
Equity Share Capital	3,00,000	4,00,000	Fixed Assets	3,00,000	3,30,000
(Face Value Rs.100)			Trade Investments	80,000	90,000
General Reserve	1,00,000	30,000	Stock	80,560	70,650
Profit & Loss A/c	20,500	30,400	Debtors	1,35,650	1,20,740
Proposed Dividend	30,000	40,000	Cash at Bank	40,500	30,500
Provision for Taxation	40,000	50,000	Preliminary Expenses	10,000	5,000
Bills Payable	10,000	10,000	Prepaid Expenses	–	4,000
Sundry Creditors	1,46,210	90,490			
	6,46,710	6,50,890		6,46,710	6,50,890

Additional information :

1. Bonus shares have been issued @ 1 for 5 shares held, out of General Reserves (Ratio 5 : 1)
2. The Fixed Assets are depreciated @ 10% on the opening balance.
3. An interim dividend of Rs.20,000 has been paid.
4. Trade investments of Rs.20,000 are written off against the General Reserve and investments of Rs.10,000 are sold at 10% loss which is debited to Profit and Loss Account.
5. A machine costing Rs.15,000 having depreciated upto 6,000 was sold at 10% profit.
6. Taxes paid during the year are Rs. 30,000.

Solution 9

Equity Share Capital A/c

	Rs.		Rs.
To Balance c/d	4,00,000	By Balance b/d	3,00,000
		By General Reserve	60,000
		By Bank	40,000
	4,00,000		4,00,000

General Reserve A/c

	Rs.		Rs.
To Equity Share Capital	60,000	By Balance b/d	1,00,000
To Trade Investments	20,000	By Profit & Loss A/c	10,000
To Balance c/d	30,000		
	1,10,000		1,10,000

Fixed Assets A/c

	Rs.		Rs.
To Balance b/d	3,00,000	By Depreciation	30,000
To Profit & Loss A/c	600	By Bank	6,600
To Bank	66,000	By Balance c/d	3,30,000
	3,66,600		3,66,600

Trade Investment A/c

	Rs.		Rs.
To Balance b/d	80,000	By General Reserve	20,000
To Bank	40,000	By Bank	9,000
		By Profit & Loss A/c	1,000
		By Balance c/d	90,000
	1,20,000		1,20,000

Provision for Taxation A/c

	Rs.		Rs.
To Bank	30,000	By Balance b/d	40,000
To Balance c/d	50,000	By Profit & Loss A/c	40,000
	80,000		80,000

Cash Flow Statement
for the year ended 31st March, 2002

	Rs.	Rs.
Cash Flow from operating activities		
P & L A/c Balance at the end of the year	30,400	
Less : P & L A/c Balance at the beginning of the year	20,500	
Net Profit before Adjustment	9,900	
Transfer to General Reserve	10,000	
Depreciation	30,000	
Profit on Sale of Fixed Assets	(600)	
Loss on Sale of Investments	1,000	
Provision for Taxation	40,000	
Provision for Dividend	40,000	
Interim Dividend	20,000	

	Rs.	Rs.
Preliminary Expenses Written Off	5,000	
Operating Profit before Working Capital changes	1,55,300	
Changes in Working Capital :		
Decrease in Stock	9,910	
Decrease in Debtors	14,910	
Increase in Pre-paid Expenses	(4,000)	
Decrease in Creditors	(55,720)	
	1,20,400	
Payment of Income Tax	(30,000)	
Net Cash from operating activities		90,400
Cash Flow from investing activities :		
Sale of Machinery	6,600	
Sale of Investments	9,000	
Purchase of Fixed Assets	(66,000)	
Purchase of Investments	(40,000)	(90,400)
Cash Flow from financing activities :		
Issue of Equity Share Capital	40,000	
Payment of Dividend	(30,000)	
Payment of Interim Dividend	(20,000)	(10,000)
Net increase in Cash and Cash equivalent		(10,000)
Add : Cash and Cash equivalent at the beginning of the year		40,500
		30,500
Cash and Cash equivalent at the end of the year		30,500

Questions

Objective Type

A. State whether the following Statements are True or False :

1) Purchase of Stock-in-trade is an application of Funds.
2) A decrease in current liabilities increases Working Capital.
3) Fund flow refer to changes in long-term funds.
4) The Fund Flow Statement shows the position of business as on the closing date of business period.
5) Working Capital is the difference between fixed assets and current assets.
6) Fund Flow Statement show changes in the individual items comprising working capital.
7) Cash or credit sales increases working capital.
8) Purchase of fixed assets is a use of Funds.

9) Amortisation of preliminary expenses is a use of Funds.

10) Payment of dividend is a use of Funds.

11) For Fund Flow Statement, provision for taxation will be treated as an item of internal sources.

Answers :

1) False   2) True   3) False   4) False   5) False   6) False

7) True   8) True   9) False   10) True   11) True

B) State whether the following statements are True or false :

1) Cash Flow Statement reveals the effect of transactions involving movement of cash.

2) The term 'Funds' mean 'Current Assets' in case of a cash flow analysis.

3) A Cash Flow Statement can very well be equated with an 'Income Statement.'

4) A Company should keep large balance of cash in hand to meet all contingencies.

5) Increase in provision for doubtful debts should be added back in order to find out cash from Operations.

6) Fund Flow Statement and Cash Flow Statement are one and the same.

Ans : 1) True 2) False 3) False 4) False 5) True 6) False

C) Fill in the blanks :

1) Fund flow refers to changes in ..... Capital.

2) Building sold on credit is ...... of funds.

3) Goods purchased on credit ...... in flow of funds.

4) Commission outstanding is ..... of funds.

5) Any gain on sale of non-current assets should be ..... from the net profit for determining funds from Operations.

6) Difference between Current Assets and Current Liabilities is known as ......

7) Depreciation is sometimes treated as ...... funds.

Ans. : 1) Working 2) a source 3) does not result 4) an application 5) deducted 6) Working capital 7) a source

D) Fill in the blanks :

1) Cash from Operations is equal to .....

2) Increase in the amounts in Debtors is .....

3) Increase in the amount of Bills Payable results in ......

4) Cash Flow Statement show ..... in cash position from one period to another.

5) Creation of Reserves is an .... source.

6) Raising long-term loans is an ..... source.

Ans. : 1) increase in cash 2) decrease in cash 3) no change in cash 4) changes 5) internal 6) external

Essay Type

1) What is a 'Fund Flow Statement?' Examine its managerial uses.

2) 'A Fund Flow Statement' is a better substitute for an Income Statement.

3) Explain the various concepts of Fund in the context of Fund Flow Analysis.

4) What do you understand by Fund Flow Statement? How are they prepared? What are their uses?

5) What are the main advantages of Fund Flow Statement? Also describe its limitations.

6) Explain the meaning of a Cash Flow Statement. Discuss its utility.

7) Explain the technique of preparing a Cash Flow Statement with imaginary figures.

8) Distinguish between Cash Flow Statement and Fund Flow Statement.

9) What is a Cash Flow Statement? Discuss briefly the major classification of cash flows as per AS-3.

10) Write Short Notes on :–
   a) Examples of Operating Activities
   b) Uses of Cash Flow Statement
   c) Application of Funds.
   d) Importance of Fund Flow Statement.
   e) Statement of changes in Finanical Position.
   e) Non-current Assets
   f) Internal Sources of Cash
   g) External Sources of Cash
   h) Limitations of Cash Flow Analysis.
   i) Utility of Cash Flow Analysis
   j) Difference between Cash Flow Statement and Fund Flow Statement

Practial Exercises

1. Following are the summarised Balance Sheets of Indira Ltd., as at 31-3-08 and 31-3-07. You are required to prepare a Statement of Source and Application of Funds for the year ending 31st March, 1977.

Balance Sheets

Liabilities	31-3-08 Rs.	31-3-07 Rs.	Assets	31-3-08 Rs.	31-3-07 Rs.
Share Capital	2,60,000	2,00,000	Goodwill	5,000	10,000
General Reserve	50,000	50,000	Land & Building	1,75,000	1,80,000
Profit & Loss A/c	85,000	25,400	Plant & Machinery	3,29,000	2,49,000
Debentures	2,00,000	2,50,000	Investments	60,500	78,000
Sundry Creditors	1,80,000	1,45,000	Stock	1,23,000	78,000
Provision for Taxation	1,50,000	40,000	Sundry Debtors	1,80,000	64,000
Dividend Outstanding	6,500	–	Cash at Bank	45,000	40,000
			Discount on Debenture	6,000	6,500
			Pre-payments	8,000	4,900
	9,31,500	7,10,400		9,31,500	7,10,400

Additional information :

	31-3-08 Rs.	31-3-07 Rs.
1. Balances of accumulated depreciation		
a) Land & Buildings	80,000	75,000
b) Plant & Machinery	2,41,000	2,45,000
2. Depreciation charged during the year		
a) Land & Buildings	5,000	–
b) Plant & Machinery	21,000	–

3. a) During the year 2007-08, Plant standing in the books at written down value of Rs. 20,000. Accumulated depreciation thereon being Rs. 25,000 was sold for Rs. 15,000. Loss adjusted to Profit & Loss A/c.

   b) Investment costing Rs. 15,000 was sold for Rs. 18,000. Profit & Loss A/c.

   c) Dividend paid during the year Rs. 6,500.

Ans. : 1. Increase in Working Capital Rs. 1,34,100.

2. Income from Operations Rs. 2,56,100.

3. Funds Flow Total Rs. 3,51,600.

Hints i) Dividend o/s Rs. 6,500 + Dividend paid during the year Rs. 6,500 totals to Rs. 13,000 is to be taken on debit of P & L A/c. and application Rs. 6,500 only.

ii) Add accumulated depreciation in opening and closing balance of Building & Machinery while preparing those accounts.

iii) Purchase of Plant Rs. 1,21,000.

iv) On Investment A/c after taking all items, yet there is a difference on credit side of Rs. 2,500 which is treated as second sale of investments at cost. So, the total of investment sold comes to Rs. 18,000 + 2,500 = 20,500.

v) Source = Rs. 60,000, 15,000, 20,500, 2,56,100
   Application = Rs. 50,000, 1,21,000, 6,500, 40,000

2. The summarised Balance Sheets of "VEE LTD.," as on 31-12-2005 and 2006 are as follows:

Balance Sheets

Liabilities	2005 Rs.	2006 Rs.	Assets	2005 Rs.	2006 Rs.
Share Capital	3,00,000	4,00,000	Fixed Assets	5,70,000	6,60,000
Capital Reserve	–	10,000	Trade Investments	1,00,000	80,000
General Reserve	1,70,000	2,00,000	Current Assets	2,80,000	3,30,000
Profit & Loss A/c	60,000	75,000	Preliminary Exp.	20,000	10,000
Debentures	2,00,000	1,40,000			

Liabilities	2005 Rs.	2006 Rs.	Assets	2005 Rs.	2006 Rs.
Liabilities for Goods & Services	1,20,000	1,30,000			
Provision for Income Tax	90,000	85,000			
Proposed Dividend	30,000	36,000			
Unpaid Dividend	–	4,000			
	9,70,000	10,80,000		9,70,000	10,80,000

Prepare a Fund Flow Statement after considering the following information :

During the year, 2006, the company

i) sold one Machine of Rs. 25,000, the book value of which was Rs. 29,000, loss being adjusted to Profit & Loss A/c;

ii) provided Rs. 95,000 as depreciation;

iii) redeemed 30% of the Debentures at Rs. 103;

iv) sold some Trade Investments at a profit, it being credited to Capital Reserve; and

v) decided to value the Stock at cost whereas previously the practice was to value Stock at cost less 10%. The Stock according to books on 31-12-2005 was Rs. 54,000, the Stock of 31st December, 2006, Rs. 75,000 was correctly valued at cost.

Ans. : 1. Increase in Working Capital Rs. 34,000.

2. Income from Operations Rs. 2,74,800.

3. Funds Flow Total Rs. 4,29,800.

Hints : a) Increase opening Current Assets by Rs. 6,000 being proper valuation of opening at 10% less than cost.

Again, Rs. 6,000 increase in value of last year's closing stock will increase profit of last year by Rs. 6,000, i.e. to be credited to P & L A/c.

b) Purchase of Fixed Assets Rs. 2,14,000.

c) Capital Reserve Rs. 10,000 to be debited to Investments A/c only.

d) Redemption of Debentures Rs. 60,000 + 3%, Premium Rs. 1,800. Total amount of redemption Rs. 61,800 on. Application. Further, Rs. 1,800 to be debited to P & L A/c.

e) Source = Rs. 2,74,800, 1,00,000, 25,000, 30,000.

Application = Rs. 34,000, 61,800, 90,000, 30,000, 2,14,000.

3. The book figures of Bhagyoday Ltd., as on 31st March, 2007 and 31st March, 2008 are as follows:

	31-3-07 Rs.	31-3-08 Rs.
Share Capital :		
Shares of Rs. 100 each.	1,50,000	1,75,000
Share Premium	–	5,000
Profit on Sale of Freehold	–	1,450
Profit & Loss A/c (Cr.)	16,000	30,000
Debentures	25,000	–
Current Liabilities	32,000	34,000
Freehold Properties	10,000	8,000
Plant less Depreciation	1,43,000	1,54,000
Preliminary Expenses	800	400
Current Assets	69,200	83,050

The Share Capital issued in 2007-08, was entirely for cash. Plant depreciation for the year ending 31st March, 2008, was Rs. 14,000. Dividend paid during the year Rs. 7,500.

Prepare a statement showing :
  a) net increase in working capital during the year ended 31-3-08; and
  b) the Sources and Application of the funds during the year.

Ans.: i)   Increase in working capital Rs. 11,850,
     ii)   Income from Operations Rs. 35,900.
     iii) Funds Flow Total Rs. 69,350.

Hints : a) Profit on Sale of Freehold is to be debited only to Freehold Property A/c. Do not take on credit of P & L A/c.
     b)   Take depreciation of Plant Rs. 14,000 on credit of Plant A/c & debit of P & L A/c.
     c)   Purchase of Plant Rs. 25,000 & Sale of Freehold Rs. 3,450
     d)   Sources = Rs. 35,900, 25,000, 5,000, 3,450.
         Application = Rs. 11,850, 25,000, 7,500, 25,000.

4. The summarised Balance Sheets of 'AB' Ltd., are set out below :

Balance Sheets

Liabilities	31-12-07 Rs.	31-12-08 Rs.	Assets	31-12-07 Rs.	31-12-08 Rs.
Equity Shares			**Fixed Assets :**		
of Rs. 10 each	1,00,000	2,00,000	Building at Cost	60,000	70,000
General Reserve	–	10,000	Machinery at Cost	50,000	55,000
Share Premium	2,000	12,000	Investment	5,000	45,000
Profit & Loss	10,000	14,000	**Current Assets :**		
5% Debentures	1,00,000	50,000	Stock	80,000	1,00,000
			Bills Receivable	5,000	13,000

Liabilities	31-12-07 Rs.	31-12-08 Rs.	Assets	31-12-07 Rs.	31-12-08 Rs.
Current Liabilities					
Loan	20,000	–	Debtors	58,000	75,000
Bills Payable	15,000	7,000	Cash in Hand	7,000	2,000
Creditors	20,000	40,000	Cash at Bank	40,000	30,000
Accrued Exp.	5,000	7,000	Pre-paid Expenses	2,000	3,000
Provision : Depreciation on			**Miscellaneous Exp. :**		
Building	25,000	35,000	Preliminary Exp.	5,000	–
Machinery	15,000	20,000	Loss on Sale		
			of Machinery	-	2,000
	3,12,000	3,95,000		3,12,000	3,95,000

Profit & Loss A/c for 2008

	Rs.		Rs.
To Depreciation	19,000	By Trading Profit	46,500
To Debenture Interest	2,500	By Balance b/d from last year	10,000
To Preliminary Expenses	5,000		
To General Reserve	10,000		
To Interim Dividend paid	6,000		
To Balance c/d	14,000		
	56,500		56,500

Further Information :

    1. Debentures were redeemed on 1-7-2008 and the debentureholders were paid as follows :

       a) Rs. 22,500 plus amount of accrued interest in cash.

       b) 2,500 equity shares of Rs. 10 each issued as fully paid at a Premium of Re. 1 per share.

    2. The Balance of the equity shares were issued for cash at a premium of Re. 1 per share.

    3. Certain machinery was sold during 2008 for which the following entry was made :–

       Cash A/c   Dr.   Rs. 6,000.

       Provision for Depreciation A/c   Dr.   Rs. 4,000.

       Loss on Sale of Plant A/c   Dr.   Rs. 2,000.

          To Machinery A/c   Rs. 12,000

Prepare the Statement showing the Sources and Application of Funds during the year 2008. Also, prepare the Statement Showing changes in Working Capital.

Ans : 1. Income from Operations Rs. 44,000.

      2. Increase in Working Capital Rs. 37,000.

      3. Funds Flow Total Rs. 1,32,500.)

Hints : 1. Prepare P & L A/c by taking Opening Balance, Closing Balance & all items from given

P & L A/c except Debenture Interest & Trading Profit.

2. Issue of Shares for Cash Rs. 75,000. (increase Rs. 1,00,000 - Rs. 25,000 Shares to Debentureholders.)
3. Purchase of Machinery Rs. 17,000.
4. Sources = Rs. 44,000, 75,000, 7,500, 6,000.
    Application = Rs. 22,500, 17,000, 6,000, 40,000, 10,000, 37,000.

5) The following are the summaries of the Balance Sheets of a limited company on 31-12-2007 and 2008.

Balance Sheets

Liabilities	2007 Rs.	2008 Rs.	Assets	2007 Rs.	2008 Rs.
Sundry Creditors	39,500	41,135	Cash at Bank	2,500	2,700
Bills Payable	33,780	11,525	Sundry Debtors	85,175	72,625
Bank Overdraft	59,510	–	Sundry Advances	2,315	735
Provision for Taxation	40,000	50,000	Stock	1,11,040	97,370
Reserves	50,000	50,000	Plant & Machinery	1,12,950	1,16,200
P & L A/c	39,690	41,220	Land & Buildings	1,48,500	1,44,250
Share Capital	2,00,000	2,60,000	Goodwill	–	20,000
	4,62,480	4,53,880		4,62,480	4,53,880

The following additional information is obtained from the general ledger :

i) During the year ended 31-12-2008, an interim dividend of Rs. 26,000 was paid.
ii) The assets of another Co., were purchased for Rs. 60,000 payable in fully paid shares of the Company. These assets consisted of stock Rs. 2,640, Machinery Rs. 18,360 and Goodwill Rs. 20,000. In addition, sundry purchases of Plant were made totaling to Rs. 5,650.
iii) Income Tax paid during the year Rs. 25,000.
iv) The net profit for the year before Tax was Rs. 62,530.

Prepare a Fund Flow Statement.

Ans : i) Increase in Working Capital Rs. 52,530
        ii) Fund Flow Statement Total Rs. 1,09,180
        iii) Income from Operations Rs. 87,540.)

Hints : a) Bank Overdraft is a Current Liability,
           b) The total increase in share capital is of Rs. 60,000 (2,60,000 - 2,00,000) but we have to take only increase in share capital at Rs. 21,640 (for Stock taken from another Co.); because the amount of Machinery Rs. 18,360 and Goodwill is a part Non-current Assets.

So, source of funds from share capital to be taken at Rs. 21,640 and not Rs. 60,000.

c) Sundry Advances is a Current Asset.

6) Following are the summaries of the Balance Sheets of a limited company as on 31-12-2007 and 2008

	2007 Rs.	2008 Rs.
Paid-up Capital	1,00,000	1,00,000
General Reserve	21,400	26,000
P & L A/c	17,000	16,000
Creditors	9,750	6,380
Provision for Taxation	19,000	21,000
Provision for Doubtful Debts	1,000	1,200
	1,68,150	1,70,580
Building	46,800	45,000
Machinery	38,280	42,030
Goodwill	13,000	13,000
Investments	10,000	11,250
Stock	30,000	28,000
Debtors	22,000	22,000
Pre-paid Expenses	70	300
Cash	8,000	9,000
	1,68,150	1,70,580

Adjustments

i) The profit for the year - 2008 was Rs. 8,600 which has been arrived at after charging Rs. 3,050 by way of depreciation and increase in provision for doubtful debts Rs. 200.

ii) An interim dividend of Rs. 5,000 was paid in October, 2008.

iii) Additional Machinery was purchased in May, 2008 for Rs. 5,000.

iv) Investments (Cost Rs. 5,000) were sold in Nov., 2008 for Rs. 4,800 and on 1-1-2008, another Investment was made for Rs. 6,250.

v) Income Tax of Rs. 18,000 was paid during the year and charged against the provsion.

Prepare a Fund Flow Statement.

Ans. : i) Increase in Working Capital Rs. 2,400,

ii) Fund Flow Statement total Rs. 36,650,

iii) Income from Operations Rs. 31,850.)

7) The following are the summarised Balance Sheets of 'X' Ltd., as on 31st March, 2007 and 2008.

Balance Sheets

Liabilities	31-3-07 Rs.	31-3-08 Rs.	Assets	31-3-07 Rs.	31-3-08 Rs.
Share Capital	4,50,000	4,50,000	Fixed Assets	4,00,000	3,20,000
General Reserve	3,00,000	3,10,000	Investments	50,000	60,000
P & L A/c	56,000	68,000	Stock	2,40,000	2,10,000
Sundry Creditors	1,68,000	1,34,000	Debtors	2,10,000	4,55,000
Mortgage Loan	–	2,70,000	Bank	1,49,000	1,97,000
Provision for Taxation	75,000	10,000			
	10,49,000	12,42,000		10,49,000	12,42,000

Additional information :

1. Investments costing Rs. 8,000 were sold during the year for Rs. 8,500 and further investments were purchased during the year for Rs. 18,000.
2. The net profit for the year was Rs. 62,000 after charging depreciation on fixed assets Rs. 70,000 for the year and provision for taxation Rs. 10,000.
3. During the year, part of fixed assets costing Rs. 10,000 was disposed off for Rs. 12,000 and the profit is included in the P & L A/c
4. Dividend paid during the year Rs. 40,000.

Prepare a Fund Flow Statement as on 31-3-08

Ans.: i) Increase in Working Capital Rs. 2,97,000.

ii) Fund Flow Statement Total Rs. 4,30,000.)

Hint : a)

Profit & Loss A/c

Dr. Cr.

	Rs.		Rs.
To Depreciation	70,000	By Balance b/d (2007)	56,000
To Provision for Taxation	10,000	By Profit on Sale of Fixed Assets	2,000
To Dividend paid (Application)	40,000		
To General Reserve (Transfer)	10,000	By Profit on Sale of Investments	500
To Balance c/d (2008)	68,000	By Source from Operations	1,39,500
(Balancing figure)		(Balancing figure)	
	1,98,000		1,98,000

Hint : b) Do not consider the amount of net profit Rs. 62,000 given in the adjustments.

c) Mortgage loan is a non-current item.

d) Investment is for a long-term one, and hence, a non-current item.

8) The comparative Balance Sheets of Alka Trading Corporation Ltd., are indicated in a condensed form as under :–

	31-12-2008 Rs.		31-12-2007 Rs.	
Fixed Assets	5,20,000		4,80,000	
Less : Depreciation todate	1,40,000		1,08,000	3,72,000
		3,80,000		
Investment at Cost		50,000		1,00,000
Stocks		90,500		55,600
Sundry Debtors		1,67,800		1,18,300
Cash at Bank		47,500		49,800
Preliminary Expenses	-	–		7,200
		7,35,800		7,02,900
Equity Share of Rs. 100		4,00,000		3,60,000
General Reserve		60,000		1,10,000
Surplus in P & L A/c		33,450		20,450
Sundry Creditors		1,95,350		1,33,650
Proposed Dividend		15,000		28,800
Provision for Taxation		32,000		50,000
		7,35,800		7,02,900

The net profit for the year (after providing for depreciation Rs. 40,000, writting off preliminary expenses Rs. 7,200 and making provision for taxation Rs. 32,000,) amounting to Rs. 38,000. The Company sold during the year an old machinery costing Rs. 9,000 for Rs. 3,000. The accumulated depreciation on the said machinery was Rs. 8,000.

A portion of the company's investment became worthless and was written off to General Reserve. The cost of such Investments Rs. 50,000.

During the year the Company paid an Interim Dividend of Rs. 10,000 and directors have recommended a final dividend of Rs. 15,000 for the year 2008.

Prepare –

a) Fund flow statements for the year, 2008; and

b) Schedule of Working Capital changes

Ans.: i) Increase in Working Capital Rs. 20,400

ii) Fund Flow Statement Total Rs. 1,58,200

iii) Income from Operations Rs. 1,15,200

9) From the information provided you are required to prepare a Cash Flow Statement according to AS-3

Liabilities	2008 Rs.	2009 Rs.	Assets	2008 Rs.	2009 Rs.
Issued Share Capital	1,00,000	1,50,000	Freehold Property		
Share Premium	15,000	35,000	at Cost	1,10,000	1,30,000
Profit & Loss	28,000	70,000	Plant & Machinery		
Debentures	70,000	30,000	at Cost	1,20,000	1,51,000
Bank Overdraft	14,000	–	Fixtures & Fittings		
Creditors	34,000	48,000	at Cost	24,000	29,000
Proposed Dividend	15,000	20,000	Stocks	37,000	51,000
Depreciation -			Debtors	43,000	44,000
Plant	45,000	54,000	Bank Balance	–	16,000
Fixtures	13,000	15,000	Premium on		
			Redemption of		
			Debentures	–	1,000
	3,34,000	4,22,000		3,34,000	4,22,000

The following additional information is relevant –

i) There had been no disposal of freehold property in the year.

ii) A machine tool which had cost Rs. 8,000 and in respect of which Rs. 6,000 depreciation had been provided for was sold for Rs. 3,000 and fixtues which had cost Rs. 5,000 in respect of which depreciation of Rs. 2,000 had been provided was sold for Rs. 1,000. The profits and losses on these transactions had been dealt with through the profit & Loss A/c

iii) The actual premium on the redemption of debentures was Rs. 2,000, of which Rs. 1,000 had been written off to the profit & loss account.

iv) No interim dividend had been paid.

Ans. : 1) Cash from Operations Rs. 82,000.

      2) Purchase of Machinery Rs. 39,000.

      3) Depreciation on Machinery Rs. 15,000.

10) Following are the comparative Balance Sheets of Spraylac Paint Ltd., for the year ended 31st Dec., 2007. and 31st Dec., 2008. Prepare a Cash Flow Statement.

	2007 Rs.	2008 Rs.
Cash	43,000	58,000
Pre-paid Expenses	2,000	2,000
Debtors	80,000	90,000
Stock	32,000	40,000
Investments (Long-term)	50,000	30,000
Machinery at Cost	25,000	40,000
Building at Cost	75,000	90,000
Land	10,000	10,000
	3,17,000	3,60,000
Provision for Doubtful Debts	2,000	3,000
Accumulated Depreciation		
Machinery	3,000	7,500
Building	12,000	18,000
Creditors	33,000	40,000
Outstanding Expenses	3,500	4,500
Debentures	40,000	35,000
Equity Share Capital	2,00,000	2,00,000
Profit & Loss A/c	23,500	52,000
	3,17,000	3,60,000

Additional information

i) Dividend paid during the year 2008 was Rs. 26,500

ii) Investments costing Rs. 20,000 were sold in 2008 for Rs. 25,000.

iii) Machinery costing Rs. 5,000, on which Rs. 1,000 depreciation has been accumulated was sold for Rs. 6,000 in 2008.

Ans. i) Cash from Operations Rs. 50,500

ii) Purchase of Machinery Rs. 20,000.

11) The following are the summarised Trial Blances of 'PQ' Ltd., at 31st March, 2007 and 2008 :

	31-03-2007		31-03-2008	
	Rs.	Rs.	Rs.	Rs.
30,000 Shares of Rs. 10 each, fully paid	.....	3,00,000	....	3,00,000
Capital Reserve	......	....	......	49,200
8% Debentures	....	.....	.....	50,000
Debenture Discount	.....	....	1,000	....
Freehold Property at Cost	1,22,000	.....	....	....
Freehold Property at Valuation	.....	.....	1,65,000	.....
Plant and Machinery at Cost	2,23,000	....	2,83,000	......
Depreciation on Plant & Machinery	....	1,07,600	......	1,22,000
Debtors	1,04,600	.....	1,54,600	......
Stock and Work-in-progress	1,24,000	....	1,62,500	......
Creditors	.....	37,400	....	49,200
Profit & Loss Account	.....	1,12,000	.....	1,12,000
Net Profit for the year	....	....	.....	76,500
Dividend paid in respect of 2007	......	.....	30,000	.....
Provision for Doubtful Debts	.....	3,100	.....	6,400
Trade Investment at Cost	.....	.....	47,000	....
Bank	.....	13,500		77,800
Total Rs.	5,73,600	5,73,600	8,43,100	8,43,100

You are informed that :
   i) The Capital Reserve on 31-03-2008 represented the realised profit on the sale of one freehold property together with the surplus arising on revaluation.
   ii) During the year ended 31-3-2008, plant costing Rs. 18,000 against which a depreciation provision of Rs. 13,500 had been made was sold for Rs. 7,000.
   iii) On 1-04-2007, Rs. 50,000 debentures were issued for cash at a discount of Rs. 1,000.
   iv) The net profit for the year is arrived at after crediting the profit on the sale of machinery and charging debenture interest.
   You are required to prepare a Cash Flow Statement according to AS-3 showing how the borrowing has increased by Rs. 64,300* during the year ended 30-6-2008.
   Taxation has been and is to be ignored.
Ans. : 1) Cash from Operations Rs. 28,500.
   2) Increase in Overdraft Rs. 64,300.
   3) Purchase of Plant Rs. 78,000.

■ ■ ■

CHAPTER 4

Working Capital

● 4:1 Meaning of Working Capital ● 4:2 Objectives of Working Capital ● 4:3 Importance of Working Capital ● 4:4 Factors Determining Requirements of Working Capital ● 4:5 Sources of Working Capital ● 4:6 Estimation of Working Capital ● 4:7 Computation of Working Capital ● 4:8 Illustrations of Working Capital requirements ● 4:9 Exercises

Working capital is required by all industries irrespective of whether they are engaged in manufacturing or service industries. It stands for that part of capital which is required for financing the working or current needs of the company or industry. Working capital is also called as short-term capital or circulating or floating capital. It is usually invested in current assets like raw materials, partly-finished stocks, account receivables, in saleable securities and cash. Capital in all these forms is constantly being converted into cash and this cash flows out again in exchange for other forms of working capital As this capital is revolving, it is rightly called as circulating capital. In short, apart from investment in fixed assets, every industry has to arrange for adequate funds for meeting day-to-day expenses.

4:1 Meaning of Working Capital

The term 'working capital' is defined by various authors keeping in mind the various views. Some of the definitions of working capital are as follows :–

1) According to **Lincoln and Doris :** "Working capital is the excess of current assets over current liabilities as designated in the following equation :
   Working Capital = Current Assets - Current Liabilities

2) In the words of **Gerestenberg :** "Circulating capital means current assets of the Company that are changed in the ordinary course of business from one form to another as for example from cash to inventories, inventories to receivables and receivables into cash."

3) **Hoagland** gives a simple definition of the term working capital. According to him, "Working capital is descriptive of that capital which is not fixed. The more common use of working capital is to consider it as the difference between the book value of the current assets and current liabilities.

From the above definitions, the term 'working capital' may be used in two different ways.

1) Gross Working Capital or Total Working Capital :

The gross working capital refers to the firm's investment in all the current assets taken together. The total of investments in all the individual current assets is the gross working capital. For example, if a firm has a cash balance of Rs. 40,000, bank balance of Rs. 30,000, debtors of Rs. 60,000 and inventory of raw materials and finished goods has been assessed at Rs. 1,50,000, then the gross working capital of the firm is Rs. 2,80,000 i.e. Rs. 40,000 + Rs. 30,000 + Rs. 60,000 + Rs. 1,50,000).

2) Net Working Capital :

The net working capital may he defined as the excess of total current assets over total current liabilities. Current assets are those assets that in the ordinary course of business can be or will be tumed into cash within a short period (not exceeding one year) without undergoing diminution of value and without disrupting the organisation. Examples of current assets are given below. (i) Cash in hand and cash at bank, (ii) Debtors, (iii) Bills Receivables, (iv) Stock or inventories of raw materials, Work-in-progress and finished goods, (v) Marketable securities held as temporary investment, and (vi) Accrued income etc.

Current liabilities refer to those liabilities which are payable within a period of one year out of current assets or the income of the business. Its examples may be listed as below. (i) Accounts payable to Creditors. (ii) Notes or bills payable. (iii) Accrued expenses such as accrued taxes, salaries and interest. (iv) Liability reserves of the nature of accrued expenses, such as reserve for income taxes (provision for income tax). (v) Bonds to be paid within one year and (vi) dividends payable. etc.

The net working capital may either be positive or negative. If the total current assets are more than total current liabilities, then the difference is known as positive net working capital, otherwise the difference is known as negative net working capital. The net working capital measures firm's liquidity. The greater the margin. (i.e. net working capital) by which the firm's current assets over its current liabilities, the better will it be. Although the firm's current assets may not be converted into cash precisely when they are needed, still greater net working capital assures that in all likelihood some current assets will be converted into cash to pay the current liabilities.

4:2 Objectives of Working Capital

The need and importance of adequate working capital for day-to-day operations can hardly be underestimated. Every firm must maintain a sound working capital position - otherwise, its business activities may be adversely affected. The financial manager must see that the firm has sufficient working capital as and when required so that the fixed assets of the firm are optimally used. The objective of financial management to maximise the wealth of shareholders cannot be attained if the operations of the firm are not optimised. Hence, every firm or business must have adequate capital. It should have neither excessive working capital nor inadequate working capital. Both situations are risky and dangerous to business. In short, adequacy of working capital is the life-blood and nerve centre that controls the business.

The basic **objectives of working capital management** are as follows :

1) By optimising in investment in current assets and by reducing the level of current liabilities, the Company or firm can reduce the locking up of funds in working capital thereby, it can improve the return on capital employed in the business.

2) The second important objective of working capital management is that the Company should

always be in a position to meet its current obligations which should properly be supported by the current assets available within the firm. But maintaining excess fund in working capital means locking up of funds without any productive return.

3) The firm should manage its current assets in such a way that the managerial returns on investment in these assets is not less than the cost of capital employed to finance the current assets.

4:3 Importance of Working Capital

The main advantages of having sufficient amount of working capital may be enumerated as follows :

1) Feeling of security and confidence : If the business has adequate amount of working capital, the proprietor, officers, creditors, customers etc., feel secure and safe. The day-to-day payment like wages and salaries, cost of raw materials can be paid in time. This ensures confidence among the various parties concerned with the business.

2) Creation of sound goodwill : Goodwill means reputation of the business. It is a common experience that goodwill can be maintained or increased if the payments are made in time. The prompt payment of bills to suppliers of material will not only ensure a continued supply of raw materials but also establish credit for future or for seasonal operations.

3) Quick and steady returns to investors : All investors expect quick and steady returns on their investments. The shareholders have invested their capital in the shares of the company. Banks and creditors have given loans to the company. Shareholders expect returns in the form of dividend and creditors expect prompt payment of interest and principal. In case of insufficiency of working capital, major portion of profits are retained in the business. But, in case of their adequacy, ample dividend can be paid to the shareholders and, similarly, payments of creditors too can be made in time.

4) For maintaining solvency and continuity in production : Adequate capital is a must for maintaining solvency and continuing production. For doing so, it is essential that sufficient amount of funds be available to purchase raw materials, pay the wage and salary bill, stock finished goods and meet other administrative expenses. Manufacturing concerns or commercial enterprises may collapse if sufficient working capital is not available.

5) Easy loans from banks : The banks generally provide loan to those industry or business, which runs in profit and maintain liquidity. Banks are also favourably inclined in granting seasonal loan if the business is adequately financed and has a good credit standing and reputation. In order to borrow from banks, a business or industry must keep itself in a fairly liquid condition. Thus, adequacy of working capital contributes a lot in raising the credit standing of the company.

6) Easy availability of cash discount : Due to the availability of adequate working capital, purchases are made on cash basis. This ensures cash and trade discount. Thus, the advantage may be taken of cash discounts in the purchase of raw materials, resulting in saving in interest charges on the amount of working capital employed.

7) Facility of off-season purchasing : Only the business concerns with adequate working capital can take advantage of purchasing raw materials, coal or other factory supplies in a sharply advancing market or in off season periods, resulting in substantial savings where storage costs are not prohibitive.

8) Quick and prompt target sales : There is a obvious and inevitable relationship between the sales growth and the level of current assets. The target sales can be achieved only if supported by adequate working capital. The increase in sales volume requires an increase in working capital and, hence a financial manager must be able to respond quickly in providing and arranging additional working capital. Insufficient working capital may result in loss of sales and, consequently, in the decline in profits of the firm.

9) Periods of slump can easily be overcome : Business fluctuations are not in common in the life of an undertaking. It is no credit obtaining adequate amount of capital during boom periods, but during the period of depression when the demand for working capital usually shoots up, only concerns having ample resources can tide over such circumstances.

10) Steady work and efficiency in production : A continuous supply of raw materials and production means steady work for the employees which raises their morale, increases their efficiency, lowers costs besides creating goodwill in the community.

In short, an efficient working capital management is important from the point of view of both liquidity and profitability. Poor and inefficient working capital management means that the funds are unnecessarily tied up in idle assets. This reduces the liquidity as well as the ability to invest funds in productive assets, thus affecting the profitability. The financial manager must frame a suitable working capital policy, keeping in view the importance of working capital.

4.4 Factors Determining Requirements of Working Capital

Fixed capital requirements of a Company can be determined easily but it is very difficult to determine the working capital needs of a Company. The working capital needs of a Company are determined and influenced by various factors. A wide variety of considerations may affect the quantum of working capital required and these considerations may vary from time to time. Hence, no definite formula can be advocated for the determination of working capital. The determination of working capital requirement is a continuous process and must be undertaken on a regular basis in the light of changing situtations. Some of the important determinants of working capital requirements are as follows : These determinants can be classified as Internal factors and External factors.

a) Internal determinants of working capital

1) Nature of business : The working capital needs are closely related to the nature of the business of the firm. In certain types of enterprises like public utilities and railways, as compared to manufacturing concerns, lesser amount of working capital is required. It is because such concerns, by their very nature need more fixed capital and less raw materials. On the other hand, trading and manufacturing concerns have to invest large part of their total funds in the purchase of raw materials, payment of wage and salary bills and such other working expenses. Hence, large amount of working capital is required for trading or merchandising institutions. Working capital requirements of manufacturing concerns lie between the above two extreme requirements of trading concerns and public utilities. Such concerns require a large amount of working capital depending upon their total asset structure and other variables.

2) Size of business : Size of business is a significant factor for determining the proportion of working capital to fixed capital. The general principle in this connection is that the bigger the size of the unit, the more will be the amount of working capital required. But it is quite likely that bigger sized business units like consumer goods industry may require a large amount of fixed capital than working capital. Small firms having cash inflows from relatively fewer services are more affected by the defaults on the part of customers to pay in time. Larger firms with many resources of funds may require less working capital in relation to total assets or sales.

3) Manufacturing cycle : The quantum of working capital needed is influenced by the length of the manufacturing cycle. Manufacturing process always involve a time lag between the time when the raw materials are fed into the production line and finished products that are finally turned out by it. The length of the period of manufacture, in turn, depends on the nature of product as well as production technology used by the concern. For example, in ship building industry, a big ship takes 4 to 5 years for its construction, so large amount of working capital is required. On the other hand, in bakery industry, a very little time is required for processing the final product, and hence, lesser working capital is required.

4) Credit policy : The credit policy means the totality of terms and conditions on which goods are sold and purchased. A firm has to interact with two types of credit policies at a time. One, the credit policy of the supplier of raw materials, goods etc., and, two the credit policy relating to credit which it extends to customers. In both cases, however, the firm while deciding its credit policy has to take care of the credit policy of the market. For example, a firm might be purchasing goods and services on credit terms but selling only for cash. The working capital requirements of this firm, will be obviously lower than that of a firm which is purchasing on cash but has to sell the same on a credit basis.

5) Depreciation policy : The depreciation policy influences the level of working capital by affecting tax liability and retained earning of the enterprise. Since depreciation is tax deductible expenses item, higher amount of depreciation result in lower taxes and greater profits. Similarly, the amount of net profit will be less if higher amount of depreciation is charged. If dividend policy is linked with net profits, the firm can pay less dividend by providing for more depreciation. This will result in increased earnings and strengthen the firm's working capital position.

6) Time consumed between order and delivery : An important influence on the inventory size is the time involved size is the time involved between order and delivery of the goods. When time element is uncertain, a larger amount must be invested in raw materials. Efficiency in handling inventories and getting deliveries from railroads and other transport agencies to and from market makes it possible to carry comparatively low inventories.

7) Growth and expansions of business : Working capital requirements of an enterprise tend to increase in correspondence with the growth in volume of sales. Although there is no definite relationship between the volume of a company's business and growth in its working capital, it is usually found in actual practice that the growing firms require additional funds to acquire additional fixed assets so as to sustain its growing production and sales. Besides, additional current assets will support the increased scale of production. It can be further noted that a growing enterprise requires additional funds continuously to fulfil the increased needs of its business.

8) Turnover of circulating capital : Turnover of working or circulating capital plays an important and decisive role in judging the adequacy of working capital. By turnover is meant the ratio of annual gross sales to average working assets. It is that figure which shows how many times the amount invested in working assets has been traded in our 'turnover' during a year. As a principle, it may be enunciated that greater the turnover, the larger the volume of business that can be conducted with a given working capital. On the other hand, if the sales are slow and irregular, a great amount of working capital will have be blocked up in purchase of stock. Thus, demand is the most important factor in determining the rapidity of turnover.

9) Current assets : If the Company follows conservative asset policy, it will operate with a high level of current assets relative to its sales volume. It has to carry large stocks of raw materials, inventories and finished goods, offer liberal terms of credit to customers and carry a large amount of cash to meet its current expenditure, all of which, in turn, demand a larger working capital. On the other hand, a Company following an aggressive current assets policy has to operate with a relatively lower level of working capital.

10) Co-ordination of activities in firm : Where production and distribution activities are co-ordinated, pressure on working capital will be minimised. On the other hand, in the absence of co-ordination in production and distribution policies, demand for working capital increases.

b) External factors :

11) Business cycle fluctuations : Different phases of business cycle i.e. boom, recession, recovery etc., also affect the working capital requirements. In case of boom conditions, inflationary pressure appears and business activities expand. As a result, the overall need for cash, inventories increases, resulting in more and more funds getting blocked in the current assets. In case of a recession period, however, there is usually a dullness in business activities and there will be an opposite effect on the level of working capital requirement. There will be a fall in inventories and cash requirements.

12) Technological developments : Technological developments in the area of production have a sharp effect on the need of working capital. If a firm or industry switches over to new manufacturing process and instals new equipments with which it is able to cut time periods involved in converting raw materials into finished goods, permanant working capital requirements of the firm will decrease. If the new machine can utilise less expensive raw materials, the inventory needs may be reduced.

13) Seasonal operations : If the firm is operating in goods and services having seasonal fluctuations in demand, then the working capital requirement will also fluctuate with every change. There are certain industries, wherein it becomes essential to purchase raw materials in bulk during a particular season and utilise them throughout the year. Such industries will require more working capital during the particular season. On the other hand, if the operations are smooth and even throughout the year, then the working capital requirements will be constant and will not be affected by the seasonal factors.

14) Taxation policy : Working capital needs of business enterprises are affected sharply by the taxation policy of the government. It heavy taxes are imposed on industries, more working capital will be required. On the other hand, if liberal taxation policy is adopted by the government, the pressure of working capital needs may be minimised.

4:5 Sources of Working Capital

The working capital needs can be bifurcated into permanent working capital and temporary working capital.

1) Permanent working capital : There is always a minimum level of working capital which is continuously required by a firm in order to maintain its activities. Every firm must have a minimum cash, stock and other current assets to meet its business requirements irrespective of the level of operations. Even during a slack season, every firm maintains some current assets. This minimum level of current assets which must be maintained by any firm at all times is known as the permanent working capital of that firm. This amount of working capital is constantly and regularly required in the same way as fixed assets are required, and hence it may also be called as fixed working capital. This fixed working capital may be procured by issuing shares, debentures and public deposits.

2) Temporary working capital : Over and above the permanent working capital, the firm may also require additional working capital in order to meet the requirements arising out of fluctuations in the sales volume. This extra working capital needed to support the increased volume of sales is known as temporary or fluctuating working capital. For example, in case of spurt in sales, more stocks must be manitained in order to meet the growing demand. Temporary working capital can be procured from commercial banks, money lenders and indigenous bankers.

In short, the sources of working capital can be depicted as follows :–

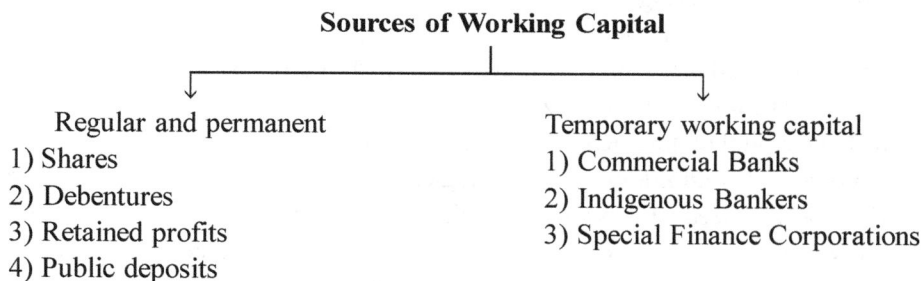

Sources of Working Capital

Regular and permanent	Temporary working capital
1) Shares	1) Commercial Banks
2) Debentures	2) Indigenous Bankers
3) Retained profits	3) Special Finance Corporations
4) Public deposits	

Sources of Regular or Permanent Working Capital :

There are three important sources of procuring the regular or fixed working capital viz., (a) Issue of shares (2) Issue of debentures and retained profits. According to well-defined canons of corporate finance, the minimum working capital requirements should be anticipated at the time of drafting the initial capital structure of the company and adequate provisions should be made in it for a long-term basis. Permanent or fixed working capital can be procured by the following sources :

1) Issue of Shares :

A Company can obtain permanent or fixed working capital by issuing different shares. It is the most common and important method of raising capital. The Company can issue following types of shares to raise the capital.

a) Ordinary or Equity Shares : A major portion of the capital of a Company is usually in the form of equity shares. These shares have no preferential right in the matter of payment of dividend or repayment of capital. The denomination of an equity share is too low, and hence, are purchased even by a layman. The Company has no obligation to return the amount of shares after a fixed period. Dividend on equity shares is not fixed and may vary from year to year depending upon the amount of profits available.

b) Preference Shares : Preference Share capital means that part of share capital of the company which fulfils both the following requirements :–

i) Preference shareholders have a priority in respect of receiving dividend. They get assured income in the form of dividend.

ii) Preference shareholders have a right to receive the paid-up value before anything is paid to equity shareholders.

In short, the Company may issue equity or perference shares for raising the permanent working capital.

2) Issue of Debentures :

Regular working capital can also be procured by way of issuing debentures. But it should be remembered in this connection that the method is resorted to only for satisfying the permanent working capital requirements and not the seasonal needs. The amount raised by issue of debentures is treated as borrowed capital. The debentureholders get a fixed rate of interest on the amount invested and debenture capital is repaid after the expiry of a certain period. The Company can issue different types of debentures, as per its requirement.

The only advantage in the issue of debentures is that after paying the fixed interest to debenture holders, the remaining amount can be utilised for paying equity shareholders, and thus, the rate of dividend for ordinary shareholders can be sufficiently increased. But the redemption of regular instalment of debentures remains a constant headache for the management. Hence, the company prefers to issue shares instead of debentures.

3) Retained Profits :

It is considered as a sound practice to finance the fixed and working capital requirements from the retained profits of an existing unit. It is the cheapest and most convenient method of securing capital by an enterprise. Retained profit is also known as ploughing back of profits or internal financing. An established undertaking can meet its financial needs out of its own profits, some profits are transferred to reserves, some is distributed as dividend and remaining is reinvested in the business as a capital. Thus the profit, which is reinvested in business is called as ploughing back of profits or retained earnings. In this method, capital is raised from internal sources and hence, called as internal financing. This type of financing is used to meet the regular requirements of working capital. Though this method is economical and convenient for the company, the funds so raised through internal savings may be misused, besides posing a danger of over Capitalisation.

4) Public Deposits :

The other source of working capital which has been particularly popular in the textile industry of Bombay and Ahmedabad as well as in the tea gardens of Bengal and Assam, is the public deposits. Public deposits are preferred by the companies because : (a) these deposits carry a lower rate of interest, (b) these are unsecured deposits; (c) less formalities are needed; and (d) the period of deposits is shorter, etc. Public deposits are directly accepted by companies from the members of the public. Their period may vary from six months to seven years. The rate of interest is fixed and generally lower than other loans. In normal times, this method of borrowing has the advantage of enabling a company to keep its share capital low and to borrow at cheap rates and thus pay higher dividends than would be possible, if entire money were in the shape of share capital.

Temporary Working Capital :

Temporary working capital needs may be satisfied by means of following sources :–

1) Commercial Banks :

Commercial banks including State Bank of India are the most important sources of short term funds to business enterprises. In India, bank credit has the main institutional source of short-term financing requirement. This short-term financing to business firm is regarded as self-liquidating, in the sense, that the user to which the borrowing firm is expected to put the fund are ordinarily expected to generate cash flows adequate to repay the loan for meeting seasonal demands of the industries. The amount of credit extended by the bank is referred to as a credit limit which the firm can avail from the bank. The bank provides short-term working capital through the following sources.

a) Loan : This is the oldest and simplest form of providing working capital. In this case, the entire amount of a loan is disbursed at one time only either in cash or by transfer to the company's account. It is a single advance. The loan is repaid in instalments or even in one lumpsum. If loan is to be repaid in instalments, then interest will be charged on outstanding balance.

b) Overdraft : In this case, the borrowing firm which already has a current account with the bank is allowed to withdraw more (upto a specified limit) over and above the balance in its current account. The firm is not required to seek approval of the bank authority every time it is overdrawing, but a one time approval may work for a particular period, say for a year. The firm has to pay interest at a specified rate for the period during which the amount was overdrawn.

c) Cash credit : In practice, the operations in cash credit facility are similar to those of overdraft facility expect the fact that the Company need not have a formal current account. Here, also a fixed limit is stipulated beyond which the Company is not able to withdraw the amount. Legally, cash credit also is a demand facility, but in practice, it is on continuous basis. Here too, interest is payable on the actual amount withdrawn. Recently, the Reserve Bank of India has issued guidelines which provide that a Company has to maintain a margin of 25% and cash credit limit may be sanctioned only upto 75% of the cash purchased inventories and book-debts.

d) Bill purchased and discounted : This form of assistance is of comparatively recent origin. This facility enables the Company to get the immediate payment against the credit bills / invoices raised by the company. The bank holds the bill as security till the payment is made by the customer. The entire amount of bill is not paid to the Company. The Company gets only the present worth of the amount of the bill, the difference between the face value of the bill and the amount of assistance being in the form of discount charges. However, on maturity, the bank collects the full amount of the bill from the customer while granting this facility to the Company after satisfying itself about the creditworthiness of the customer and the genuineness of the bill. A fixed limit is stipulated in the case of Company, beyond which the bills are not purchased or discounted by the bank.

e) Working capital term loan : Generally, the banks while granting working capital facility to a customer stipulates that a margin of 25% would be required to be provided for by the customers, and hence, the bank borrowings remain only limited to 75% of the security offered. In other words, against the security of Rs.100, the bank gives a loan upto Rs.75 only. The shortfall is generally treated as working capital term loan. This loan is to be repaid in a phased manner which may vary between a period of two to five years.

f) Packing credit : This type of loan may be considered by the bank to take care of specific needs of the Company, when it receives some export order. Packing credit is a facility given by the bank to enable the Company to buy or manufacture the goods to be exported. If a Company holds a confirmed export order placed by the overseas buyer or an irrecoverable Letter of Credit in its favour, it can approach to the bank for packing credit facility. Packing credit facility may be :

i) pre-shipment credit facility; and

ii) post-shipment packing credit facility. Both these facilities are of short-term facilities. The Company may be required to repay the same within a pre-decided time span or out of the export proceeds of the goods exported.

2) Indigenous banks :

Prior to the establishment of banking companies on modern lines, the shroffs, money-lenders and other country bankers had an unrivalled sway over the whole country. With the development of organised banks, indigenous banks have been pushed into the background and their activities are usually confined to giving loans for personal consumption and trading purposes. In certain cases, even small scale industries obtain their short-term credits from indigenous bankers. However, they charge a prohibitive rate of interest, thereby making things difficult even for a small scale enterprise to get them at affordable rates.

3) Loans from specialised Institutions :

The industrial development of a country is dependent upon industrialisation. In underdeveloped countries, industrialisation is beset with organisational and financial difficulties. The progress of industrialisation is hampered due to absence of organised capital market and inadequacy of financial facilities. Hence, there was a need for exploring the industrial potential by attracting and encouraging new entrepreneurs through financial promotion and expansion of enterprise. The usual banking institutions are not able to provide adequate working capital to industrial organisations. These institutions are as under : Industrial Finance Corporation of India, Industrial Credit and Investment Corporation of India, State Finance Corporations. Industrial Development Bank of India, Unit Trust of India. etc. Although funds can be obtained from these corporations - yet this option, ought to be exercised only in the case of emergencies.

4:6 Estimation of Working Capital

We have seen various aspects of working capital planning, management and control. The efficiency of the planning and management is subject to the correct estimate of the working capital requirements. Irrespective of the planning exercise made and control mechanism adopted, the correct estimation of working capital requirement is the fundamental necessity of a good and efficient working capital management. The present chapter looks into the steps and calculations required to estimate the working capital requirements of a firm.

Estimation process : A Company must estimate in advance as to how much net working capital will be required for the smooth operations of the business. Only then, can bifurcation help in deciding the financing pattern i.e. how much working capital should be financed from long-term sources and how much from short-term sources. There are different approaches available to estimate the working capital requirements of a firm which are as follows :

1) Working capital as a percentage of net sales :

This approach to estimate the working capital requirements is based on the fact that the working capital for any Company is directly related to its sales volume. Therefore, the working capital requirements expressed thus are solely dependent on the sales forecast. This approach is based on the assumption that the higher the sales level, the greater would be the need for working capital. There are three steps involved in the estimation of working capital.

a) To estimate total current assets as a percentage of estimated net sales.

b) To estimate current liabilities as a percentage of estimated net sales, and

c) The difference between the above two, is the net working capital as a percentage of net sales.

So, the Company has to find out on the basis of its past experience or on the basis of other companies' experience, in the same competitive environment as to how much total current and total current liabilities should be maintained for a given level of expected sales. The step (a) above i.e., total current assets as a % of net sales will give the gross working capital requirement and step (b) above i.e., current current liabilities as a % of net sales will give the funds provided by current liabilities. The difference between the two is the net working capital which the firm has to arrange for. For example, the following information is available from ABC Ltd., for past three years, on the basis of which, the working capital requirements for the next year is to be estimated, given that the sales are expected to increase by 10% over sales level of the current year.

	Year 1 Rs.	Year 2 Rs.	Year 3 Rs.
Net Sales	10,00,000	12,00,000	14,00,000
Total Current Assets	2,00,000	2,52,000	3,08,000
Total Current Liabilities	50,000	60,000	70,000
Current Assets as a % of sales	20%	21%	22%
Current Liabilities as a % of sales	5%	5%	5%

In this case, the average of current assets as a % of sales is 21% i.e., (20% + 21% + 22%) ÷ 3; and the average of current liabilities as a % of sales is 5% so, the net working capital as a % of sales is 16% i.e., 21%-5%. Now, if the Company expects an increase of 10% in sales next year, then its working capital requirements can be estimated as follows :

Expected Sales = Rs.14,00,000 + 10% thereof = 14,00,0000 +1,40,0000
= Rs. 15,40,000.

Net working capital as a % of sales = 16%.
= Rs. 15,40,000 × 16% = Rs. 2,46,400

The company is expected to have gross working capital of Rs. 3,23,400 (i.e. 21% of Rs. 15,40,000), out of which financing by current liabilities is expected to be Rs. 77,000 (i.e. 5% of Rs. 15,40,000). It may be noted that in the above situation, the simple arithmetic average of current assets and current liabilities as a % of sales have been taken. If there is a consistent trend (increase or decrease) in current assets or current liabilities, or both, then the weighted average may be preferred.

2) Working capital as percentage of total assets or fixed assets :

This approach of estimation of working capital requirement is based on the fact that the total assets of the company are consisting of fixed assets and current assets. On the basis of past experience, a relationship between (i) total current assets i.e. gross working capital ; or net working capital i.e. Current assets - Current liabilities, and (ii) total fixed assets or total assets of the company is established. For example, a company is maintaining 20% of its total assets in the form of current assets and expects to have total assets of Rs. 50,00,000 next year. Thus, the current assets of the company would be Rs. 10,00,000 (i.e. 20% of Rs. 50,00,000).

In this approach, the working capital may be estimated as a % of fixed assets. The company basically plans the future level of fixed assets in terms of capital budgeting decisions. In order to use these fixed assets in an efficient and optimal way, the company must have sufficient working capital. So, the working capital requirements depend upon the planned level of fixed assets. The estmation of working capital, therefore, depends upon the estimation of fixed capital which, in turn, depend upon the capital budgeting decisions.

Both the above approaches to the estimation of working capital requirements are relatively simple in approach but difficult in calculation. The main shortcoming of these approaches is that these require to establish the relationship of current assets with the net sales or fixed assets, which is quite difficult. The past experience either may not be available, or even if available, may not help much in correct estimation. There is yet another approach to estimate the working capital requirements based on the concept of operating cycle.

3) Working capital based on operating cycle :

The concept of operating cycle helps in determining the time scale over which the current assets are maintained. The operating cycle for different components of working capital gives the time for which an asset is maintained, once it is acquired. However, the concept of operating cycle does not talk of funds invested in maintaining these current assets. The concept of operating cycle can definitely be used to estimate the working capital requirements of any company.

In this approach, the working capital estimate depends upon the operating cycle of the company.

A detailed analysis is made for each component of working capital and estimation is made for each of these components. The different components of working capital may be enumerated as follows :

Current Assets	**Current Liabilities**
Cash and Bank Balance	Creditors for Purchases
Stock of Raw Materials	Creditors for Expenses
Stock of Work-in-progress	
Stock of Finished Goods	
Bills - Receivables	
Debtors	

4:7 Computation of Working Capital / Estimate of Working Capital

The working capital estimation as per the method of operating cycle is the most appropriate, systematic and logical approach. In this case, the working capital estimation is made on the basis of analysis of each and every component of working capital. The following items are usually included in the calculation required at a particular level of business operation.

1) Total cost incurred on the materials, wages and overheads as obtained from cost records.

2) Time lag during which raw materials are to remain in stock before they are issued for productive purposes.

3) Duration of production cycle, the longer the duration of the cycle, the larger will be the capital required.

4) Length of the sales cycle indicating the duration of time during which finished products have to stay in the warehouse before sale. For certain business concerns having seasonal sales of goods, stocks have to be maintained throughout the rest of the year, and hence, working capital requirements will be very low.

5) Period of credit allowed to debtors. If longer periods of credit are allowed to the customers by a company without the same being extended to it by its suppliers, a larger working capital will be required.

6) If the period of credit extended by the creditors / suppliers of a company is for a longer period than that extended by the latter to its customers, then in such a case, the working capital requirements will be considerably reduced.

7) Time lag involved in the payment of wages and other overheads.

8) Find out the rate per unit for each of the elements. For example, rate of raw materials, work-in-progress, finished goods are to be ascertained.

9) Find out the amount expected to be blocked in each element. For example, in raw materials, the fund blocked is : Average holding period × No. of units required per period × Rate per unit.

10) Thus, prepare the working capital estimation and find out the working capital requirement.

The quantum of working capital required will be determined by taking all the above factors into account and by adding finally a flat percentage to this amount by way of provision for meeting contingencies. This provision for meeting contingencies must be effected since the forecast of working capital is compiled on the basis of estimates only. The provision helps in cushioning all uncertainties involved in making the estimates.

Proforma for estimation of Working Capital requirements

Particulars	Rs.	Rs.
1) **Current Assets**		
Minimum Cash Balance	×××	
Inventories (Stocks)	×××	
Raw Materials	×××	
Work-in-progress	×××	
Finished Goods	×××	
Receivables :	×××	
Debtors	×××	
Bills Receivables	×××	
Gross Working Capital		××××
(Total Current Assets)		
Less		
2) **Current Liabilities**	×××	
Creditors for Purchases	×××	
Creditors for Wages	×××	
Creditors for Overheads	×××	
Bank Overdraft	×××	
Bills Payable	×××	
Provisions for Expenses	×××	
i.e. Dividends		××××
Total Current Liabilities		
Excess of Current Assets		××××
over current Liabilities		
Add : Margin of Safety		×××
Net Working Capital		××××

Notes - Depreciation on fixed assets, which are used in production process or other activities, is not considered in working capital estimation.

The depreciation is a **non-cash expense** and as there are no funds locked up in depreciation as such, it is ignored.

2) Double-shift working : If the firm is operating in double shift, it affects the working capital requirements. The reason being that extra working (production) would require additional raw materials resulting in higher stock of finished goods. Sometimes, the firm may be required to pay a higher rate of wages to labour. Therefore, the calculations of working capital requirements for double shift should be made depending on the information.

4:8 Illustrations on Working Capital Requirement

Illustration 1

Jay Industrial Enterprises proposes to manufacture a cosmetic product which has been developed by its research and development department. The cost of production is estimated as follows.

Particulars	Cost per unit Rs.
Raw Materials	80
Direct Labour	40
Overheads	40
Total	160

The new product will be sold at Rs. 200 per unit. For the first year, sales are estimated at 1,04,000 units. The Company is a going concern with marketing network and it thinks that the maximum credit to be allowed to the customers will be 8 weeks. Other relevant data are given below :-

Raw material stocks required	4 weeks.
Processing time (work-in-progress Stage)	2 weeks.
Finished goods stock	6 weeks.
Credit allowed by suppliers	4 weeks.
Cash and bank balances required	Rs. 50,000.

Prepare a statement showing the amount of working capital required by the Company. You may make assumptions that are necessary.

Solution :

Statement showing requirements of Working Capital

Working Capital items	Requirement in weeks	No. of Units per week	Cost per Unit (Rs.)	Amount required Rs.
Current Assets				
Cash and bank balance	—	—	—	50,000
Raw Materials	4	2,000	80	6,40,000
Work-in-progress	2	2,000	120	4,80,000
Finished goods	6	2,000	160	19,20,000
Debtors	8	2,000	200	32,00,000
Current Assets Total				62,90,000
Less : Current Liabilities				
Credit from Suppliers	4	2,000	80	6,40,000
Total amount of Working Capital required				56,50,000

Working Notes :

1) No. of units per week $= \dfrac{1,04,000}{52} = 2,000$ units.

2) Work-in-progress has been valued at raw materials in full and 50% of Labour and Overheads i.e. Rs. 120 per unit.

Illustration 2

The following are the extracts from the Balance Sheet of a Company as on 31-12-2008. You are required to compute the additional Working Capital required by the Company for the next year.

Particulars	Rs.	Rs.	Rs.
Fixed Assets	(Asset side)		
Land and Buildings	5,00,000		
Plant & Machinery	3,00,000		8,00,000
Working Capital			
Current Assets			
Stock	8,00,000		
Debtors	3,00,000		
Cash at Bank	2,00,000	13,00,000	
Less :			
Current Liabilities	(Liability side)		
Creditors	3,40,000		
Provision for Taxation	80,000		
Bank Overdraft	1,40,000		
Outstanding Liabilities	1,60,000	7,20,000	5,80,000

Additional information :-

   i) It is estimated that sales will increase by 25% next year.

  ii) Maximum amount of Bank Overdraft will be only Rs. 1,60,000

 iii) There will be no increase in tax liability due to increase in export.

 iv) Period of credit allowed to the customers and the Stock turnover will remain unaltered.

  v) Period of credit allowed by Creditors will also remain same. Bills Payable will remain at the same relative position.

 vi) There will be no increase in the total amount of Cash and Bank balances.

Solution :

Estimation of additional Working Capital

Particulars		Current level (Rs.)	Estimated Increase (Rs.)	Requirement for next year (Rs.)
Current Assets				
Cash and Bank balance		2,00,000	–	2,00,000
Stock		8,00,000	2,00,000	10,00,000
Debtors		3,00,000	75,000	3,75,000
Current Assets	Total	13,00,000	2,75,000	15,75,000
Less :				
Current Liabilities				
Creditors		3,40,000	85,000	4,25,000
Provision for Taxation		80,000	–	80,000
Bank Overdraft		1,40,000	20,000	1,60,000
Bills Payable		1,60,000	40,000	2,00,000
Current Liabilities	Total	7,20,000	1,45,000	8,65,000
Total Asset - Total Liabilities i.e. Working Capital		5,80,000	1,30,000	7,10,000

The additional working capital required is (Rs. 7,10,000 - Rs. 5,80,000) = Rs. 1,30,000

Working Notes :

Increase in Sales by 25% will result in increase of Debtors balance and Stock by 25% assuming that the debtors collection period and Stock turnover ratios remain the same. Purchases, Creditors and Bills Payable will also increase by 25%.

Illustration 3

The management of Good Luck Industries has called for a statement showing the working capital to finance a level of activity of 1,80,000 units of output for the year.

The cost strucuture for the Company's product for the above mentioned activity is detailed below :–

Particulars	Cost per Unit
Raw materials	20
Direct Labour	5
Overheads (including depreciation of Rs. 5 per unit)	15
Total	40
Profit	10
Selling Price	50

Additional information

1) Minimum desired cash balance is Rs. 20,000.
2) Raw materials are held in stock, on an average, for two months.
3) Work-in-progress (assume 50% completion stage) will approximate to half-a-month's production.
4) Finished goods remain in warehouse, on an average, for a month.
5) Suppliers of materials extend a month's credit and debtors are provided two month's credit, cash sales are 25% of the total sales.
6) There is a time lag in payment of wages of a month; and, half-a-month in case of overheads. From the above facts, you are required to prepare a statement showing working capital requirements.

Solution :

Statement of Total Cost

Particulars	Rs.
Raw materials (1,80,000 units × Rs. 20 per unit)	36,00,000
Direct Labour (1,80,000 units × Rs. 5 per unit)	9,00,000
Overheads (excluding depreciation)	18,00,000
(1,80,000 units at Rs. 10 per unit)	
Total	63,00,000

Statement of Working Capital Requirements

Particulars	Rs.
Current Assets	
Cash balance	20,000
Raw materials ($\frac{1}{6}$ of 36,00,000 i.e. for 2 months)	6,00,000
Work-in-progress (Total Cost ÷ 24 × 50%)	1,31,250
(63,00,000 ÷ 24 × 50%)	
(only for $\frac{1}{2}$ month and 50%)	
Finished goods = Total cost ÷ 12	
∴ 63,00,000 ÷ 12 =	5,25,000
(Finished goods remain in godown for one month	
Debtors (75% fo 63,00,000 × $\frac{1}{6}$)	7,87,500
Total Current Assets	20,63,750

Particulars		Rs.
Less :		
Current Liabilities		
Creditors (Rs. 36,00,000 × $\frac{1}{12}$) (one month credit)		3,00,000
Direct Labour (Rs. 9,00,000 × $\frac{1}{12}$) (Time lag of one mouth)		75,000
Overheads (Rs. 18,00,000 × $\frac{1}{24}$) (Half month and 50%)		75,000
Current Liabilities	Total	4,50,000
Total Current Assets - Total Current Liabilities i.e. (20,63,750 - 4,50,000)		
Net Working Capital requirements		16,13,750

Note : Depreciation is a non-cash item. Therefore, it has been excluded from total cost as well as working capital provided by overheads. Work-in-progress has been assumed to be 50% complete in respect of materials as well as labours and overhead expenses.

Illustration 4

ABC Ltd., sells goods on a gross profit of 25%. Depreciation is considered as a part of cost of production. The following are the annual figures given to you :

	Rs.
Sales (2 month credit)	18,00,000
Materials consumed (1 month credit)	4,50,000
Wages paid (1 month lag in payment)	3,60,000
Cash manufacturing expenses (1 month lag in payment)	4,80,000
Administrative expenses (1 month lag in payment)	1,20,000
Sales promotion expenses (paid quarterly in advance)	60,000

Tha Company keeps one month's stock each of raw materials and finished goods. It also keeps Rs. 1,00,000 in cash. You are required to estimate the working capital requirements of the Company on cash cost basis, assuming 15% safety margin.

Solution :

Working Notes :

1) Cost Structure

		Rs.
Sales		18,00,000
Less : Gross profit 25% on Sales		4,50,000
Cost of Materials		13,50,000
Less : Cost of Materials	4,50,000	
Wages	3,60,000	8,10,000
Total Manufacturing Expenses		5,40,000
Less : Cash Manufacturing Expenses		4,80,000
Therefore, Depreciation		60,000

2) Total Cash Cost

	Rs.
Cost of Production	13,50,000
Less : Non-cash item i.e. Depreciation	60,000
Cash cost production	12,90,000
Add : Administrative Expenses	1,20,000
Add : Sales Promotion Expenses	60,000
Total Cash Cost	14,70,000

Note : Finished goods have been valued at cash cost of production Rs. 12,90,000 and Debtors have been valued at total cost of sales i.e. Rs. 14,70,000.

Statement of Working Capital requirements

Particulars		Rs.
Cash in hand		1,00,000
Debtors (Cost of Sales $14,70,000 \times \frac{2}{12}$)		2,45,000
Pre-paid Sales Promotion Expenses (Rs. $60,000 \times \frac{1}{4}$)		15,000
Inventories (Stocks)		
Raw Materials ($4,50,000 \times \frac{1}{12}$)		37,500
Finished goods ($12,90,000 \times \frac{1}{12}$)		1,07,500
Current Assets	Total	5,05,000

Particulars		Rs.
Less : Current Liabilities		
Sundry Creditors $(4,50,000 \times \frac{1}{12}) =$ 37,500		
Outstanding Manufacturing Expenses		
$(4,80,000 \times \frac{1}{12}) =$ 40,000		
Outstanding Administrative Expenses		
$(1,20,000 \times \frac{1}{12}) =$ 10,000		
Outstanding Wages		
$(3,60,000 \times \frac{1}{12}) =$ 30,000		
Current Liabilities 1,17,500	Total	1,17,500
Expenses of Current Assets		
Over Liabilities (5,05,000 - 1,17,500)		3,87,500
Add : 15% for Contingencies		58,125
Working Capital required		4,45,625

4.9 Exercises
Objective Type Questions :

a) State whether the following statements are True or false.
1) Working Capital is the difference between fixed assets and current assets.
2) Decrease in Current Liabilities increases working capital.
3) Cash Sales increases working capital.
4) Current Assets are realised within a short period of time.
5) Outstanding Expenses are a fixed liability.

Ans. : 1) False 2) True 3) True 4) True 5) False

b) Fill in the gaps :–
1) Current Assets-Current Liabilities = ...
2) Depreciation is ..... item.
3) Stock of finished goods is .... asset.
4) Pre-paid expenses is current ......
5) Current Liabilities are paid within a period of ..... year.

Ans. : 1) Working capital 2) non-cost 3) current assets 4) Liability 5) one

Essay Type Questions :
1) Explain the factors considered while determining the need for Working Capital.
2) State the major sources of Working Capital.
3) State the significance of Working Capital.

4) Explain briefly the concept of Working Capital and mention the important objectives of Working Capital.

5) What factors should the Finance Management take into consideration while estimating the working capital needs of a firm.

Practical Problems :

1) The Cost Sheet of a manufacturing company provides the following particulars :–

Elements of Cost	Amt. per Unit Rs.
Raw Materials	80
Direct Labour	30
Overheads	60
Total Cost	170
Profit	30
Selling Price	200

The following further particulars are available :–

1) Raw Materials are in Stock for one month.
2) Credit allowed by suppliers is one month.
3) Lag in payment of wages 1.5 weeks.
4) Lag in payment of overheads-one month.
5) Materials are in process for an average of half month.
6) Finished goods are in stock for an average of one month.
7) $\frac{1}{4}$ th of output is sold against cash.

Cash in hand and at bank is expected to be Rs. 25,000. You are requested to prepare a statement showing the capital needed to finance a level of activity of 1,04,000 units of product.

You may assume that the production is carried on evenly throughtout the year. Wages and overheads accrued similarly and a period of 4 weeks is equivalent to a month.

Ans. : Working capital requirements = Rs. 35,35,000

2) The following information has been extracted from the records of a Company :–

Product Cost Sheet

	Rs.
Raw Materials	45
Direct Labour	20
Overheads	40
Total	105
Profit	15
Selling Price	120

Raw materials are in stock on an average for two months. The materials are in process on an average for one month. The degree of completion is 50% in respect of all elements of cost. Finished goods stock on an average is for one month. Time lag in payment of wages and overheads is 1.5 weeks.

Time lag in receipts of proceeds from debtors is 2 months. Credit allowed by suppliers is one month 20% of the output is sold against cash. The Company expects a cash balance of Rs. 1,00,000.

The Company is Poised for a manufacture of 1,44,000 units in the next year.

You are required to prepare a statement showing the working capital requirements of the Company.

Ans. : Working Capital Rs. 42,76,000.

3) Prepare a Working Capital forecast from the following information :–

Product during the previous year was 10,00,000 units. The same level of activity is intended to be maintained during the current year. The expected ratios cost to selling price are :

Raw Materials	40%
Direct Wages	20%
Overheads	20%

The raw materials ordinarily remain in store for 3 months before production. Every unit of production remains in process for two months and is assumed to be consisting of 100% raw materials, wages and overheads. Finished goods remain in the warehouse for 3 months. Credit allowed by creditors is for 4 months from the date of delivery of raw materals and credit given to debtors is 3 months from the date of despatch.

The estimated balance of cash to be held Rs. 2,00,000

Lag in payment of wages – ½ month.

Lag in payment of expenses – ½ month.

Selling price is Rs. 8 per unit. You are required to make a provision of 10% for contingency (except cash) Relevant assumptions may be made.

Ans. : Amount of Contingency Rs. 3,86,667.

Working Capital requirements Rs. 44,53,334.

4) Calculate the amount of working capital requirements of Sudarshan & Company Ltd., from the following information :–

	Amt per Unit (Rs.)
Raw Materials	160
Direct Labour	60
Overheads	120
Total Cost	340
Profit	60
Selling Price	400

Raw materials are held in stock on an average for one month. Materials are in process on an average for half a month. Finished goods are in stock on an average for one month.

Credit allowed by suppliers is for one month. Credit allowed to debtors is two months. Lag in payment of wages – 1½ weeks. Lag in payment of overhead expenses is one month.

One-fourth of the finished stock is sold against cash. Cash on Hand and at Bank is expected to be Rs. 50,000. Expected level of production amounts to 1,04,000 units.

You may assue that the production is carried on evenly throughout the year. Wages and overheads accrued similarly and the time period of 4 weeks is equivalent to a month.

Ans. : Estimated Working Capital requirements Rs. 70,70,000.

5) If you are appointed as a financial manager of a Company and asked to estimate the working capital of the said Company from the following information :–

	Cost per Unit
Raw Materials	200
Direct Materials	100
Overheads (excluding depreciation)	250
Total	550

Estimated data for the forthcoming period is given as under :

Raw materials in stock	average 6 weeks
Work-in-progress (assume 50% completion)	
State with full material completion	average 4 weeks
Finished goods in stock	average 4 weeks
Credit allowed to suppliers	average 6 weeks.
Credit allowed to Debtors	Rs. 75,000
Cash at bank expected to be	Rs. 800 per Unit
Output per annum	52,000 Units
Selling price	Rs. 800 per Unit

Assume the production is sustained on an even pace during 52 weeks of the year. All the sales are on credit basis. Provide any other assumption that you make while estimation.

Ans. : Net Working Capital – Rs. 67,25,000

■ ■ ■

CHAPTER 5

Marginal Costing

● 5:1 Meaning and Definitions of Marginal Cost and Marginal Costing ● 5:2 Advantages of Marginal Costing ● 5:3 Limitations of Marginal Costing ● 5:4 Various Concepts ● 5:4.1 Fixed Cost ● 5:4.2 Variable Cost ● 5:4.3 Contribution ● 5:4.4 Profit Volume Ratio ● 5:4.5 Break-even Point ● 5:4.6 Margin of Safety. ● 5:5 Illustrations on Marginal Costing ● 5:6 Exercises

Introduction

Marginal costing is a new technique and not a method of cost accounting unlike Job or Process costing, Operating costing etc. As a special technique, it provides the management with timely information, which in turn, enables the management to measure the profitability of an undertaking by considering the behaviour of costs. Hence, profit planning, cost control and decision-making requires the application of marginal costing technique in all industries. Further, it can ablso be used in conjunction with other methods of costing to produce one complete system of cost accounting or with other techniques, such as – budgeting and standard costing. In short, marginal costing deals with the effects on cost or profits of changes in the volume or range of output and sales.

5:1 Meaning and Definitions

1. Marginal Cost :- Marginal cost is the cost of producing one extra unit of the output. It is the amount by which total cost increases when one extra unit is produced, or the amount of cost which can be avoided by producing one unit less.

The ICMA, London, has defined marginal cost as "The amount at any given volume of output is increased or decreased by one unit. In practice, this is increased by the total variable costs attributable to one unit."

For example, if the cost of production of 100 units is Rs. 1,000 and that of 110 units is Rs. 1,100 the marginal cost is Rs. 100. Thus, marginal cost is the variable cost comprising the cost of direct materials consumed, direct wages paid, direct expenses and the variable overheads incurred for producing the extra additional unit. Hence, marginal cost may be defined as the total variable cost incurred due to a specific activity.

2. Marginal Costing :- Marginal costing may be defined as the ascertainment of marginal costs and of the effect on profit of changes in volume or type of output by differentiating between fixed costs and variable costs. The official terminology of Management Accounting has described marginal costing as "a principle whereby variable costs are charged to cost units and the fixed costs are attributable to the relevant period are written off in full against the contribution for that period."

Thus, marginal costing is a costing technique which distinguishes between fixed costs and variable costs. In marginal costing, variable costs are charged to cost units and the surplus derived from setting variable cost of production against sales revenue is termed as "Contribution". Such surplus is used to make up the fixed costs of the period to arrive at the net profit. Thus, marginal costing is a special technique based upon the behavioural cost classification and its strategic use in the decision-making process.

In short -

Marginal Cost	= Variable Cost
Hence, Marginal Cost	= Direct Material+ Direct Labour + Direct Expenses +
	Variable Overheads.
In brief, Marginal Cost	= Prime Cost + Variable Overheads.
Similarly, Sales	= Variable Cost + Fixed Cost + Profit (or - loss)
So, Sales	= Variable Cost + Fixed Cost + Profit
But, by Marginal Costing	
Sales - Variable Cost	= Contribution. Again, Contribution - Fixed Costs
	= Profit, Contribution = Fixed Cost + Profit.

The abovementioned are the fundamental relations in the technique of marginal costing and strategic use of the same enable the management in the decision-making process.

Several other terms like Direct Costing, Variable Costing, Differential Costing, Incremental Costing are also used in place of marginal costing.

Basic Characteristics/Features of Marginal Costing

The main characteristics and technique of Marginal Costing may be summed up as follows :

1. All costs are classified into fixed and variable components. Semi-variable costs are also segregated into fixed and variable elements.
2. The marginal (variable) costs are treated as the cost of the products manufactured.
3. The stocks of finished goods and work-in-progress are also valued at marginal cost only.
4. Fixed costs are treated as period costs and charged to costing Profit and Loss Account of the period. Fixed costs, therefore, find no place in the cost of products or in the valuation of stocks.
5. The difference between selling price and variable cost is termed as "Contribution". In marginal costing, prices are based on variable cost plus contribution.
6. The relative profitability of various products or departments is determined by a study of contributions made by respective products or departments.
7. In marginal process costing, products are transferred from one process to another and are valued at marginal costs only.
8. Prices are determined with reference to marginal cost and contribution margin.
9. It is a technique of cost recording and cost reporting.

MARGINAL COSTING Vs. ABSORPTION COSTING

Absorption costing is a traditional method of costing whereby the total costs (fixed and variable) are charged to products. The more progressive cost accountants argue that marginal costing is the correct technique and that absorption costing is obsolete. However, the points of distinction between the two are given as under :

1. Treatment of fixed and variable costs : In marginal costing, only variable costs are charged to products, processes or operations. Fixed costs of the period are charged to costing profit and loss account.

Absorption costing is a total cost technique. It is the practice of charging all costs, both fixed and variable, to products, processes or operations.

2. Valuation of stock : In marginal costing, stocks of finished goods and work-in-progress are valued at variable cost only. In absorption costing, stocks are valued at total cost, which includes both fixed and variable costs. This results in a higher valuation of stocks in absorption costing than in marginal costing.

3. Under and over-absorption of overheads : Marginal costing excludes fixed cost, and therefore, the problem of apportionment of fixed overheads does not arise. There is no question of under/over-absorption of overheads.

In absorption costing, fixed costs are apportioned on an arbitrary basis. This results in under/over-absorption of overheads.

4. "Contribution" and "Profit" : In marginal costing, managerial decisions are guided by 'Contribution' which is the difference between sales value and variable cost. Absorption costing focusses its attention on 'Profit' which is the excess of sales over total cost.

Objectives of Marginal Costing :-

1) To enable taking decision on important matters by the management.
2) To make profit planning from the past records.
3) To find out the controllable and uncontrollable costs, so that the controllable costs can be controlled to achieve reduction in costs.
4) To ascertain the correct costs and fix the exact price of the products.
5) To help in studying the profitability of different products so that 'the non-profit making products can be discontinued.'
6) To take decisions about accepting or rejecting new orders by using contribution analysis.
7) To study break-even analysis and cost-volume profit analysis.

2) Advantages/Uses of Marginal Costing :-

The advantages to be gained from a system of marginal costing may be summarised as follows:

1. Valuable aid of management : The most useful contribution of marginal costing is the assitance it renders to the management in vital decision-making. In marginal costing system, the cost data required for decision-making and profit planning is readily available from accounting records. A few managerial problems that are simplified by the use of marginal costing are - make or buy decisions, pricing of products, selection of suitable sales mix, choosing from among alternative methods of production etc.

2. Facilitates cost control : By seperating the fixed and variable costs, marginal costing provides an excellent means of controlling costs.

3. Avoids arbitrary apportionment of overheads : Marginal costing avoids the complexities of allocation and apportionment of fixed overheads which is really arbitrary.

4. No under/over-absorption : In marginal costing, there is no complication of under-absorption and over-absorption of overheads.

5. Basis for pricing : Marginal costing furnishes a better and more logical basis for fixation of selling prices and tendering for contract, particularly when business is dull.

6. Relative profitability : In case a number of products are being manufactured, marginal costing facilities the study of relative profitability of different products. It will show where the sales effort should be concentrated.

7. Realistic valuation of stocks : In marginal costing, stocks of finished goods and work-in-progress are valued at their variable cost only. This prevents the carry forward in stock valuation of a proportion of current year's fixed overheads.

8. Valuable adjunct to other techniques : Marginal costing is a valuable adjunct to budgeting and standard costing techniques.

9. Aid to profit planning : The technique of marginal costing helps the management in profit planning. The management can plan the value of sales for earning a required profit.

10. Consistency : The marginal cost per unit of output remains the same irrespective of the volume of output.

11. Simplicity : Marginal costing technique is simple in application and an easy to exercise cost control.

12. Cost analysis possible : Profit volume analysis is facilitated by the use of break-even charts and profit volume graphs.

5:3 Limitations of Marginal Costing

Marginal costing suffers from the following limitations :

1. Difficulty in analysis : It may be very difficult in practice to segregate all costs into fixed and variable. Moreover, certain expenses are purely caused by managerial decisions and cannot be strictly classified as fixed or variable. For e.g., amenities to staff, bonus to workers, etc.

2. Difficulty in application : The technique of marginal costing is difficult to apply in industries like ship building, contracts, etc., where the value of work-in-progress is large in proportion to turnover. Thus, if fixed overheads are not included in the closing value of work-in-progress, losses on contracts may result every year, while on completion of a contract there may be large profits.

3. Improper basis for pricing : In marginal costing, prices are based on contribution which does not cover fixed costs. This may prove dangerous in the long run.

4. Ignores time factor : In marginal costing, time factor is ignored. For instance, the marginal cost of two jobs may be identical, but if one job takes twice as long to complete as the other, the true cost of job taking longer time is higher than that of the other. This is not disclosed by marginal costing.

5. Less effective cost control : Marginal costing ignores the fact that fixed costs are also controllable. By placing fixed overheads in a separate category, the importance of their controllability is reduced.

Moreover, marginal costing is not as effective as standard costing and budgetary control in controlling costs.

6. Limited Scope : With the increased use of automatic machinery, the proportion of fixed costs (maintenance, depreciation etc.) increases. As marginal costing ignores fixed costs, this system becomes less effective in capital-intensive industries.

7. Unrealistic statements : The exclusion of fixed overhead from stock valuation affects the profit and loss account and also produces an unrealistic balance sheet.

8. Unacceptable by taxation authorities : The income tax authorities do not recognise the marginal cost for inventory valuation.

9. Faulty conclusions : Exclusion of fixed overheads from costs may lead to erroneous conclusions. It may create problems in inter-firm comparison.

10. Not useful for long-run : The distinction between fixed and variable costs hold good only in the short-run. In the long-run however, all costs become variable. As in marginal costing only variable costs are considered, it is useful for short-term assessment of profitability.

Marginal Cost Statement

Particulars	Rs.	Rs.
Sales		....
Less : Marginal Cost :		
Direct Material	.....	
Direct Labour	.....	
Direct Expenses	....	
Variable Overheads	.....	....
Contribution		....
Less : Fixed Costs		....
		....
Net Profit		....

5:4 Various Concepts

5:4.1 Fixed Cost

The Terminology defines fixed cost as "A cost which accrues in relation to the passage of time and which, within certain output and turnover limits, tends to be unaffected by fluctuations in the level of activity (output or turnover). Examples of fixed costs are – rent, rates, insurance, executive salaries. Other terms used include period cost and policy cost."

In simple words, fixed costs are those costs, which remain unaffected by the changes in the production units or sales units. So, the fixed costs are also called as "period costs or "policy costs".

The features of the fixed costs are -

1) Fixed costs remain unaffected by changes in the level of activity.

2) Fixed costs are time-based

3) Fixed costs are not directly associated with the production. They remain fixed / constant in total.

4) In long-term period, fixed costs can be changed as price levels in the market are always subject to the changes.

5:4.2 Variable Cost

The term variable cost is defined by the Terminology as "A cost which, in the aggregate, tends to vary in direct proportion to changes in the volume of output or turnover." Examples of variable costs are direct material cost, packing cost, power, sales commission etc. In simple words, variable costs keep changing as per the changes in the number of units of the output / turnover. If output / turnover increases, the variable cost also increases in the exact proportion of its increase and vice-versa. If the output / turnover is stopped, this costs tends to be nil. Hence, it is sometimes described as 'Linear Cost'.

The features of variable costs are -

1) Variable costs are directly related to the level of activity, and they keep changing as per the changes in the activity.

2) Variable costs are not time-based.

3) Variable costs are directly related to the output/turnovers, and hence, described as 'Direct Costs'.

4) In short-term as well as in long-term, they remain as variable.

Semi-variable costs stand mid-way between fixed and variable costs. These costs vary with volume but not in proportion to changes in volume. The terminology defines semi-variable costs as "A cost containing both fixed and variable elements and which is thus partly affected by fluctuations in the level of activity." Accordingly, semi-variable costs do not change within the limits of small range of activity, but may change when the output reaches a new level in some direction on which the output changes. However, the changes are not in proportion to the output. Electricity charge, Telephone bill, Depreciation etc., are examples of semi-variable costs.

5:4.3 Contribution

Contribution is of vital importance in marginal costing system. It is defined as "the difference between selling price and variable cost." It is some times referred to as "gross margin."

In marginal costing, determination of profit per unit of product is not possible because fixed overheads are charged in total to the profit and loss account rather than recovered in product costing. Contribution is a pool of amount from which total fixed costs will be deducted to arrive at the profit or loss. If contribution is equal to fixed costs, there is neither profit nor loss. It is called contribution because it contributes to the recovery of fixed costs and assessment of the amount of the net profit. Thus, by equation it can be described as -

Contribution	= Sales - Variable Cost (i.e. S - V)
	OR
Contribution	= Fixed Cost + Profit (i.e. F + P)
∴ Profit	= Contribution - Fixed Cost (i.e. C - F)
	OR
	= Selling Price - Variable Cost - Fixed Cost
∴ Selling Price / Sales	= Variable Cost + Fixed Cost + Profit

If, for example, the selling price of a chair is Rs. 300 and its marginal cost is Rs. 200, there is a contribution of Rs. 100. This means that every time we make and sell a chair, we receive Rs. 300 from the customer, pay Rs. 200 for variable costs and have Rs. 100 over. This Rs. 100, is not of course profit, since fixed costs remain to be paid. Indeed, until we have sufficient costs of Rs. 100 to pay all fixed costs, there can be no profit. For instance, if fixed cost is Rs. 6,000, then we need to produce and sell 60 chairs to pay all fixed costs. At this point, there will be no profit no loss. This is known as break-even point. After break-even point, contribution will be all profit as fixed costs have already been fully recovered.

The concept of contribution is useful in determining break-event point, fixation of selling price, ascertainment of profitability of products, departments and managerial decision-making.

Illustration :

	Rs.
Sales	20,000
Variable Cost	16,000
Calculate Contribution	

Solution :

Contribution	= Sales - Variable Cost
	= 20,000 - 16,000
	= Rs. 4,000

5:4.4 Profit -Volume Ratio (P/V Ratio) -

The Profit Volume Ratio (P/V Ratio) is the ratio of contribution to sales. It is also called as contribution to sales ratio. The ratio, expressed as a percentage, indicates the relative profitability of different products, processes or departments.

A high P/V ratio indicates that a slight increase in the volume without a corresponding increase in fixed costs would yield higher profits. In such a case, the management may do well to spend more on advertising to boost up sales so that the contribution therefrom might more than cover the fixed costs.

The P/V ratio may also give a clue to the extent to which price reduction is possible during depression. Apart from the profitability of products, the ratio is also used to calculate the break-even point, the profit at a given level of sales (desired sales), sales volume required to earn a given profit and the volume of sales required to maintain the present level of profit if the selling price is reduced by a specific percentage.

The P/V ratio can be improved by increasing the contribution. This can be done by (a) increasing the selling price, (b) reducing the variable costs, and (c) altering the sales mixture and selling more profitable products. Since the P/V ratio is the ratio of contribution to sales, the formula for calculating the ratio is :

$$\text{P/V Ratio} = \frac{\text{Contribution}}{\text{Sales}} \times 100$$

$$\text{So, P/V Ratio} = \frac{\text{Sales} - \text{Variable Cost}}{\text{Sales}} \times 100$$

By transposition, we have

$$\text{i) Sales} = \frac{\text{Contribution}}{\text{P / V Ratio}}$$

ii) Contribution $= \text{Sales} \times \text{P/V Ratio}$

There is also one important algebraic relation available for this ratio as –

$$\text{P/V Ratio} = \frac{\text{Change in the Profit}}{\text{Change in the Sales}} \times 100$$

$$\text{OR P/V Ratio} = \frac{\text{Change in Contribution}}{\text{Change in the Sales}} \times 100$$

Illustration :

Fixed Cost   Rs. 8,000
Variable Cost   Rs. 24,000
Sales   Rs. 60,000
∴ Contribution   = Sales - Variable Cost
                 = 60,000 - 24,000
                 = 36,000

$$\therefore \text{P/V Ratio} = \frac{36,000}{60,000} \times 100$$

$$= 60\%$$

Limitations of P.V. Ratio

1) P.V. Ratio heavily leans on excess of revenues over variable costs.
2) P.V. Ratio fails to take into consideration the capital outlays required by the additional productive capacity and the additional fixed costs that are added.
3) It gives only an indication of relative profitability of product/product lines and it will not help to take a final decision.

4) It requires proper segregation of costs into fixed and variable costs. Over-simplification may lead to erroneous conclusion.

5) High P/V ratio per unit of sales or per unit of production will indicate the most profitable item only when other conditions are constant.

5:4.5 Break-even Analysis (Break-even Point) :-

The term 'break-even analysis' is interpreted in two senses – narrow sense and broad sense. In its narrow sense, it refers to finding out break-even point, i.e., a point of no profit and no loss. Taken in its broad sense, break-even analysis means a system of analysis that can be used to determine the probable profit at any level of production. The following figure is a graphical presentation of break-even analysis.

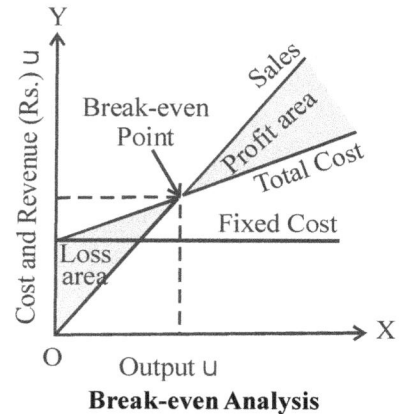

Assumption of Break-even Analysis

Break-even analysis is based on certain assumed conditions. These assumptions are not realistic and rarely found in practice. Some of these assumptions are as follows :

1. All costs can be segregated into fixed and variable components.
2. Fixed costs remain constant at all levels of output.
3. Variable costs fluctuate in direct proportion to the volume of output.
4. Selling prices do not change as volume changes.
5. There is only one product and in case of multiple products, the sales mix remains constant.
6. There will be no change in general price level.
7. Productivity per worker will remain unchanged.
8. There is synchronisation between production and sales, i.e., whatever is produced is sold out.

Uses of Break-even Analysis

Some of the important uses to which break-even analysis may be put are given below :
1. Determination of that level of production where there is no profit and no loss, i.e., Break-even point.
2. Determination of the selling price which will give the desired profit.
3. Determination of the sales volume that gives a desired return on capital employed.
4. Forecasting costs and profits as a result of change in volume.
5. Determining of costs and sales at various levels of output.
6. Determining the most profitable sales mix.
7. Effect of changes in fixed and variable costs on profit.
8. Inter-firm comparison of profitability.

Limitations of Break-even Analysis

1) Break-even analysis is based on the assumption that costs can be classified into fixed and

variable. In practice, it is very difficult to have such a clear-cut distinction.

2) In practice, assumption that fixed costs remains constant may not hold true.
3) Variable costs may not vary in direct proportion to the volume.
4) Selling price may not remain constant.
5) The analysis is static. However, circumstances are dynamic.
6) The cost of capital and the concept of capital employed in business is not taken into account.
7) It does not consider the outside foctors such as Government policy, market conditions, social and economic changes etc.
8) The assumption regarding production and sales does not realise in practice.

Break-even Point :

This is that level of output at which there is neither profit nor loss. It is a point where total costs are equal to total sales. This is also a point where profit begins. Loss will begin to be made as soon as sales fall below this level.

Determination of Break-even Point
1. Algebraic Method.
2. Graphic Method (Break-even Chart)

Calculation of Break-even point (Algebraic Method)

a) **Contribution Margin Approach :-**

The break-even point may be found by use of the following formulae :-

1. **Based on Unit costs :**

$$\text{B. E. point (in Units)} = \frac{\text{Total Fixed Cost}}{\text{Contribution per Unit}}$$

OR

$$\text{Break-even point (in Units)} = \frac{\text{Fixed Cost}}{\text{Selling Price Per Unit-Variable Cost per Unit}}$$

OR

$$\text{Break-even point (in Units)} = \frac{\text{Break-even Sales (Rs.)}}{\text{Selling Price per Unit}}$$

2. **Based on budget totals :**

$$\text{Break-even point (in Units)} = \frac{\text{Total Fixed Cost}}{\text{P/V Ratio}}$$

$$\text{or} = \frac{\text{Total Fixed Cost}}{\text{Contribution}} \times \text{Sales}$$

$$\text{or} = \frac{\text{Total Fixed Cost}}{1 - \frac{\text{Variable Cost per Unit}}{\text{Selling Price per Unit}}}$$

$$\text{or} = \frac{\text{Fixed Cost} \times \text{Selling Price per Unit}}{\text{Contribution per Unit}}$$

$$\text{or} = \frac{\text{Fixed Cost} \times \text{Selling Price per Unit}}{\text{Selling Price Per Unit-Variable per Unit}}$$

or = Break-even Point (Units) × Selling Price per Unit

$$\text{or} = \frac{\text{Fixed Cost} \times \text{Sales}}{\text{Sales - Variable cost}}$$

b) Equation Approach : -

Sales - Total Cost = Net Profit

Sales - Fixed Cost - Variable Cost = Net Profit

Sales = Fixed Costs + Variable Costs + Net Profit

Sales - Variable Cost = Fixed Cost + Profit

Contribution = Fixed Cost + Profit

At Break-even Point :-

Contribution = Fixed Cost + 0

Sales - Variable Cost - Fixed Cost = 0

OR

Contribution - Fixed Cost = 0

Calculation of required (desired) Sales (Rs.)

$$\text{Required (desired) Sales} = \frac{\text{Fixed Cost} + \text{Desired Profit}}{\text{P/V Ratio}}$$

Illustration :

Calculate the break-even point (in units and in value) from the following information :

Selling Price per Unit	Rs. 20
Variable Cost per Unit	Rs. 4
Fixed Cost for the year	Rs. 80,000
Estimated Sales for the period	Rs. 2,00,000

Solution :

Break-even Point (Units)

1) B.E.P. (Units) $= \dfrac{\text{Fixed Cost}}{\text{Selling Price per Unit - Variable Cost per Unit}}$

$$= \frac{\text{Rs. } 80,000}{\text{Rs. } 20 - 4}$$

$$= \frac{\text{Rs. } 80,000}{\text{Rs. } 16}$$

$$= 5,000 \text{ Units}$$

OR

2) B.E.P. (Units) $= \dfrac{\text{Fixed Cost}}{\text{Contribution Per Unit}}$

$$= \dfrac{\text{Rs.} 80,000}{\text{Rs.} 16}$$

$$= 5,000 \text{ Units}$$

OR

3) B.E.P. (Units) $= \dfrac{\text{Break-even Sales}}{\text{Selling Price Per Unit}}$

$$= \dfrac{\text{Rs.} 1,00,000}{\text{Rs.} 20} = 5,000 \text{ Units}$$

Note : - B.E.P. Sales is calculated as follows :
Break-even Units × Selling Price per Unit
5,000 Units × Rs. 20 = Rs. 1,00,000.
Break-even Point (in value Rs.)

1) B.E.P. (in Value) $= \dfrac{\text{Fixed Cost}}{\text{P/V Ratio}}$

Note : P.V. Ratio is calculated as under :

$$\dfrac{\text{Contribution Per Unit}}{\text{Selling Price Per Unit}} \times 100$$

$$= \dfrac{\text{Rs.} 16}{\text{Rs.} 20} \text{ (Rs. } 20 - \text{Rs. } 4) \times 100$$

$$= 80\%$$

Hence, B.E.P. in Rs. $= \dfrac{80,000}{80\%}$

$$= \text{Rs.} 1,00,000$$

OR

2) B.E.P. in Rs. $= \dfrac{\text{Fixed Cost} \times \text{Selling Price P.U.}}{\text{Selling Price P.U.-Variable Cost P.U.}}$

$$= \dfrac{\text{Rs.} 80,000 \times \text{Rs.} 20}{\text{Rs.} 20 - \text{Rs.} 4}$$

$$= \dfrac{\text{Rs.} 16,00,000}{\text{Rs.} 16}$$

$$= \text{Rs.} 1,00,000$$

OR

3) B.E.P. in Rs. $= \dfrac{\text{Fixed Cost} \times \text{S. P. per Unit}}{\text{Contribution P.V.}}$

$= \dfrac{\text{Rs. } 80,000 \times \text{Rs. } 20}{\text{Rs. } 16 \,(\text{Rs. } 20 - \text{Rs. } 4)}$

$= \dfrac{\text{Rs. } 16,00,000}{\text{Rs. } 16}$

$= \text{Rs. } 1,00,000$

OR

4) B.E.P. in Rs. $= \dfrac{\text{Fixed Cost}}{1 - \dfrac{\text{Variable Cost P.V.}}{\text{Selling Price P.V.}}}$

$= \dfrac{\text{Rs. } 80,000}{1 - \dfrac{\text{Rs. } 4}{\text{Rs. } 20}}$

$= \dfrac{\text{Rs. } 80,000}{1 - 0.20}$

$= \text{Rs. } 1,00,000$

OR

Break-even Sales - Fixed Cost - Variable Cost = 0

Let Break-even Units be 'X' then

$\text{Rs. } 20\text{X} - \text{Rs. } 80,000 - \text{Rs. } 4\text{X} = 0$

$16\text{X} - \text{Rs. } 80,000 = 0$

$16\text{X} = \text{Rs. } 80,000$

$\text{X} = 5,000 \text{ Units}$

Break-even Sales (Rs.) $= 5,000 \text{ Units} \times \text{Rs. } 20$

$= \text{Rs. } 1,00,000$

Calculation of Break-even Point (Graphic Method)

Break-even chart is a graphic presentation of break-even point and also shows the profit or loss at different levels of output.

Stages in preparing Break-even Chart

Break-even chart is simple to compile provided the basic principles are understood. A chart has two sides which are known as 'axis'. The left-hand vertical side is 'Y-axis', and the horizontal side at the bottom of the chart is 'X-axis'.

On the Y-axis, it is usual to show costs and revenue in rupee value, whereas on the X-axis one or more of the following factors may be employed :

Volume of Sales (Units)

Volume of Production (Units)

Volume of Sales (Rs.)

Volume of Production (Rs.)

Production capacity in percentage.

Illustration

	Rs.
Fixed Cost	40,000
Variable Cost per Unit	2
Selling Price per Unit	10

Draw a break-even chart and find out the break-even point.

Solution

The principal stages in the preparation of a break-even chart are shown below.

Stage 1 : First, draw X-axis and Y-axis on a suitable graph paper and insert the cost and sales values. Then, draft the fixed cost line at the appropriate point on the chart i.e. Rs, 40,000 on the Y-axis.

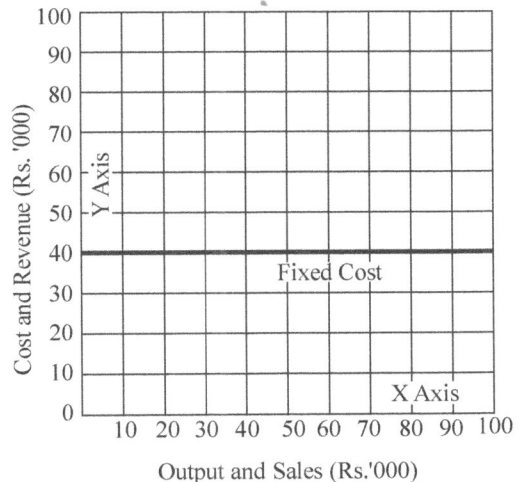

Break-even Chart - Stage 1

Stage 2 : After having drawn a fixed cost line, the total cost line is inserted above the fixed cost line. Total cost is found at different assumed levels and then is plotted on the graph. This is shown below :

Units	Fixed Cost	Variable Cost	Total Cost	Sales
0	40,000	4	40,000	0
4,000	40,000	8,000	48,000	40,000
8,000	40,000	16,000	56,000	80,000
10,000	40,000	20,000	60,000	1,00,000

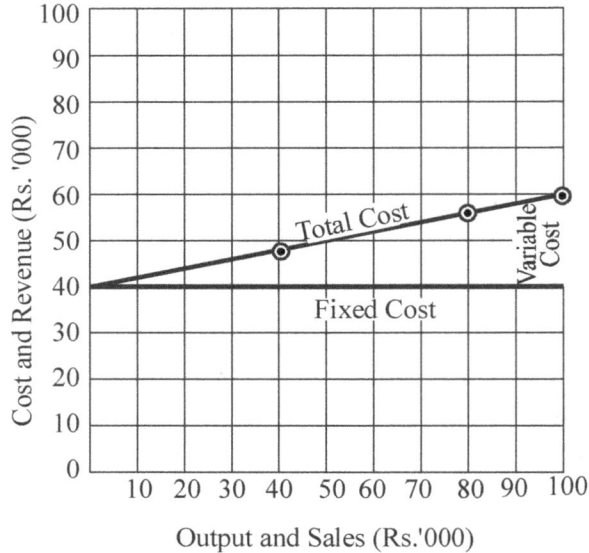

Break-even Chart - Stage 2

Stage 3 : The last step is drawing the sales line. This line starts from zero and finishes at Rs. 1,00,000 point on the chart. (As shown in the table prepared in Stage 2). When X-axis and Y-axis scale is the same, the sales line should be at 45° angle. This is shown as under :

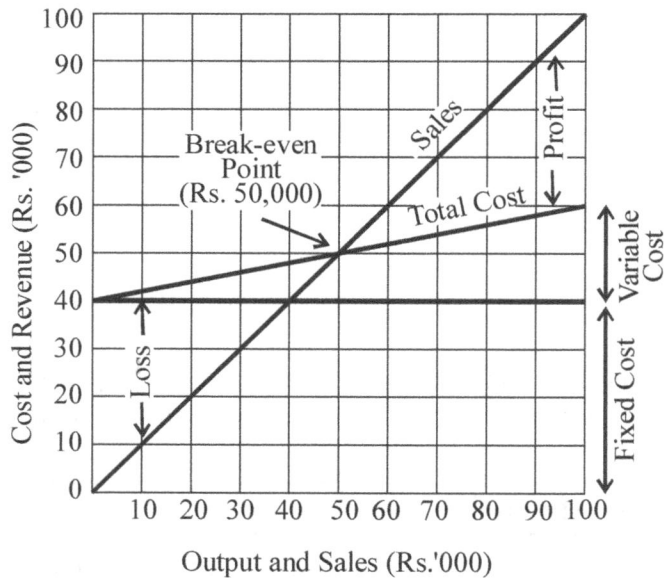

Break-even Chart - Stage 3

The point, at which total cost line and sales line intersect each other, is known as Break-even Point.

Contribution Break-even Chart

One shortcoming of the above type of break-even chart is that amount of contribution cannot be known from the chart. 'Contribution Break-even Chart' starts with the variable costs. Fixed costs are represented by a line drawn above the variable cost line. This method has the advantage of indicating the recovery of fixed cost at various levels of production before profits are realised. Therefore, 'Contributions' at various levels of output are automatically depicted in the chart.

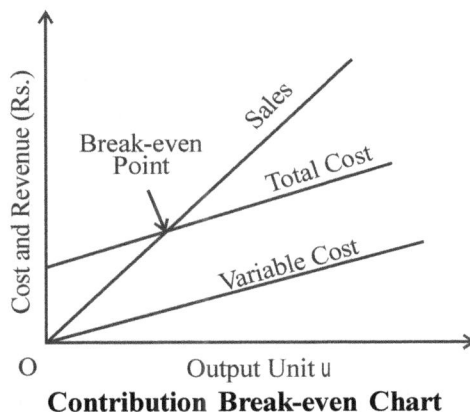

Contribution Break-even Chart

Illustration

The following figures relate to one year's working at 100 per cent capacity level in a manufacturing business :

	Rs.
Fixed Overhead	30,000
Variable Overhead	50,000
Direct Wages	40,000
Direct Materials	1,00,000
Sales	2,50,000

Represent the above figures on a break-even chart and determine from the chart the break-even point. Verify your result by calculations.

Solution

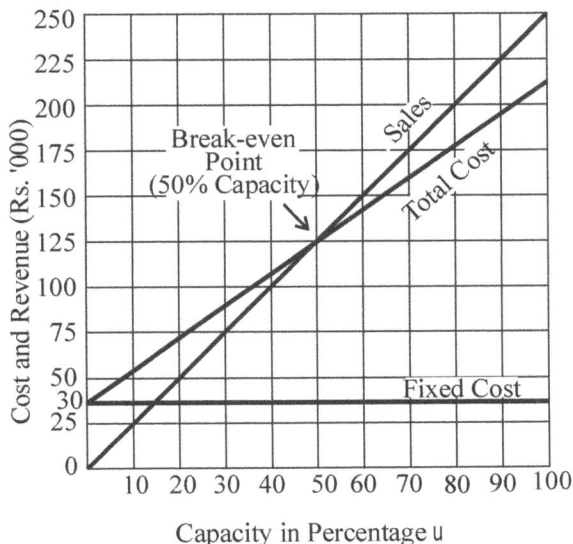

Break-even Chart

	Rs.
Variable Overhead	50,000
Direct Wages	40,000
Direct Materials	1,00,000
Total Variable Cost	1,90,000
Sales	2,50,000

Contribution $= 2,50,000 - 1,90,000$

$= \text{Rs. } 60,000$

P/V Ratio $= \dfrac{C}{S} = \dfrac{60,000}{2,50,000} \times 100 = 24\%$

Break-even Point $= \dfrac{30,000}{24\%} = \text{Rs. } 1,25,000 \text{ or } 50\% \text{ capacity}$

5:4.6 Margin of Safety (M/S)

The difference between actual sales and break-even point is known as margin of safety. A company operating at break-even point, makes neither profit nor loss. The margin of safety at break-even point is, therefore, nil. The knowledge of margin of safety is important for the management. The management should realise how close to the break-even point, the company is operating. If margin of safety is small, any fall in sales may be a serious matter. If the margin of safety is high, it shows that break-even point is much below. The actual sales and business is safe. Thus, the margin of safety indicates the soundness of a business.

Margin of Safety = Actual Sales - Break-even Sales

OR   Margin of Safety $\times$ P/V Ratio = Profit

$\therefore$ Margin of Safety $= \dfrac{\text{Profit}}{\text{P/V Ratio}}$

OR

$= \dfrac{\text{Profit} \times \text{S.P. Per Unit}}{\text{S.P. Per Unit - Variable Cost Per Unit}}$

So,   M/S $\times$ P.V. Ratio = Profit

Margin of Profit Ratio :-

Margin of Profit Ratio $= \dfrac{\text{Margin of Safety}}{\text{Total Sales}} \times 100$

The margin of safety can be improved by -

(i) Increasing sales volume.

(ii) Increasing selling price.

(iii) Reducing fixed cost.

(iv) Reducing variable cost.

(v) Improving contribution by changing sales mix.

The following break-even chart shows the margin of safety :

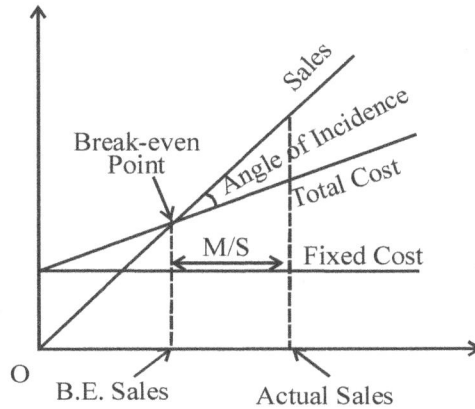

Break-even Chart

Illustration :

From the following data, calculate Margin of Safety

Sales   Rs. 2,50,000

Profit   Rs. 80,000

Fixed Cost   Rs. 1,20,000

Working :

1) P.V. Ratio $= \dfrac{\text{Contribution}}{\text{Sales}} \times 100$

But, Contribution = Fixed Cost + Profit

$= 1,20,000 + 80,000$

$= 2,00,000$

$\therefore$ P.V. Ratio $= \dfrac{2,00,000}{2,50,000} \times 100$

$= 80\%$

2) B.E.P. (Sales) :-

B.E.P. (Sales) $= \dfrac{\text{Fixed Cost}}{\text{P.V. Ratio}}$

$= \dfrac{1,20,000}{80} \times 100$

$= 1,50,000$

$\therefore$ Margin of Safety = Actual Sales - BEP (Sales)

$$= 2,50,000 - 1,50,000$$
$$= Rs. 1,00,000$$

OR

$$\text{Margin of Safety} = \frac{\text{Profit}}{\text{P.V. Ratio}}$$

$$= \frac{80,000}{80} \times 100$$

$$= Rs. 1,00,000$$

Angle of Incidence

The angle formed by the intersection of total cost line and sales line at the break-even point is known as 'Angle of Incidence'. This is shown in the break-even chart. This angle is an indicator of the rate at which profits are being earned. A small angle of incidence indicates a low rate of earnings; whereas a large angle of incidence indicates high rate of profits.

A large angle of incidence with a high margin of safety indicates an extremely favourable position.

Key Factor or Limiting Factor

Although every business wants to maximise its profits, there is always something that prevents it from earning unlimited profits. It may not be able to sell as much as it can produce or due to reasons of limited production capacity and/or non-availability of raw materials etc., to do the same. These factors limit the volume of production and thus prevent a business from earning unlimited profits. Such a factor is known as key factor or limiting factor or governing factor.

It is essential that the key factor is correctly ascertained. When a key factor is operating, the best position is reached when contribution per unit of key factor is maximum.

Marginal Costing and Managerial Decistions

The most useful contribution of marginal costing is that it helps the management in vital decision-making which essentially involves a choice between various alternatives. Marginal costing assists in choosing the best alternative by furnishing all possible facts. The information supplied by marginal costing technique is of special importance where information obtained from total absorptions costing method is incomplete. Further, the information revealed by total costing method, at times, is misleading.

The following are some of the managerial problems which are simplified by the use of marginal costing techniques :

1. Fixation of selling prices.
2. Make or buy decisions.
3. Selection of a suitable product mix.
4. Alternative methods of production.
5. Profit planning.
6. Suspending activities i.e., closing down.

1) Fixation of Selling Price - Although prices are regulated more by market conditions of demand and supply than by management, yet fixation of selling prices is one of the most important functions of management. While fixing prices, the management has to keep in view the level of profits to be earned.

In normal circumstances, the selling price fixed must cover total cost, as otherwise the profit cannot be earned. But under certain circumstances, products may have to be priced below total cost. This type of situation may arise in trade depression when there is a serious fall in the demand for the products. Though prices fixed during depression may be below total cost, it still, should be equal to or more than marginal cost. This is because fixed costs will have to be incurred even if production is discontinued for a short period. If the product can be sold at a price above marginal cost, the loss on account of fixed costs can be reduced to that extent. In other words, any contribution towards the recovery of fixed costs will reduce the losses which, otherwise, will be incurred if production is stopped. As a word of caution, fixation of prices below total cost should be made only on a short–term basis, since no firm can afford losses on a long-term basis.

However, under the following circumstances, selling prices may have to be fixed even below the marginal cost :

(i) When competitors are to be eliminated from the market.

(ii) When a new product is introduced in the market and it has to be made popular.

(iii) When goods are of perishable nature and there is a stock of such goods.

(iv) When depression seems temporary and closure of business may mean breaking of business connections that can be re-established only at a heavy expenditure.

(v) When plant and machinery has to be kept in gear as idle machines are liable to deteriorate.

Marginal costing presents information in such a way so as to enable the management to know the price limits within which it can operate.

2. Make or Buy Decisions - Marginal costing helps the management to decide whether the firm should itself manufacture a component part or buy it from an outside firm. This is particularly so, when a component part is available in the market at a price below the firm's own cost. This decision can be arrived at by comparing the supplier's price with the firm's own marginal cost. For example, if total cost of making a component part is Rs. 18, consisting of Rs. 15 as variable cost and Rs. 3 as fixed cost. Suppose, the same component part is available in the market at Rs. 17. The *prima facie* conclusion is that it is cheapter to buy the component part from outside. But, a study of cost analysis shows each unit produced also contributes Rs. 3 towards the fixed cost. If purchased from outside, it will cost Rs. 20 i.e., Rs. 17 + 3 (Fixed Cost). This fixed cost incurred influences the decision - whether to make or buy. Thus, this component should not be purchased from outside unless it is available at below Rs. 15, which is its marginal (variable cost.)

However, while arriving at a final decision in this regard, it should also be considered that the production facilities (plant capacity) released by the non-manufacture of a component may be put to some alternative use. In such a case, the above argument does not hold good.

3. Selection of a suitable product mix - When a concern manufactures more than one product, the management has to decide the proportion in which these products should be manufactured. This is known as product mix or sales mix. The production and sales of those products should be pushed up which give maximum profits and production of comparatively less profitable products should be reduced. Marginal costing helps the management in deciding the best product mix so that profits can be maximised. The best product mix is the one that yields maximum contribution.

4. Alternative methods of production - When management is faced with the problem of choosing from amongst alternative methods of production, marginal costing helps by furnishing relevant cost information for taking a right decision. For example, management may be faced with the problem of using an automatic machinery or manufacturing entirely by manual labour. The method of manufacture which yields the greatest contribution should be selected, of course, keeping in view certain other factors.

5. Profit planning - The aim of each business is to maximise profits. Marginal costing with the help of break-even analysis guides management about the profit position at various levels of output so that management can operate the business at an optimum level where profit is maximum. Thus, it is helpful in profit planning.

6. Closure of business - The management, under certain circumstances, may be faced with the problem of suspending the activities, i.e., closing down the business. This type of situation usually arises when sufficient volume of business cannot be secured. The closure of business may take one of the two forms :

(i) Temporary closure

(ii) Permanent closure

Temporary closure of business is a short-term concept. The object is usually to stop operations until trade depression has passed. But, if products are making a contribution towards fixed cost, then generally speaking, production should continue. In other words, if prices exceed marginal (variable) cost, losses will tend to be minimised by the continuing production.

Permanent closure of business is decided, when in the long run business is not earning sufficient profits to cover the risks involved.

5:4 Illustrations :

While solving the problems, following short forms may be used.

S = Sales, F = Fixed Cost

V = Variable Cost, S.P = Selling Price

C = Contribution, P/V Ratio = Profit Volume Ratio

P = Profit, B.E.P = Break-even Point

M.S = Margin of Safety

Illustration 1.

From the following information, find out the amount of profit earned during the year using marginal costing technique.

Fixed Cost Rs. 5,00,000

Variable Cost Rs. 10 per Unit

Selling price | Rs. 15 per Unit
Output | 1,50,000 Units

Solution :

Statement of Marginal Cost and Profit

		Rs.
Sales (1,50,000 × 15)		22,50,000
Marginal Cost (1,50,000 × 10)		15,00,000
Contribution (Sales - Marginal Cost)		7,50,000
Less : Fixed Cost		5,00,000
	Profit	2,50,000

Illustration 2 :

Ambitious Enterprises is currently working at 50% capacity and produces 10,000 Units.

At 60% working; raw material cost increases by 2% and selling price falls by 2%. At 80% working, raw materials cost increases by 5% and selling price falls by 5%.

At 50% capacity working, the product costs Rs. 180 per Unit and is sold at Rs. 200.

The Unit cost of Rs. 180 is made up as follows :

	Rs.
Materials	100
Wages	30
Factory Overheads	30 (40% Fixed)
Administration Overheads	20 (50% Fixed)

Prepare a Marginal Cost Statement showing the estimated profit of the business when it is operated at 60% and 80% capacity.

	60% Capacity (Output 12,000 Units)		80% Capacity (Output 16,000 Units)	
	Per Unit Rs.	Total Rs.	Per Unit Rs.	Total Rs.
A) Sales	196	23,52,000	190	30,40,000
Materials	102	12,24,000	105	16,80,000
Wages	30	3,60,000	30	4,80,000
Variable Overheads :				
Factory	18	2,16,000	18	2,88,000
Administration	10	1,20,000	10	1,60,000
B) Marginal Cost	160	19,20,000	163	26,08,000

	Per Unit Rs.	Total Rs.	Per Unit Rs.	Total Rs.
C) **Contribution** (A-B)	36	4,32,000	27	4,32,000
Fixed Overheads :				
Factory	10	1,20,000	7.50	1,20,000
Administration	8.33	1,00,000	6.25	1,00,000
D) **Fixed Cost**	18.33	2,20,000	13.75	2,20,000
Net Profit (C - D)	17.67	2,12,000	13.25	2,12,000

Notes :

1. At 60% capacity, material cost is Rs. 100 + 2% = Rs. 102
2. At 80% capacity, material cost is Rs. 100 + 5% = Rs. 105
3. At 60% capacity, selling price is Rs. 200 - 2 % = Rs. 196
4. At 80% capacity, Selling price is Rs. 200 - 5% = Rs. 190
5. Factory Overhead - per Unit Rs.   30

        Less 40% Fixed   12

        Variable per Unit   18

    Total Fixed Factory Overhead   = 12 × 10,000

                                = Rs. 1,20,000

6. Administration Overhead - per Unit - Rs.   20

           Less Fixed 50%   10

          Variable per Unit   10

    Total Fixed Administration Overhead -

    10 × 10,000 = Rs. 1,00,000

B. Illustrations on Break-even Points :-

Illustration 3 :

From the following data, calculate :

(i) Break-even Point expressed in amount of sales in rupees.

(ii) Number of Units that must be sold to earn a profit of Rs. 60,000 per year.

	Rs.
Sale Price	20 per Unit
Variable Manufacturing Cost	11 per Unit
Variable Selling Cost	3 per Unit
Fixed Factory Overheads	5,40,000 per year
Fixed Selling Costs	2,52,000 per year

Solution

(i) Calculation of Break-even Point

Variable Cost per Unit = Variable Manufacturing Cost + Variable Selling Cost

        = Rs. 11 + Rs. 3 = Rs. 14

Contribution   = Selling Price - Variable Cost

        = Rs. 20 - Rs. 14 = Rs. 6 per Unit

Total Fixed Cost = Fixed Factory Overheads + Fixed Selling Costs

        = 5,40,000 + 2, 52,000

        = Rs. 7,92,000

Break-even Point $= \dfrac{\text{Fixed Cost}}{\text{Contribution per Unit}} \times \text{Selling Price}$

       $= \dfrac{7,92,000 \times 20}{6} = \text{Rs. } 26,40,000$

(ii) Number of Units to be sold to earn a Profit of Rs. 60,000 per year:

       $= \dfrac{\text{Fixed Cost} + \text{Desired Profit}}{\text{Contribution per Unit}}$

       $= \dfrac{7,92,000 + 60,000}{6} = 1,42,000 \text{ Units.}$

Illustration 4 : The following data is given :

Fixed expenses Rs. 1,00,000, Variable expenses Rs. 10 per Unit, Selling Price Rs. 15 per Unit.

(a) Indicate the number of Units to be manufactured and sold (i)To break-even; (ii) To earn a Profit of Rs. 10,000

(b) What additional Units would be necessary to increase the above Profit by Rs. 5,000.

Solution

(a) Break-even Point $= \dfrac{\text{Fixed Cost}}{\text{Contribution per Unit}}$

 Contribution = Selling Price - Variable Cost

      = 15 - 10

      = Rs. 5

(i) B.E. Point $= \dfrac{1,00,000}{5} = 20,000 \text{ Units.}$

 or $= 20,000 \times \text{Rs. } 15 = \text{Rs. } 3,00,000$

(ii) Sales to earn a Profit of Rs. 10,000

      $= \dfrac{1,00,000 + 10,000}{5}$

$$= 22,000 \text{ Units}$$

or $\quad = 22,000 \times \text{Rs. } 15 = \text{Rs. } 3,30,000$

(b) Sales to earn an additional Profit of Rs. 5,000

$$= \frac{1,00,000 + 15,000}{5}$$

$$= 23,000 \text{ Units.}$$

Thus, in order to increase the Profit by Rs. 10,000 by Rs. 5,000. Additional Sales of 1,000 Units (i.e. 23,000 - 22,000) is required.

Finding Missing Figures

Illustration 5:

Break-even Point $\quad = 1,000$ Units

Sales $\quad = 1,500$ Units at Rs. 6 each

Fixed Cost $\quad = \text{Rs. } 2,000$

Find out the Variable Cost per Unit and Profit.

Solution

$$\text{Break-even Point (Units)} = \frac{\text{Fixed Cost}}{\text{Contribution per Unit}}$$

$\therefore \qquad 1,000 = \dfrac{2,000}{\text{Contribution per Unit}}$

$\therefore \quad \text{Contribution per Unit} = \dfrac{2,000}{1,000} = \text{Rs. } 2$

And since Selling Price is Rs. 6, the Variable Cost per Unit must be

$$6 - 2 = \text{Rs. } 4$$

And total Contribution must be $1,500 \times 2 = \text{Rs. } 3,000$

$\therefore \qquad\qquad \text{Profit} = \text{Contribution - Fixed Cost}$

$$= 3,000 - 2,000$$

$$= \text{Rs. } 1,000$$

Illustration : 6

Find out : PV Ratio, B.E.P., Net profit on the sales of Rs. 3,00,000 and required sales for the net profit of Rs. 70,000.

Position of 'A' Ltd., for the year 2009

	Rs.
Sales	2,00,000
Variable exp.	1,50,000
Gross Profit	50,000
Fixed exp.	15,000
Net Profit	35,000

Solution

i) $\text{P. V. Ratio} = \dfrac{\text{Contribution}}{\text{Sales}} \times 100 = \dfrac{2,00,000 - 1,50,000}{2,00,000} \times 100$

$= \dfrac{50,000 \times 100}{2,00,000} = \mathbf{25\%}$

ii) $\text{B.E.P.} = \dfrac{\text{Fixed cost}}{\text{P.V. Ratio}} = \dfrac{15,000}{25\%}$

$= \dfrac{15,000 \times 100}{25} = \mathbf{60,000}$

iii) Net Profit from Sales of Rs. 3,00,000

$\text{S (P. V. Ratio)} = F + P$

$\dfrac{3,00,000 \times 25}{100} = 15,000 + P$

$75,000 = 15,000 + P$

$P = \mathbf{60,000}$

iv) Sales for the net Profit of Rs. 70,000

$\text{D (P. V. Ratio)} = F + P$

$\text{S (25\%)} = 15,000 + 70,000$

$\dfrac{S}{4} = 85,000$

$\text{Sales} = \mathbf{3,40,000}$

Illustration : 7

Amount of Profit on a Specific Sale

	Rs.
Sales	1,80,000
Less : V. C.	1,44,000
Contribution	36,000
Less : Fixed Overheads	24,000
Net Profit	12,000

You are required to calculate (i) P/V Ratio, B.E.P., net Profit for the sales of Rs. 2,70,000 and required sales to earn a Profit of Rs. 24,000

Solution

i)
$$\text{P. V. Ratio} = \frac{C}{S} \times 100$$

$$= \frac{36,000}{1,80,000} \times 100 = \mathbf{20\%}$$

ii)
$$\text{B.E.P.} = \frac{\text{Fixed Cost}}{\text{P.V.Ratio}}$$

$$= \frac{24,000}{20} \times 100 = \mathbf{1,20,000}$$

iii) Net Profit for the Sales of Rs. 2,70,000

$$\text{Net Profit} = \text{Contribution - F.C.}$$

$$\text{P.V. Ratio} = \frac{C}{S} \times 100$$

$$20 = \frac{C}{2,70,000}$$

$$C = 2,70,000 \times \frac{20}{100} = \mathbf{54,000}$$

$$\text{Profit} = 54,000 - 24,000 = 30,000$$

iv) Required to earn a Profit of Rs. 24,000

$$\text{Sale} = \frac{F + P}{\text{P.V. Ratio}}$$

$$= \frac{24,000 + 24,000}{20\%} = \mathbf{2,40,000}$$

Illustration : 8

You are given the following data for the costing year of a factory.

	Units Rs.
Budget Output	1,00,000 Units
Fixed Exp.	Rs. 5,00,000
Variable Exp. per Unit	Rs. 10
Selling Price per Unit	Rs. 20

Draw B.E.P. showing the B.E.P., if the selling price is reduced to Rs. 18 per Unit, what 'll be the new break-enven point?

Solution

$$\text{B.E.P in Units} = \frac{F}{P-V} = \frac{5,00,000}{20-10} = 50,000 \text{ Units}$$

i) B.E.P. @ Rs. 20 per Unit is 50,000 Units. The margin of safety is 1,00,000 - 50,000 = 50,000 Units.

ii) $\text{B.E.P.} = \dfrac{F}{P-V} = \dfrac{5,00,000}{18-10} = 62,500 \text{ Units}$

iii) B.E.P. @ Rs. 18 per Unit is 62,500 Units. The margin of safety is 1,00,000 - 62,500 = 37,500 Units

Illustration : 9

	Rs.
Sales	5,00,000
Variable Cost	3,00,000
Fixed Cost	1,00,000

Calculate the B.E.P. in rupees.

Solution

$$\text{B.E.P. in rupees} = \frac{F \times S}{S - V}$$

$$= \frac{1,00,000 \times 5,00,000}{5,00,000 - 3,00,000}$$

$$= \textbf{Rs. 2,50,000}$$

Illustration : 10

	Rs.
Sales	2,00,000
Fixed Cost	20,000
Selling Price per Unit	20
Variable Cost per Unit	16

Solution

i) B.E.P. in Units $= \dfrac{F}{P-V}$

$= \dfrac{20,000}{20-16} = 5,000$ Units.

ii) B.E.P. in rupees $= \dfrac{F}{1-\dfrac{V}{P}} = \dfrac{20,000}{1-\dfrac{16}{20}}$

$= \dfrac{20,000}{\dfrac{4}{20}}$

$= 20,000 \times \dfrac{20}{4} = \mathbf{1,00,000}$

Illustration : 11

Ajay Enterprises present before you the following information :-

Year	**Sales Rs.**	**Profit Rs.**
2008	30,000	800
2009	38,000	2,000

Compute P.V Ratio, the profit when sales are Rs. 24,000, and the sales that are required to earn a profit of Rs. 3,800.

Solution :

Change in Sale $= 38,000 - 30,000 = 8,000$

Change in Profit $= 2,000 - 800 = 1,200$

i) PV Ratio $= \dfrac{1,200}{8,000} \times 100 = 15\%$

ii) Fixed Cost $=$ Sales $\times$ P/V Ratio - Profit

$= 38,000 \times \dfrac{15}{100} - 2,000$

$= 5,700 - 2,000 = \mathbf{3,700}$

iii) Profit when Sales are Rs. 24,000 profit + Contribution − Fixed Cost
= 3,600 - 3,700 = 100 (loss)

Contribution on Sales of Rs. 24,000 $= \dfrac{24,000 \times 15}{100} = \textbf{3,600}$

iv) The Sale required to earn a Profit of Rs. 3,800

Sales $= \dfrac{F+P}{\text{P.V. Ratio}} = \dfrac{3,700 + 3,800}{15\%}$

$= \dfrac{7,500}{15} \times 100 = \textbf{Rs. 50,000}$

Illustration : 12

	Rs.
Fixed Cost	50,000
Variable Cost per Unit	5
Sale Price per Unit	10

i) Determine the break-even Point.
ii) What is the sale price, if B.E.P. is 8,000 Units.
iii) What is the B.E.P., if sale price is reduced by 10%

Solution

i) B.E.P $= \dfrac{F}{C}$ Here, C per Unit = 10 - 5 = Rs. 5

so, $\dfrac{F}{C} = \dfrac{50,000}{5} = 10,000$ Units

Or 10,000 Units $\times$ 10 = **Rs. 1,00,000**

ii) Contribution at 8,000 Units of B.E.P.

$$\text{B.E.P} = \dfrac{E}{C} \text{ or } C = \dfrac{F}{\text{B.E.P.}} = \dfrac{50,000}{8,000}$$

= 6.25 per Unit.

Selling price = Variable Exp. + Contribution = 5 + 6.25 = 11.25

iii) B.E.P. at reduced selling price by 10% S.P. is Rs. 10. Reduction by 10% means selling price Rs. 9.

$$C = S - V$$
$$= 9 - 5$$
$$= 4$$

$$B.\ E.\ P.\ =\frac{F}{C}=\frac{50,000}{4}=\textbf{12,500 Units}$$

In terms of amount, B.E.P. = 12,500 × 9 = **1,12,500**

Illustration : 13

a) Fixed Costs Rs. 40,000, Variable Costs 60% on Sales. Determine the B.E.P.

b) Find out the new B.E.P., if

i) Fixed Costs increase by Rs. 10,000

ii) Variable Costs increase by 15% on Sales.

iii) Sale Price increase by 20%

iv) Variable Costs are reduced by 10%

Solution :

a)
$$C = S - V$$
$$= 100 - 60 = 40\%$$

$$B.E.P.\ =\frac{F}{C\%}=\frac{40,000\times100}{40}=\textbf{1,00,000}$$

b) i)
$$B.E.P.\ =\frac{F}{C\%}=\frac{50,000}{40}\times100=\textbf{1,25,000}$$

Contribution = 100 - 75 = 25%

So, $$B.E.P\ =\frac{40,000}{25}\times100=\textbf{1,60,000}$$

c) The increase or decrease of S.P. will not affect the amount of Variable Costs.

$$B.E.P.\ =\frac{F\times S}{S-V}=\frac{40,000\times120}{120-60}=\textbf{80,000}$$

d) Contribution = S - V
$$= 100 - 50 = 50\%$$

$$B.E.P.\ =\frac{F}{C\%}=\frac{40,000}{50\%}$$

$$=\frac{40,000\times100}{50}=\textbf{80,000}$$

Illustration : 14

Company 'A' and Company 'B' both under the same management make and sell the same type of product. Their budgeted profit and loss account for January to June 2008, are as under :

	Company 'A'		Company 'B'	
	Rs.	Rs.	Rs.	Rs.
Sales	—	3,00,000	—	3,00,000
Less: Variable Cost	2,40,000	—	2,00,000	—
Fixed Cost	30,000	2,70,000	70,000	2,70,000
Profit	—	30,000	—	30,000

You are required to :

i) Calculate the Break-even Point for each.

ii) Calculate the Sales volume at which each of the two companies will make a profit of Rs. 10,000.

iii) Assess how their profitability will change with increase or decrease in volume.

Solution

i) $$\text{Break-even Point} = \frac{\text{Fixed Cost}}{\text{P/V Ratio}}$$

$$\text{PV Ratio} = \frac{\text{Contribution}}{\text{Sales}}$$

Contribution = Sales - Variable Cost

Contribution - Company 'A' = 3,00,000 - 2,40,000 = Rs. 60,000

'B' = 3,00,000 - 2,00,000 = Rs. 1,00,000

$$\text{PV Ratio - Company 'A'} = \frac{60,000}{3,00,000} \times 100 = 20\%$$

$$\text{'B'} = \frac{1,00,000}{3,00,000} \times 100 = 33\frac{1}{3}\% \text{ or } 33.33\%$$

$$\text{B.E. Point of Company 'A'} = \frac{30,000}{20\%} = \textbf{Rs. 1,50,000}$$

$$\text{B.E. Point of Company 'B'} = \frac{70,000}{33\frac{1}{3}} = \textbf{Rs. 2,10,021 (or 33.33\%)}$$

ii) $$\text{Sales to earn a desired Profit} = \frac{\text{Fixed Cost} + \text{Desired Profit}}{\text{P/V Ratio}}$$

$$\text{For Company 'A'} = \frac{30,000+10,000}{20\%} = \textbf{Rs. 2,00,000}$$

$$\text{For Company 'B'} = \frac{70,000+10,000}{33\frac{1}{3}\%} = \textbf{Rs. 2,40,024}$$

iii) When there is an increase in volume of business, a Company with larger PV ratio can earn greater profit. In this case, Company 'B', would have larger profits in conditions of heavy demand.

When there is decrease in volume of business, a Company with lower break-point is better off. In this case, Company 'A' will start earning profits when its sales reach the level of Rs. 1,50,000, whereas profit will start at Rs. 2,10,021 in the case of Company 'B'. Thus, in conditions of lower demand, Company 'A' will be better off.

Illustration : 15

The Sales turnover and Profit during Ist and IInd year was as follows :

	Sale	Profit
I	2,40,000	18,000
II	2,80,000	26,000

Find out : P.V. Ratio, Fixed Exp., B.E.P., Margin of Safety, when Sales are Rs. 3,60,000.

Solution

i) $\quad$ P. V. Ratio $= \dfrac{\text{Change in Contribution in two years}}{\text{Change in Sales in two years}}$

$$= \dfrac{\text{Change in Profit}}{\text{Change in Sales}} \times 100$$

$$= \dfrac{26{,}000 - 18{,}000}{2{,}80{,}000 - 2{,}40{,}000} = \dfrac{8{,}000}{40{,}000} \times 100$$

$$= \textbf{20\%}$$

ii) Taken IInd year (Fixed Expenses)

$$C = \text{Sale} \times \text{PV Ratio}$$

$$= 2{,}80{,}000 \times \dfrac{1}{5}$$

$$= 56{,}000$$

Since $\quad C = F + P$

$$F = C - P$$

$$= 56{,}000 - 26{,}000$$

$$= \textbf{30,000}$$

iii) B.E.P. Sales

$$\text{B.E.P. Sales} = \dfrac{\text{Fixed Cost}}{\text{PV Ratio}}$$

$$= \dfrac{30{,}000 \times 5}{1} = \textbf{1,50,000}$$

iv) Margin of Safety :

$$M/S \ = \frac{\text{Profit}}{\text{PV Ratio}} = \frac{18,000 \times 5}{1}$$

$$= \textbf{90,000}$$

$$M/S \ = \text{Sale - B.E.P. Sale}$$

$$= 2,40,000 - 1,50,000$$

$$= \textbf{90,000}$$

v) Margin of Safety at a Sales of Rs. 3,60,000

$$M/S \ = \text{Given Sale - B.E.P. Sale}$$

$$= 3,60,000 - 1,50,000$$

$$= \textbf{2,10,000}$$

Illustration : 16

From the following information, calculate the B.E.P., and turnover required to earn a Profit of Rs. 30,000

Fixed Overheads	Rs. 21,000
Variable Costs	Rs. 2 per Unit
Selling Price	Rs. 5 per Unit

If the Company is earning a Profit of Rs. 30,000, express the margin of safety available to it.

Solution

$$\text{B.E.P. (Units)} \ = \frac{\text{Fixed Overheads}}{\text{Selling Price = Variable Cost per Unit}}$$

$$= \frac{21,000}{\text{Rs. 5 - Rs. 2}} = \textbf{7,000 Units}$$

$$\text{B.E.P. Rs.} \ = 7,000 \times 5 = \textbf{Rs. 35,000}$$

Turnover to earn a profit of Rs. 30,000

Contribution = Sales - Variable Cost

$$\text{Rs. 5 - Rs. 2} \ = \text{Rs. 3}$$

$$\text{Required Sales} \times \text{Contribution} \ = \text{Fixed Cost + Profit}$$

$$S \times \frac{3}{5} \ = 21,000 + 30,000$$

$$S \ = \frac{3}{5} = 51,000$$

$$S \ = 51,000 \times \frac{5}{3} = 85,000$$

$$\text{Sales in Units} \ = \textbf{17,000 Units}$$

$$\text{Margin of Safety} \ = \text{Annual Sale - Sale at B.E.P.}$$

$$= 17,000 - 7,000 = 10,000 \text{ Units}$$

$$S - V = F + P$$
$$85,000 - 34,000 = 21,000 + 30,000$$
$$B.E.P. = 35,000$$

$$M/S = \frac{\text{Actual Sale - B.E.P. Sales}}{\text{Sales}} \times 100$$

$$= \frac{85,000 - 35,000}{85,000} \times 100$$

$$= \mathbf{58.82\%}$$

Illustration : 17

Following figures have been taken from the financial records of M/s Ramesh and Co

	2008 (Rs)	2009 (Rs)
Fixed Costs	1,00,000	1,50,000
Variable Costs	2,40,000	3,00,000
Sales	4,00,000	6,00,000

From the abobve information, you are required to calculate –
i) P. V. Ratio, ii) B.E.P., iii) Margin of Safety.

Solution

	2008 (Rs)	2009 (Rs)
Sales	4,00,000	6,00,000
Less : Variable Costs	2,40,000	3,00,000
	1,60,000	3,00,000
Less : Fixed Costs	1,00,000	1,50,000
Net Profits	60,000	1,50,000

i) Profit Volume Ratio $= \dfrac{C}{S} \times 100$

For 2008 $= \dfrac{1,60,000}{4,00,000} \times 100 = \mathbf{40\%}$

For 2009 $= \dfrac{3,00,000}{6,00,000} \times 100 = \mathbf{50\%}$

ii) Break-even Point $= \dfrac{\text{Fixed cost}}{\text{P.V. Ratio}}$

$$\text{For 2008} = \frac{1,00,000}{40\%} = \text{Rs. } 2,50,000$$

$$\text{For 2009} = \frac{1,50,000}{50\%} = \text{Rs. } 3,00,000$$

iii) Margin of Safety = Totals - Sales at B.E.P.
For 2008 year = Rs. 4,00,000 - Rs. 2,50,000 = Rs. 1,50,000
For 2009 year = Rs. 6,00,000 - Rs. 3,00,000 = Rs. 3,00,000

Illustration : 18

	Sales Rs.	Profit Rs.
2008	16,000	800
2009	20,000	2,000

Calculate P. V. Ratio, Profit when sales are Rs. 18,000, and the Sales required to earn a Profit of Rs. 2,400

Solution

Change in Sales = Rs. 20,000 - Rs. 16,000 = Rs. 4,000
Change in Profit = Rs. 2,000 - Rs. 800 = Rs. 1,200

i) $\quad$ PV Ratio $= \dfrac{1,200}{4,000} \times 100 = 30\%$

ii) $\quad$ Fixed Cost = Sales × PV Ratio - Profit

$$= 16,000 \times \frac{30}{100} - 800$$

$$= \text{Rs. } 4,800 - \text{Rs. } 800 = \text{Rs. } 4,000$$

iii) Profit when Sales are of Rs. 18,000
Profit = Contribution - Fixed Cost

Contribution on Sales of Rs. 18,000 $= 18,000 \times \dfrac{30}{100}$

$$= \text{Rs. } 5,400$$

Profit = Rs. 5,400 - Rs. 4,000 = **Rs. 1,400.**

iv) The Sales required to earn a Profit of Rs. 2,400

$$\text{Sales} = \frac{\text{Fixed Cost + Profit}}{\text{PV Ratio}}$$

$$= \frac{4,000 + 2,400}{30\%}$$

$$= \frac{6,400 \times 100}{30} = \textbf{81,333.33 approx.}$$

Illustration : 19

	Sales Rs.	Profit Rs.
2008	2,00,000	10,000
2009	1,80,000	2,000

You are required to predict the expected profit and loss with sales of -

(a) Rs. 1,50,000,   (b) 3,00,000

Determine the P. V. Ratio and Sales at B.E.P

Solution

i)　　　　　　P.V. Ratio $= \dfrac{\text{Change in Profit}}{\text{Change in Sales}} \times 100$

$$= \dfrac{8,000}{20,000} \times 100 = \mathbf{40\%}$$

$S \times$ P.V. Ratio $= F + P$

$2,00,000 \times \dfrac{40}{100} = F + 10,000$

$F = 80,000 - 10,000 = 70,000$

ii) Sale at B.E.P. point

Fixed Exp. $\times$ P.V. Ratio $= 70,000 \times \dfrac{40}{100}$

$$= 70,000 \times \dfrac{100}{40} = \mathbf{Rs.\ 1,75,000.}$$

(a) Profit or Loss at the Sale of Rs. 1,50,000

$$S \times \dfrac{P}{V} = F + P; \ 1,50,000 \times \dfrac{2}{5} = P + 70,000$$

$60,000 = P + 70,000$

$P = \mathbf{10,000\ (Loss)}$

(b) Profit or Loss at the Sale of Rs. 3,00,000

$$30,000 \times \dfrac{2}{5} = P + 70,000$$

$1,20,000 = P + 70,000$

$P = \mathbf{50,000}$

Illustration : 20

The following data relating to a Company. Calculate :

i) The break-even Sales

ii) Sales required to earn a Profit of Rs. 6,000 per period.

Period	Total Sales	Total Cost
1	42,500	38,700
2	39,200	36,852

Solution

$$= \frac{\text{Change in Cost}}{\text{Change in Sales}} = \frac{1,848}{3,300} \times 100$$

$$= 56\%$$

Fixed cost = Total Cost - Variable Cost

$$= 38,700 - 23,800 = 14,900$$

$$\text{V.C} = \frac{56}{100} \times 42,500 = 23,800$$

$$\text{P.V. Ratio} = \frac{3,300 - 1,848}{3,300} = \frac{1,452}{3,300} \times 100 = 44\%$$

i) Break-even Sales $= \dfrac{\text{Fixed Cost}}{\text{P/V Ratio}}$

$$= \frac{14,900}{44} \times 100 = \mathbf{33,864}$$

ii) Sales on Profit of Rs. 6,000

$$= \frac{\text{Fixed Cost + Direct Profit}}{\text{P.V. Ratio}}$$

$$= \frac{14,900 + 6,000}{44} \times 100 = \mathbf{47,500}$$

Illustration : 21

The Sales and Profit for Timbuktoo Pvt. Ltd., during 2008 and 2009 were as follows :

Year	Sales	Profit
2008	1,00,000	10,000
2009	1,50,000	20,000

Find out (i) B. E. P., (ii) Sales required to produce a Profit of Rs. 40,000, (iii) What will the profit be if Sales are Rs. 1,20,000?

Solution

$$\text{Change in Sales} = 1,50,000 - 1,00,000 = 50,000$$

$$\text{Change in Profit} = 20,000 - 10,000 = 10,000$$

$$\text{Profit Volume Ratio} = \frac{10,000}{50,000} \times 100 = 20\%$$

$$\text{Contribution} = \text{Sales} \times \text{PV Ratio}$$

$$= 1,00,000 \times \frac{20}{100} = \mathbf{20,000}$$

$$\text{Fixed Cost} = \text{Contribution - Profit}$$

$$= 20,000 - 10,000$$

$$= \mathbf{Rs.\ 10,000}$$

i) $\qquad$ B.E.P $= \dfrac{\text{Fixed Cost}}{\text{P/V Ratio}}$

$$= 10,000 \times \frac{10}{20} = \mathbf{50,000}$$

ii) Sales required to produce a Profit of Rs. 40,000

$$= \frac{F + P}{\text{P.V. Ratio}} = \frac{10,000 + 40,000}{20\%}$$

$$= \frac{50,000}{20} \times 100 = \mathbf{2,50,000}$$

iii) Profit when Sales are Rs. 1,20,000

$$P = \text{Contribution - Fixed Cost}$$

Contribution on Sales of Rs. 1,20,000

$$= 1,20,000 \times \frac{20}{100} = 24,000$$

$$= 24,000 - 10,000 = \mathbf{14,000}$$

Illustration : 22

Calculate B.E.P. and Turnover required to earn a Profit of Rs. 36,000 :

Fixed Overheads	Rs. 1,80,000
Variable Cost per Unit	Rs. 2
Selling Price	Rs. 20

If the Company is earning a profit of Rs. 36,000, express the margin of safety.

Solution

$$\text{B.E.P. (Units)} = \frac{\text{Fixed Exp.}}{\text{S.P.} - \text{V.C.}}$$

$$= \frac{1,80,000}{18} = \mathbf{10,000} \text{ Units}$$

B.E.P. (Amt) = 10,000 Units @ Rs. 20 per Unit
= **Rs. 2,00,000**

Turnover required to earn a Profit of Rs. 36,000

$$\text{Turnover in Units} = \frac{\text{Fixed Exp. + Profit}}{\text{S.P. per Unit - V.C. of Unit}}$$

$$= \frac{1,80,000 + 36,000}{20-2} = \frac{2,16,000}{18}$$

= 12,000 Units

Turnover in (Amt) = 12,000 Units @ Rs. 20 per Unit
= Rs. 2,40,000

$$\text{Margin of Safety} = \frac{\text{Profit}}{\text{P.V. Ratio}}$$

$$= \frac{36,000}{\dfrac{18}{20}}$$

$$= \frac{36,000}{18} \times 20 = 40,000 \text{ Units}$$

Illustration : 23

The following figures are available for 2 successive years of a Company.

	2008 (Rs)	2009 (Rs)
Sales Volume	6,00,000	9,00,000
Variable Overheads	3,60,000	4,50,000
Fixed Overheads	1,50,000	1,80,000

The management is interested to know the profit volume ratio, B.E.P., and margin of safety.

	2008 (Rs)	2009 (Rs)
Sales volume	6,00,000	9,00,000
Less : Variable Overheads	3,60,000	4,50,000
Contribution	2,40,000	4,50,000
Less : Fixed Costs	1,50,000	1,80,000
Net Profit	90,000	2,70,000

1) Profit Volume Ratio $= \dfrac{C}{S} \times 100$

$$(2008) \quad = \dfrac{2,40,000}{6,00,000} \times 100 = \mathbf{40\%}$$

$$(2009) \quad = \dfrac{4,50,000}{9,00,000} \times 100 = \mathbf{50\%}$$

2) Break-even Point $= \dfrac{\text{Fixed Cost}}{\text{P.V. Ratio}}$

$$(2008) \quad = \dfrac{1,50,000 \times 100}{40} = \mathbf{3,75,000}$$

$$(2009) \quad = 1,80,000 \times \dfrac{100}{50} = \mathbf{3,60,000}$$

3) Margin of Safety $= \dfrac{\text{Profit}}{\text{P.V. Ratio}}$

$$(2008) \quad = 90,000 \times \dfrac{100}{40} = \mathbf{2,25,000}$$

$$(2009) \quad = 2,70,000 \times \dfrac{100}{50} = \mathbf{5,40,000}$$

Illustration : 24

You are given the following data for the year 2008 of PQR Ltd.

	Rs.
Variable Cost	6,00,000
Fixed Cost	3,00,000
Sales	10,00,000
Net Profit	1,00,000

Find out :
a) P / V Ratio
b) B. E. P.
c) Profit when Sales amounted to Rs. 12,00,000
d) Sales to earn a Profit of Rs. 2,00,000.

(P.U.)

Solution

MARGINAL COST STATEMENTS

	Rs.
Sales	10,00,000
Less : Variable Cost	6,00,000
Contribution	4,00,000
Less : Fixed Cost	3,00,000
Profit	1,00,000

a)
$$\text{P/V Ratio} = \frac{\text{Contribution}}{\text{Sales}} \times 100$$

$$= \frac{4,00,000}{10,00,000} \times 100$$

$$= \textbf{40\%}$$

b)
$$\text{Break-even Point} = \frac{\text{Fixed Cost}}{\text{P.V. Ratio}}$$

$$= \frac{3,00,000}{40\%}$$

$$= 3,00,000 \times \frac{100}{40}$$

$$= \textbf{Rs. 7,50,000}$$

c) Sales Rs. 12,00,000

P/V Ratio 40%

40% of Rs. 12,00,000 = Rs. 4,80,000

Contribution = F + P

4,80,000 = 3,00,000 + Profit

Profit = 4,80,000 - 3,00,000

= **Rs. 1,80,000**

d) Sales required to earn a Profit of Rs. 2,00,000

$$\frac{\text{Fixed Cost} + \text{Direct Profit}}{\text{P.V. Ratio}} = \frac{3,00,000 + 2,00,000}{40\%}$$

$$= 5,00,000 \times \frac{100}{40}$$

$$= \textbf{Rs. 12,50,000}$$

Illustration : 25

The following information is obtained from Gulmohar Company Ltd., in a certain year.

	Rs.
Sales (1,00,000 Units)	1,00,000
Variable Cost	60,000
Fixed Cost	30,000

Calculate :

a) P / V Ratio,

b) Break-even Point Sales value,

c) Sales to earn a Profit of Rs. 15,000,

d) Profit when Sales amounted to Rs. 1,40,000. (P.U.)

Solution

a)
$$\text{P / V Ratio} = \frac{\text{Contribution}}{\text{Sales}} \times 100$$

$$\text{But, Contribution} = \text{Sales - Variable Cost}$$

$$\frac{\text{Sales - Variable Cost}}{\text{Sales}} \times 100 = \frac{\text{Rs.} 1,00,000 - \text{Rs.} 60,000}{1,00,000} \times 100$$

$$= \frac{\text{Rs.} 40,000}{\text{Rs.} 1,00,000} \times 100$$

$$= \mathbf{40\%}$$

b)
$$\text{Break-even Point (Sales Value)} = \frac{\text{Fixed Cost}}{\text{P.V. Ratio}}$$

$$= \frac{\text{Rs.} 30,000}{40\%}$$

$$= \text{Rs.} 30,000 \times \frac{100}{40}$$

$$= \mathbf{Rs.\ 75,000}$$

c) Sales to earn a Profit of Rs. 15,000

$$\therefore \qquad \text{P / V Ratio} = \frac{\text{Contribution}}{\text{Sales}}$$

$$\text{But, Contribution} = \text{Fixed Cost + Profit}$$

$$\therefore \qquad \text{P / V Ratio} = \frac{\text{Fixed Cost + Profit}}{\text{Sales}}$$

$$\therefore \quad Sales = \frac{Fixed\ Cost + Profit}{P/V\ Ratio}$$

$$= \frac{Rs.\,30,000 + Rs.\,15,000}{40\%}$$

$$= 45,000 \times \frac{100}{40} = \textbf{Rs. 1,12,500}$$

d) Profit when Sales amounted to Rs. 1,40,000

$$\therefore \quad P/V\ Ratio = \frac{Contribution}{Sales}$$

But, Contribution = Fixed Cost + Profit

$$\therefore \quad P/V\ Ratio = \frac{Fixed\ Cost + Profit}{Sales}$$

$\therefore \quad P/V\ Ratio \times Sales = Fixed\ Cost + Profit$

$$\therefore \quad \frac{40}{100} \times 1,40,000 = 30,000 + Profit$$

$$Profit = (P/V\ Ratio \times Sales) - Fixed\ Cost$$

$$\therefore \quad Profit = \left(\frac{40}{100} \times 1,40,000 \right) - 30,000$$

i.e. Rs. 56,000 - Rs. 30,000

= **Rs. 26,000**

Illustration : 26

A Limited Co., has prepared the following budget estimates for the year 2008-2009 :

	Rs.
Sales (Units)	15,000
Fixed Expenses	34,000
Sales Value	1,50,000
Variable Cost per Unit	6

You are required to calculate :

a) P / V ratio, Break-even Point and Margin of Safety in each of the following cases :-

b) i) Decrease of 10% in selling price.

   ii) Increase of 10% in variable cost.

Solution

a) i) $P/V\ Ratio = \dfrac{C}{S} \times 100$ But, $C = S - V$

$\therefore$ P / V Ratio $= \dfrac{S - V}{S} \times 100$

Here, $S = \dfrac{\text{Sales Rs. } 1,50,000}{\text{Units } 15,000} = \text{Rs. 10 per Unit}$

$\therefore$ P / V Ratio $= \dfrac{\text{Rs.} 10 - \text{Rs.} 6}{\text{Rs.} 10} \times 100$

$= \dfrac{\text{Rs. } 4}{\text{Rs.} 10} \times 100$

$= \mathbf{40\%}$

ii) B.E.P. (Sales)

$\dfrac{F}{\text{P/V Ratio}} = \dfrac{\text{Rs.} 34,000}{40\%} = \text{Rs.} 34,000 \times \dfrac{100}{40}$

$= \mathbf{Rs.\ 85,000}$

iii)   Margin of Safety $=$ Annual sales - B.E.P.

i.e. Rs. 1,50,000 - Rs. 85,000

$= \mathbf{Rs.\ 65,000}$

B) i) Decrease of 10% in Selling Price

     Original SP   +   Decrease of 10%   +   New SP

       Rs. 10   +   Re. 1   +   Rs. 9

$\therefore$ P / V Ratio $= \dfrac{S - V}{S} \times 100 = \dfrac{\text{Rs.} 9 - \text{Rs.} 6}{\text{Rs.} 9} \times 100$

i.e. $= \dfrac{\text{Rs.} 3}{\text{Rs.} 9} \times 100$

$= 33\dfrac{1}{3}\% \text{ or } \mathbf{33.33}$

B.E.P. (Sales) $= \dfrac{F}{\text{P/V Ratio}} = \dfrac{\text{Rs.} 34,000}{33\dfrac{1}{3}\% \text{ or } \dfrac{1}{3}}$

$= \dfrac{\text{Rs.} 34,000}{\dfrac{1}{3}}$

$= \text{Rs.} 34,000 \times \dfrac{3}{1}$

$= \mathbf{Rs.\ 1,02,000}$

$$\text{Margin of Safety} = \text{Accrued Sales - B.E.P. (S)}$$
$$= \text{Rs. } 1,50,000 - \text{Rs. } 1,02,000$$
$$= \textbf{Rs. 48,000}$$

i) Increase of 10% in Variable Cost

Original VC	+	Increase of 10%	=	New VC
Rs. 6	+	Re. 0.60	=	Rs. 6.60

$$\text{P / V ratio} = \frac{S-V}{S} \times 100 = \frac{\text{Rs.}10 - \text{Rs.}6.60}{\text{Rs.}10} \times 100$$

$$= \frac{\text{Rs.}3.40}{\text{Rs.}10} \times 100$$

$$= \textbf{34\%}$$

$$\text{B.E.P. (Sales)} = \frac{F}{\text{P/V Ratio}} = \frac{\text{Rs. }34,000}{34\%}$$

$$= \text{Rs. }34,000 \times \frac{100}{34}$$

$$= \textbf{Rs. 1,00,000}$$

$$\text{MS} = \text{AS - BEP (S)}$$
$$= \text{Rs. }1,50,000 - \text{Rs. }1,00,000$$
$$= \textbf{Rs. 50,000}$$

Illustration : 27

Western Radio Company produced and sold 10,000 radios last year at a price of Rs. 500 each, the cost structure per radio is as follows :

	Rs.
Materials	100
(+) Labour	50
(+) Variable Overheads	+25
Marglnal Cost	175
(+) Fixed Overheads	+200
Total Cost	375
(+) Profit	+125
Price	500

Due to heavy competition, the price has to be reduced to Rs. 425 for the coming year. Assuming that there will be no change in costs, find out how many radios shall be sold to ensure the same amount of total profits as last year. (P.U.)

Solution

Statement showing Marginal Cost and Contribution for 10,000 radios in the last year

Particulars		Total Cost Rs.	Cost per Radio Rs.
Sales	(A)	50,00,000	500
(10,000 Radios × Rs. 500)			
Variable Expenses :			
i) Materials		10,00,000	100
ii) Labour		5,00,000	50
iii) Variable Overheads		2,50,000	25
∴ **Marginal Cost**	(B)	**17,50,000**	**175**
C = S - V			
= 50,00,000 - 17,50,000 (A - B)		32,50,000	325
C = F + P			
∴ P = C - F ..... Fixed Overheads		20,00,000	200
∴ **Profit**		**12,50,000**	**125**
Calculation of new Contribution			
C = S - V			
Sales			425
Variable Cost			175
∴ **Contribution**			**250**

Sales volume to earn the required Profits

i.e. Rs. 125 × 10,000 = Rs. 12,50,000

$$\frac{F + RD}{C} = \frac{Rs.\ 20,00,000 + Rs.\ 12,50,000}{Rs.\ 250}$$

$$= \frac{Rs.\ 32,50,000}{Rs.\ 250}$$

$$= \textbf{Rs. 13,000 Radio sets}$$

Illustration : 28

'R' Ltd., furnished you the following information relating to half year ended 30. 6. 2008

	Rs.
Fixed Expenses	45,000
Sales Value	1,50,000
Profit	30,000

During the second half of the year, the Company has projected a loss of Rs. 10,000.

Calculate :

1. Variable Cost   (For 1st half year)
2. P / V Ratio   (For 1st half year)
3. B. E. P.   (For 1st half year)
4. Margin of Safety   (For 1st half year)
5. Expected Sales volume for the 2nd half of the year assuming that the P/V ratio and fixed expenses remain constant in the 2nd half year also.

Solution

1. Variable Cost

$$SP = CP + P \text{ But, } CP = F + V$$
$$SP = F + V + P$$
$$V = SP - (F + P)$$
$$= \text{Rs. } 1,50,000 \, (\text{Rs. } 45,000 + 30,000)$$
$$= \text{Rs. } 1,50,000 - \text{Rs. } 75,000$$
$$= \textbf{Rs. 75000}$$

2.   **P / V Ratio** $= \dfrac{C}{S} \times 100 \text{ But, } C = F + P$

∴   P / V Ratio $= \dfrac{F + P}{S} \times 100$

$$= \dfrac{\text{Rs. } 45,000 + \text{Rs. } 30,000}{\text{Rs. } 1,50,000} \times 100$$

$$= \dfrac{\text{Rs. } 75,000}{\text{Rs. } 1,50,000} \times 100 = \dfrac{1}{2} \times 100$$

$$= \textbf{50\%}$$

3.   **B. E. P. (Sales)** $= \dfrac{F}{\text{P/V Ratio}} = \dfrac{\text{Rs. } 45,000}{5\%}$

$$= \text{Rs. } 45,000 \times \dfrac{100}{50}$$

$$= \textbf{Rs. 90,000}$$

4. Margin of Safety

$$MS = AS - \text{B. E. P. (S)}$$
$$= 1,50,000 - \text{Rs. } 90,000$$
$$= \textbf{Rs. 60,000}$$

5. Expected Sales volume for 2nd half year

$$P / V \text{ Ratio} = \dfrac{C}{S} \qquad \text{But, } C = F + P \text{ or } F - L$$

$$P / V \text{ Ratio} = \frac{\text{Fixed Expenses - Loss}}{\text{Sales}}$$

$$\therefore \quad S = \frac{F - L}{P/V \text{ Ratio}} = \frac{Rs.\,45,000 - Rs.\,10,000}{50\%}$$

$$= \textbf{Rs. 70,000}$$

Illustration : 29

The turnover and profits during the two period were as follows :

Particulars	Sales Rs.	Profit Rs.
Period I	40 lakhs	4 lakhs
Period II	60 lakhs	8 lakhs

Assuming that the cost structure and selling prices remain the same in the two periods. Calculate :

(A) P/V Ratio

(B) B.E.P. Sales

(C) Sales required to earn a profit of Rs. 10 lakh

(D) Margin of Safety in period II

(E) Profit when Sales are Rs. 50 lakhs.   (P.U.)

Solution :

 A) Profit Volume Ratio

$$\frac{P}{V} \text{ Ratio} = \frac{\text{Contribution}}{\text{Sales}}$$

$$= \frac{\text{Changes in Contribution in the periods}}{\text{Changes in Sales in two periods}}$$

$$= \frac{\text{Changes in Profits in two periods}}{\text{Changes in Sales in two periods}}$$

(Because after Break-even Point, Entire Contribution is equal to the Profit as fixed costs have already been recorded).

$$\therefore \quad \frac{P}{V} \text{ Ratio} = \frac{8 \text{ lakhs - 4 lakhs}}{60 \text{ lakhs - 40 lakhs}} = \frac{4 \text{ lakhs}}{20 \text{ lakhs}}$$

$$= \frac{4}{20}$$

$$= \frac{1}{5} \text{ i.e } 20\%$$

$$= \textbf{20\%}$$

B) Break-even Point Sales -

In order to find out Break-even Point, Fixed Costs are to be found out first

$$\text{Contribution} = \frac{P}{V} \text{ Ratio} \times \text{Sales.}$$

$$= 20\% \text{ of } 60 \text{ lakhs}$$

$$= \textbf{Rs. 12 lakhs}$$

$$\text{Fixed Cost} = \text{Contribution - Profits}$$

$$= 12 \text{ lakhs - 8 lakhs (Period II)}$$

∴ $$\text{Fixed Cost} = \text{Rs. 4 lakhs}$$

$$\text{B.E.P. Sales} = \frac{\text{Fixed Cost}}{\frac{P}{V}\text{Ratio}} = \frac{4 \text{ lakhs}}{\frac{1}{5}}$$

$$= \text{Rs. 4 lakhs} \times 5$$

$$\text{B.E.P. Sales} = \text{Rs. } \textbf{20 lakhs.}$$

C) Sales required to earn Profits of Rs. 10 lakhs

$$\frac{P}{V} \text{ Ratio} = \frac{\text{Contribution}}{\text{Sales}}$$

$$\text{Sales} = \frac{\text{Contribution}}{\frac{P}{V}\text{Ratio}} = \frac{\text{Fixed Cost + Profit}}{\frac{P}{V}\text{Ratio}}$$

$$= \frac{\text{Rs. 4 lakhs} + 10 \text{ lakhs}}{20\% \text{ or } \frac{20}{100}}$$

$$= \frac{14 \text{ lakhs} \times 100}{20}$$

$$\text{Sales} = \textbf{Rs. 70 lakhs.}$$

D) Margin of Safety in Period II

$$= \frac{\text{Profit}}{\text{P/V Ratio}}$$

$$= \frac{8 \text{ lakhs}}{20} \times 100$$

$$= \textbf{Rs. 40 lakhs}$$

(Varification = Actual Sales - B.E.P. Sales = Margin of Safety)

E) Profit when Sales are Rs. 50 (lakhs)

$$\text{Contribution} = \text{P/V Ratio} \times \text{Sales}$$

i..e 20% of 50 lakhs

$$= 10 \text{ lakhs}$$

Less : Fixed Costs = 4 lakhs

$$\therefore \textbf{Profit Rs. = 6 lakhs}$$

Illustration : 30

Calculate from the following information:

a) Fixed Cost
b) Break-even Point Sales
c) The number of Units to be sold to earn a Profit of Rs. 40,000
d) Profit when Sales are 20,000 Units.
   Period I Sales - 7,000 Units, Rs.10,000 Loss
   Period II Sales - 9,000 Units, Rs. 10,000 Profit.
   The Selling Price per Unit Rs. 100.   (P.U.)

Solution

N.B. : Additional Sales of Rs. 2,00,000 in Period II has given an additional Contribution i.e. change in profits of Rs. 20,000 which has wiped off the loss of Rs. 10,000 of Period I and given a profit of Rs. 10,000 for Period II.

a) Calculation of Fixed Cost :

i) Calculation of P / V Ratio $= \dfrac{\text{Change in Profits}}{\text{Change in Sales}} \times 100$

$$= \dfrac{\text{Rs.} 20,000}{\text{Rs.} 2,00,000} \times 100\%$$

$$= \textbf{10\%}$$

ii) Calculation of Contribution = Sales × P / V Ratio
    of Period I = Rs. 7,00,000 × 10%
    $$= \textbf{Rs. 70,000}$$

iii) Calculation of Fixed Cost, where C = F - L
    $$F = C + L$$
    $$= \text{Rs. } 70,000 + \text{Rs. } 10,000$$
    $$= \textbf{Rs. 80,000}$$

b) Break-even Point (Sales) $= \dfrac{F}{\text{P/V Ratio}} = \dfrac{\text{Rs.} 80,000}{10\%}$

$$= \text{Rs. } 80,000 \times \dfrac{100}{10}$$

$$= \text{Rs. } \textbf{8,00,000}$$

c) The number of Units to be sold to earn a Profit of Rs. 40,000

$$\text{P / V Ratio} = \dfrac{C}{S} \qquad \text{But, C } = F + P$$

$$\therefore \text{ P / V Ratio } = \frac{F + P}{S}$$

$$S = \frac{F + P}{P/V \text{ Ratio}}$$

$$= \frac{Rs. 80,000 + Rs. 40,000}{10\%}$$

$$= \frac{Rs. 1,20,000}{10\%}$$

$$= Rs. 1,20,000 \times \frac{100}{10}$$

$$= Rs. 12,00,000 \text{ Sales}$$

$$\text{Sales of Units} = \frac{Rs. 12,00,000}{Rs. 100}$$

$$= \textbf{12,000 Units}$$

d) Profit when Sales are 20,000 Units

20,000 Units $\times$ Rs. 100 = Rs. 20,00,000

$$\text{P / V Ratio} = \frac{C}{S} \quad \text{But, C} = F + P$$

$$\therefore \text{ P / V Ratio} = \frac{F + P}{S}$$

$$\therefore \text{ S} \times \text{P / V Ratio} = F + P$$

$$P = (S \times P / V \text{ Ratio}) - F$$

$$= (Rs. 20,00,000 \times 10\%) - Rs. 80,000$$

$$= \textbf{Rs. 1,20,000}$$

Illustration : 31

The Sales and Profit during two years were :

Year	Sales Rs.	Profit Rs.
2008	15,00,000	2,00,000
2009	17,00,000	2,50,000

Fixed Cost is Rs. **1,75,000** p.a

You are required to calculate :

a) Break-even Point,

b) P / V Ratio,

c) the profit made when Sales are Rs. 25,00,000,

d) Sales required to earn Profit of Rs. 4,00,000

(P.U.)

Solution

a) P / V Ratio :

$$= \frac{\text{Change in Profits}}{\text{Change in Sales}} \times 100$$

$$= \frac{\text{Rs.} 50,000}{\text{Rs.} 2,00,000} \times 100$$

$$= \mathbf{25\%}$$

b) Break-even Point (Sales) :

$$= \frac{F}{\text{P/V Ratio}} = \frac{\text{Rs.} 1,75,000}{25\%}$$

$$= \text{Rs.} 1,75,000 \times \frac{100}{25}$$

$$= \textbf{Rs. 7,00,000}$$

c) The Profit made when Sales are Rs. 25,00,000

$$\text{P / V Ratio} = \frac{C}{S} \qquad \text{But, } C = F + P$$

$\therefore \qquad \text{P / V Ratio} = \dfrac{F + P}{S}$

$\therefore \qquad \text{P / V Ratio} \times S = F + P$

$$P = (\text{P / V Ratio} \times S) - F$$

$$= (\text{Rs.} 25,00,000 \times 25\%) - \text{Rs.} 1,75,000$$

$$= \text{Rs.} 6,25,000 - \text{Rs.} 1,75,000$$

$$= \textbf{Rs. 4,50,000}$$

d) Sales required to earn Profit of Rs. 4,00,000

$$\text{P / V Ratio} = \frac{C}{S} \qquad \text{But, } C = F + P$$

$$\therefore \text{P / V Ratio} = \frac{F + P}{S}$$

$$\therefore S = \frac{F + P}{\text{P/V Ratio}}$$

$$= \frac{\text{Rs.} 1,75,000 + \text{Rs.} 4,00,000}{25\%}$$

$$\text{i.e. Rs. } 5,75,000 \times \frac{100}{25}$$

$$= \textbf{Rs. 23,00,000}$$

Illustration : 32

From the following find out :

a) P / V Ratio,

b) Break-even Point

c) Net Profit if the Sales were Rs. 2,50,000

d) Sales to get a net Profit of Rs. 70,000

Position of Rama and Co. Ltd., for the year ending 31.12.2008

	Rs.
Sales	2,00,000
Marginal Cost	1,50,000
Contribution	50,000
Less : Fixed Cost	15,000
Net profit	35,000

(P.U)

Solution

a) **P / V Ratio :**

$$= \frac{\text{Contribution}}{\text{Sales}} \times 100 = \frac{\text{Rs. } 50,000}{\text{Rs. } 2,00,000} \times 100$$

$$= \textbf{25\%}$$

b) **Break-even Point (Sales)**

$$= \frac{\text{Fixed Cost}}{\text{P.V. Ratio}} = \frac{\text{Rs.} 15,000 \times 100}{25}$$

$$= \textbf{Rs. 60,000}$$

c) **Net profit if sales were Rs. 2,50,000**

$$S (P / V) = F + P = 2,50,000 \times \frac{25}{100} = 62,500$$

$$62,500 = 15000 + P$$

$$P = 62,500 - 15,000$$

$$\text{Profit} = \textbf{Rs. 47,500}$$

d) **Sales to get a N. P. of Rs. 70,000**

$$S \times 25\% = F + P$$

$$\frac{S}{4} = 15,000 + 70,000$$

$$\frac{S}{4} = 85,000$$

$$\therefore S = 85,000 \times 4$$
$$= \textbf{Rs. 3,40,000}$$

Illustration : 33

An analysis of 'S'. Ltd., cost records gives the following information :

	Variable Cost (% of Sales)	Fixed Cost Rs.
Direct Materials	32.8	
Direct Labour	28.4	
Factory Overheads	12.6	1,89,000
Distribution Overheads	4.1	58,400
General Administration Overheads	1.1	66,700

Budgeted Sales for the next year Rs. 18,50,000. You are required to determine –
a) Break-even Sales value
b) Profit at the budgeted Sales volume
c) Profit, if the actual Sales
    i)   drop by 10%
    ii) increase by 5%   (P.U.)

Solution

Total Variable Cost as % of Sales = 79

Sales	Rs. 100
Less :	
Variable Cost	79
Contribution	21

$$P / V \ Ratio = \frac{Contribution}{Sales} \times 100$$

$$= \frac{21}{100} \times 100$$

$$= \textbf{21\%}$$

a)   Break-even Sales volume $= \dfrac{Fixed\ Cost}{P.V.\ Ratio}$

$$= \frac{3,14,100}{21} \times 100$$

$$= \textbf{Rs. 14,95,714}$$

b) Profit at the budgeted Sales volume :

Budgeted Sales Volume	Rs. 18,50,000
Less : Variable Cost : 79% of Sales	14,61,500
Contribution	3,88,500
Fixed Cost	3,14,100
Profit	**74,400**

(c) (i) Profit, if the actual sales drop by 10%

Budgeted Sales volume	Rs. 18,50,000
Less : 10% drop	1,85,000
Actual Sales	16,65,000
Contribution (16,65,000 - 13,15,350 i.e. 79%)	3,49,650
Less : Fixed Cost	3,14,100
Profit	**35,550**

The same answer may also be got by using the forumula –

$$S (P / V) = F + P$$

$$18,50,000 - 10\% \times \frac{21}{100} = 3,14,100 + P$$

$$16,65,000 \times \frac{21}{100} = 3,14,100 + P$$

$$3,49,650 = 3,14,100 + P$$

$$P = \textbf{Rs. 35,550}$$

ii) Profit, if the actual sales increase by 5%

$$S (P / V) = F + P$$

$$18,50,000 + 5\% \times \frac{21}{100} = 3,14,100 + P$$

$$19,42,500 \times \frac{21}{100} = 3,14,100 + P$$

$$4,07,925 = 3,14,100 + P$$

$$P = \textbf{Rs. 93,825}$$

Illustration : 34

The Sales turnover and Profit during two years were as follows :

Year	Sales Rs.	Profit Rs.
2008	1,50,000	20,000
2009	1,70,000	25,000

You are required to calculate :

(a) P.V Ratio, (b) Break-even Point, (c) Sales required to earn a Profit of Rs. 40,000, (d) Profit made when Sales are Rs. 2,50,000, (e) Margin of Safety at a Profit of Rs. 50,000, (f) Variable Costs of the two periods.

Solution

a)
$$P / V \text{ Ratio} = \frac{\text{Change in Profits}}{\text{Change in Sales}} \times 100$$

$$= \frac{5,000}{20,000} \times 100$$

$$= \mathbf{25\%}$$

Fixed Cost : S (P / V) = F + P

$$1,50,000 \times \frac{25}{100} = F + 20,000$$

$$37,500 = F + 20,000$$

$$F = \mathbf{Rs.\ 17,500}$$

b)
$$\text{Break-even Point} = \frac{\text{Fixed cost}}{\text{P.V. Ratio}}$$

$$= \frac{17,500}{25} \times 100$$

$$= \mathbf{Rs.\ 70,000}$$

c) Sales for a Profit of Rs. 40,000

$$S (P / V) = F + P$$

$$S \times \frac{25}{100} = 17,500 + 40,000$$

$$\frac{S}{4} = 57,500$$

$$\therefore S = \mathbf{Rs.\ 2,30,000}$$

d) Profit when Sales are Rs. 2,50,000

$$S (P / V) = F + P$$

$$2,50,000 \times \frac{25}{100} = 17,500 + P$$

$$62,500 = 17,500 + P$$

$$P = \mathbf{Rs.\ 45,000}$$

e) Margin of Safety at a Profit of Rs. 50,000 :

$$M.S = \frac{\text{Profit}}{\text{P/V Ratio}}$$

$$= \frac{50,000}{25} \times 100$$

$$= \textbf{Rs. 2,00,000}$$

f) Variable Costs of the two periods :

if P / V Ratio is 25%, Variable Cost should be 75% of Sales.

2008 : Sales Rs. 1,50,000

Variable Cost 75% of Rs. 1,50,000 = Rs. 1,12,500

2009 : Sales Rs. 1,70,000

Variable Cost 75% of Rs. 1,70,000 = Rs. 1,27,500

	OR	S - V = C and F + P = C
2008 :	17,500 + 20,000	= 37,500
	1,50,000 - V	= 37,500
	V	= **1,12,500**
2009 :	F + P	= C
	17,500 + 25,000	= C
	C	= 42,500
	S - V	= C
	1,70,000 - V	= 42,500
	V	= **1,27,500**

Exercises

A. Indicate whether the following statements are true or false:

1) All Costs are controllable

2) Variable Cost per Unit varies with the increase in the volume of output.

3) Fixed Cost per Unit remains constant.

4) Marginal Costing can be used with process costing

5) In Marginal Costing, valuation of stock is done on total cost basis

6) Profit = Sales - Contribution

7) Variable Cost + Profit = Sales

8) Profit = Contribution - Fixed Cost

9) P/V Ratio = Profit/Sales

10) Marginal Costing and Direct Costing are the same.

11) Marginal Costing is based on the distinction between Fixed and Variable Cost.

12) For decision-making, Absorption Costing is more suitable than Marginal Costing.

13) Marginal Costing cannot be applied in job costing.

14) Marginal Costing is a technique of cost control.

15) A firm earns profit when contribution is equal to fixed cost under Variable Costing.

16) Marginal Cost includes prime cost plus fixed overhead.

17) Contribution is the difference between selling price and variable cost

18) Margin of Safety is the difference between Actual Sales and B.E.P. Sales.

19) Break-even Point indicates the position of no profit, no loss.

20) Sales commission is an example of fixed cost.

Answers : (1) True (2) False (3) False (4) True (5) False (6) False (7) False (8) True (9) False (10) True (11) True (12) False (13) False (14) True (15) False (16) False (17) True (18) True (19) True (20) False

B. Fill in the blanks :

1) In cost accounting, marginal cost does not include....

2) In absorption costing... cost is added to inventory.

3) Sales minus Variable Cost = Fixed Cost plus...

4) Contribution minus... cost is profit.

5) At break-even point ... is equal to total fixed cost.

6) Total fixed costs remain... at all levels of production.

7) A high P/V Ratio indicates... profitability.

8) The break-even chart is a... representation of marginal costing.

9) The size of the margin of safety indicates... of a business.

10) While calculating marginal cost... are added.

11) Marginal costing is a... and not a... of costing.

12) Marginal cost is the cost of producing... extra unit of the output.

13) Executive salaries is an example of... cost.

14) Contribution = Sales......

Answers : (1) fixed cost (2) total (3) profit (4) fixed cost (5) total contribution (6) constant (7) high (8) graphical (9) soundness (10) variable overheads (11) technique, method (12) one (13) fixed (14) Variable Cost.

C) i) Match the following :-

Group A	Group B
1) P/V Ratio	a) Prime Cost + Variable Overheads
2) Marginal Cost	b) Contribution to Sales Ratio
3) Variable Cost per Unit	c) Sales × P/V Ratio
4) Contribution	d) Is fixed
5) Margin of Safety	e) $\dfrac{F}{P/V\ Ratio}$
6) Break-even Point	f) $\dfrac{Profit}{P/V\ Ratio}$

Answers : 1 (b), 2 (a), 3 (d), 4 (c), 5 (f), 6 (e).

ii) **Match the following :-**

Group A

i) Total Fixed Cost
ii) Total Variable Cost
iii) Unit Variable Cost

iv) Unit Fixed Cost
v) Standard Cost
vi) Period Cost
vii) Actual Cost
viii) Labour and Overheads
ix) Incremental Cost
x) Budget Cost

Group B

1) What cost should be
2) Incurred cost
3) Increases in proportion to output
4) Cost of conversion
5) What costs are expected to be
6) Decreases with rise in output
7) Remains constant in total
8) Remains constant per unit
9) Cost not assigned to products
10) Added value of a new product

Answers : (i) 7 (ii) 3 (iii) 8 (iv) 6 (v) 1 (vi) 9 (vii) 2 (viii) 4 (ix) 10 (x) 5

D. Choose the correct alternative answer :-

1) .... is the difference between Sales and Variable Cost
   (a) Contribution   (b) P/V Ratio   (c) Margin of Safety
2) If production is nil, the loss will be equal to...
   (a) Variable Cost   (b) Fixed Cost   (c) Marginal Cost
3) Contribution + Variable Cost = ...
   (a) Profit   (b) Loss   (c) Selling price
4) The Margin of Safety may be improved by.... Sales volume.
   (a) decreasing   b) increasing   (c) keeping constant.
5) When break-even point is 1,000 Units and Contribution per Unit is Rs. 5, then total Fixed Cost is Rs. ....
   (a) Rs. 5,000   (b) Rs. 500   (c) Rs. 50,000
6) At break-even point, total cost is equal to...
   (a) total Variable Cost   (b) total Revenue   (c) total Sales volume
7) Marginal costing technique follows the ... classification of costs
   (a) Behaviour-wise   (b) Element-wise   (c) Function-wise
8) Contribution margin is equal to ....
   (a) Fixed - Variable Cost   (b) Sales - Variable Cost   (c) Sales - fixed Cost
9) Variable Cost ....
   (a) remains fixed in total   (b) varies per Unit   (c) remain fixed per Unit
10) Margin of safety is ...
   (a) Actual sales - B.E.P. Sales   (b) Sales - Contribution   (c) Sales - Fixed Cost

Answers : 1 (a) 2 (b) 3 (c) 4 (b) 5 (a) 6 (b) 7 (a) 8 (b) 9 (c) 10 (a).

Essay Type

1. What is meant by 'Marginal Costing'? Explain the main features and limitations of Marginal Costing.
2. Define 'Marginal Cost' and 'Marginal costing'. How variable costs and fixed costs are treated in Marginal Costing?
3. What do you mean by Marginal Costing? Discuss its usefulness and limitations.
4. "The technique of Marginal Costing is a valuable aid to management". Comment.
5. What is the significance of "Contribution" in Marginal Costing"?
6. What do you understand by the term 'Break-even analysis'? Enumerate its uses.
7. What do you understand by the term 'Break-even Point'? Why should it be calculated?
8. State the assumptions underlying a 'Break-even Chart'. Give five points.
9. Define Profit- Volume Ratio and explain its significance. In what ways can the P/V Ratio be improved upon?
10. Explain the term 'Break-even Point'. Give an example illustrating your answer.
11. What do you mean by a 'Break-even Chart'? What are its advantages?
12. Discuss the importance of the following in relation to Marginal Costing :
    (a) Break-even Point.   (b) Margin of Safety.
    (c) P/V Ratio   (d) Contribution.
13. Explain the significance and objective of a Break-even Chart and state the factors which would cause the break-even point to change.
14. Write notes on the following :
    (a) Angle of Incidence.   (b) Contribution Sales ratio.   (c) Key factor.
15. Write a lucid note on Marginal Costing indicating its effect on Profit.
16. Explain the principles of Marginal Costing. How does Marginal Costing differ from total costing?

Practical Exercises

1) a) Calculate the Break-even Point from the following figures:

	Rs.
Sales	5,00,000
Fixed Cost	60,000
Direct Materials	2,05,000
Direct Labour	75,000
Variable Overhead	1,00,000

   b) What is the new Break-even Point when fixed cost increases by 10%.

[**Ans.** (a) Rs. 2,50,000, (b) 2,75,000]

2) a) From the following particulars, draw a Break-even Chart and find out the Break-even Point :

	Rs.
Variable Cost per Unit	15
Fixed Expenses	54,000
Selling Price per Unit	20

(b) What should be the Selling Price per Unit, if the Break-even Point is brought down to 6,000 Units?

[**Ans.** (a) 10,800 Units, (b) Rs. 24]

3) A Company budgets a production of 5,00,000 Units at a variable cost of Rs. 20 each. The fixed costs are Rs. 20,00,000. The selling price is fixed to yield 25 per cent profit on cost. You are required to calculate : (i) Profit-Volume Ratio, and (ii) Break-even Point.

[**Ans** : (i) 33 $\frac{1}{3}$ %, (ii) 60,00,000]

4) You are required to calculate the Break-even Point in the following case :
The fixed costs for the year are Rs. 80,000; variable cost per unit for the single product being made is Rs. 4.
Estimated sales for the period are valued at Rs. 2,00,000. The number of units involved coincides with the expected volume of output. Each unit sells at Rs. 20.

[**Ans.:** Rs. 1,00,000; Units 5,000]

5) From the following information available, calculate the Break-even Point and the turnover required to earn the Profit of Rs. 36,000 :

	Rs.
Fixed Overheads	1,80,000
Variable Cost per Unit	2
Selling Price	20

[**Ans** : (a) B.E.P. 10,000 Units; (b) Turnover required 12,000 Units]

6) Polestar Electronics decides to effect a 10% reduction in the price of its product because it is felt that such a step may lead to a greater volume of sales.
It is anticipated that there are no prespects of a change in total fixed costs and variable costs per unit.
The directors wish to maintain net profits at the present level.
The following information has been obtained from its books:

	Rs.
Sales - 10,000 Units	2,00,000
Variable Costs	Rs. 15 per Unit
Fixed Costs	40,000

How would the management proceed to implement this decision?

[**Ans.:** Sales required to earn current amount of Profit Rs. 3,00,000]

7) The Sales turnover and Profit during the two periods were as follows :

Period No. 1. - Sales Rs. 20 lakhs, Profit Rs. 2 lakhs

Period No. 2. - Sales Rs. 30 lakhs, profit Rs. 4 lakhs.

Calculate (i) P/V ratio and (ii) The sales required to earn a profit of Rs. 5 lakhs.

[**Ans.:** (i) 20% (ii) Rs. 35 lakhs]

8) The following information relating to a Company is given to you.

	Rs.
Sales	4,00,000
Fixed Cost	1,80,000
Variable Cost	2,50,000

Ascertain how much the sales value must be increased for the Company to break-even.

[**Ans.:** 80,000]

9) Two businesses 'Y' Ltd., and 'Z' Ltd., sell the same type of product in the same type of market. Their budgeted profit and loss accounts for the coming year are as follows :

	'Y' Ltd. Rs.		'Z' Ltd. Rs.	
Sales		1,50,000		1,50,000
Less: Variable Costs	1,20,000		1,00,000	
Fixed Costs	15,000		35,000	
		1,35,000		1,35,000
Budgeted Net Profit		15,000		15,000

You are required to :

(a) calculate the Break-even Point of each business; and

(b) calculate the Sales volume at which each of the business will earn Rs. 5,000 Profit.

[**Ans.:** (a) 'Y' Ltd. Rs. 75,000, 'Z' Ltd. Rs. 1,05,000

(b) 'Y' Ltd. Rs. 1,00,000, 'Z' Ltd. Rs. 1,20,000]

10) You are given the following data for the year 2007 of 'X' Company :

	Rs.	%
Variable Cost	6,00,000	60
Fixed Cost	3,00,000	30
Net Profit	1,00,000	10
Sales	10,00,000	100

Find out : (a) Break-even Point

(b) P/V Ratio, and

(c) Margin of Safety Ratio.

Also, draw a Break-even Chart indicating Contribution.

[**Ans.** (a) Rs. 7,50,000 (b) 40%, (c) 25% of Sales]

CHAPTER - 6

Budget and Budgetary Control

● 6:1 Meaning and Nature of Budget and Budgetary Control ● 6:2 Objectives of Budget and Budgetary Control ● 6:3 Essentials of Budgetary Control ● 6:4 Advantages and Limitations of Budgetary Control ● 6:5 Steps in Budgetary Control. ● 6:6 Types / Classification of Budgets ● 6:7 Illustrations on Flexible Budgets ● 6:8 Exercises

Budget and budgetary control are perhaps the oldest tools of financial control. Across various civilisations, we find ample references of it. In European history, we find king Augustus preparing budget for his kingdom. Indian history too is replete with references to it right from the days of *Mahabharat* to Kautilya's *Arthshastra* regarding the control procedure terms like budgets. However, the importance and procedure of budgetary control in Cost Accountancy have a recent origin of not more than a century period. Of course, the nature, procedure and the purpose of this control technique is much different than that of the fiscal policies in modern Economics. Here, we have to understand the budgetary control technique used in the business world.

Business Budget is at present used as one of the most important tool of managerial control. Due to the increasing complexity of the organisation and managerial problems, the accountants have developed this tool for the assistance of the Management. Thus, budgeting is essentially a tool for internal control in the organisation. Though, the budgeting and financial year is closely associated, modern management science looks at the budgetary control as a blue print of the financial year prepared in advance. Actually, it is regarded as a scientific planning exercise based on well-known management principle, 'MBO - Management By Objectives.'

Budgeting may be a partial or a comprehensive one depending on the size, objectives and need of the organisation. Partial application means the budgeting may be adopted for a single or few important operational areas of the organisation i.e., only for advertising, purchasing, etc., whereas comprehensive application means, budgets are prepared for every operation and function of the business prior to the 'Master Budget' with projected financial statements of the business are prepared. Whatever may be the nature and scope of the budgeting, undoubtedly, it is an excellent tool for planning, co-ordination and control.

6.1 Meaning and Nature of Budget and Budgetary Control

To comprehend this technique, we have to understand the meaning of terms - budget and budgetary control.

1) Budget -

The term 'budget' is defined by the ICMA, London, as follows :-

"A budget is a financial and / or quantitative statement, prepared and approved prior to a defined period of time, of the policy to be pursued during that period for the purpose of attaining a given objective."

'Budget is also defined as" a blue print of a projected plan of action of business, for a definite period of time."

The above definition reveals the following essentials of a budget (Nature of budget)

1) The budget is a monetary and / or quantitative statement.
2) It is prepared prior to a defined period of time.
3) It is prepared for a definite period in the future.
4) It is based on the policies to be pursued.
5) It lays out the objectives to be attained in unambiguous terms.

2) Budgeting :-

Budgeting refers to the mechanism of preparing budgets. According to **J.Betty** - "The entire process of preparing the budgets is known as budgeting." Preparation of business budget involves a careful study of the conditions of the business, the objectives of the management and the capacity of the business concern for attaining those objectives.

3) Budgetary Control :-

Budgetary control is a system of controlling costs which includes the preparation of budgets. In budgetary control, the budgets are used as a means of planning and controlling costs. There are various definitions given by experts.

(i) The I.C.M.A., London :- "The establishment of budgets relating to the responsibilities of executives of a policy and the continuous comparison of actual with budgeted results, either to secure by individual action the objectives of that policy or to produce a basis for its revision."

(ii) J.L. Brown and L.R. Howard :- "Budgetary control systems are a system of controlling costs, which includes the preparation of budgets, co-ordinating the departments and establishing responsibilities by comparing actual performance with the budgeted, and acting upon results to achieve maximum profitability."

(iii) J.A. Scott :- "Budgetary control is applied to the system of management control and accounting in which all operations are forecasted and as far as possible planned ahead and the actual results compared with the forecast and planned ones."

(iv) May Cushing Niles :- "Budgetary control is an important tool of management. It is in fact, a tool in the hands of planning which reaches through co-ordination into control and ties the three aspects firmly together. It stimulates thinking in advance by requiring specific planning and the anticipation of operating problems."

(v) W.W. Big - "The term budgetary control is applied to a system of management control by which all operations and output are forecast as far as ahead as possible and the actual results when known, are compared with the budget estimates."

From the above definitions, it is clear that - budgetary control operates through different budgets. The targets set up under the system are such that they can be directly compared with the actual performances and the difference, if any, can be traced to an individual who is responsible for the same.

The above definitions can reveal the essential features of Budgetary control, i.e. Nature of budgetary control as follows :-

(i) Establishment of budgets for each department / function.

(ii) Measurement of actual performance.

(iii) Comparison of actual performance with budgeted performance to find out variations, if any.

(iv) Ascertainment of the reason for such variations and taking suitable remedial action.

6:2 Objectives of Budget and Budgetary Control

The main objectives of budgetary control may be summarised as follows :

1) Planning : A budget is nothing but a plan. It is a planning device. Without planning, a business cannot run. By means of planning, the management tries to look ahead, anticipate eventualities, prepare for contingencies and provide an orderly sequence for achieving the firm's objectives. Budgets present the plan, objectives and policies of an enterprise and expresses them in numerical terms. A detailed budgetary control system is one, where the plans are written down and these plans are circulated to all the levels of management. Budgets boost the morale of managers and foster a spirit of co-operation amongst them.

2) Co-ordination : A business organisation is always divided into a number of departments, sections and sub-sections. There is division of work among them. All work is linked amongst themselves in a definite order so that the desired goal can be achieved. To have co-ordination, there should be proper communication. Communication can be effected through the budgets. Planning helps co-ordination, and hence, if the planning is good, there is effective co-ordination. Thus, budgetary control forces the executives to think and feel responsible at an individual as well as group level.

3) Control : To accomplish the desired goals, it is necessary to establish control measures at different levels of the activities. Control consists of action necessary to ensure that the performance of the organisation conforms to the plan and objectives. This is not possible without pre-determined standards. Budgetary control makes it possible by comparing the actual performance with those pre-determined in the budgets. It indicates variances and identifies the causes for the same. Thus, it enables to determine and fix responsibility and take the necessary corrective action well in advance to prevent losses or damages to the organisation.

4) Communication - A budget is a communication device. It communicates information about the plans and policies of the organisation.

5) Revision - In budgetary control, it is possible for the revision of future budgets in the light of experience gained.

Thus, the overall objective of the budgetary control is to exercise effective managerial control over the different activities in the organisation.

6:3 Essentials of Budgetary Control

The successful implementation of a budgetary control system depends on certain factors. They can be summarised as follows :

1) Support of top Management : Budgetary control requires the wholehearted participation of every part of the organisation. It makes changes in the working styles and methodology in the organisation. Right from its preparation to implementation, it needs honest contribution by every manager. This is only possible if there is total support from the top management of the business. Otherwise, it may lead to a very poor show.

2) Sound organisation : Clearly defined duties, authorities and responsibilities are the important characteristics of a sound organisational structure. Only such a type of organisation can facilitate the success of the budgetary control system. Because in this, every manager must know his authorities, duties and responsibilities in clear terms.

3) Responsibility centres : Every manager responsible in the preparation and implementation of the budget is considered as a responsibility centre. Hence, every opportunity must be given to the manager to take an active part in the preparation and implementation of the budget. He should be given every opportunity to explain the reasons for the failure to achieve the target set for him/her.

4) Objectives and goals : The budgetary control system must be capable of putting the objectives before executives in clear-cut terms. There should not be any confusion or ambiguity about the objectives to be attained. The goals translated in terms of the target must be reasonably attainable in the normal condition. Ambiguous objectives and targets that are too ideal will only result in failure of the system.

5) Budget committee : There should be a budget committee to look after the preparation and implementation of the budgets. It should include all the concerned executives responsible for the preparation and implementation of budgets. To send the right signals regarding the total support of the management across the organisation, a top member of the management should be appointed as the chairman of the committee.

6) Nature of budgeting : Budgeting may be either a partial or a comprehensive one. It basically depends on the size and needs of the organisation. But normally, it should be a comprehensive system to explore maximum benefits from it. Again, it should be a permanent exercise and not an occasional one.

7) Accounting and Reporting : Standard accounting system is a prerequisite for any reliable reporting system. Of course, budgetary control system needs both of them. It aims at a continuous comparison of budgeted targets with the actual performance. Hence, it needs efficient accounting and a regular and periodic reporting system in the organisation.

8) Acceptance of the system : There should be an appreciation of the uses and limitations of the system by everybody in the organisation. It helps to understand the difficulties and problems in the working of the system. If red tapism or personal ego prevails, the system will certainly suffer adversely.

9) Cost of implementation : The cost of the execution of the system must be reasonable and affordable to the organisation. The benefits that accrue to the organisation from the execution of the system must be more than the cost incurred for it. Otherwise, it may be a meaningless exercise.

10) Budget education : For successful implementation of the system, there should be an active interest of every participant in the system. This can only be achieved by giving budget education to the concerned part/persons of the organisation. It should be part of the training programme of every executive. It certainly affects the performance of the system.

6:4 Advantages and Limitations of Budgetary Control

Advantages of Budgetary Control

Budgetary control is basically built upon the 'Management by Objective' principle in the management science. Therefore, it derives all benefits of that strategy automatically. However, as an important tool of cost control, it underlines the following merits –

1) Guidance to the management : Budgetary control defines the objectives and policies of the concern in very clear terms. It also helps to quantify the objectives along with time limit. Thus, it compels it to think ahead of every action. Through such process, it guides the management in planning and formulation of policies for the organisation in a more practical way.

2) Compels participation : Thinking ahead compels all members in the organisation to participate in setting of goals and objectives for their respective levels of management. As an effective means of communication, budgets help the lower levels of management to understand the allotted share of the objectives to them.

3) Delegation of authority : The preparation process of budget needs identification and clarification of the responsibilities of each executive. They need to work together as a team and depend on each other. It creates a sense of harmony. Such a situation facilitates the delegation of authority.

4) Efficient and economic use of resources : All managers are required to think over the probable problems, to identify the alternative courses of action in an optimum way and to seek out further opportunities for profitable activities. Thus, it ensures the optimum use of available resources and avoids wastages. Of course, it needs standardising of equipments, processes and functions.

5) Operational efficiency : Budget sets up the targets in quantitative terms in a given time limit. Thus, it helps to create awareness among all members of the organisation to achieve the same in time, besides promoting operational efficiency.

6) Sufficient working capital : Budgetary control looks after the availability of working capital by directing capital expenditure to the most profitable area. It also acts as a sales guide by providing accurate sales forecasting of market demand in highly competitive situations. This helps in suspending the sale of loss-making or less-profit making products besides facilitating the correct sales mix to be introduced in the market.

7) Acceptance of responsibility : Budgets act as a compass needle pointing towards the targets to be achieved continuously. It requires each manager to compare his/her actual performance against budget. It creates commitment amongst them. This sense of responsibility works as force of incentive to attain the target. It also helps the top management to decentralise responsibilities to lesser executives without losing control over them.

8) Timely corrective action : This control technique facilitates management by exception and timely correction of significant deviations from the target. It needs adequate attention of the management towards the effect of expected trends of general business conditions, seasonal and cyclical fluctuations in the business. These provide opportunity to take corrective steps to adjust the actual conditions of the business with that of the market and industry.

9) Other costing technique : It facilitates use of marginal costing in regard to price fixation and decision-making. Whenever needed, it also creates a basis for the introduction of standard costing.

10) Wage systems : More effective, just and fair wage system with incentive plans can be introduced with the help of budgetary control.

Disadvantages or Limitations of Budgetary Control

Though the budgetary control is a meritorious and probably the oldest technique of control, it suffers from the following limitations :–

1) Rigidity : Business conditions are fast changing and needs immediate responses. The budgetary control tries to do so through the flexible budgeting. However, it is observed that it also suffers from rigidity. It is particularly so, where technology is developing fast and fashions form the core marketing.

2) Estimations : Budgets are estimates. Their success depends on the forecasts. Forecasting is a highly individual trait. Further, forecasts are based on data and information available. Hence, reliability and accuracy of such data and information makes an effect on the forecast. So, it is dangerous to depend on it every time.

3) No automatic execution : This technique does not provide an in-built system of control. Firstly, it needs the preparation of budgets and its execution. Since, they are related to different managers, their individual efficiency has an effect on them. If there are problems in its effective communication and co-ordination, then this system will face the risk of failure.

4) Expensive tool : It requires training and continuous education of all members in the organisation. It also results into huge clerical work. Again, its execution requires conducting meetings, brainstorming, etc. All this results in high costs for the working of this system. Hence, it is considered as an expensive tool.

5) Extensive decentralisation : The system of budgetary control involves an extensive decentralisation of authority and processes which require proper co-ordination of different business activities.

6) Only a tool of Management : Budgeting cannot take the place of management, since it can not do away with the necessity of a superior executive's role in decision-making. Hence, it can only be regarded as an aid or tool of the Management.

7) Opposition by staff : Budgets provide yardsticks against which the performance of the executives and workers are measured. As such, inefficient executives and workers generally create difficulties in the way of operating this system.

8) Lack of flexibility : Budgets are prepared after a lot of groundwork is done by different departments. The executives treat the budget's figures as the final figures.

6:5 Procedure of Budgetary Control - Steps in Budgetary Control

The procedure of budgetary control can be viewed in three broad phases.

A) Procedure of preparation and establishment of the budgets.

B) Procedure of recording and reporting the results.

C) Action taken under budgetary control.

Let us review these procedures in detail.

A) Procedure of preparation and establishment of the budgets :

This phase of preparation and establishment of the budgets include following preliminaries and activities :–

1) Establishment of budget centres : A budget centre is a section of the organisation of an undertaking defined for the purpose of the budgetary control. It must be defined in clear-cut terms and exactly. For every budget centre, separate budgets have to be prepared. For e.g. sales budget, production budget, etc.

2) Preparation of the organisation chart : Carefully designed organisational chart show inter-relationship among the different sections in the organisation. Such a chart without any confusion is a necessary requisite for the success of budgetary control. Further, it is also essential for recording and reporting of the results. (See fig. below)

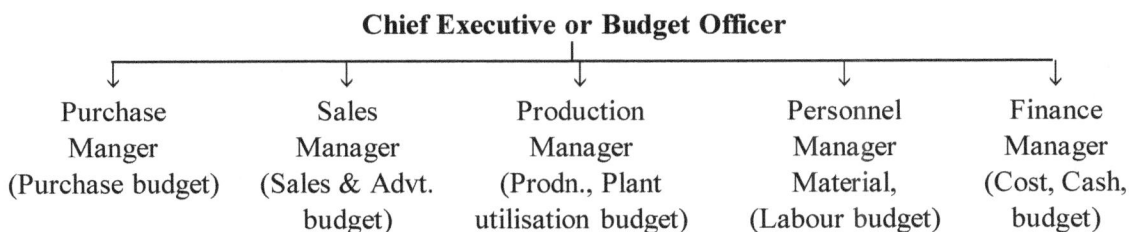

Chief Executive or Budget Officer

| Purchase Manger (Purchase budget) | Sales Manager (Sales & Advt. budget) | Production Manager (Prodn., Plant utilisation budget) | Personnel Manager Material, (Labour budget) | Finance Manager (Cost, Cash, budget) |

3) Maintaining accounting records : Accurate accounting system is essential for reporting and decision - making. Hence, adequate accounting records with accuracy should be prepared by adopting scientific accounting system. For e.g. 'a chart of accounts', 'accounting code' etc., should be prepared corresponding to the budget centres.

4) Establishing the budget committee - In small concerns, the budget officer looks after all budgeting activities. However, in medium and large concerns, it is physically impossible for a single individual to do so. Hence, a 'Budget Committee' needs to be established.

The Committee should consist of the chief executive and the all functional heads in the organisation. Normally, the chief executive is the Budget Officer, but in very large concerns, there may be a separate budget officer to coordinate the functions of the committee.

The important functions of the committee are as follows -

1) To define general policies of the Management.
2) To provide help to the departmental managers to forecast the activities.
3) To receive and review the individual budget estimates of different concerned departments.
4) To suggest budget revisions.
5) To approve the revised budgets.
6) To receive budget reports and actual performances report.
7) To conduct comparisions between them and to discuss the variances if any, in detail.
8) To fix responsibilities for the variances and recommend the corrective actions necessary.
9) To co-ordinate budget programmes.
10) To maintain the historical data and to provide wherever necessary.

The functions of the budget officer can be listed as follows -

1) To act as a secretary to the budget committee.
2) To advise the committee on all budget matters.
3) To prepare and edit the budget manual.
4) To issue budget instructions to departmental heads.
5) To prepare all forms of the schedules, reports of the budgeting reporting system.
6) To receive the budgets from departmental heads.
7) To prepare summary budget.
8) To prepare commentary reports on draft budgets.
9) To provide reference to the budget committee and members of it.
10) To act as friend and philosopher of the entire budgetary system and organisation.

5) Preparation of the Budget Manual : ICMA defines budget manual as, "a document which sets out the responsibilities of the person engaged in, the routine of, and the forms and records required for budgetary control."

Thus, it is a schedule, document or booklet containing the different forms to be used, procedures to be followed by budgeting organisation and set of instructions to be followed in the budgeting system. It also lists out details of the responsibilities of different persons and the managers involved in the process.

A typical Budget Manual contains -

1) Objectives and managerial policies of the business concern.
2) Internal lines and linkages of authority and responsibility in the organisational structure.
3) Functions of the budget committee including that of the budget officer, if any.
4) Broad time schedule to be followed in budget preparation.
5) Instructions and forms.
6) Detailed programme of budget preparation.
7) Procedure of budget approvals.
8) Accounting codes and numbering.
9) Budget periods and reporting periods.
10) Follow-up procedures, etc.

The advantages that accrue from the budget manual are -

i) It highlights the duties and responsibilities of every manager clearly. Hence, there is no ambiguity in the working procedure.
ii) It provides the correct mechanism to resolve the operational problems arising from the implementation of the system.
iii) It helps a lot of the newly entered officers to work along with other officers.
iv) All procedures and work of the budgetary system is standardised.
v) It avoids the overlapping of work or instructions. Thus, it saves time, money and labour. Hence, a budget manual is always a prerequisite of a budgetery system.

6) Ascertaining the suitable budget period : Before starting the process of budget preparation, it is very necessary to ascertain the budget period. All budget recordings and reporting are subject to the budget period. Hence, it is very essential to decide upon it.

The term 'budget period' can be defined as, "the period for which a budget is prepared and employed."

There is no general rule for ascertaining a specific period as budget period. Decision about such a period depends upon the nature and type of business, seasonal fluctuations, type of budgeting system, etc. Normally, the accounting year is accepted as budget period. However, for multinational companies or for capital expenditure budget, such a period may be more than one year. For cash budget, it may be a week or a month, etc. The important factors affecting this decision are-

1) Nature of the demand of the product.
2) Length of the trade cycle.
3) The product cycle.
4) Functional area geographically covered by the product.
5) Need for control operations.
6) Time interval necessary for financing production well in advance of actual needs.
7) The accounting cycle, etc.

Whatever may be the period selected, it should relate to the objectives of the budgeting and actual operations of the business concern. Otherwise, the entire budgeting process may end up as a futile exercise.

7) Key factor or budget factor : It is nothing but the limiting factor, principal factor or governing factor, discussed in Marginal Costing.

It can be defined as, "the factor, the extent of whose influence must be assessed first in order to ensure that functional budgets are reasonably, capable of fulfilment."

Suppose a Company has a production capacity to produce 20,000 units p.a., but if the market can absorb only 15,000 units p.a., then the 'sales' is a factor. But, if the market demand is more than 20,000 units, then the present production is not capable of satisfying the demand, and in this case, the 'production' will be the limiting factor.

Thus, this factor puts limitation on other functions, and hence, must be considered carefully well in advance. It is to be noted that as situation changes, these factors also change. Hence, continuous assessment of changing business environment is necessary to identify such factors. Many times, there are more than such factors influencing the budgeting process. In all conditions, these factors are the starting point in this process. Following is the illustrative list of such factors :–

a) Sales :	i)	Consumer demand
	i)	Shortage of salesmen
	ii)	Inadequate advertising.
b) Materials :	i)	Supply availability
	ii)	Restrictions like licence, quota, etc.

c) Labour :
    i) General shortage.
    ii) Shortage of skilful workers, etc.

d) Plant :
    i) Insufficient capacity of plant.
    i) Bottlenecks in the key processes, etc.

e) Management :
    i) Lack of capital
    ii) Pricing Policy
    iii) Shortage of efficient executives
    iv) Lack of Know-how
    v) Faulty design of the product, etc.

Only an accurate identification of the limiting factors, and thereafter, putting them in their due preference, will help ensure the success of the budgeting system.

Thus, budgetary control involves the entire organisation. After taking the above policy decision, budgets are to be established as per selected types of the budgets. Normally, functional budgets are more popular. Budgets can be either prepared for a single activity or for few particular activities. However, all functional budgets necessary to the organisation should be prepared, and at last, a 'Master budget' should be prepared, so that a complete blue print of the financial position at the end of the budget period is available. Such a master budget includes 'the budgeted P & L A/c' and 'the budgeted Balance Sheet.'

B) Procedure of recording and reporting the results

To achieve the objectives of the budgetary control, actual costs and performances are to be compared and reported at regular intervals. For this purpose, generally 'Departmental Operating Statement' is regularly prepared. It is a statement relating to the operating performance of a departmental manger during a specific period and includes listing all the relevant data of the actual performance of the concerned department. It also shows the variances and classifies them as favourable-unfavourable, controllable-uncontrollable, etc. Further, it is also interpreted in terms of ratio, such as standard capacity ratio, actual usage of budgeted capacity ratio, etc.

Detailed discussions are held in the budget committee on such reports and suggest the necessary corrective actions. Of course, for an effective implementation of the same, a regular and accurate reporting system must be in place within an organisation.

C) Action taken under budgetary control

When the budget reports are presented before the appropriate authorities, steps are suggested to take timely corrective action, wherever necessary. Generally, such an action, may involve a discussion with person/persons responsible, discussions with other seniors, and/or arranging the revisions in budgets, etc. The budget officer or budget committee, as the case may be, carries out such activities.

6:6 Types of Budgets (Classification of Budgets)

Budgets may be classified as follows :

Budgets

1) According to Time	2) According to Activity Level	3) According to Functions	4) According to Control Instruments

1) According to Time
(i) Long-Term Budget
(ii) Short-Term Budget
(iii) Current Budget

2) According to Activity Level
(i) Fixed Budgets
(ii) Flexible Budgets

3) According to Functions
(i) Purchase Budget
(ii) Production Budget
(iii) Production Cost Budget
(iv) Sales Budget
(v) Cash Budgets
(vi) Plant Utilisation Budgets
(vii) Selling and Distribution Cost Budget
(viii) Capital Expenditure Budget
(ix) Labour Cost Budget
(x) Factory Overhead Budget
(xi) Administration Cost Budget
(xii) Research and Development Cost Budget
(xiii) Master Budget

4) According to Control Instruments
(i) Programme Budgeting
(ii) Performance Budgeting
(iii) Zero-Base Budgeting

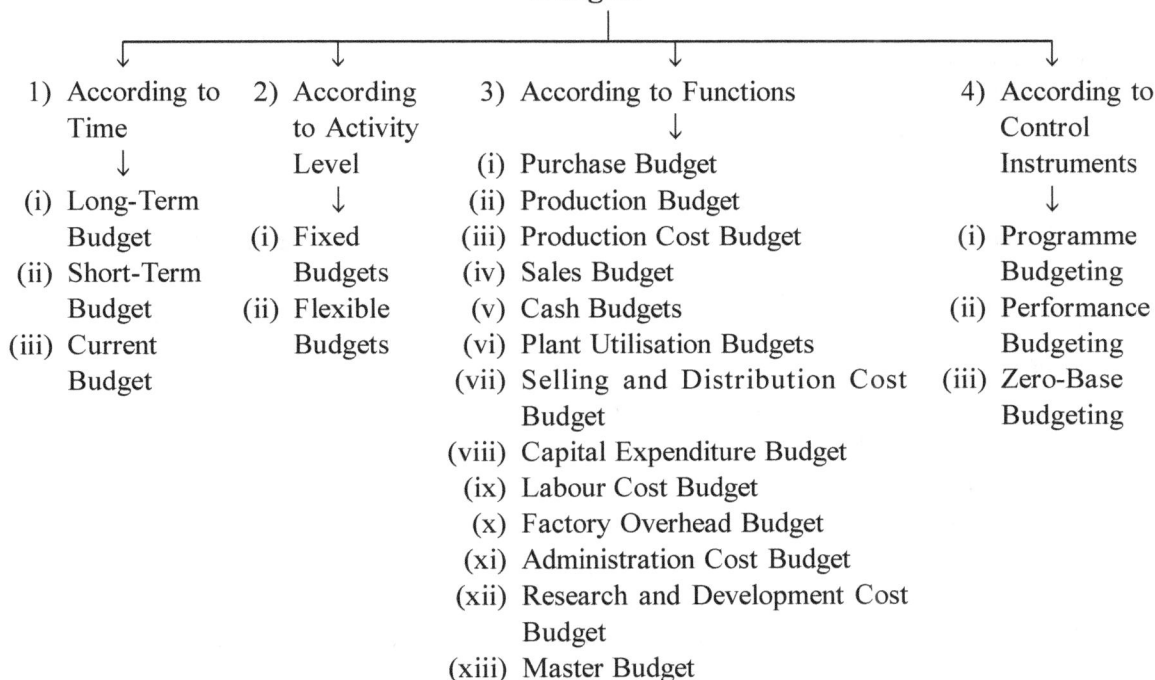

Note : As the syllabus of S.Y. B.C.A, B.B.A., is restricted only to the first two types of budgets, the practical problems are given only on flexible budget. The third and fourth type of budgets are given only for the information of students.

Let us discuss all these budgets in brief –

1) According to time - On the basis of the budget period, they are classified as -

(i) Current budget - The budget prevailing and relating to a given time is called the current budget. It is generally a period of current week, current month, quarter etc.

(ii) Long-term budget - A long term budget is that which is prepared for a period longer than a year. Capital Expenditure Budget and Research and Development Expenditure Budget are the examples of long-term budgets.

(iii) Short-term Budget - A short-term budget is that which is prepared for a period of one year or less than one year. Cash Budget and Materials Budget are the examples of short-term budgets.

2) According to activity level flexibility - On the basis of activity levels or capacity, the budgets may be classified as -

(i) Fixed Budget is "a budget which is designed to remain unchanged irrespective of the level of activity actually attained." (ICMA, London). Its purpose is to lay down the major objectives of the organisation and co-ordinate the activities to achieve the objectives. The fixed budget will remain the same and will not take note of changed circumstances which may compel to change the level of activity.

(ii) Flexible Budget is "a budget designed to change in accordance with the level of activity actually attained." (ICMA, London). This type of budget provides costs budgeted at different levels of activity. It facilitates comparison of actual performance with the budget at any level of activity. It enables the assessment of what any individual cost should have been at the actual level of activity attained. This type of budget is necessary for control. A manager's actual performance or achievement can be compared with what should have been achieved in the conditions preaviling and not with what should have been achieved under different circumtances.

To prepare a flexible budget, all costs should be classified into variable, semi-variable and fixed costs. If variable and semi-variable and fixed costs also vary, the extent or degree of their variability should also be determined. However, the fixed costs remain unchanged.

Preparation of Flexible Budget

There are two methods followed for preparation of flexible budget
1) Formula Method
2) Multi-activity Method.

Formula Method : Before the period begins, the fixed budget for a normal activity should be prepared. The fixed and variable cost should be separated. Then, the variable cost per unit of activity should be computed.

At the end of the period, the actual activity is ascertained and the variable cost allowed for this level of activity is computed on the basis of per unit activity and the fixed costs are added to give the budget cost allowance.

Formula -

Allowed Cost = (Actual Units of Activity for period) ×

(Variable Costs per unit of activity) + (fixed Cost)

Multi-activity Method - Under this method, a budget for every major level of activity is prepared. When the actual level of activity is known, the allowed cost is ascertained by interpolation between the budgets of activity levels on either side. If the actual level of activity, is, say 72%, the variable costs allowed would be ascertained by interpolating between 70% and 80% of budget levels, i.e., by adding two-tenths of the difference between 70% and 80% to the 70% figures. These allowed costs would be compared with the actual costs incurred and the variance computed.

Uses of flexible budget -

 (i) It is a dynamic tool for controlling overheads.
 (ii) It is a useful tool for planning and controlling costs.
(iii) Analysis of performance provides a feedback for more realistic plans of costs in future.
 (iv) It facilitates development of departmental overhead costs budgets for profit plan.
 (v) It provides adjusted budget allowances for comparison purposes.

Proforma of Flexible Budget
Flexible Budget

Normal level of Activity - 70%   Period ending -

Units	Capacity		
	40%Rs.	70%Rs.	90%Rs.
1. Prime Cost			
Direct Materials	-	-	-
Direct Labour	-	-	-
Direct Expenses	-	-	-
2. Variable Overheads			
Indirect Materials	-	-	-
Indirect Labour	-	-	-
Repairs & Maintenance	-	-	-
3. Marginal Cost (1 + 2)	-	-	-
4. Sales	-	-	-
5. Contribution (4 - 3)	-	-	-
6. Fixed Costs			
Production	-	-	-
Administration	-	-	-
Selling and Distribution	-	-	-
7. Profit / Loss (5 - 6)	-	-	-

3. According to functions : A functional budget is one which relates to any of the functions of an organisation. For e.g. purchases, sales, production, etc. The Master Budget is prepared based on the functional budget. The following are generally the types of functional budgets prepared -

1) Purchase Budget : This budget lays down the quantity of materials to be purchased from month to month. It is necessary to ensure smooth production. Preparation of purchase budget requires drawing a complete list of raw materials required to produce goods, the opening and closing inventories. Unless such a comprehensive list of requirement is prepared, purchases cannot be done properly.

This budget is to be prepared for each type of material.

2) Production Budget : This budget is prepared by the production manager. It shows the quantity of products to be manufactured. It is based on –

(i) The sales budget.

(ii) The factory capacity.

(iii) The budgeted stock requirements.

(iv) Policy of the management.

(v) Samples required for free issue.

The budget is classified into the following categories :
(i) Products
(ii) Manufacturing departments
(iii) Months.

While preparing a production budget, allowance is made for a normal loss in production. This is required in order to see whether the net output is sufficient to meet the sales requirements and the year-end inventories.

Production budget is used for computing the requirements of raw materials and components.

Year	Product		Department
		Forecast closing stock	-
	Add :	Sales requirement	-
		Samples requirement	-
	Less :	Forecast Opening Stock	-
		Net Production requirements	-
	Add :	Normal Loss	-
			-

3) Production Cost Budget - This budget is also known as manufacturing budget and one based on cost standards. It is the quantity of goods to be manufactured, expressed in terms of cost. This budget consists of three subsidiary budgets :
(i) Material budget
(ii) Labour cost budget
(iii) Manufacturing overhead budget

Production Cost Budget

Prod-ucts	Materials			Labour				Overheads			Cost
	Qty.	Rate Rs.	Cost Rs.	Oper-ation	Hours	Rate Rs.	Cost Rs.	Dept.	Cost Rs.	Total Rs.	per Unit Rs.
X											
Y											
Z											
Total											

4) Sales Budget : This budget is prepared by a sales manager. Preparation of sales budget is the most difficult job since it is very difficult to estimate the future demands for a product. This is probably the most important budget as all other budgets depend upon the sales budget.

Sales budget is usually prepared in terms of quantities. It is based on the following :

  (i) Products

 (ii) Territories

(iii) Type of Customers

(iv) Salesmen

    The sales manager has to consider the following factors while preparing the sales budget :

  (i) Analysis of post sales

 (ii) Market analysis

(iii) Type of Customers

(iv) General trade and business conditions

 (v) Special conditions.

Format of Sales Budget (Product-wise)

Year :

Month	Product X		Product Y		Product Z		Total Rs.
	Qty.	Value Rs.	Qty.	Value Rs.	Qty.	Value Rs.	
Total							

5) Cash Budget : This represents the cash receipts and cash payments and estimated cash balance for each month of the period for which a budget is prepared. Cash budget is a device for controlling and co-ordinating the financial side of a business. Cash budget serves the following purposes :

  (i) to ensure that sufficient cash is available whenever required;

 (ii) to point out any possible shortage of cash so that necessary steps can be taken to meet the shortage by making arrangements with the bank for overdraft or loan; and

(iii) to point out any surplus cash so that management can invest it in interest-fetching securities.

Preparation of Cash Budget

    Usually the reponsibility of preparing the cash budget lies with the Treasurer or other Financial Executive. Cash budget has to be prepared by estimating cash receipts and cash payments.

Estimating Cash Receipts

    Cash is received on the following accounts :

  (i) Cash sales

 (ii) Collection from debtors

(iii) Interest / Dividends on investment

(iv) Sale of assets etc.

 (v) Loans, Advance, Deposits etc.

The person who is responsible for the budget has to estimate how much cash is likely to be received month-by-month during the budget period on the above accounts.

Estimating Cash Payments

Cash payment is made on the following accounts :

(i) Payment for purchases

(ii) Payment for overheads

(iii) Purchase of assets

(iv) Payment to creditors

(v) Payment for taxes

(vi) Payment for dividends / interest etc.

(vii) Repayment of Loans / Advances / Deposits etc.

This budget is based on several factors, such as :

1) Several functional budgets, particularly - sales, purchase etc.

2) Credit terms on sales, purchases and expenses.

Specimen : Cash Budget

	Jan. Rs.	Feb. Rs.	March Rs.	Total Rs.
Balance				
Receipts				
1.	–	–	–	–
2.	–	–	–	–
3.	–	–	–	–
4.	–	–	–	–
Total				
Payments				
1.	–	–	–	–
2.	–	–	–	–
3.	–	–	–	–
4.	–	–	–	–
5.	–	–	–	–
6.	–	–	–	–
Total Payments				
Balance	–	–	–	–
Cash Required	–	–	–	–

6) Plant Utilisation Budget - This budget indicates the capacity of plant required to execute the production programme as per the production budget. This budget is prepared simultaneously with production budget. It determines :

(i) The machine load in each department during the budget period.

(ii) the problem of overloading. Overloading may be sorted out by taking actions such as shift working, purchase of new machinery, overtime working, sub-contracting etc.

Plant Utilisation Budget

Product	Units	Cost Centre X			Cost Centre Y		
		Hrs. per Unit	Total Machine hours	No. of Machines required	Hrs. per Unit	Total Machine hours	No. of Machines required

Plant utilisation and production budgets are inter-connected.

7) Selling and Distribution Cost Budget : This is a forecast of selling and distribution cost during a stipulated period i.e., the budget period. This budget is based on the sales budget. In addition to sales volume, other points to be considered while preparing this budget are – advertising planned during the budget period, distribution expenses etc. This budget is prepared by grouping the costs, according to elements as under :

(i) Direct Selling Expenses : This consists of salaries of salesmen, commission of salesmen, motor car expenses, travelling expenses of salesmen etc.

(ii) Sales Office Expenses : This consists of salaries, rent, rates, electricity, depreciation, postage, stationery, telephone, general expenses etc.

(iii) Distribution Expenses : This consists of wages of warehouse staff, rent and rates of warehouse, electricity, insurance, export duty, transport expenses, packing, insurance etc.

(iv) Advertising Expenses : This consists of expenses of advertisements on T.V, radio etc, window display, coupon, offers, leaflets, etc.

Specimen : Budget
Selling and Distribution Cost Budget

Elements of Cost	Area		
	North Rs.	South Rs.	Total Rs.
A. Direct Selling Expenses :			
1.	–	–	–
2.	–	–	–
3.	–	–	–
B. Sales Office Expenses :			
1.	–	–	–
2.	–	–	–
3.	–	–	–

Elements of Cost	Area		
	North Rs.	South Rs.	Total Rs.
C. Distribution Expenses :			
1.	–	–	–
2.	–	–	–
3.	–	–	–
D. Advertising Expenses :			
1.	–	–	–
2.	–	–	–
3.	–	–	–
E. Total (A + B + C + D)	–	–	–

8) Capital Expenditure Budget -

This budget is prepared for estimating the expenditure on fixed assets required during the budget period. This is based on the following :

(i) Overloading indicated by plant utilisation budget

(ii) Report of the production manager requesting new machinery.

(iii) Report from distribution manager requesting new transport.

(iv) Report from works engineers requesting new machinery.

(v) Report from Accounts and Other Departments requesting new office equipmens, etc.

(vi) Decisions of management to expand.

9) Labour Cost Budget

This budget represents, in terms of money, number and grades of personnel, number of working hours or other appropriate units, the direct and indirect labour required to carry out the programme laid down in the Sales, Production, Capital Expenditure and Research and Development Expenditure Budget. Thus, this budget is a forecast of planned outlay on direct and indirect labour of a concern during the budget period.

10) Factory Overhead Budget

Factory overheads consists of indirect material, indirect labour and indirect expenses. These items are classified as fixed overheads and variable overheads. For this classification, it is necessary to study cost behaviour.

Since departmental heads are held responsible for expenses incurred by them, this budget is prepared by the departmental heads. This budget is very useful for computing pre-determined overhead recovery rates.

11) Administration Cost Budget

This budget is a forecast of general administration costs of the undertaking during the budget period. General administration cost includes the cost of formulating the policies, directing the organisation and controlling the operations of an undertaking.

12) Research and Development Cost Budget

This budget is a planned outlay on research and development activities of an undertaking, and is expressed in terms of money, the permissible limits within which the research and development activities are to be pursued and the directions for the same.

13) Master Budget

It is defined as, "the summary budget, incorporating its component - functional budgets, which is finally approved, adopted and employed." Master budget summarises all the functional budgets. It means a master budget can be prepared only when all the functional budgets are prepared and approved. A Master budget is the overall plan of operations to be followed during the budget period. It also takes the form of budgeted profit and loss account and the balance sheet.

XYZ Ltd.
Master Budget for the year ending...

Normal Capacity ....   Standard Hours (100%) ....
Capacity Budgeted ...   Standard Hours .....

	Product X Rs.	Product Y Rs.	Product Z Rs.
Sales	××	××	××
Cost of Sales	××	××	××
Direct Materials	××	××	××
Direct Labour	××	××	××
Factory Overheads	××	××	××
Add : Opening Stock	××	××	××
Less : Closing stock	××	××	××
Gross Profit	××	××	××
Administration Cost	××	××	××
Selling and Distribution Cost	××	××	××
Net Profit	××	××	××
Fixed Assets	××	××	××
Current Assets	××	××	××
Total Capital Employed	××	××	××

Recent trends in Budgeting

There are different types of budgeting techniques evolved over a span of time. We have seen traditional budget technique. It is carried out with reference to the organisational set-up of the business concern. Then, every department is supposed to forecast its functional needs in terms of quantity and turn them into financial forecasts. By combining the departmental budgets with reference to the constraints, the Master Budget is prepared and is looked after as the exterior limit of working.

There are a lot of flaws in this technique and that is why these new techniques are to be studied.

(A) Programme Budgeting

It was developed in the U.S.A. in 1962. It was accepted in different departments of U.S.A. Government for more effective and efficient operations.

Features of Programme Budgeting

The important features of this system can be viewed as follows :-

1. This system considers each activity in relation to effects of its programmes like health, defence, education, etc. The accounting expenditure under each activity is categorised in respect of the output from it. Therefore, this system reconstructs the budgets not by the objectives but by the output category.

2. Programme budgets are prospective and not retrospective like other budgets.

3. Is not an annual ritual. Though fund allocation is similar to traditional budgeting, programme budgeting covers the entire period of programme completion. Such a period may be more than one year also.

4. Programme budgeting is based upon the cost-benefit analysis of the programmes and sub-programmes.

Procedure for developing Programme Budgeting

It involves four phases -

(i) Programme accounting : To identify and define exact numbers of the different programmes is the first step. The expenses of each programme are listed in detail. The total expenditure for all of them is worked out. This is termed as 'Programme Accounting.'

(ii) Multi-year costing : It is related with a project to the programmes spread over more than a year. It is useful in the case where the initial expenditure is low and there may be large variations in the future and the management of the business may be misled or the programmes undertaken are on an experimental basis.

(iii) Description and measurement of the activities : In this technique, importance is given to the objectives, targets, alternatives considered, choices made, output, costs and effectiveness of the programme. So, before approval of any programme, all these aspects are considered in detail and wherever possible, quantitative measurement yardsticks are adopted.

(iv) Cost-benefit analysis : In this technique, the cost benefit analysis is used as a ranking tool. This technique is deployed in a situation where funds are scarce and different projects are competing with each other to receive funding. In such a situation, the cost benefit analysis of each programme helps to assign the ranking for fund allocation.

Advantages of Programme Budgeting

1) It makes for a **better decision-making procedure.** The decision-makers know the total expenditure for each programme. So, funds are properly allocated.

2) It renders **effective decision-making process,** as each alternative programme is properly

defined in terms of alternatives.

3) It helps **better co-ordination and control** by cutting across the organisational lines. So, departmental ego problems are kept away.

Limitations of Programme Budgeting

1) Difficuties in clear-cut identification of the programmes is the main problem, particularly where the activities are interwoven.
2) Excessive centralisation of decision-making process takes away the interest of middle management level.
3) High degree of rigidity makes this technique ineffective, in situations that are dynamic and unpredictable.

Therefore, this technique has limited application in the business world.

(B) Performance Budgeting

Performance budgeting is a budgetary system where the input costs are related to the performances or the end results of the programme or the activity. Unlike traditional budgeting, the performance budgeting begins with a broad classification of the functions, programmes and sub-classification of the activities and considers the end results of each of them.

Features of Performance Budgeting

The important features of this system can be viewed as follows -

(a) Classification into function, programme, or activity.
(b) Specification of the objectives of each programme.
(c) Establishing suitable methods for the measurement of work as far as possible.
(d) Fixation of work targets for each programme.

Procedure of Performance Budgeting

It may have three phases -

1) Allocation of resources : After classification functions, programme is computed. Objectives for each programme are identified and quantified. End results are expected and the resources are allocated on this basis only.

2) Execution of the budgets : After allocation of the resources, annual, quarterly and monthly targets are determined for each of the programme and activity selected. Cost and revenue data are given for each 'activity centre' and for the entire organisation. Different productivity or performance ratios are set up for each of them. Targets are compared with that of actual results produced.

(3) Budget reporting : Progress reports are prepared periodically at regular intervals and submitted to the higher level. The reports indicate the physical performances achieved, the expenditure resulted, the variances from the targets and the explanation thereof.

Differences between Programme and Performance budgeting - The important differences in these techniques can be viewed as follows :

Programme Budgeting	Performance Budgeting
1. It is mainly related with the purpose of the work.	1. It is mainly related with the process of work.
2. It is prospective.	2. It is retrospective.
3. It means detailed planning.	3. It means the evaluation of would-be performance.
4. It is objective-oriented technique.	4. It is methodology-oriented technique.
5. It relates to top management level.	5. It relates to middle and lower level management.

Thus, performance budgeting is a natural expansion of the programme budgeting to overcome its limitations.

(c) Zero-Based Budgeting

Popularly, it is termed as ZBB. It is interesting to know the history of evalution of this technique. It originated in U.S.A. It was first invented and introduced by Mr. Peter A. Pyhrr. He was a staff control manager at Texas Instruments Corporation in U.S.A. After popularising this technique in the private sector, he wrote a detailed article on the subject in *'Harward Business Review'* (Nov-Dec, 1970 issue.) Later, he also wrote a book on this same subject. Mr Jimmy Carter, then Governor of the State of Georgia read the article and the book and called on Mr. Peter Pyhrr to introduce in the state, budgetary control system. Later, when Mr. Jimmy Carter become the President of U.S.A., he strongly supported the use of ZBB in national fiscal policy formulation. Let us have a basic understanding of the technique.

Application of ZBB

It is a very different technique than that of traditional budgeting system. In conventional system, the budget figures are estimated and adjusted on the basis of the trends or historical figures and other expected conditions. However, the process of ZBB differs. It uses the same conventional budget centres. But, preparation of budget starts from zero or scratch. It means it is considered that if the allocation is made zero to the concerned activity, what will be the effect. In other words, every activity needs to establish and justify the demands it has requested for budget allocation. Thus, every process or activity has to justify the budget allocation in its entirety. Thus, the burden of proof of such justification is shifted to the concerned activity manager. The manager has to justify why the money should be spent on the activity.

In practice actually, the managers begin justification at current level of expenditure and work and not from the zero. The managers explain what will happen if the expenditure is cut off or stopped. Basically, he is explaining the cost-benefit analysis of every aspect of the demanded allocation, so that selection of the better alternative is possible to the management. Successful ZBB is, thus nothing but the identification and evaluation of all possible alternatives in their entirety. It provides sufficient scope for choice from amongst the available alternatives. Of course, it results in saving of money from inefficient activities and diverting the same to efficient activities.

Procedure of ZBB

The most common procedure adopted in this technique is described in brief as follows :-

1) Identifying the decision units. (i.e. the budget centres) in the organisation.

2) Listing the activities, programmes or other functions of each decision unit.

3) Mentioning the objectives of each activities of each decision unit in clear-cut terms. (Here, it is similar to the programme and performance budgeting.)

4) Identifying and evaluating alternative methods of achieving the objectives of each activity.

5) Designing decision packages. A decision package is a document, which identifies and describes the specific activity in such a way that the management can evaluate it, and rank it in order of priority against their activities. Such packages may be of two types -

(a) Mutually exclusive packages, means the alternative methods of getting the same job done. The best option is to be selected on the basis of the cost-benefit analysis; and

(b) Incremental packages means the work or the activity is divided into different levels of efforts. The base package will describe the minimum work to be carried out and other packages describe additional work to the base work and explain the effect in the incremental order. Of course, these packages must be prepared for all activities of the budget centres identified in the first step.

6) Evaluating each decision package and ranking it by cost-benefit analysis.

7) Allocating resources in the budget according to the funds available and the evaluation and ranking of the competing packages. The alternative most near to the objective defined should be selected.

Advantages of ZBB

The important objectives can be narrated as follows -

1) Insufficient and obsolete operations can be removed from the budgeting.

2) Employees tend to avoid wasteful expenditure.

3) As cost-benefit is the main criteria, the optimum utilisation of the resources is promised.

4) It provides maximum flexibility to the top decision-makers in the allocation of resources among different competing demands of activities.

5) It is freely applicable in all types of the organisation like profit organisations, non-profit organisation, Government as well as non-Government organisation, etc.

Limitations of ZBB

1) ZBB involves large clerical work.

2) The cost of implementing and execution of the ZBB is very high.

3) Where ethical or social responsibility and performances are the tests of conducting the activities, ZBB is useless as these performances cannot be evaluated wisely in the terms of cost-benefit analysis.

4) It is mostly affordable by large organisations only. Irrespective of these limitations, it is regarded as a successful budgeting technique and widely accepted in the modern business field.

Illustration on Flexible Budgets -

Illustration 1

Prepare a flexible budget for overheads on the basis of the following data. Ascertain the overhead rates at 50%, 60% and 70% capacity.

	At 60% Capacity (Rs.)
Variable Overheads :	
Indirect Materials	6,000
Indirect Labour	18,000
Semi-Variable Overheads :	
Electricity (40% fixed, 60% variable)	30,000
Repairs (80% fixed, 20% variable)	3,000
Fixed Overheads :	
Depreciation	16,500
Insurance	4,500
Salaries	15,000
Total Overheads	93,000
Estimated Direct Labour hours	1,86,000

Solution :

Items	50% Capacity Rs.	60% Capacity Rs.	70% Capacity Rs.
Variable Overheads :			
Indirect Materials	5,000	6,000	7,000
Indirect Labour	15,000	18,000	21,000
Semi-Variable Overheads :			
Electricity	(1) 27,000	30,000	(1) 33,000
Repairs and Maintenance	(2) 2,900	3,000	(2) 3,100
Fixed Overheads :			
Depreciation	16,500	16,500	16,500
Insurance	4,500	4,500	4,500
Salaries	15,000	15,000	15,000
Total Overheads	85,900	93,000	1,00,100
Estimated Direct Labour hours	1,55,000	1,86,000	2,17,000
Overhead Rate	Re. 0.55	Re. 0.50	Re. 0.46

Working Notes :

1. **Electricity:** Rs. 30,000 is the cost of electricity of 60% capacity, of which 40% is fixed overhead; i.e. Rs. 12,000 and variable is Rs. 18,000.

   For 60% capacity Variable Overhead   = Rs. 18,000

   For 60% capacity Variable Overhead $= \left(\dfrac{18,000}{60} \times 60 \right)$

                    = 18,000

   Therefore, electricity cost at 50% capacity = Rs. 12,000 + 18,000

                    = Rs. 30,000

   For 70% capacity, Variable Overhead $= \dfrac{18,000}{60} \times 70$

                    = Rs. 21,000

   Therefore, electricity cost at 70%   = Rs. 12,000 + Rs. 21,000

                    = Rs. 33,000

2. **Repairs and Maintenance :** Rs. 3,000 is the cost of repairs and maintenance at 60% capacity, of which 80% is fixed overhead, i.e. Rs. 2,400 and variable is Rs. 600.

   For 60% capacity Variable Overhead   = Rs. 600

   For 50% capacity Variable Overhead $= \dfrac{600}{60} \times 50 =$ Rs. 500

   Therefore, the total cost of repairs and maintenance at 50%

                    = Rs. 2,400 + Rs. 500

                    = Rs. 2,900

   For 70% capacity, the Variable Overhead $= \dfrac{600}{60} \times 70$

                    = Rs. 700

   Therefore, the total cost of repairs and maintenance

                    = Rs. 2,400 + Rs. 700

                    = Rs. 3,100

Illustration 2

A company working at 50% capacity manufactures 10,000 units of a product. At 50% capacity, the product cost is Rs. 180 and sale price Rs. 200. The break-up on the costs is as below:

	Cost per Unit
Materials	100
Wages	30
Factory Overheads	30 (40% fixed)
Administration Overheads	20 (50% fixed)

At 60% working, raw materials cost goes up by 2% and sales price falls by 2%. At 80% working, the raw materials cost increases by 5% and sale price decreases by the same percentage i.e., 5%.

Prepare a statement to show profitability at 60% and 80% capacity.

Solution :

Flexible Budget

Particulars Production (Units)	at 50% 10,000 (Units)		at 60% 12,000 (Units)		at 80% 16,000 (Units)	
	Per Unit	Total	Per Unit	Total	Per Unit	Total
Sales	200	20,00,000	196	23,52,000	190	30,40,000
Materials	100	10,00,000	102	12,24,000	105	16,80,000
Wages	30	3,00,000	30	3,60,000	30	4,80,000
Factory Overheads :						
Variable (60%)	18	1,80,000	18	2,16,000	18	2,88,000
Fixed (40%)	12	1,20,000	10	1,20,000	7.50	1,20,000
Administration Overheads :						
Variable (50%)	10	1,00,000	10	1,20,000	10	1,60,000
Fixed (50%)	10	1,00,000	8.33	1,00,000	6.25	1,00,000
Total	180	18,00,000	178.33	21,40,000	176.75	28,28,000
Profit	20	2,00,000	17.67	2,12,000	13.25	2,12,000

It is not advisable to increase the production to 80% capacity because the profits are the same at 60% and 80% capacities.

Illustration 3

For the production of 10,000 electric automatic irons; the following are the budgeted expenses :

	Per Unit Rs.
Direct materials	60
Direct Labour	30
Variable Overheads	25
Fixed overheads (Rs. 1,50,000)	15
Variable Expenses (direct)	5
Selling expenses (10%) fixed	15
Administration Expenses (Rs. 50,000 rigid for all levels of production)	5
Distribution Expenses (20%) fixed	5
The total cost of sale per Unit	5
	165

Prepare a budget for the production of 6,000, 7,000 and 8,000 Irons, showing distinctly the marginal cost and the total cost. (P.U.)

Solution

Flexible Budget

	6,000 Units		7,000 Units		8,000 Units	
	Per Unit Rs.	Total Rs.	Per Unit Rs.	Total Rs.	Per Unit Rs.	Total Rs.
Expenses :						
Direct Materials	60.00	3,60,000	60.00	4,20,000	60.00	4,80,000
Direct Labour	30.00	1,80,000	30.00	2,10,000	30.00	2,40,000
Direct Expenses	5.00	30,000	5.00	35,000	5.00	40,000
Variable Overheads:						
Production	25.00	1,50,000	25.00	1,75,000	25.00	2,00,000
Selling	13.50	81,000	13.50	94,500	13.50	1,08,000
Distribution	4.00	24,000	4.00	28,000	4.00	32,000
Marginal Cost	137.50	8,25,000	137.50	9,62,500	137.50	11,00,000
Fixed Overheads :						
Production	25.00	1,50,000	21.43	1,50,000	18.75	1,50,000
Administration	8.34	50,000	7.14	50,000	6.25	50,000
Selling	2.50	15,000	2.14	15,000	1.88	15,000
Distribution	1.66	10,000	1.43	10,000	1.25	10,000
Fixed Cost	37.50	2,25,000	32.14	2,25,000	28.13	2,25,000
Total Cost	175.00	10,50,000	169.64	11,87,500	165.63	13,25,000

Illustration 4

From the following data for a 60% activity, prepare a budget for production at 80% and 100% capacity :

Production	600 Units
Material cost	Rs. 100 per Unit
Direct wages	40 per Unit.
Direct Expenses	10 per Unit.
Factory Overheads	40,000 (40% fixed)
Administration Overheads	30,000 (50% fixed)

Solution

XYZ Co.
Flexible Budget

Capacity Utilised	60%	80%	100%
Units Produced	600	800	1000
Variable Cost			
Direct Materials Rs. 100/- per Unit	60,000	80,000	1,00,000
Direct wages Rs. 40/- per Unit	24,000	32,000	40,000
Direct Expenses 10/- per Unit	6,000	8,000	10,000
PRIME COST	90,000	1,20,000	1,50,000
Factory Overheads	24,000	32,000	40,000
60% variable (60% of 40,000)			
Variable Administrative Overheads 40%	12,000	16,000	20,000
TOTAL	**1,26,000**	**1,68,000**	**2,10,000**
FIXED COST			
Factory Overheads 40%	16,000	16,000	16,000
Administrative Overheads 60%	18,000	18,000	18,000
	34,000	34,000	34,000
TOTAL COST	**1,60,000**	**2,02,000**	**2,44,000**

Illustration : 5

Prepare a flexible budget from the following data for half-yearly period and forecast the results @ 70%, 85% and 100% capacity. When the respective sales are Rs. 50,00,000, Rs. 60,00,000 and Rs. 85,00,000 while fixed expenses remain constant, semi-variable expenses are constant between 55% and 75%, increase by 10% between 75% and 90% and by 20% between 90% and 100%.

The expenses @ 60% capacity are as under :–

Semi-variable 60%	In lakhs Rs.
Maintenance and Repairs	1.25
Indirect Labour	5.00
Sales Department Expenses	1.50
Sundry Expenses	1.25

Variable Expenses	In lakhs Rs.
Materials	12.00
Labour	13.00
Direct Expenses	02.00

Fixed Expenses	In lakhs Rs.
Wages and Salaries	4.20
Rates and Taxes	2.80
Depreciation	3.50
Sundry Expenses	4.50
Total Rs.	**51.00**

Solution

Fiexible Budget for the period of ......

Items	60%	70%	85%	100%
(A) Variable Expenses				
Materials	12.00	14.00	17.00	20.00
Labour	13.00	15.17	18.42	21.67
Direct Expenses	2.00	2.33	2.83	3.33
	27.00	**31.50**	**38.25**	**45.00**
(B) Semi-Variable Expenses				
Maintenance and Repairs	1.25	1.25	1.38	1.50
Indirect Labour	5.00	5.00	5.50	6.00
Sales Dept. Expenses	1.50	1.50	1.65	1.80
Sundry Expenses	1.25	1.25	1.38	1.50
	9.00	**9.00**	**9.91**	**10.80**
(C) Fixed Expenses				
Wages and Salaries	4.20	4.20	4.20	4.20
Rates and Taxes	2.80	2.80	2.80	2.80
Depreciation	3.50	3.50	3.50	3.50
Sundry Expenses	4.50	4.50	4.50	4.50
	15.00	**15.00**	**15.00**	**15.00**
Capacity		70%	85%	100%
Total cost of Production (A+B+C)		55.50	63.16	70.80
Sales		50.00	60.00	85.00
Profit(+) Loss (-)		**-5.50**	**-3.16**	**+14.20**

Illustration 6 :

The cost of an article at a capacity level of 5,000 Units is under 'A' below. For a variation of 25% in capacity above or below this level, the expenses vary as indicated under 'B' below :

Items	A Rs.	B Variation
Materials Cost	25,000	100% Varying
Labour Cost	15,000	100% Varying
Power	1,250	80% Varying
Repairs and Maintenance	2,000	75% Varying
Stores	1,000	100% Varying
Inspection	500	20% Varying
Depreciation	10,000	100% Varying
Administrative Overheads	5,000	25% Varying
Selling Overheads	3,000	25% Varying
Total	**62,750**	

Prepare a Flexible Budget at production levels of 4,000 Units and 6,000 Units.　　　(P.U.)

Solution

Flexible Budget

	4,000 Units		5,000 Units		6,000 units		
	Per Unit Rs.	Amt Rs.	Per Unit Rs.	Amt Rs.	Per Unit Rs.	Amt Rs.	Nature of Cost
Materials Cost	5.00	20,000	5.00	25,000	5.00	30,000	Variable
Labour Cost	3.00	12,000	3.00	15,000	3.00	18,000	Variable
PRIME COST	**8.00**	**32,000**	**8.00**	**40,000**	**8.00**	**48,000**	
Power	0.26	1,050	0.25	1,250	0.24	1,450	Semi-variable
Repairs & Maintenance	0.43	1,700	0.40	2,000	0.38	2,300	Semi-variable
Stores	0.20	800	0.20	1,000	0.20	1,200	Variable
Inspection	0.12	480	0.10	500	0.09	520	Semi-variable
Depreciation	2.50	10,000	2.00	10,000	1.67	10,000	
COST OF PRODUCTION	**11.51**	**46,030**	**10.95**	**54,750**	**10.58**	**63,470**	
Administration Overheads	1.19	4,750	1.00	5,000	0.87	5,250	Semi-Fixed
Selling Overheads	0.67	2,700	0.60	3,000	0.55	3,300	Semi-Fixed
TOTAL COST	**13.37**	**53,480**	**12.55**	**62,750**	**12.00**	**72,020**	

Variability of an item of expense will be found out as follows :

Fixed Portion + Variable Portion $\times \dfrac{4,000 \,(\text{or}\, 6,000)}{5,000}$

For example, 80% of power is variable and 20% fixed. The power expenses for 4,000 Units will be calculated as :

$= 250 + 1,000 \times \dfrac{4,000}{5,000}$

$= 250 + 800$

$= \text{Rs. } 1,050$

Illustration 7 :

	At 100% Capacity (Rs.)
Materials	6,00,000
Labour	2,00,000
Variable Expenses (direct)	40,000
Variable Overheads	2,00,000
Fixed Overheads	80,000
Administrative Expenses (fixed)	40,000
Selling Expenses (10% fixed)	1,20,000
Distribution Expenses (20% fixed)	60,000

Prepare a budget for the production of : (a) 60% capacity, (b) 80% capacity.

Solution

In the books of a Factory
Fiexible Budget

Particulars Units% Capacity	60	80	100
	Total Rs.	Total Rs.	Total Rs.
Materials	3,60,000	4,80,000	6,00,000
Labour	1,20,000	1,60,000	2,00,000
Variable Expenses (direct)(+)	24,000	32,000	40,000
PRIME COST (1)	**5,04,000**	**6,72,000**	**8,40,000**
(+) Factory Expenses :			
(i) Variable Overheads	1,20,000	1,60,000	2,00,000
(ii) Fixed Overheads	80,000	80,000	80,000
WORKS COSTS (2)	**7,04,000**	**9,12,000**	**11,20,000**

Particulars Units% Capacity	60	80	100
	Total Rs.	Total Rs.	Total Rs.
(+) Administrative Expenses (fixed)	40,000	40,000	40,000
COST OF PRODUCTION (3)	**7,44,000**	**9,52,000**	**11,60,000**
(+) Selling Expenses -1,20,000			
F-10% - 12,000	12,000	12,000	12,000
V-90% - 1,08,000 (+)	64,800	86,400	1,08,000
(+) Distribution Expenses 60,000			
F-20% - 12,000	12,000	12,000	12,000
V-80% - 48,000 (+)	28,800	38,400	48,000
Total Cost (4)	**8,61,600**	**11,00,800**	**13,40,000**

Illustration 8 :

Draw up a flexible budget for overhead expenses on the basis of the following data and determine the overhead rates at 70% and 90% plant capacity.

Expenses	At 80% Capacity (Rs.)
Variable Overheads :	
Indirect Labour	12,000
Stores including spares	4,000
Semi-variable Overheads :	
Power (30% fixed, 70% variable)	20,000
Repairs & Maintenance (60% fixed, 40% variable)	2,000
Fixed Overheads :	
Depreciation	11,000
Insurance	3,000
Salaries	10,000
Total Overheads	62,000

Estimated Direct Labour hours at 80% capacity 1,24,000 hrs.

Solution

In the books of a Company
Flexible Budget

Particulars Units% Capacity		70	80	90
		Total Rs.	Total Rs.	Total Rs.
Variable Overheads :				
Indirect Labour		10,500	12,000	13,500
Stores including spares		3,500	4,000	4,500
Semi-Variable Overheads :				
Power	20,000			
(a) Fixed 30%	6,000	6,000	6,000	6,000
(b) Variable 70%	14,000	12,250	14,000	15,750
Repairs and				
Maintenance	2,000			
(a) Fixed 60%	1,200	1,200	1,200	1,200
(b) Variable 40%	800	700	800	900
Fixed Overheads :				
Depreciation		11,000	11,000	11,000
Insurance		3,000	3,000	3,000
Salaries		10,000	10,000	10,000
Total Overheads		58,150	62,000	65,850
Overhead recovery rate (On the basis of direct Labour hours)		Total Overheads Direct Labour Hours		
		Rs. 58,150	Rs. 62,000	Rs. 65,850
		Hrs. 1,08,500 Re. 0.535	Hrs. 1,24,000 Re. 0.500	Hrs. 1,39,500 Re. 0.472

Illustration - 9

A Factory produces 20,000 Units. The budgeted expenses are given below :-

	Per Unit (Rs.)
Raw Materials	75
Direct Labour	20
Direct Expenses	25
Overheads	15
Fixed Overtheads (Rs. 4,00,000)	20
Administration Overheads (Fixed)	10
Selling Expenses (10% Fixed)	15
Distribution Expenses (25% Fixed)	20
Total cost of sale per Unit	**200**

You are required to prepare a budget for 15,000 Units and 10,000 Units. (P.U.)

Solution -

A Budget

	20,000 Units		15,000 Units		10,000 Units	
Particulars	**Per Unit Rs.**	**Amount Rs.**	**Per Unit Rs.**	**Amount Rs.**	**Per Unit Rs.**	**Amount Rs.**
Production Expenses						
Raw Materials	75.00	15,00,000	75.00	11,25,000	75.00	7,50,000
Direct Labour	20.00	4,00,000	20.00	3,00,000	20.00	2,00,000
Overheads	15.00	3,00,000	15.00	2,25,000	15.00	1,50,000
Direct Expenses	25.00	5,00,000	25.00	3,75,000	25.00	2,50,000
Fixed Overheads (Rs. 2,00,000)	20.00	4,00,000	26.67	4,00,000	40.00	4,00,000
Administrative Expenses :						
Fixed	—	2,00,000	13.33	2,00,000	20.00	2,00,000
Selling Expenses :						
Variable	13.50	2,70,000	13.50	2,02,500	13.50	1,35,000
Fixed	1.50	30,000	2.00	30,000	3.00	30,000
Distribution Expenses :						
Variable	15.00	3,00,000	15.00	2,25,000	15.00	1,50,000
Fixed	5.00	1,00,000	6.67	1,00,000	10.00	1,00,000
Total Cost of Sales	190	40,00,000	212.17	31,82,500	236.50	23,65,000

Illustration - 10

The statement given below gives the flexible budget at 60% capacity. Prepare a tabulated statement giving the budget figures at 75% capacity and 90% capacity.

Where no indication has been given, make your own classification of expenses between fixed and variable overheads.

Expenses	At 60% Capacity (Rs.)
Direct Materials	1,60,000
Direct Labour	40,000
Indirect Materials and Spares	48,000
Depreciation	60,000
Indirect Labour	40,000
Rent	12,000
Electric Power (40% fixed)	8,000
Repairs and Maintenance (40% Variable)	20,000
Insurance of Machinery (F)	12,000

(P.U.)

Solution -

Flexible Budget

Expenses	Basis	60%	75%	90%
(A) Variable Cost :				
Direct Materials	100% Variable	1,60,000	2,00,000	2,40,000
Direct Labour	100% Variable	40,000	50,000	60,000
Indirect Materials and Spares	100% Variable	48,000	60,000	72,000
Indirect Labour	100% Variable	40,000	50,000	60,000
B) Semi-Variable Overheads :				
Electric Power	40% Fixed			
	60% Variable	8,000	9,200	10,400
Repairs and Maintenance	60% Fixed			
	40% Variable	20,000	22,000	24,000
(C) Fixed Overheads :	100% Fixed			
Depreciation	100% Fixed	60,000	60,000	60,000
Rent	100% Fixed	12,000	12,000	12,000
Insurance	100% Fixed	12,000	12,000	12,000
	Total	4,00,000	4,75,200	5,50,400

Working Notes :

1) Semi-variable Overhead - **Electricity.**

Fixed portion = 40% of Rs. 8,000 = 3,200

Variable portion at 60% capacity = 8,000 - 3,200 = 4,800

Variable portion = 75% capacity = $\dfrac{4,800}{60}$ × 75 = 6,000

Total Cost = Fixed Cost portion + Variable Cost portion

Total Electricity at 75% capacity = 3,200 + 6,000 = **9,200**

Variable portion of Electricity at 90% capacity = $\dfrac{4,800}{60}$ × 90 = 7,200

Total Electricity Cost at 90% capacity = 3,200 + 7,200 = **10,400**

2) Repairs and Maintenance

Fixed portion of Cost = 60% of 20,000 = 12,000

Variable portion at 60% capacity = 40% of 20,000 = **8,000**

6:8 Exercises

Objective Type

A. State whether the following statements are true or false :

i) Sales budget is the most important and forms the basis on which all other budgets are built up.

ii) Long-term budget covers a period of less than one year.

iii) For control purpose, long-term budgets should be prepared.

iv) Budgets are action plans.

v) The key factor in a budget does not remain the same every year.

vi) A flexible budget is one that is prepared for changing level of activity.

vii) Budgetary control does not operate through different budgets.

viii) For co-ordination, there is no need of communication.

ix) For maximum profit through budgetary control, there is need of a proper organisational structure.

x) Budgets are estimates.

Answers : (i) True (ii) False (iii) False (iv) True (v) True (vi) True (vii) False (viii) False (ix) True (x) True.

B) Select the correct answer for each of the following :–

i) A budget is ....

   (a) an aid to management   (b) a post-mortem analysis   (c) institute of management.

ii) A budget is a projected plan of action in ....

   (a) physical Units   (b) monetary terms

   (c) physical as well as monetary terms

iii) The document which described the budgeting organisation procedures etc., is known as ......

    (a) budget centre   (b) key factor   (c) budget manual

iv) Operation budgets normally cover a period of ....

    (a) one year or less   (b) one to two years   (c) one to four years

v) A flexible budget takes into account ....

    (a) Fixed costs only   (b) Variable and semi-variable costs only

    (c) Fixed, variable and semi-variable costs.

vi) Which budget shows the anticipated sources and utilisation of costs?

    (a) Cash budget   (b) Sales budget   (c) Flexible budget

Answers - (i) a (ii) b (iii) c (iv) a (v) c (vi) a

C) Fill in the blanks :

i) .....budget is usually prepared for a long period of time.

ii) .....budget denotes the summary of all functional budgets.

iii) Budgets are .....

iv) Budgetary control is a .....of costing.

v) Budgets .....the morale of managers.

vi) Budgetary control is an ......tool.

vii) .....is a device for controlling and co-ordinating the financial side of business.

Answers : (i) Capital Expenditure (ii) Master (iii) estimates (iv) technique (v) boosts (vi) expensive (vi) Cash budget.

Essay Type

1) Define 'Budgetary Control'. What are its objectives?

2) What are the advantages and disadvantages of budgetary control?

3) What is budgetary control? Explain different types of budgets.

4) What do you understood by 'Budgeting'? What types of budgets are generally prepared in an organisation?

5) What do you mean by 'flexible budget'? State its procedure.

6) How cash budget is prepared? What are the advantages of cash budgeting?

7) Discuss the objectives and limitations of budgetary control.

8) What is budget centre? Whether it is desirable to prepare a budget for each budget centre?

9) What is a budget manual? Mention the centres and advantages of budget manual.

10) Discuss the main steps in budgetary control procedure.

11) Write Short Notes :-

    i) Short-term Budget   ii) Programme budgeting

    iii) Performance budgeting   iv) Budget Manual

    v) Budget Centre   vi) Master Budget

    vii) Flexible Budget

Practical Exercises :

1) With the following data for a 60 per cent activity, prepare a budget for production at 80 per cent and 100 per cent activity. Production at 60 per cent activity : 600 units.

	Rs.
Materials	100 per Unit
Labour	40 per Unit
Expenses	10 per Unit

Factory expenses Rs. 40,000 (40 per cent fixed.)

Administration expenses Rs. 30,000 (60 per cent fixed)

Ans. 80% budget : Rs. 2,20,000; 100% budget : Rs. 2,44,000

2) The following budget estimates are available from a factory working at 50% its capacity.

	Rs.
Variable Expenses	60,000
Semi-variable Expenses	20,000
Fixed Expenses	10,000

Prepare a budget for 75% of the capacity assuming that semi-variable expenses increase by 10% for every 25%.

Ans. Rs. 1,22,000

3) The following overhead expenses relate to a cost centre operating at 50% of normal capacity. Draw up a flexible budget for the cost centre for operating at 75%, 100% and 125% of normal capacity. Indicate the basis upon which you have estimated each item of expenses for the different operating levels.

	Rs.
Foreman	60
Assistant Foreman	40
Inspectors	65
Shop Labourers	40
Machinery Repairs	100
Defective Work	25
Consumable Stores	20
Machine Depreciation	110
	460

Ans. 75%, Rs. 565; 100%, 760; 125% 950

4) The expenses budgeted for production of 10,000 Units in a factory are given below :

	Per Unit Rs.
Materials	70
Labour	25
Variable Overheads	20
Fixed Overheads (1,00,000)	10
Variable Overheads (Direct)	5
Selling Expenses (10% fixed)	13
Administration Expenses (Rs. 50,000)	5
Distribution Expenses (20 % fixed)	7
	155

Prepare a budget for the production of (a) 8,000 units (b) 6,000 units. Assume that the administration expenses are rigid for all levels of production.

Ans. (a) Rs. 12,75,400; (b) Rs. 10,00,800

5) ABC Ltd., has prepared a budget for the production of a lakh units of the only commodity manufactured by them for a costing period as under :

	Per Unit Rs.
Raws Materials	2.52
Direct Labour	0.75
Direct Expenses	0.10
Works Overheads (60% fixed)	2.50
Administration Overheads (80% fixed)	0.40
Selling Overheads (50% fixed)	0.20

The actual production during the period was only 60,000 Units. Calculate the revised budgeted cost per Unit.

Ans. Rs. 7.75

■ ■ ■

$$\boxed{\textbf{Key Terms}}$$

Chapter I : Introduction

1) **Financial Accounting :** It is concerned with record keeping and preparation of final accounts i.e. P & L A/c and Balance Sheet.

2) **Cost Accounting :** It is concerned with determination of costs of manufacturing concern and/ or service providing institutions.

3) **Management Accounting :** It is concerned with the presentation of accounting information in such a way, as to assist the management in creation of policy and day-to-day operations of an undertaking.

4) **Break-even Analysis :** It is an important technique which is used to analyse the behaviour of cost viz., fixed cost and marginal cost.

5) **Break-even point :** It is that level of activity where total costs are equal to total revenue.

6) **Collection of data :** It is an activity to collect reliable data for the purpose of decision-making.

7) **Control :** It is an activity to control the performance of the organisation by using some techniques. For e.g. marginal costing, standard costing, bugetary control etc.

8) **Reporting :** It is an important function of management accounting.

9) **Co-ordination :** It is an activity which co-ordinates the activities of different sections or department. It can be done through functional budgets.

10) **Presentation of data :** It is an activity of presenting collected data in such a way that the management is able to take a right decision.

Chapter 2 : Analysis and Interpretation of Financial Data and Ratio Analysis :

11) **Trading on equity :** When equity shares and loans are used for financing the business activities, it is said that a company is to be trading on equity.

12) **Capital Gearing :** It is a proportion between ownership securities and creditorship securities.

13) **Average Stock :** It is the average of opening and closing stock.

14) **Short-term solvency :** It is the ability of a Company to pay its current obligations out of its current assets.

15) **Long-term solvency :** It is the ability of a company to repay long-term loans.

16) **Debtor's velocity :** It is the speed with which amount is collected from debtors.

17) **Stock velocity :** It is the speed of movement of stock.

18) **Capital employed :** It is the amount of own funds and owed funds invested in business.

19) **Debt-service :** It is the ability of a Company to service the debt.

20) **Immediate solvency :** It is the ability of a Company to pay its urgent obligations.

21) **Analysis :** It is a systematic and specialised arrangement of information for the purpose of interpretation.

22) **Interpretation :** It is the process of drawing inference or conclusions about the various aspects of a business.

23) **Comparative statement :** It is a technique of comparative analysis for drawing conclusions.

24) **Common-size statement :** It is a statement prepared to bring the ratio of each item with the total assets / net sales respectively.

25) **Trend percentage :** It is an analysis of the trend of data shown in a series of financial statements over several successive years.

26) **Ratio :** A Ratio is one figure expressed in terms of another figure.

27) **Ratio Analysis :** It is a process of computing, determining and presenting the relationship of items or group of items in the financial statements.

28) **Balance-Sheet Ratios :** They deal with the relationship between two items or group of items which are seen in the balance sheet.

29) **Revenue Statement Ratios :** They deal with the relationship between two items or two group of items, which are both found in the income statement.

30) **Composite Ratios :** They indicate the relationship between two items or two group of items, of which one is found in the balance sheet and the other in the income statement.

31) **Liquidity Ratios :** They analyse short-term and immediate financial position of a business organisation and indicate the ability of the firms to meet its short-term commitments out of its short-term resources.

32) **Leverage Ratios :** They measure the relationship between proprietor's funds and borrowed funds.

33) **Activity Ratios :** They indicate the effectiveness of the firm in utilising its funds and the degree of efficiency and standards of performance.

34) **Profitability Ratios :** They reflect the overall efficiency of the organisation, its ability to earn a reasonable return on capital employed or on shares issued and the effectiveness of its investment policies.

35) **Current Ratio :** It indicates the relationship between current assets and current liabilities.

36) **Liquid Ratio :** It indicates the financial, position of an enterprise.

37) **Proprietory Ratio :** It relates shareholders funds to total assets i.e. total funds. It determines the long-term ultimate solvency of the company.

38) **Capital Gearing Ratio :** It brings out the relationship between two types of capital i.e. capital carrying a fixed rate of interest/dividend and capital which does not carry a fixed rate of interest/dividend.

39) **Debt-Equity Ratio :** It expresses the relation between the external equities and internal or the relationship between borrowed capital and owner's capital.

40) **Gross Profit Ratio :** It brings out the relationship between Gross Profit and Net sales.

41) **Net Profit Ratio :** It indicates the relationship between net profit and net sales.

42) **Operating Ratio :** It is the relationship between cost of activities and net sales.

43) **Expenses Ratios :** It brings out the relationship between various elements of operating costs and net sales.

44) **Operating Profit Ratio :** It is a relationship between net operating profit and net sales which

is expressed in percentages.

45) **Inventory Ratio :** It measures the number of times stock turns or flows or rotates in an accruing/accounting period compared to the sales effected during that period.

46) **Earnings per Share :** It is calculated to find out the overall profitability of the organisation. It represents earnings of the Company whether or not dividends are declared.

47) **Fixed Assets Turnover Ratio :** It is a relationship between Sales and Fixed Assets.

48) **Working Capital :** It is the difference between current assets and current liabilities.

Chapter 3 : Fund Flow Statement and Cash Flow Statement :

49) **Fund :** It refers to working capital

50) **Flow :** It is a movement of fund.

51) **Current Items :** It includes current assets and current liabilities.

52) **Non - current items :** It includes share capital, Reserves, Loans, Fixed Assets, Investments etc.

53) **Working Capital :** Excess of current assets over current liabilities.

54) **Cash :** It includes cash and demand deposits with Bank.

55) **Cash Equivalents :** These are short-term and highly liquid investment.

56) **Cash Flow :** It is movement of cash.

57) **Revenue activities :** These are the activities which are revenue producing

58) **Investing activities :** These are related to acquisition and disposal of long-term assets.

59) **Financing activities :** These are activities relating to changes in capital and borrowings.

60) **Sources of Fund :** The transactions which increase the amount of funds is called a "Source of Fund"

61) **Use (Application) of fund :** If a transaction decreases the amount of funds, it is said to be a "Use or Application of Funds."

Chapter 4 : Working Capital

1) **Net Working Capital :** The excess of current assets over current liabilities is called net working capital.

2) **Gross Working Capital :** The total of investment in all individual current assets is gross working capital.

3) **Current Assets :** The assets which can be converted into cash within a short period of time i.e. within a year.

4) **Current Liabilities :** The liabilities which are to be paid within a year, are called current liabilities.

5) **Turnover of Working Capital :** It means the ratio of annual gross sales to average working assets.

6) **Permanent Working Capital :** The minimum level of working capital, which is continuously required by a firm in order to maintain its activities.

7) **Temporary Working Capital :** The capital required to meet seasonal demands of the business is called temporary working capital.

Chapter 5 : Marginal Costing

1) **Marginal cost :** It is an addition to total cost, that results from increasing output by one more unit.
2) **Marginal costing :** It is the ascertainment of marginal costs by differentiating between fixed and variable costs, and the effect on profit of changes in volume or type of output.
3) **Fixed cost :** It is the cost which remains fixed in 'total' and does not increase or decrease when the volume of production increases or decreases.
4) **Variable cost :** It is the cost which fluctuates in proportion to the volume of production.
5) **Contribution :** It is the difference between sales and the marginal cost of sales.
6) **Break-even analysis :** It refers to ascertainment of level of operating, where total revenue equals to total costs.
7) **Break-even Chart :** It is a chart which show the profitabilities or otherwise of an undertaking at various levels of activity, and as a result, indicates the point at which neither profit nor loss is made.
8) **Break-even Point :** It is a level of production and sales, where there in neither profit nor loss. Total sales and total cost is the same, contribution equals fixed cost.
9) **Angle of Incidence :** It is formed by the interaction of total cost line and sales line at the break-even point.
10) **Margin of Safety :** It is the sales between actual sales and Break-even-point.
11) **Key Factor :** It is the factor in the activities of production unit, which limits the volume of output at a particular point of time or over a period.
12) **Profit Volume Ratio :** It is the rate at which contribution margin increases with the increase in volume.
13) **Cost Volume Profit Analysis :** It is the study of the relationship between expenses (costs) revenue (sales) and net income (profit), with the aim to establish what will happen to financial results, if a specified level of activity or volume fluctuates.
14) **Profit Volume Chart :** It is the graphical representation of cost volume profit relationship.
15) **Absorption Costing :** It is a traditional method of costing, whereby the total fixed cost (fixed and variable) are charged to products.

Chapter 6 : Budgetary Control

1) **Budget :** It is the formal expression on the expected income and expenditure for a definite future period.
2) **Budgeting :** It is a mechanism of preparing budgets.
3) **Budgetary Control :** It is a system of controlling costs, which includes the preparation of budgets, co-ordinating the departments and establishing responsibility, comparing actual performance with the budgeted and acting upon results to achieve maximum profitability.
4) **Fixed Budgeting :** It is one which is designed to remain unchanged irrespective of the level of activity actually attained.
5) **Flexible Budgeting :** It is one, which is designed to change in accordance with the level of activities actually attained.

6) **Master Budget :** It is a budget in which various functional budgets have been prepared and summarised into one harmonious budget.

7) **Purchase Budget :-** It is concerned with purchases during the budget period. It includes purchases of direct and indirect materials and other goods.

8) **Sales Budget :** It is a budget which shows what products will be sold in what quantities and at what prices.

9) **Production Budget :** It is a forecast based on sales, production capacity and budgeted finished goods stock requirements.

10) **Plant Utilisation Budget :** It shows plant capacity required to meet the production budget.

11) **Capital Expenditure Budget :** It shows the expenditure on fixed assets during the period concerned.

12) **Cash Budget :** It shows the estimated cash receipts and payments during the budget period and also the resultant cash position as the budget period develops.

13) **Programme Budgeting :** It restructures the conventional budget by accumulating expenditure, according to the output category.

14) **Performance Budgeting :** It is a budgetary system where the input costs are related to the performances or the end results of the programme or activity.

15) **Zero-Base Budgeting :** It is a method of budgeting, whereby all activities are re-evaluated, each time a budget is set. Discreet levels of each activity are valued and a combination chosen to match funds available.

16) **Short-term Budget :** It is a budget which is prepared for a period longer than one year.

17) **Basic Budget :** It is a budget which is established for use unaltered over a long period of time.

18) **Current Budget :** It is a budget which is established for use over a short period of time and is related to current conditions.

Formulae

At a glance

Chapter 2 : Ratio Analysis
A. Balance Sheet Ratios :

1. **Current Ratio or 2:1 Ratio :** $\dfrac{\text{Current Assets}}{\text{Current Laibilities}}$

2. **Quick Ratio / Acid Test Ratio / Liquid Ratio :** $\dfrac{\text{Quick or liquid Assets}}{\text{Quick or liquid liabilities}}$

3. **Inventory to working Capital Ratio :** $\dfrac{\text{Closing Stock}}{\text{Working Capital}}$

4. **Proprietory Ratio or Tangible Net Worth to Total Assets Ratio :** $\dfrac{\text{Proprietors' Funds}}{\text{Total Assets}}$

5. Fixed Assets Ratio or Fixed Assets to Tangible Net Worth Ratio :

$$\frac{\text{Depreciation value of Fixed Assets}}{\text{Proprietor's Fund}} \times 100$$

6. Current Assets to Proprietor's Fund : $\dfrac{\text{Current Assets}}{\text{Proprietor's Funds}} \times 100$

7. Debt to Equity Ratio : $\dfrac{\text{Total Debt (Long-term)}}{\text{Net Worth (Shareholder's Funds)}}$

8. Capital Gearing Ratio : $\dfrac{\text{Equity Share Capital} + \text{Reserves \& Surplus}}{\text{Preference Share Capital} + \text{Loan Capital}}$

B. Revenue Statements or Profit and Loss Account Ratios

1. Gross Profit Ratio : $\dfrac{\text{Gross Profit}}{\text{Net Sales}} \times 100$

2. Net Profit Ratio : $\dfrac{\text{Net profit}}{\text{Net Sales}} \times 100$

3. Operating Ratio : $\dfrac{\text{Cost of goods sold} + \text{operating expenses}}{\text{Net Sales}} \times 100$

4. Interest Coverage Ratio / Fixed Charges Cover Ratio :

$$\frac{\text{Net profit before deduction of interest \& Income Tax}}{\text{Fixed Interest Charges}}$$

C. Composite Ratios :

1. Inventory Turnover Ratio : $\dfrac{\text{Cost of Goods sold}}{\text{Average Inventory}}$

2. Debtor's Turnover Ratio : $\dfrac{\text{Accounts Receivable}}{\text{Average Daily Sales}}$

3. Fixed Assets Turnover Rastio : $\dfrac{\text{Sales}}{\text{Net Fixed Assets}}$

4. Total Assets Turnover Ratio : $\dfrac{\text{Sales}}{\text{Total Assets}}$

5. Return on shareholder's Fund : $\dfrac{\text{Net Profit after Taxes}}{\text{Shareholder's Fund}} \times 100$

6. Return on Capital Employed, or Net Profit to Total Assets Ratio :

$$\frac{\text{Net Profit after Tax}}{\text{Capital Employed}} \times 100$$

7. Return on Equity Capital Ratio :

$$\frac{\text{Net Profit (after Tax and Preference Share dividend)}}{\text{Equity Capital}} \times 100$$

8. Earnings per Share : $\dfrac{\text{Net Profit (after Tax and Preference Share dividend)}}{\text{Number of Equity shares}}$

The above Formulaes may be classified as under :-

A. Liquidity Ratios :	1) Current Ratio 2) Quick Ratio 3) Inventory to working capital Ratio
B. Leverage Ratios :	1) Proprietory Ratio 2) Fixed Assets Ratio 3) Current Assets to Proprietor's Fund Ratio 4) Debt to Equity Ratio 5) Capital Gearing Ratio
C. Activity Ratio :	1) Inventory Turnover Ratio 2) Debtor's Turnover Ratio 3) Fixed Assets Turnover Ratio 4) Total Assets Turnover Ratio 5) Capital Turnover Ratio 6) Creditor's Turnover Ratio
D. Profitability Ratio : **1) Profitability Ratio in relation to Sales :**	1) Gross Profit Ratio 2) Operating Profit Ratio 3) Net Profit Ratio 4) Operating Ratio 5) Expenses Ratio
2) Profitability Ratio is relation to Investment :	1) Return on Total Assets 2) Return on Capital Employed 3) Return on Equity 4) Earnings per Share (EPS) 5) Proprietory Ratio

The formulae which are <u>not</u> covered in <u>Ratios acording to Nature</u> are given below :-

1) Capital Turnover Ratio $= \dfrac{\text{Credit Purchases}}{\text{Average Creditors}}$

2) Working Capital Turnover Ratio : $\dfrac{\text{Sales}}{\text{Working Capital}}$

3) Operating Profit Ratio : $\dfrac{\text{Operating Profit}}{\text{Net Sales}} \times 100$

4) Expenses Ratio : $\dfrac{\text{Particular Expenses}}{\text{Net Sales}} \times 100$

5) Return on Total Assets Ratio : $\dfrac{\text{Net Profit before Interest and Tax}}{\text{Total Assets}} \times 100$

Important Terms :

1) **Capital Employed or Long term Funds or Proprietors' Funds**
   = Share Capital + Reserves & Surplus + Premium + Long -term loans
   Less : (Non-Business Assets + Fictitious Assets)
   OR
   Fixed Capital (i.e Fixed Assets at W. D. V.) + Working Capital / Net Current Assets (i.e Current Assets - Current Liabilities)

2) **Operating Profits :**
   = Gross Profit <u>Less</u> Operating Expenses (i.e. Trading Exp.) before interest and tax

3) **Equity or Net worth :**
   = Pref. Share Capital + Equity Share Capital + Reserves & Surplus <u>Less</u> Losses and Fictitious Assets

4) **Liquid / Quick Assets** = Current Assets excluding Stock & pre-paid Exp.

5) **Liquid / Quick Liabilities** = Current Liabilities excluding B. O. and Accrued Exp.

6) **Working Capital** = Current Assets - Current Liabilities

Chapter 3 Fund Flow and Cash Flow Statement

Fund Flow Analysis :

   i) Sources of Funds - Application of Funds = Increase in Working Capital

   ii) Application of Funds - Sources of Funds = Decrease in Working Capital

General Rule :

   i) Transactions which involve only Current Assets do not result in a flow.

   ii) Transactions which involve only Non - Current Assets do not result in a flow.

   iii) Transactions which involve one current Asset and one Non - current Asset results in 'flow' of funds.

Cash Flow Analysis :

1) Opening Balance + Receipts - Payments = Closing balance

2) **Cash inflow from sales :**

Credit Sales	......
Add : Debtors and B. R. in the beginning of the year	......
	......
Less Debtors and B. R. at the end of the year	......
Cash Flow from Sales	......

3) **Cost of Sales on Cash Basis (Cash Outflow on Purchases)**

Purchases	......
Add : Opening Creditors	......
	......
Less : Closing Creditors	......
Cash outflow on Purchases	......

4) **Expenses on Cash Basis**

Expenses (as per P and L A/c)	......
Add : Outstanding in the beginning	......
	......
Less : Outstanding at the end	......
Cash outflow on account of Expenses	......

Note : Non-cash expenses such as depreciations, loss on sale of fixed assets, goodwill written off etc., are deleted.

Chapter 4 : Working Capital

Working Capital = Current Assets - Current Liabilities

Chapter 5 : Marginal Costing

1) **Sales -**

$$
\begin{aligned}
\text{Sales} \ &= \text{Total Cost} + \text{Profit} \qquad &\textbf{OR} \\
&= \text{Variable Cost} + \text{Fixed Cost} + \text{Profit} \qquad &\textbf{OR} \\
&= \frac{\text{Contribution}}{\text{P/V Ratio}} \qquad &\textbf{OR} \\
&= \text{Contribution} + \text{Variable Cost} \qquad &\textbf{OR} \\
&= \frac{\text{Marginal Cost}}{\text{Marginal Cost Ratio}}
\end{aligned}
$$

2) Profit -

$$\text{Profit} = \text{Sales - Total Cost} \qquad \textbf{OR}$$
$$= \text{Sales - (Variable Cost + Fixed Cost)} \qquad \textbf{OR}$$
$$= \text{Contribution - Fixed Cost}$$
$$= \text{Margin of safety} \times \text{P/V Ratio}$$

3) Loss -

$$\text{Loss} = \text{Total Cost - Sales} \qquad \textbf{OR}$$
$$= \text{Fixed Cost - Contribution}$$

4) Contribution -

$$\text{Contribution} = \text{Sales - Variable Cost (S - V)}$$
$$= \text{Fixed Cost + Profit (F + P)}$$
$$= \text{Sales} \times \text{P/V Ratio (S} \times \text{P/VR)}$$
$$= \text{Fixed Cost - Loss (F - L)}$$
$$= \frac{\text{Fixed Cost}}{\text{B. E. Unit}}$$

5) Fixed Cost -

$$\text{Fixed Cost} = \text{Total Cost - Variable Cost (TC - VC)}$$
$$= \text{Contribution - profit (C - P)}$$
$$= \text{Contribution + Loss (C + L)}$$
$$= \text{Sales - (Variable Cost + Profit) (Sales -(V - P))}$$

6) Variable Cost -

$$\text{Variable Cost} = \text{Total Cost - Fixed Cost (TC - FC)}$$
$$= \text{Sales - Contribution (S - C)}$$
$$= \text{Sales - (Fixed cost + profit) (S - (F + P))}$$

7) Break-Even Point (Units) -

$$\text{B.E.P. (Units)} = \frac{\text{Total Fixed Cost}}{\text{Contribution per Unit}} \qquad \textbf{OR}$$

$$= \frac{\text{BEP – Sales in Value}}{\text{Selling Price per Unit}}$$

8) Break - Even Point in Rs. $= \dfrac{\text{Fixed cost}}{\text{P / V Ratio}} = \dfrac{F}{\text{P / V R}}$ **OR**

$$= \frac{\text{Total Fixed Cost}}{\text{Total Contribution}} \times \text{Total Sales} \qquad \textbf{OR}$$

$$= \frac{\text{Total Fixed cost}}{\text{Contribution per Unit}} \times \text{Selling Price per Unit}$$

$$= \frac{\text{Total Fixed Cost}}{1 - \dfrac{\text{Variable Cost}}{\text{Sales}}} \qquad \textbf{OR}$$

= B.E.P. (units) $\times$ Selling Price per Unit

9) P.V. Ratio -

$$\text{P/V Ratio} = \frac{\text{Contribution}}{\text{Sales}} \times 100$$

OR

$$= \frac{\text{Sales - variable cost}}{\text{Sales}} \times 100 = \frac{S - V}{S} \times 100$$

OR

$$= \frac{\text{Change in Profit}}{\text{Change in Sales}} = \frac{\text{Change in Contribution}}{\text{Change in Sales}}$$

10) Margin of Safety (MS)

= Actual Sales - B.E.P. Sales

OR

$$= \frac{\text{Profit}}{\text{P/V Ratio}}$$

$$\text{Margin of Profit Ratio} = \frac{\text{Margin of Safety}}{\text{Actual Sales}} \times 100 = \frac{MS}{S} \times 100$$

11) Sales required for desired Profit in Units

$$= \frac{\text{Total Fixed Cost + Desired Profit}}{\text{Contribution per Unit}}$$

12) Sales required for desired Profit in Rupees =

$$= \frac{(\text{Total Fixed Cost + Desired Profit}) \times \text{Sales}}{\text{Total Contribution}}$$

$$= \frac{\text{Total Fixed Cost + Desired Profit}}{\text{P/V Ratio}}$$

13) Profit required for certain Sales -

$$\text{Profit} = \text{Contribution - Fixed Cost}$$

$$\text{But P/V Ratio} = \frac{\text{Contribution}}{\text{Certain Sales}} \times 100$$

$$\therefore C = S \times \text{P/V Ratio Desired Profit}$$
$$= \text{Contribution - Fixed Cost}$$

Bibliography

Belty J. – Management Accounting - ELBS TMH.

Choudhari, Chopade – Management Accounting - Seth Publications.

Goyal Manmohan – Management Accounting - Academic press.

Jain K. P., Khan M. R. – Management Accounting - Mc Graw Hill.

Jawarlal (Dr.) – Management Accounting - THM.

Kishore R. M – Management Accounting - Taxman.

Maheshwari S. N. – Principles of Management Accounting - Vikas Publishing House.

Nagratnam S. – Management Accounting - S. Chand.

Pandey I. M – Management Accounting - Vikas Publishing House.

Patkar M. G. – A Text book of Management Accounting - Phadke Prakashan, Kolhapur.

Paul S. K. – Management Accounting - New Century Calcatta.

Tulshan P. C. – Financial Accounting - TMH.

■ ■ ■